Devī

COMPARATIVE STUDIES IN RELIGION AND SOCIETY

Mark Juergensmeyer, editor

1. Redemptive Encounters: Three Modern Styles in the Hindu Tradition, *by Lawrence Babb*

2. Saints and Virtues, *edited by John Stratton Hawley*

3. Utopias in Conflict: Religion and Nationalism in Modern India, *by Ainslie T. Embree*

4. Mama Lola: A Vodou Priestess in Brooklyn, *by Karen McCarthy Brown*

5. The New Cold War? Religious Nationalism Confronts the Secular State, *by Mark Juergensmeyer*

6. Pious Passion: The Emergence of Modern Fundamentalism in the United States and Iran, *by Martin Riesebrodt, translated by Don Reneau*

7. Devī: Goddesses of India, *edited by John Stratton Hawley and Donna Marie Wulff*

Devī

Goddesses of India

EDITED BY
John S. Hawley
AND
Donna M. Wulff

UNIVERSITY OF CALIFORNIA PRESS
Berkeley Los Angeles London

University of California Press
Berkeley and Los Angeles, California

University of California Press, Ltd.
London, England

Library of Congress Cataloging-in-Publication Data

Devī : goddesses of India / John S. Hawley and Donna M. Wulff, editors.
p. cm. — (Comparative studies in religion and society ; 7)
Includes bibliographical references and index.
ISBN 0-520-20057-8 (alk. paper). — ISBN 0-520-20058-6 (pbk. : alk. paper)
1. Goddesses, Hindu. I. Hawley, John Stratton, 1941– . II. Wulff, Donna Marie, 1943– . III. Series.
BL1216.2.D48 1996
294.5'2114—dc20 95-46773
CIP

Printed in the United States of America
9 8 7 6 5 4 3 2 1

The paper used in this publication meets the minimum requirements of American National Standard for Information Sciences—Permanence of Paper for Printed Library Materials, ANSI Z39.48-1984.

CONTENTS

MAPS AND ILLUSTRATIONS

ACKNOWLEDGMENTS

To Douglas Abrams Arava, Marilyn Schwartz, Nola Burger, and Suzanne Samuel at the University of California Press, we are indebted for endless measures of good sense and good cheer offered in the course of producing this book, to Mark Juergensmeyer for welcoming it into his series at the Press, and to Pamela MacFarland Holway for exquisite skill in the art of copyediting, a vast knowledge of India, and such keen compassion that the book became her own. Particular thanks go to two outside readers for giving the book such careful and helpful evaluations. These readers—one anonymous; the other, Linda Hess—took the book on as if it had been their own, offering detailed suggestions as to how it could be improved. Linda Hess did so in a particularly direct way, by penciling in numerous rewrites, particularly in the prologue. These were invaluable. And the comments received from our contributors were invariably helpful and insightful.

Two of the chapters in this book were originally published in our earlier volume, *The Divine Consort: Rādhā and the Goddesses of India.* For permission to reprint these essays, we are grateful to the original publisher, the Graduate Theological Union, Berkeley. For further assistance, very cordially rendered, we are indebted to Lauren Bryant, Martha Gollup, and Rebecca Verrill of Beacon Press, which published the paperback edition of *The Divine Consort.* A number of the illustrations come from museum collections and previous publications of various kinds. We are sincerely grateful to the companies, publishers, and organizations who have granted us permission to reproduce.

We wish also to thank the institutions with which we are associated: Brown University, Barnard College, and Columbia University. Brown provided funds so that Maya Grosz could explore certain of the publications listed in our bibliography. Kathleen Pappas of the Department of Religious Studies at Brown and Tara Susman of the Religion Department at Barnard were kind-spirited and sometimes long-suffering when asked to help shoulder a variety of burdens. Robert Cessna and his staff at the Southern Asian Institute of Columbia University cheerfully assisted with tasks of duplication and coordination. Paul Arney, of the Religion Department at Columbia, checked a number of references with meticulous care.

Finally, we would express deep gratitude to our colleagues who contributed essays to the book. They have formed an especially genial and enthusiastic group, working patiently through many revisions without having the stimulus of a conference or seminar series to urge them on. We very much look forward to gathering, at last, for a "cast party" once the book has been born.

John Stratton Hawley
Donna Marie Wulff

New York and Providence,
May, 1995

A NOTE ON TRANSLITERATION AND PRONUNCIATION

For the sake of internal consistency throughout the volume, we have retained the Sanskrit or pan-Indian forms of words wherever it seemed reasonable to do so, and we have followed the standard system of transliterating Sanskrit. Although Sanskrit makes no distinction between upper- and lower-case letters, we have used capitals to indicate proper names and titles (Devī, Mātā, Vindhyakṣetra, etc.). For the terms from Malayalam and Tamil found in the chapters by Caldwell and Narayanan, respectively, we have adopted the authors' conventions.

Exceptions include terms that have been anglicized in form (Krishna, Puranic) or that have come into English usage (guru, swami, yoga, avatar); these are treated as English words. Further, modern place names are given in their current transliterated forms, but without diacritics. If references to such places are made in a literary context, however, the diacritics have been retained.

The vowels of Sanskrit and other Indian languages are pronounced much as those of Latin, Italian, or French, with the following exceptions:

a is pronounced like the short u in English cup,
ā is pronounced like the broad a in English father,
ṛ (a vowel) is a liquid sound that approximates the flipped r of British very.

Although the system of consonants is complex, the English reader can approximate their sounds using the following guidelines:

c is pronounced like the English ch, as in cherry,
h after a consonant (e.g., p) indicates that the consonant is aspirated, i.e., articulated with a puff of air, as in the English hip-hop,
ś and *ṣ* are pronounced roughly like the English sh, as in shame.

SITES ASSOCIATED WITH GODDESS WORSHIP

Sites listed include those explicitly mentioned in the text as well as those where one of the goddesses discussed in the following essays is particularly worshiped or thought to be at home.

Banaras	Holy city and pilgrimage site on the Ganges, where millions of Hindus bathe in the sacred waters of Mother Ganges to gain earthly boons as well as ultimate liberation.
Bombay	Film capital of India and home of the studio that produced the Hindi film *Jai Santoshi Ma.*
Calcutta	Major center for the worship of Kālī, notably at the famous temple of Kālīghāṭ, where her skull is worshiped.
Chottanikkara	Town in Kerala with a major temple dedicated to the goddess Bhagavati known for the cures of madness, especially of young women, that take place there.
Hardwar	Pilgrimage town high in the Himalayan foothills, in which the Vishva Hindu Parishad, a militant Hindu nationalist organization, completed and consecrated in 1983 an eight-story temple to Bhārat Mātā, "Mother India."
Jodhpur	City in Rajasthan in which a temple has been dedicated to Santoṣī Mā since 1967.
Srirangam	Location of the major Śrī Vaiṣṇava temple, in which Śrī is called Raṅganāyakī, mistress of Srirangam.
Tiruchanur	Town at the foot of the Tirumala-Tirupati hills in Andhra Pradesh that houses a temple to Padmāvatī, a local goddess identified with Śrī.
Vaishno Devi	Pilgrimage site near Katra in the district of Jammu, in the state of Jammu and Kashmir, in which the Goddess known in her iconic form as Śerāṅvālī is worshiped in the form of three stone outcroppings.
Vindhyachal	Pilgrimage town sacred to the goddess Vindhyavāsinī, located at the point where the Vindhya Mountains descend to meet the southern shore of the Ganges.
Vrindaban/Brindavan	Vaiṣṇava pilgrimage town on the bank of the Yamuna River, where Rādhā, in particular, is worshiped.

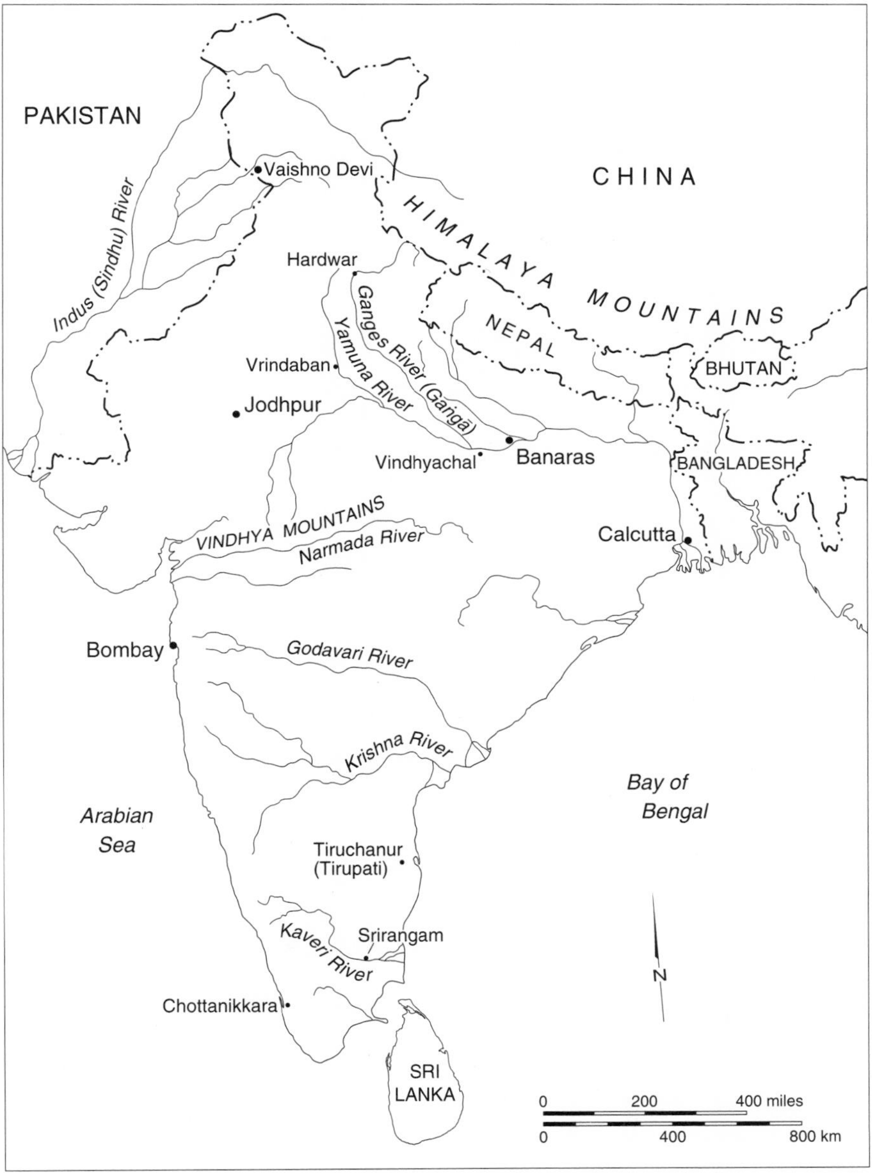
PAKISTAN
CHINA
Vaishno Devi
Indus (Sindhu) River
HIMALAYA MOUNTAINS
Hardwar
Ganges River (Gaṅgā)
Yamuna River
NEPAL
BHUTAN
Vrindaban
Jodhpur
Banaras
Vindhyachal
BANGLADESH
VINDHYA MOUNTAINS
Narmada River
Calcutta
Bombay
Godavari River
Krishna River
Bay of Bengal
Arabian Sea
Tiruchanur (Tirupati)
Srirangam
Kaveri River
N
Chottanikkara
SRI LANKA
0 200 400 miles
0 400 800 km

Map 1

PROLOGUE
The Goddess in India

John Stratton Hawley

One of the critical developments in the recent history of Western religion has been the effort to make clearer contact with the feminine dimension in religious experience. This has taken a myriad of forms. Women are now ordained ministers and rabbis in a number of communities where a few years ago the idea would have been laughed away. Gender-neutral language is mandated in many hymnals, prayer books, and new translations of the Bible. Much attention has been focused on feminine images for God in the scriptures and elsewhere. Groups of women have labored to rescue the word *witch* from its infamous past by becoming witches themselves—and demonstrating whose infamy it actually was, when witches were burned at Salem and elsewhere. Finally, there has been a determined assault on the very history of Western religion in an effort to discover at its origins a Goddess who was widely worshiped before the champions of patriarchy suppressed her. Could she not be worshiped again? Indeed, she is.

The Abrahamic faiths nonetheless place many barriers in the way of seeing the divine as feminine. Those who assert that a coherent culture of the Goddess once prevailed across the Mediterranean world and Europe acknowledge that it has long since been defiled, broken, obscured.[1] In the task of reconstruction—at the scholarly level as well as in the realm of practice—great creativity will be required before Westerners can discover the Goddess again.

Not so for India. All through the archaeological remains of the Indus Valley Civilization, which created a new standard of culture for South Asia in the third and second millennia B.C.E., one finds a distinctive set of female terracotta figurines—thousands of them. We cannot tell exactly what functions they served or what they meant to those who made and kept them, but there seems no question about their ubiquity or importance. Moreover, the styles of modeling they display were carried forward into subsequent ages. Female sculptures from the Mauryan period (fourth to second centuries B.C.E.) and even later often look very much like their Indus prototypes.[2] By that time one also has much clearer evidence of a religion that projected the divine in both masculine and feminine terms.[3] True, the Aryan civilization that became increasingly dominant in North India at the level of high culture from 1000 B.C.E. onward allotted only minor roles to goddesses, but the material evidence shows that the indigenous culture never died out. In fact, one scholar recently suggested that "the history of the Hindu tradition can be seen as a reemergence of the feminine."[4] As the Sanskrit textual tradition developed up through the seventeenth and eighteenth centuries C.E., the place of the Goddess in it became ever more firmly established.

Thus, in the religious life of Hindus today there is no need to resuscitate the Great Goddess. She is alive and well. She proliferates in ever new forms of herself (many would say, in fact, that she is fundamentally plural rather than singular), and she animates the religious lives of hundreds of millions of people. Her generic name in Sanskrit and the many Indian languages related to it is *devī*, a word that, like its Latin and Greek cognates *dea* and *thea*, means simply "goddess." This is a book about Devī, singular and plural, the Goddess and goddesses of India.

It has a forerunner. A decade ago, Donna Wulff and I published a collection of essays (five of which reappear here, in altered form) under the title *The Divine Consort: Rādhā and the Goddesses of India.*[5] That volume focused on Rādhā, the consort of the well-known Hindu god Krishna, and had as a primary aim the task of making her better known and understood outside of India. Other goddesses were arrayed around Rādhā, with the particular desire of illuminating her place in the broader Hindu tradition. The book that emerged was the first collection of essays in English on Hindu goddesses, but because of the intimate relation between Rādhā and Krishna, it inevitably laid a certain emphasis on goddesses who are understood as wives or consorts.

This time we intend to shift the balance so that independent goddesses and goddesses who dominate their male partners can take center stage. In part, this reflects the redirection of Western scholarship in the intervening decade, which is in turn partially a response to the vigorous feminist influence in the field of religious studies. But this attempt to readjust the balance in the earlier book also has a logic of its own. However wide-ranging the essays that *The Divine Consort* comprised, the name of the book quite wrongly suggested that male gods (and perhaps male religion) are the fundamental point of reference in Hinduism. Indian society may be overwhelmingly patriarchal, as is often said, but in the realm of religion the picture is far more complex.

The entrance of many women scholars into the field of Hindu studies has also facilitated another important change that is reflected in this book. These women have often been able to pursue research into aspects of the living religion of India that their male predecessors could only approach indirectly. In a society where women and men often lead separate lives, women scholars can observe and enter into conversation with Hindu women far more easily than men. Of course, it would be wrong to think that Hindu goddesses are worshiped exclusively or even primarily by women, but female devotees certainly figure importantly in the communities that revere them. Several chapters in the book—those by Cynthia Humes, Donna Wulff, Lindsey Harlan, Kathleen Erndl, Sarah Caldwell, and Rachel McDermott—especially benefit from this new mode of access to the Goddess, and in general the focus on lived religion here is stronger than it was in *The Divine Consort*, which had a predominantly textual orientation. Because most Indian texts about goddesses, whether consort or "free," have been composed by men, this increasing disengagement from the hegemony of the written word is doubly significant.

Critics may well observe that another hurdle is yet to be jumped: most of the authors represented here are not themselves Hindus. Only one has an Indian language as her mother tongue. With the rapid movement of South Asians into a Western diaspora, and with the gradual (if sometimes grudging) acknowledgment in India itself that religion is a respectable field of study, another decade will doubtless not only demand but make possible further changes of perspective in a collection such as this. More Hindu voices will be heard—and particularly, more voices of Hindu women.

ONE GODDESS AND MANY, NEW AND OLD

In 1975 the movie *Jai Santoshi Ma* emerged from the thriving network of studios that make Bombay one of the major capitals of the international film industry, and within months a new goddess was being worshiped throughout India. The name of the movie can be loosely translated as "Hail to the Mother of Satisfaction," and it heralded a divinity—"The Mother of Satisfaction," Santoṣī Mā—who had hitherto remained entirely unknown to most Indians. In fact, although a temple to her existed in Jodhpur, Rajasthan, she had evidently not been known very long under that name or in that form even there. Before 1967 the temple now dedicated to her had belonged to a goddess called Lāl Sāgar kī Mātā, "The Mother of the Red Lake," near whose banks it stands, and the characteristics of the earlier goddess diverged in important respects from those of Santoṣī Mā. Most significantly, Lāl Sāgar kī Mātā was a carnivore, to whom goats and other animals were periodically sacrificed, whereas Santoṣī Mā is a vegetarian, with chickpeas and unrefined sugar at the center of her diet.

Most who saw the movie knew nothing of this previous history, or indeed of Santoṣī Mā herself, before they walked into cinema halls throughout the subcontinent. Yet the goddess who appeared before them in celluloid form was in many ways familiar. The colors of her clothes and complexion were drawn from a palette standardized by the poster-art industry that dominates the iconographic imaginations of most modern-day Hindus (see figure 1). Her characteristic poses showed her standing or sitting on a lotus, as several other goddesses do. (See especially Vasudha Narayanan's description of Śrī in this collection.) And she shared her most prominent implements, the sword and trident, with the great goddess often named Durgā. (See the chapter by Thomas Coburn on Devī and Kathleen Erndl's essay on Śerāṅvālī.)

As her film brought her to life, however, Santoṣī Mā quickly became one of the most important and widely worshiped goddesses in India, taking her place in poster-art form in the altar rooms of millions of Hindu homes. People throughout India, especially women, kept (and still keep) a vow of fasting for sixteen consecutive Fridays. On those days they made special offerings to Santoṣī Mā, hoping to be blessed with a wish fulfilled. Then, and at other times too, they read her story and sang her songs. The annual calendar of Hindu festivals also responded to her advent. In late summer there is a celebration of brother-sister solidarity, *rākhī* or *rakṣabandhana*, which the film identified as the moment of and reason for Santoṣī Mā's birth. Not unexpectedly, then, her image began to appear on the bright paper medallions that decorate the threads (*rākhīs*) sisters tie onto the wrists of their brothers and other male relatives and friends on that day. Everywhere, Santoṣī Mā images and shrines were added to temples, and in some cases, as had already happened in Jodhpur, she took over the place of the presiding deity in temples that had previously been dedicated to other goddesses.

How was all this possible? Obviously the filmmakers had found the right story at the right time. Obviously, they were appealing to a religious culture in which visual access to the divine was understood to be both legitimate and crucial. Moreover, many said, it was devotion that had produced the film: the filmmaker's wife, after discovering Santoṣī Mā on a pilgrimage to Jodhpur, had been the one who persuaded her husband to spread the goddess's message by translating her into a new medium.

Yet it is hard to conceive that Santoṣī Mā could have granted such instant satisfaction to so many people had she not been part of a larger and already well-integrated culture of the Goddess. Her new devotees could immediately recognize many of her characteristic moods and attributes, and feel them deeply, because she shared them with other goddesses long since familiar to them. Some of these divine women were somewhat playfully depicted in the film as struggling spitefully against the growth of the cult of the new goddess—and understandably, for she had stolen their fire. In some sense, she really *was* Brahmāṇī and Pārvatī and Lakṣmī, the goddesses who

Figure 1. Santoṣī Mā. Polychrome poster-art depiction, ca. 1980, by J. B. Khanna and Company, Madras.

did their best to make life hard for Santoṣī Mā's paradigmatic devotee. In some sense, too, she prevailed because of her youth and vigor. In India, as elsewhere, there is something fascinating about the new, and the film's own plot suggested it was natural that Santoṣī Mā's youth should arouse the envy of older goddesses.

But there was another secret to her success: she was a unitive presence. At least in the context of this film, she was the Great Goddess in a way that Brahmāṇī, Pārvatī, and Lakṣmī, as wives to the classic triad of supreme Hindu gods (Brahmā, Śiva, and Viṣṇu), were not. Although she was depicted as emerging from a divine lineage, she stood on her own. Not only did she incorporate and thus summarize a certain spectrum of preexisting female divinities, but she unified them as well, amalgamating their power for her devotees.

There is much more to be said about the appeal of this new film goddess, as Stanley Kurtz has attempted to do in his recent book, *All the Mothers Are One.*[6] Yet in all of it one can scarcely miss the point that, as his title suggests, Hindu goddesses tend to be seen as close relatives of one another—even possessing a common substance—in a way that is somehow less true of the male side of the Hindu pantheon. The "high theology" of the Goddess enunciated in two classic Sanskrit texts, the *Devī Māhātmya* and the *Devī Bhāgavata Purāṇa,* provides a way of understanding why this should be so. For most Hindus, the gods, too, are ultimately understood as a unity: *bhagavān ek hī hai* ("God is one"), as the common Hindi phrase has it. Yet this unity is typically conceived to exist at a level distant from everyday life—at the "nonqualified" (*nirguṇa*) level. With goddesses, it is different. As described in the texts just named (on one of which, the *Devī Māhātmya,* see the essays by Thomas Coburn and Cynthia Humes), the unity of the Great Goddess incorporates the world as we know it, as well as transcending it. In some sense, Goddess *is* our world, in a way that God is not. Hence the multiple forms she takes are connected in a way that strikes us as more intimate than those we typically project when we understand the divine as male.

This is not to deny the variousness of the Goddess. In one of her most prevalent expressions she spreads herself across the landscape of much of India—the southern part especially—such that she becomes specific to each place she touches. Each village has its tutelary divinity, its *grāmadevatā* ("village deity"), and the personality of each is distinct: no one place is the same as any other. Yet the fact that the divine *is* ubiquitous in this manner says something generic, and Hindus have overwhelmingly conceptualized that place-specific, divine reality as female. These village deities are almost always understood as goddesses, not gods. In most instances their commonality can be acknowledged by calling each of them "Mother," and in many places in South India one can be even more specific. There, village goddesses tend to collect under the common heading of Mariyamman: the Mariyamman of this locale or that, after the fashion of "Our Lady of ——."[7]

It is important to understand that for Hindus, real differentiations, such as those that obtain among local deities, do not necessarily imply unbridgeable gaps between members of a given set of beings. As Diana Eck has commented about Indian ways of thinking, "If something is important, it is important enough to be repeated, duplicated, and seen from many angles."[8] This is true for gods, and even truer for goddesses. Not so many years ago India's vast film industry produced a movie, entitled "Sarasvatī, Lakṣmī, Pārvatī," and on billboards the three goddesses were clumped together as a triad—three similar-looking heads emerging as if from a common frame. It is hard to imagine a film taking its title from the names of three gods who would be portrayed in the same fashion.

Of course, Hindu male deities do sometimes share emblems, attributes, and properties. Viṣṇu's characteristic disc can on occasion be found in the hand of Krishna, who is often conceptualized as his avatar, and Śiva's habit of wearing snakes as garlands is often replicated in his horrific manifestation as Bhairava ("The Fearsome One"). Yet this sharing of family traits is even more pronounced on the female side of the Hindu pantheon. To begin with, goddesses observe an important ground rule that does not apply to gods: when they appear in sculpted form, as images, they are almost invariably anthropomorphic.[9] More than that, they share associations: with the auspicious, gentle lotus on the one hand, and with such powerful weapons as the sword and the trident on the other. Similar ties emerge at the level of theological analysis. For example, goddesses are characteristically described as bearing a close relation to power or energy per se (*śakti*). That energy is abundant in the physical universe we inhabit. Hence, goddesses tend to be strongly associated with the forces of nature (*prakṛti*) and the earth—sometimes in its nurturing, maternal aspect, sometimes in its natural periodicity, sometimes in its uncontrollable, destructive power. The earth itself is typically figured as a goddess: *bhū*, the earth, is Bhūdevī. Often, too, the power of a goddess (or *the* Goddess) is experienced as brilliantly hot—a quality called *tejas*. Finally, perhaps especially in the eyes of men, this goddess power is felt to be somehow miraculous, to produce illusion (*māyā*), to delude. And not surprisingly, all but one of the concepts we have just listed are grammatically feminine in Sanskrit and in other Indic languages that distinguish nouns by gender (*tejas*, the exception, is neuter).

To a certain degree, these family resemblances carry over into the ritual dimension as well. Both gods and goddesses are worshiped throughout India with a ritual vocabulary whose central elements remain more or less constant. To the accompaniment of music, offerings of praise (*pūjā*) are made to the divinity, who is typically present in the form of a clothed image (*mūrti*), and certain of the offerings are standard: incense, flowers, lighted candles or flames of burning camphor, and various sorts of food. These, once touched or tasted by the divinity, are returned to the worshipers as ritual leftovers, called *prasād*. The word means literally "grace" and signifies that the original giver in this transaction is actually the deity, who is the real author of the materials being offered—and, indeed, of the offerers. A similar thing holds true for the act of visual attention (*darśan*, "seeing" or "sight") that accompanies these acts of worship. On the one hand, the worshiper sees the divinity, in an imagistic expression. Yet on the other, the worshiper is seen by the deity, the image, for the image has been ritually enlivened and thus has eyes. As with *prasād*, there is the conviction that in this visual transaction the deity's act of seeing actually precedes the devotee's. Ontologically, it has a prior status.

All this is standard for deities of either sex. It is noteworthy, however, that certain kinds of symbols and rituals are particularly associated with female divinities. For example, goddesses are often represented by pots; the pot overflowing with vegetation is an ancient Indian symbol of fructification. Further, goddesses tend to possess their devotees to the point of total identification, which is much rarer for gods. Possession is not entirely absent in the worship of male divinities, but it is especially characteristic of the worship of goddesses. In a similar way, it would seem likely, although the evidence is far from complete, that women are more frequently possessed by goddesses than are men.[10] Certainly, women figure more prominently in possession performances associated with goddesses than they do as lead actors in the general run of public Hindu rites. Finally, and quite importantly, some goddesses (but emphatically not all) share a taste for blood sacrifice. Sacrificial violence is endemic to the worship of many goddesses, especially the village deities and local guardians mentioned above, so it was no small matter when the carnivorous Lāl Sāgar kī Mātā was converted into the vegetarian Santoṣī Mā. The elimination (or sublimation) of blood sacrifice in Hindu religion is a long-standing historical trend that applies to both gods and goddesses.[11] But it is notable that where "real" sacrifice persists, a female divinity is apt to be involved.[12]

Given this pattern of multiplicity and convergence, it is often hard to know how best to refer to Devī in English. Sometimes the singular feels more accurate, sometimes the plural. When we are speaking in the singular, it seems sexist and perhaps even imperialist to stick to English convention and withhold the capital "G" that we so readily award to a single male divinity. Hence, readers of this book will encounter not only "goddesses" and "goddess," but "Goddess"—both with and without the definite article. Since Indic languages observe no distinction between capital and lowercase letters, and since they lack the definite article, the g/G and "the" problems are clearly ours, not India's. But the quandary as to singular or plural is shared.

In similar fashion, there is no "right" way to array the extraordinary range of goddesses who will appear in the pages that follow. The present ordering of chapters reflects only one possible alignment, and even it is the product of several compromises. Readers are invited to imagine other configurations. Given the complicated web of ties that binds these goddesses together—and, equally, the many features that keep them apart—no one arrangement can be definitive.

THE GODDESS AS SUPREME, THE GODDESS AS CONSORT

In the first part of this book, we follow one major gradient: the contrast between goddesses who are conceived as supreme, independent, and comprehensive, and those whose character is shaped by relationships—especially the relations they bear to the male gods who are their consorts. Two chapters are devoted to exploring each type, and a transitional chapter links these two sets of two. At the independent end of the spectrum we encounter the generic Devī and her closely related aspect, the locally grounded Vindhyavāsinī. These goddesses are characterized by their supremacy over all other forms of life, whether animal, human, or divine. At the other end of the spectrum we have Śrī (or Lakṣmī, as she is sometimes called) and Rādhā, both of whom are defined by their relationships to their mates, although in markedly divergent ways. In between, we meet Kālī, a goddess who fits into neither of these sets and in a strange way mediates between the transcendent and the consort goddesses. On the one hand, Kālī unquestionably manifests herself as supreme—whether as a mother demanding submission or as uncanny, uncontrollable force—but, on the other hand, her supremacy is paradigmatically measured by the power she exerts over her consort, the great god Śiva. As her myths of origin reveal, she is both the same as and different from the Great Goddess.

With this Great Goddess, then, we begin: Devī, the transcendent and all-encompassing. In the book's opening chapter Thomas Coburn describes the earliest known Hindu text in which, as he puts it, "ultimate reality is understood as Goddess": the sixth-century *Devī Māhātmya* ("Glorification of the Goddess"). Coburn points to the many ways in which the theologian(s) who composed it combined and reshaped earlier formulations to make them serve the cause of a single, supreme Goddess. He retells three of Devī's most important martial encounters, in which she defeats demons who threaten the stability of the world, to illustrate how she exemplifies the powers of illusion and redemption from it (*māyā*), earthiness and materiality (*prakṛti*), and power or energy (*śakti*). As we have seen, each of these Sanskrit concepts is feminine, and Coburn shows how they all serve a female-focused vision of both cosmic and earthly reality. At the same time, however, he demonstrates how the *Devī Māhātmya* associates these female properties with the Great Goddess in such a way as to avoid the conclusion that they have male counterparts, as they are assumed to have in other expressions of the Hindu tradition. For the *Devī Māhātmya, māyā* is not complementary or subordinate to Viṣṇu, as other texts would have it. Nor is *prakṛti* balanced—or superseded—by the principle of maleness, *puruṣa,* with which it is so often paired. Nor is *śakti* paired with, or subsumed in, the male god Śiva. In Devī, these qualities stand on their own, constituting reality in a manner that is independently female.

Toward the conclusion of his chapter, Coburn takes up the various ways in which this independent theology of the Great Goddess relates to elements of the Hindu tradition that are not so entirely focused on the feminine. As we have already hinted, these include communities devoted to the worship of Śiva (the Śaivas) or Viṣṇu (the Vaiṣṇavas) or gods such as Krishna who are frequently conceptualized as being avatars of Viṣṇu (Vaiṣṇavas again). Coburn also distinguishes between some of the perspectives of the *Devī Māhātmya* and those that developed later within communities devoted primarily to the Goddess and her many forms, communities broadly referred to as Śākta, a term deriving from the concept of *śakti.*

In the chapter that follows, by Cynthia Ann Humes, we have a chance to see what happens to the idea of the Great Goddess when it is taken up by one of these Śākta traditions, as practiced in a particular place. The place is a village called Vindhyachal. It marks the spot at which the Vindhya mountain range, which stretches across the center of India, comes to an end at the banks of the Ganges. As we shall see, the Ganges itself is understood by Hindus to be a goddess—hence the place has unusual power—and the goddess who reigns there is known as Vindhyavāsinī, "The One Who Dwells in the Vindhyas." The tradition of her worship is old. Humes shows, in fact, that it contributed to the general formulation of "goddessness" that is found in the *Devī Māhātmya.* Yet it is also given voice in a text specific to the Vindhya locale itself, the *Vindhya Māhātmya* ("Glorification of the Vindhyas"). This work praises the Vindhya mountain range and the town that serves as its emblem, while at the same time extolling the goddess Vindhyavāsinī who enlivens them both and, in a deep sense, *is* them.

Humes offers a memorable account of what it is like to join the pilgrims who come to worship Vindhyavāsinī: milling crowds, the sound of temple gongs, blood sacrifices, and the following of ritual diagrams. Here we see—and hear, touch, and smell—what it is to encounter this transcendent goddess in real time and space. We come to sense how Hindus in one specific context taste the affirmation that the Great Goddess's transcendence must be experienced through her simultaneous immanence in the world we inhabit.

Humes also shows that the meaning of this conflation of transcendent and immanent is undergoing a process of continuous renegotiation. She highlights the manner in which the text describing this particular place, the *Vindhya Māhātmya*, is progressively being displaced by the *Devī Māhātmya*, even in local usage. As they increasingly seek to appeal to pilgrims drawn from far-flung places, the priests and pilgrim guides of Vindhyavāsinī tend to express her transcendence in a language that implicitly subordinates the here-and-now goddess Vindhyavāsinī to the more generalized Devī of the *Devī Māhātmya*. For their more cosmopolitan clients in particular, they reorient the old passions of Vindhyavāsinī in the direction of an emerging pan-Hindu orthodoxy that emphasizes Vedic roots, vegetarian habits, and a universalist theology.

Some of these same transitions can be seen in the worship of Kālī ("The Black One"). Recent field study by Rachel Fell McDermott, some of which she reports in her chapter at the end of this collection, shows that in modern-day Bengal, at least, the Black Goddess is predominantly conceived as a kind and beautiful maternal force.[13] Yet, as her distinctly nonvegetarian patterns of worship and apparently horrific iconography reveal, there was a time not long ago when Kālī was experienced as a terrifying reality. Sarah Caldwell's description of Kālī as she appears in a South Indian locale under the name Bhagavati ("The Blessed One") conveys some sense of how this violent Kālī feels to present-day worshipers, and David Kinsley's portrait of her as she appears in several key Sanskrit texts—the third chapter of our book—echoes many of the same themes.

Kinsley shows how Devī's three great aspects—*māyā, prakṛti,* and *śakti*—take on a new form when expressed through Kālī. Kālī provides startling glimpses of what can happen when powers of illusion, natural forces, and energy exist in a pure form, beyond the control of any governing, restraining structure. For example, there is the paradigmatic moment when Kālī dances wild on the prone, ithyphallic corpse of her husband Śiva. It seems clear that such images of Kālī were shaped by men, and male roles are what give structural definition to most segments of Hindu society. Hence it is no surprise that, as Lawrence A. Babb some years ago observed, goddesses bear a seemly, auspicious demeanor when they are subjected to the will of their husbands or consorts—that is, when they serve within the structures that their spouses provide. But they appear dangerous and threatening when they do not.[14]

Men know that women possess a power that exceeds the structures they would like to impose, structures that have collectively been called dharma: the way things should be, at least according to the dominant men. As Kinsley demonstrates, one influential account of Kālī's origins gives shape to this knowledge: the gods need her to confront demons they cannot contain, but once they release her from their own beings and allow her to consolidate herself beyond the boundaries that their personalities provide, she becomes uncontrollable. Or, in a parallel tale, once she escapes the control of her aroused mate, Śiva (*śiva* means literally "the auspicious one"), she expands her form and relaxes her behavior to the point where she dances a crazed dance on Śiva's corpse (*śava*, the most inauspicious of things). In these stories she is, as Kinsley says, "blood and death out of place." In confronting her, we are not only horrified but potentially saved. A vision of Kālī takes us beyond the constraints through which and within which we live. Kālī releases.

In this paradoxical meeting of affliction and liberation, Kālī establishes a paradigm that fits many other goddesses, especially goddesses who express themselves as diseases. There is Śītalā, for example, the goddess of pustular diseases who is worshiped all across North India and has counterparts elsewhere, too.[15] In her main incarnation as smallpox, she maims, disfigures, kills. Yet her name means "The Cool One," as if she connoted something far more soothing than her diminutive demon-consort Jara ("Fever"), the burning, delusion-causing reality that every smallpox victim knows. Poems to Śītalā demonstrate the paradox that disease is not just curse but release—release from life in its humdrum channels, a journey into levels of sensitivity that seem now illusory, now realer than real. Even death can be a release of this sort—release from life itself—and because death and life are often seen by Hindus as contrasting moments along a single gradient of experience, a single goddess may govern them both. Śītalā does this, as both the disease and its cure. And, on a grander scale, so does Kālī: her name means not only "black" but "deathly." Sarah Caldwell's chapter later in the book describes how her affliction and deliverance are dramatized and experienced in one regional setting. Kathleen Erndl's chapter provides comparative material for Devī; and in Vindhyavāsinī, too, we encounter a goddess whose independence can sometimes lead to excess.

In chapters 4 and 5 we turn to a much less frightful, less paradoxical pair of divinities—Śrī and Rādhā. As Babb's typology of malevolent and benevolent goddesses would predict, these are deities who relate to their mates in more characteristically amenable ways than Kālī or Śītalā. Both are consorts of Viṣṇu, but in different roles. As Vasudha Narayanan shows, Śrī (or Lakṣmī) is his wife, serving him predictably, eternally. True, she is sometimes shown independent of Viṣṇu, standing on the auspicious lotus, showering benefits on her human devotees, her children. But Śrī has another pose that more clearly represents what theologians regard as her ontological (as against soteriological) status and that serves as background for most devotees' understanding of the goddess, even when she stands alone. In this second pose, Śrī appears as the "breast-jewel" of Viṣṇu, ever cradled in his arms, nurturing him with her warmth and sharing his essence. According to the Śrī Vaiṣṇava community of South India, who especially revere her, it is because of this intimate, submissive association with Viṣṇu, the lord of all reality, that she is able to dispense the benefits she does. Śrī is Viṣṇu's smiling, maternal side, the caring dimension that balances the authority symbolized by his maleness.

One can, however, take this emphasis too far. Narayanan is very interested in slippages between the reigning theology of the Śrī Vaiṣṇava community, as represented in what we have just said, and the ways in which certain groups of worshipers celebrate Śrī as if she were a force fully coequal to Viṣṇu—on rare occasions, almost independent. Yet there is never any question about the importance of the bond of marriage that ties her to Viṣṇu. That bond, which mandates that a wife be subservient to husband, symbolizes the stability of the relation between the accessible (female) and the transcendent (male) sides of the divine. Śrī is Viṣṇu's wife. She is not his only wife: Bhūdevī, the Earth, in whom we participate directly, is also there.[16] But Śrī, the pure principle of cosmic auspiciousness, goes beyond the mixed earthly realm in which we live, and thus shares fully in the divine. Nevertheless, she does so without challenging the hierarchical order that is intrinsic to it. However transcendent, she continues to serve her husband—far more than he serves her.

Rādhā's relation to Krishna, who is often interpreted as an avatar of Viṣṇu but whom many of his devotees regard as the ultimate form of divinity, is different. Krishna takes to its logical conclusion the quality of free play (*līlā*) through which Viṣṇu manifests the world. In the paradigmatic form in which most of his devotees worship him, he is no king and no husband. Instead he is a youth. Although inherently powerful, he plays freely, letting his appetites carry him where they will, far beyond any constraints that might be implied by propriety, duty, or what many people conceive as religion. The word *dharma* means each of these things, and in his playfulness Krishna eternally transcends dharma.

Necessarily, then, Krishna's relation to his primary consort, Rādhā, can hardly have the quality of a marriage. By far the majority of their devotees interpret Rādhā as Krishna's lover and beloved, but not his wife. She is "another's" (*parakīyā*), not "his own" (*svakīyā*). With the constraints of structure irrelevant or contravened, theirs can be a bond of pure love (*prema*). It is without progeny; it exists for itself. Unprotected by the expectations that accompany marriage, and free from the confines of family, the relationship between Rādhā and Krishna is a sweet but stormy one. Its setting is pastoral: the Braj countryside, where he and Rādhā dwell. As Krishna's appetites take him to other women, she pines and angers, approaches and withdraws. Because of the force of their love, he, too, is often seen to be subject to these moods, and there are times when he abases himself at her feet; it is not just the other way around. When he does so, in fact, he is paying obeisance to erotic love itself (*mādhurya*), which Rādhā so fully symbolizes.

In her chapter on Rādhā, Donna Wulff explores such themes by examining the portraits of this goddess that emerge in the sixteenth-century Sanskrit plays of the major Vaiṣṇava theologian Rūpa Gosvāmī and in the modern Bengali performance tradition called *padāvalī kīrtan.* As Vasudha Narayanan found, despite what the texts say, Śrī is understood by many worshipers to be coequal with Viṣṇu. Similarly, Wulff discovers that both for Rūpa and for the Bengali *kīrtan* troupes, Rādhā is truly Krishna's equal, no matter what Sanskrit classics like the *Bhāgavata Purāṇa* would seem to imply. Indeed, in certain ways she transcends him. In a setting where embodied love is regarded as the supreme avenue to religious realization, Rādhā's steadfast devotion to Krishna (even in anger) exalts her above her mate. Wulff shows that what is in many ways Rādhā's most human feature—her intense longing for Krishna, displayed with particular force when they are apart and throbbing with the pique and anger that any neglected lover might feel—is the very measure of her divinity.

In an influential chapter of *The Divine Consort,* Frédérique Apffel Marglin discussed the meanings of different patterns of sexual union between gods and goddesses, as seen through the eyes of women she interviewed in Puri, Orissa.[17] Three patterns emerge. In one, the male is dominant and is often portrayed as larger than the woman; in another, the two sexes are equal and are often equal in size; in the third, the female prevails and is often shown larger than the male, or above him (see figure 2). The first is typified by the relation between Viṣṇu and his consort Lakṣmī (or Śrī); the second is illustrated in the love of Rādhā and Krishna; and the third is archetypally present in the union between Śiva and Kālī.

At first glance, this method of sorting out the ways in which goddesses relate to the male side of the pantheon would seem to support the typology articulated by Lawrence Babb: "small" goddesses, controlled by males, are beneficent and auspicious; "big" goddesses threaten, and may bring death. Yet Marglin moves beyond Babb's typology in two ways. First, she devotes particular attention to the intervening category, Rādhā's, which floats between the other two and which her informants see as unique. Second, in an earlier essay, Marglin directly challenges Babb's interpretation of "big" and "small" by proposing that what is dangerous in the "big" goddesses is not their female sexuality per se (as perceived by men) but their celibacy, their separation from erotic interaction. Female power (*śakti*), Marglin argues, is neither threatening nor benign. If not grounded in a sexual relation, it can oscillate freely between the two, sometimes nurturing and sometimes destroying. It is thus "the power of life and death."[18]

Be this as it may—and Babb's own interpretation acknowledges this potential ambivalence—it is hard to consider Hindu visions of how the sexes may interact at the divine level without developing a powerful sense of men's fear of women.[19] Such fear is often expressed as the desire to control. Yet Marglin's perspective in this disagreement with Babb alerts us to a different, equally important conclusion. Namely, it is insufficient merely to

Figure 2a. The following illustrations depict three kinds of relations between goddesses and gods, as typified by their relative sizes and mode of sexual interaction. Above is an image of Lakṣmī in the lap of Narasiṃha. Painted sculpture, Lakṣmī-Narasiṃha temple, Puri, Orissa.

categorize Hindu goddesses according to a schema that focuses entirely on their connections with male divinities. It is a simple fact that not all goddesses can be described in this way. Devī herself, as portrayed in the *Devī Māhātmya,* stands apart from even the "big" goddesses in that she has no consort at all, and the same can be said of many other goddesses who

Figure 2b. Rādhā and Krishna intertwined. Polychrome poster-art depiction, ca. 1990, by S. S. Brajbasi and Sons, Delhi.

are described in this volume. Śerāṅvālī, Gaṅgā, and Bhagavati belong to this set: their maternal functions make their bonds of consortship pale in importance, and in some cases no such bonds exist. Indeed, stories about Hindu goddesses, as well as conventions that govern their worship, make it clear that almost every goddess's relationships extend far beyond sex and consortship. As we have just hinted, it is especially the maternal dimension

Figure 2c. Folk painting representing the goddess Kālī straddling the erect *liṅga* of Śiva's corpse. Gouache on cloth, Orissa, 19th century. From Philip Rawson, *The Art of Tantra*, copyright 1973 by Thames and Hudson, Ltd., London. Used by permission.

that often exceeds the matrimonial, and this dimension comes to the fore in the chapters that comprise the second part of this book.

GODDESSES WHO MOTHER AND POSSESS

Diana Eck inaugurates the second half of the book with a portrait of Gaṅgā, the river Ganges. Often referred to as Gaṅgā Mātā, "Mother Ganges" (as in the hymn with which Eck commences her essay), this goddess can be experienced in both living and conceptual form. She is a tangible river but simultaneously a personage whose full dimensions can be revealed only in icon, story, and song. She is characterized as the very embodiment of *śakti*, energy in its liquid form, and her power brings life to the wide plain she nourishes. Yet not only there. As Eck shows, Mother Ganges is understood to be everywhere that water is—in all the rivers (and therefore oceans) of the earth, and throughout the cycle of evaporation and condensation that ties earth to heaven. She is the female power that connects all things: the heavenly Ganges (*ākāś gaṅgā*) above, the river Ganges and all water beneath, and the descent (*avataraṇa*) that makes them part of a single system. The ability to encompass is what makes this goddess a mother in a special way: through her power to flow and to join, she creates and sustains life. Appropriately, therefore, her mythology associates her as a consort not only with Śiva, who is the dominant male in her life, but also with Viṣṇu; and in an important sense she is greater than them both.

The chapter that follows, by Wendy Doniger, presents a portrait of the goddess known sometimes as Saraṇyū and sometimes as Saṃjñā. Although she is, like the Ganges, in a certain capacity the nurturer of the human race—the stories concerning Saraṇyū make her our actual progenitor—she is a mother and goddess of connections in an entirely different manner from that of Gaṅgā. Doniger traces the story of Saraṇyū, wife of the sun, all the way from the *Rig Veda*, India's oldest text, to the "classic comic" series (*Amar Chitra Katha*) of the modern day, and as she does so a wealth of interrelated variants unfolds.

Doniger shows how the myths of Saraṇyū/Saṃjñā return many times to a common set of themes. First and foremost, they explore the truth that humanity was born in a moment of alienation from the gods. Saraṇyū herself, our mother, rejected us and, in a series of ambiguous gestures, also rejected (and was sometimes rejected by) our celestial father, the sun. According to the oldest forms of the story, a delicate balance exists between these two. She is immortal; he is merely mortal, for he dies daily. Yet he is worshiped and she is not. Out of this ambiguous mix our species emerges, and language and representation, masquerade and illusion, are intimately involved. Saraṇyū's own name comes to be closely associated with doubles (*savarṇā*) and images (*saṃjñā*). These are her resources as a bad mother. Using them, she rejects her own human progeny, abandoning her son(s), and sometimes causes injury and death, the marks of mortality. Here, then, is a mother goddess whose power to connect has its dark side, and in some myths she is explicitly aligned with the blackness of Kālī—even as she seeks to be Kālī's bright counterpart, Gaurī, instead.

Perhaps precisely because she is conceived as so profoundly enmeshed in the ambiguities of human origins, Saraṇyū has never been a goddess whom Hindus actually worship. Her qualities as a mother may not be sufficiently distinct from our own natures to make her a promising focus for human appeals. In this regard Śerāṅvālī ("She of the Lion"), the great goddess Durgā whose independent power is so forcefully represented in the lion she rides, could not be more different. Yet Śerāṅvālī does not remain distant. In fact, as Kathleen Erndl shows in the chapter that follows, one of her most characteristic activities is to draw people to herself through the phenomenon we usually call possession. Here, too, in the experience of the Goddess the line between the human and the divine blurs.

Erndl offers us portraits of two "mothers" who illustrate this point vividly. They are human—women living in the northwest Indian state of Haryana who frequently travel to the Punjab and Himachal Pradesh—yet through a process of learning and experience they have come to be regarded by their devotees as in some sense divine as well, for the Goddess regularly "plays" in them. As is sometimes said in describing how possession works elsewhere in the world, she "rides" them—rides them as she rides her lion. These women have become the focus of organized cults, and possession regularly occurs in all-night vigils (called *jagrātā*) that feature their presence. Erndl explores the various techniques by which the women mediate between the Goddess and their clients: people sometimes need words of interpretation to understand what the Goddess means to say. That these women themselves—not just the Goddess—receive the title "mother" (Mātā) would seem to reflect not only respect and affection on the part of their devotees, and not only a close identification with the Goddess, but also a recognition that these are women who can, because of their special capabilities, both nurture and heal.

Erndl explains that in the world these "mothers" inhabit there is a healthy skepticism about possession. Not every trance is judged to be genuine. At the same time, however, the people of northwest India do expect possession by Devī to occur in women more often than in men, and these women benefit from that expectation. Erndl touches briefly on the point sometimes made by outside observers that possession affords a convenient language of protest and self-expression—and a vehicle of catharis—for groups (women, the poor, outcastes) who are given only a small share in controlling the societies in which they participate.[20] But as she also explains, from a point of view closer to that of indigenous exegesis, the nature of the Goddess herself makes it likely that women will be possessed more frequently than men. According to Śākta theology, the Goddess, however ultimate, is by nature physically immanent in this world. Women partake of her female nature, and also her *śakti,* in a greater measure than men; hence, they are more apt to be possessed by her. Similarly, the Great Goddess is more likely to manifest herself through possession than are any of the Hindu "great gods."

In the succeeding chapter, by Sarah Caldwell, we see the Great Goddess active in possession in quite a different corner of India—Kerala, the southwesternmost state. Caldwell describes and analyzes the dramatic rite of *mudiyettu,* in which the goddess Kāḷi (or Bhadrakāḷi, "Gracious Kālī"; or Bhagavati, "The Blessed One") does battle against the demon king Dārika (who is much like his counterparts elsewhere: Tāraka, Śumbha, Niśumbha, or Mahiṣa, the buffalo-demon). The rite ends in a symbolic beheading of Dārika, complete with much symbolic blood.

Many features of *mudiyettu* will seem familiar from the environment Erndl describes: the all-night ritual, the flame used to represent and worship Kāḷi, the bloody sword she carries as her principal weapon, the drums and ecstatic possession, and the "carrying" of the Goddess (who therefore "rides"). Yet there are differences. Here the entire community is assembled in a fully public ritual, the stage is a well-established shrine central to local worship, and Kāḷi's vehicles are exclusively men, not women (although in other contexts, more peripheral to the life of modern Kerala, women yield to possession more than men). This nocturnal *mudiyettu* event, interwoven so closely with the dominant social segment, is clearly understood as a way both to release the Goddess's energies and to control them. Darkness is dared, forests are entered, ghosts are called up to serve in her army. Although liquor and the passions of desire and anger flow, the men who participate are protected by a long-standing and highly stylized language of ritual performance. The action follows a familiar goddess-versus-demon story line that surfaces many times in this book, from the first chapter onward.

Caldwell devotes much attention to the fact that in *mudiyettu,* unlike in Erndl's *jagrātā* vigils, the logic of the ritual and its benefits seem to serve primarily the needs of men. She shows how the goddess is both virgin and mother for both sexes, but in different ways, and stresses the somewhat divergent reactions of men and women to the taboo on menstruation in the goddess's presence. Both sexes use the worship of the goddess as a means of cooling the dangerously repressed energies of anger and sexuality, but in the men's case this is accomplished by publicly venting these passions. In contrast, women may express these overpowering emotions only in extreme circumstances—the *tuḷḷal* dance—and when they do, their actions are viewed as insanity, as a form of possession inspired by evil spirits. Kāḷi is given the task of taming these demonic passions, not articulating them. When, in a very different mood, Kāḷi is ritually present in the possessed, cross-dressed men who perform *mudiyettu*, women guard their behavior even more carefully than usual.

Thus, in this Kerala context, at least, the power of the Goddess to possess has apparently been channeled so as to represent and benefit men, not women. Part of the ritual's function seems to be to enable men to deal with their fears of women's sexual and reproductive power. Perhaps this male cooptation helps explain why, for women especially, the dominant emotion in Kāḷi's presence is fear, not love. Before Kāḷi, Kerala women seem to reject precisely the anger and defiance that are taken as a source of strength by goddess-worshiping women in the West.

Lindsey Harlan presents us with a third perspective on possession by the Goddess. Taking us to the western state of Rajasthan, she explores the character of one of a number of *satīs*, that is, "good women" or "truthful women," who earn that title by being profoundly faithful to their husbands—even to the point of death. A genuine *satī* is believed to be overcome by a determination to place her own body on the funeral pyre of her recently deceased husband, thus keeping her *śakti* at his side not only in life but in death. For many Rajasthanis, a young bride, or even a virgin who is only betrothed and not yet married, is the ideal *satī*. As she moves forward to the act of self-sacrifice that demonstrates outwardly what she inwardly already is—a woman of pure virtue and truth—she is believed to radiate the nurturant benefits of motherhood upon her family, community, and those who come to worship her. This power is felt to persist after death, as well. Hence, like Bhagavati in Kerala, she wields that powerful combination of the virginal and the motherly. Her "children" are not her own biological offspring; rather, they are any persons who embrace her in childlike devotion.

A specific conviction about possession—and self-possession—is important here. Those who revere *satīs* believe that a woman's resolve to commit suicide in this way, if it is genuine, can only be explained as resulting from the intense, protective energy of her own *sat*: her virtue, her truthfulness to the ideals of womanhood and marriage. Her *sat* possesses her, making her *satī* (a "truthful one," in the feminine). In many contemporary Rajasthani accounts of incidences of *satī*, this possession of *sat* is depicted as having actual physical force. It ignites the pyre, shields the *satī* from pain, and repels any who would prevent her from realizing her intent. But in the story of Satī Godāvarī, which Harlan describes in its audiocassette version, the emphasis falls less on physical possession than on the total identification of the *satī* with her *sat*: she is a creature of immovable resolve. The brunt of the story is to show how Satī Godāvarī repulses any who would stand in her way, cursing them. In the effectiveness of her curses she demonstrates her *sat* and her own divinity. Yet, if she curses her enemies, she also blesses her devotees and supporters with equal force.

In the simultaneous intensity of these two acts we hear echoes of the fierce maternity of many other goddesses who appear in this book. It is dark on the one hand, bright on the other. And in the consummately close association of human and divine that Satī Godāvarī exhibits, we encounter another general pattern: the suspicion or affirmation, at least by men, that the *śakti* of goddesses is also implicit in mortal women. But there is a special question here: why should this ultimate identification of humanity with the divine lead to death when it is a woman who experiences the connection? Taking up this gender issue, Harlan explains how it is inseparable from issues related to caste and class.

Despite the general resonances, Satī Godāvarī, like each "mother" we meet in the book, has a personality all her own. The same is certainly true for the mother who appears in the essay that follows: Bhārat Mātā, Mother India. Godāvarī and other *satīmātā* ("*satī* mothers") are worshiped in part because they serve as emblems of social entities, communities of caste and place. Bhārat Mātā does this on a grand scale, for India as a whole—or such, at least, is the hope of those who have promoted her cult.

As Lise McKean shows in the chapter that concludes this second section of the book, in fashioning her as they do, the patrons of Bhārat Mātā have specific social and political objectives in mind. Like Santoṣī Mā, she is a relatively new goddess, although of a very different kind; and again like Santoṣī Mā, she earns her quick accessibility by building on connections her patrons seek to forge with other, older forms of the Goddess in India. This is evident in the massing of images of other goddesses and heroines (*satī*s) in the impressive Bhārat Mātā temple recently completed in Hardwar, a great pilgrimage center on the Ganges, north of Delhi. McKean not only provides a vivid description of this building—half temple, half museum—but also offers a close analysis of the motives of those who have constructed it, especially as revealed in guidebooks distributed at the temple itself.

More than any other expression of the Goddess, except the great Devī with whom we began, Bhārat Mātā is fashioned so as to unite. Those who would spread her cult, particularly members of the Vishva Hindu Parishad (World Hindu Council) and its close political associate, the Bharatiya Janata Party (Indian People's Party), are making a conscious effort to use in a new way the unitive power of the Goddess as Mother. Although they do not always say so explicitly, they seem to hope that Bhārat Mātā, like the Devī of the *Devī Māhātmya*, will eventually be recognized as reigning supreme over the many other manifestations of female divinity in India. If they succeed in eliciting such recognition, they will have mobilized the immanent, pantheistic power of the Goddess in the cause of religious nationalism—a weighty, and potentially dangerous, achievement.

Many feminists, both in India and abroad, have hoped that other forms of empowerment would flow from the Hindu worship of goddesses. They have hoped—indeed, have sometimes believed or even assumed—that to participate in a religious tradition that addresses divinities as female is to impart strength to real, human women. On this point, alas, the Indian record is far from consistent. Kathleen Erndl shows how women possessed by "The Lion-Rider" are sought out as leaders and healers by others, and reports that people in this area of India typically detect the Goddess's power in all women. Indeed, many observers have found the women of northwest India to be among the country's strongest and most independent. Similar assessments have also been made of the women of Kerala, whose level of education, for example, exceeds that of any other regional group in India. Yet in her study of possession by the Goddess in Kerala, Sarah Caldwell cannot but conclude that the *mudiyettu* ritual does little to empower women. Instead, the great benefits go to the men.

Similar contradictions emerge as one compares the work of other contributors to this volume. Interviews with female performers of *padāvalī kīrtan* in Bengal have led Donna Wulff to conclude that women not only delight in Rādhā's strenuous opposition to Krishna but derive strength from it.[21] Likewise, Cynthia Humes's interviews with male and female reciters of the *Devī Māhātmya* at Vindhyacal in north-central India revealed a widespread conviction that the Goddess shares with human women the power that goes under the name of *śakti,* as well as the "natural maternal instincts" that enable women, whether human or divine, to love and forgive children. Yet Humes also discovered an equally articulate conviction that there remains an unbridgeable chasm between goddesses and human women, since female bodies are irremediably permeated by evil and pollution. A few persons, however, did take exception to this widely shared view—and each, significantly, was a woman. Although Humes was able to unearth instances both in India and abroad where isolated women saw the *Devī Māhātmya* as a source of empowerment for their sex, she cautioned that all these women either had been educated in westernized Christian schools or had actually lived in the West. Moreover, each already occupied a privileged position in society.[22]

The picture is surely very mixed, and sometimes almost viciously paradoxical. As regards the latter, *satī* offers the classic example, for the strength that leads to the popular acclamation of a *satī*'s inner and peculiarly feminine divinity, the power that culminates in the ritual of her apotheosis, is fully known only in the ceremony where she sacrifices her life. The price of becoming manifest as a goddess is thus to die as a woman. Happily, not every instance of a woman's becoming or being possessed by the Goddess is a version of *satī*. Not every act of maternity—even the mothering of one's husband, as in *satī*—requires such sacrifice.

In a far more typical pattern, women make adjustments (often significant ones) within the predominant patriarchal ethos of Hindu society that allow women space for internal autonomy and growth. Sometimes these involve open challenges to the "accepted" order; sometimes the challenge is more oblique. For instance, women who sing a collective meditation on the role of Sītā in the *Rāmāyaṇa* epic seize the chance to focus on a goddess and see how things look from her point of view. This leads to an empowerment and even a subversiveness that grow from within—or in tandem with—the social system itself.[23] Under such circumstances, it is hard to tell whether challenges to the patriarchal status quo are gifts from Sītā to the women who revere her or acts whereby a goddess (here Sītā) is reclaimed or given new meaning and force by the women who sing her song.

Actually, this is a quandary we might expect from reading Kathleen Erndl's analysis of the radically interactive nature of possession by Devī, where the Goddess and human women meet. In such circumstances, who possesses whom? Which "mother" mothers which? Must the empowerment flow in one direction only? If we keep such questions in mind as we move from India into an international arena, we may wonder whether perhaps we are seeing today the emergence of a natural and healthy symbiosis of Hindu goddesses, on the one hand, and Western or Western-influenced women, on the other. This symbiosis may serve to increase the *śakti* of both—and at the same time, one hopes, to imbue men with a kind of energy they have often lacked in the past.

TURNING WEST

We began this introduction by contrasting the search for female divinity in the modern West with the worship of the Goddess—and goddesses—in India, from the time of the *Devī Māhātmya* to the present. At the end of the book, these two worlds converge, as Rachel McDermott explains how the goddess Kālī has gained a prominent place in the American and European religious movement sometimes called women's spirituality. By the time readers arrive at McDermott's essay, they will have encountered Kālī many times, especially in the chapters by Humes, Kinsley, Erndl, and Caldwell. But here is a new Kālī, a Kālī whose profile, if not whose very existence, depends upon some of the scholarship that precedes her here. The work of David Kinsley has been particularly influential.

McDermott presents this new Kālī as a goddess of transformation: Western women have turned to her as a goddess who has the power to heal—in particular, through the reintegration of alienated rage. At the extreme, one finds novel rituals and ritual paraphernalia, in which Kālī's taste for revenge and sexual pleasure are highlighted. The use of the worshiper's own menstrual blood is conspicuously prescribed. Seemingly less pointed are poems and litanies in which a verbal appeal for transformation is made, as in May Sarton's "The Invocation to Kali":

> Kali, be with us.
> Violence, destruction, receive our homage.
> Help us bring darkness into the light,
> To lift out the pain, the anger,
> Where it can be seen for what it is—
> The balance-wheel for our vulnerable, aching love.
> Put the wild hunger where it belongs,
> Within the act of creation,
> Crude power that forges a balance
> Between hate and love.[24]

McDermott explains how, like Sarton, most Euro-American women who have called upon Kālī feel that her power derives from an embracing of opposites—maternal compassion and a distinctly female kind of rage.[25] It also derives from what some feminists perceive to have been Kālī's own suppression at the hands of Indian patriarchy. McDermott examines these perceptions and finds both to be partly true, partly false; but the historical analysis, she thinks, is deeply flawed. In a view that is consonant with the many historical transformations of goddesses that we observe elsewhere in the book, as well as with the variety of forms that goddesses assume in the present day, McDermott vigorously affirms the right of Kālī (and, by implication, any Hindu goddess) to change as she moves from one culture to another. Such changes are the very stuff of India's religious history, and they can be seen to represent the energy of the divine itself.

Yet in an age of transnational culture, when religions are moving into ever more complex interactions with one another, McDermott sounds a cautionary note. The worship of Kālī in the West rests in a special way on reports—reports of what it is like to live and pray on the other side of the world. Those reports, she insists, should be as accurate as possible, and they should be used with discrimination, after wide reading and much thought. McDermott laments that not enough real scholarship has buttressed the Western worship of Kālī. Sometimes, in fact, scholarship has almost purposely been pushed aside. McDermott reflects:

> But in denying scholarly accounts of history a legitimate place in the discussion of goddess figures, it would seem that the potential for intimacy and depth is lost. Is it sufficient, in developing a love relationship with a divine being, just to "take a few minutes of research" to acquaint oneself with her characteristics? From the standpoint of devotionalism, a thorough investigation into the many backgrounds of the beloved in her land of origin would be a true sign of love and reverence.

It will take more than "a few minutes" to read this book. We hope that those who do spend the time will find genuine rewards in the panoply of goddesses—and fullness of the Goddess—that are presented here. The many particular goddesses and divine mothers, springing from soil, flowing in rivers, apotheosized from earthly women, possessing women and men, celebrated in texts and performances, remain irreducible in their diversity. She/they will not admit of any convenient oversimplification.

Devī, the Goddess in India, is one of the guiding forces of Indian civilization. In the whole world, a more complete rhapsody on the divine feminine would be hard to conceive—or one that resounds with so many happily discordant notes.

NOTES

1. The most influential text on ancient Goddess worship is Marija Gimbutas, *The Language of the Goddess: Unearthing the Hidden Symbols of Western Civilization* (San Francisco: HarperSanFrancisco, 1989).

2. See, for example, the female figurine from Sonkh, near Mathura, dating to about the second century B.C.E. and now in the Mathura Museum (acquisition number 66.2); see also the terracotta *yakṣī* from Tamluk (ancient Tamralipti) in Bengal, which dates to about the same time. The latter is now preserved in the Ashmolean Museum, Oxford (acquisition no. X.201), and has been published in J. C. Harle and Andrew Topsfield, *Indian Art in the Ashmolean Museum* (Oxford: Ashmolean Museum, 1987), pp. 6–7 and color plate 2.

3. See Ananda K. Coomaraswamy, *Yakṣas*, 2 vols. (1928 and 1931; repr. New Delhi: Munshiram Manoharlal, 1971), esp. 1:9–11, 30–36; and 2: 64–71.

4. C. Mackenzie Brown, *The Triumph of the Goddess: The Canonical Models and Theological Visions of the Devī-Bhāgavata Purāṇa*, (Albany: State University of New York Press, 1990), p. 1.

5. The first edition was published in 1982 by the Berkeley Religious Studies Series, Berkeley, California, and reprinted in 1984 by Motilal Banarsidass, Delhi. A paperback edition followed in 1986 from Beacon Press in Boston.

6. Stanley N. Kurtz, *All the Mothers Are One: Hindu India and the Cultural Reshaping of Psychoanalysis* (New York: Columbia University Press, 1992). By way of caution, however, see also the review by Cynthia Ann Humes in the *Journal of Asian Studies* 53(1): 256–58.

7. See C. J. Fuller, *The Camphor Flame: Popular Hinduism and Society in India* (Princeton: Princeton University Press, 1992), pp. 42–43.

8. Diana L. Eck, *Encountering God: A Spiritual Journey from Bozeman to Banaras* (Boston: Beacon Press, 1993), p. 60.

9. This is an observation made by Christopher Fuller (*Camphor Flame*, p. 41). The only exception I can think of is the lotus-headed goddess studied by Carol Radcliffe Bolon in *Forms of the Goddess Lajja Gauri in Indian Art* (University Park: Pennsylvania State University Press, 1992).

10. For the Punjab, see Kathleen M. Erndl, *Victory to the Mother: The Hindu Goddess of Northwest India in Myth, Ritual, and Symbol*, (New York: Oxford Uni-

versity Press, 1993), p. 105. For Maharashtra, and much more anecdotally, compare the examples offered by John M. Stanley in "Gods, Ghosts, and Possession," in *The Experience of Hinduism*, ed. Eleanor Zelliot and Maxine Berntsen (Albany: State University of New York Press, 1988), pp. 47, 50, and also p. 40. A brief overview of scholarship on the high incidence of spirit possession among women, both worldwide and in India, is provided by Elisabeth Schoembucher, "Gods, Ghosts, and Demons: Possession in South Asia," in *Flags of Fame: Studies in South Asian Folk Culture*, ed. Heidrun Brückner, Lothar Lutze, and Aditya Malik (Delhi: Manohar, 1993), pp. 244–45; see also Ruth S. Freed and Stanley A. Freed, *Ghosts: Life and Death in North India* (New York: American Museum of Natural History, 1993), p. 270.

11. See David Pocock, *Mind, Body, and Wealth* (Oxford: Basil Blackwell, 1973), pp. 74–75. Pocock notes, however, that the existence of this broad trend does not mean that any particular form of worship need be exclusively vegetarian or nonvegetarian: the two interpenetrate (pp. 72–79). Fuller describes this interpenetration, in connection with the worship of a single deity, as typically taking the form of levels or layers (*Camphor Flame*, pp. 91–92).

12. See, for example, David R. Kinsley, *Hindu Goddesses: Visions of the Divine Feminine in the Hindu Religious Tradition* (Berkeley: University of California Press, 1986), pp. 112–14, 144–47, 205–7.

13. Rachel Fell McDermott, "Kālī's Tongue: Historical Reinterpretations of the Blood-lusting Goddess," paper presented at the Mid-Atlantic Conference of the American Academy of Religion, New York, March 1991.

14. See Lawrence A. Babb, "Marriage and Malevolence: The Uses of Sexual Opposition in a Hindu Pantheon," *Ethnology* 9, no. 2 (1970): 137–48; see also his *The Divine Hierarchy: Popular Hinduism in Central India* (New York: Columbia University Press, 1975), pp. 215–29, esp. pp. 225–26, 229.

15. See Edward C. Dimock, Jr., "A Theology of the Repulsive: The Myth of the Goddess Śītalā," in *The Divine Consort*, ed. Hawley and Wulff, pp. 184–203.

16. Narayanan seems to highlight this somewhat feistier, more ambivalent, "earthy" element in retelling stories of goddesses associated with particular sacred places in South India. Their status as consorts of Viṣṇu occasionally seems to challenge that of Śrī, but ultimately they and she are shown to be the same.

17. Frédérique Apffel Marglin, "Types of Sexual Union and Their Implicit Meanings," in *The Divine Consort*, ed. Hawley and Wulff, pp. 298–315.

18. Frédérique Apffel Marglin, "Female Sexuality in the Hindu World," in *Immaculate and Powerful: The Female in Sacred Image and Social Reality*, ed. Clarissa W. Atkinson, Constance H. Buchanan, and Margaret R. Miles (Boston: Beacon Press, 1985), pp. 39–59, at p. 55.

19. Babb, *Divine Hierarchy*, p. 229.

20. See I. M. Lewis, *Ecstatic Religion: An Anthropological Study of Spirit Possession and Shamanism* (Harmondsworth: Penguin Books, 1971), esp. pp. 31–32.

21. See Donna M. Wulff, "Images and Roles of Women in Bengali Vaiṣṇava *Padāvalī Kīrtan*," in *Women, Religion and Social Change*, ed. Yvonne Y. Haddad and Ellison B. Findly (Albany: State University of New York Press, 1985), pp. 234–37. Worthy of comparison are the findings of Parita Mukta with regard to the celebration of Mīrābāī—whose status is somewhere between human and divine—on the part of

poor and lower-caste singers in Rajasthan and Gujarat. See *Upholding the Common Life: The Community of Mirabai* (Delhi: Oxford University Press, 1994).

22. Cynthia Ann Humes, "Glorifying the Great Goddess or Great Woman? Hindu Women's Experience in Ritual Recitation of the *Devi-Mahatmya*," in *Women and Goddess Traditions*, ed. Karen King (Minneapolis: Fortress Press, forthcoming).

23. Velcheru Narayana Rao, "A *Rāmāyaṇa* of Their Own: Women's Oral Tradition in Telugu," in *Many Rāmāyaṇas: The Diversity of a Narrative Tradition in South Asia*, ed. Paula Richman (Berkeley: University of California Press, 1991), pp. 114–36.

24. Published in Janine Canan, ed., *She Rises Like the Sun: Invocations of the Goddess by Contemporary American Women Poets* (Freedom, Calif.: Crossing Press, 1989), p. 153.

25. For a review of psychological perspectives on this apparent coincidence of opposites, see David M. Wulff, "Prolegomenon to a Psychology of the Goddess," in *The Divine Consort*, ed. Hawley and Wulff, pp. 283–97; for a sharply contrasting evaluation, see Kurtz, *All the Mothers Are One*, pp. 91–131.

PART ONE

Goddess as Supreme and Goddess as Consort

DEVĪ
The Great Goddess

Thomas B. Coburn

There are multiple dimensions to posing the apparently straightforward question of who is the Great Goddess of India, the Devī, and how she is related to other Hindu deities. Depending on who is asking the question, and who is answering it, very different features of divinity, both male and female, come to the fore. At least two reasons exist for the easy, but multifaceted, coexistence of oneness and manyness that we observe in Hindu conceptions of Devī. One is the richness of vision that the classic text of Hindu Goddess worship, the *Devī Māhātmya,* offers; the other is the variety of significances that have been ascribed to this text in the Indian context. It is the purpose of this essay to explore the former of these—the vision of the *Devī Māhātmya*—in some detail and then to indicate some of the larger interpretive issues.

It has long been recognized, by both devotees and academics, that the *Devī Māhātmya* is a text of unique significance to the Hindu religious tradition. The text, which forms a portion of one of the early Sanskrit Purāṇas, the *Mārkaṇḍeya,* was probably composed in or somewhat north of the Narmada river valley sometime in the fifth or sixth century C.E.[1] Yet it is no mere antiquarian curiosity. The *Devī Māhātmya* has, through the centuries, been copied by the faithful with such regularity that it now exists in virtually innumerable manuscripts. Its recitation forms part of the daily liturgy in temples dedicated to Durgā, as well as occupying a central place in the great autumnal festival of Durgā Pūjā.[2] In a lecture delivered in 1840, H. H. Wilson ranked it "amongst the most popular works in the Sanskrit language," and to this day its hymns, in particular, are familiar to vast numbers of Hindus.[3] In 1823 it became the second Purāṇic text ever translated into a European language (English).[4] By the turn of the century excerpts had appeared in

French, and another full English translation had been produced, along with one in Latin and one in Greek.[5]

Of the various features of the *Devī Māhātmya*, one stands preeminent. The ultimate reality in the universe is here understood to be feminine: Devī, the Goddess.[6] Moreover, the *Devī Māhātmya* appears to be the first Sanskrit text to provide a comprehensive—indeed, well-nigh relentless—articulation of such a vision. From the time of the *Rig Veda* onward, of course, various goddesses had figured in Sanskrit tradition. But never before had ultimate reality itself been understood as Goddess.

Since the Goddess's varied and often highly nuanced relationship to male deities is particularly revealing of her nature, we shall first explore three "moments"—one from each of the three episodes in the *Devī Māhātmya*—that present this relationship in a particularly vivid fashion. As we shall see, although Devī is understood to bear a special relation to each particular deity, this is never a mere consort relation. She is beyond being a consort to anyone. Then, in an effort to situate the *Devī Māhātmya* in the broader realm of Indian religious history, we will consider how certain of its myths and symbols had previously been employed in Sanskrit. As it turns out, certain affinities exist between the worship of Devī, as expounded in the *Devī Māhātmya*, and other, quite various theological currents involving Agni and Skanda, Śiva, Viṣṇu, and Krishna Gopāla. Finally, against the backdrop of this inquiry into the text's content and historical context, we shall take brief note of the ongoing hermeneutics of the *Devī Māhātmya*, exploring how later Hindus and others have engaged with the text and its vision.

THREE MOMENTS IN DEVĪ'S IDENTITY

The structure of the *Devī Māhātmya* is both simple and beautifully symmetrical, consisting of a frame story and three myths that tell of Devī's various salvific activities. The first half of the frame story recounts how a king and a merchant, beset by mundane adversity, seek refuge from the turmoils of the world by retiring to the forest. There they encounter a sage, who informs them that their woes are due to the power of *mahāmāyā*, a term that can mean either "she who possesses great deceptiveness" or "she who *is* the great deception." Pressed for further details, the sage then recounts the three myths. The first, that of Madhu and Kaiṭabha, offers a succinct delineation of the cosmic status of Devī. The second, a more extensive account of her origins on earth and her initial martial activities, culminates in her conquest of the dread buffalo-demon Mahiṣa. The third and longest myth is an exuberant celebration of her various forms and their role in her victory over the minions of the demons Śumbha and Niśumbha. Finally, in the second half of the frame story, we learn how the king and the merchant then worship

Devī. Their devotion merits her appearance, and she proceeds to answer their prayers.

The feature of the first episode that commands our attention here is its characterization of Devī as *mahāmāyā*, a designation that should probably be understood as a proper name. A preliminary indication of its significance can be found in the words with which the sage describes the goddess to the woebegone king and merchant:

> O best of men, human beings have a craving for offspring, out of greed expecting those [loved ones] to reciprocate; do you not see this? Just in this fashion do they fall into the pit of delusion, the maelstrom of egotism, giving [apparent] solidity to life in this world (*saṃsāra*) through the power of Mahāmāyā. . . . This blessed Devī Mahāmāyā, having forcibly seized the minds, even of men of knowledge, leads them to delusion. . . . She is [also] the supreme eternal knowledge (*vidyā*) that becomes the cause of release (*mukti*) from bondage to mundane life. (1.39–40, 42, 44)[7]

The *Devī Māhātmya* seems here to reflect the view of the early Upaniṣads that it is mystical knowledge of ultimate truth that extricates one from the process of rebirth. But something else is clearly afoot as well, for Devī is not simply the knowledge that sets one free. She is also the great illusion (*mahāmāyā*) that keeps one bound. The *Devī Māhātmya* is not given to systematic philosophical exposition, so it does not endeavor to resolve this paradox. Rather, it rejoices in it, for paradox is close to the heart of the *Devī Māhātmya*'s view of Devī. In this regard, two features of earlier Sanskrit usage of the word *māyā* help clarify what the *Devī Māhātmya* means when it calls Devī "Mahāmāyā."

First, the word *māyā* is as old as the *Rig Veda*, where it means "wile" or "magic power," a power that is frequently associated with the *asuras*, beings who, in all but the earliest strata of Sanskrit literature, are understood as enemies of the gods (*devas*). If *māyā* is thus associated with the demons, we might expect the *Devī Māhātmya* to affirm that she who is Mahāmāyā is also the great demoness. This turns out to be precisely the manner in which Devī is praised later in this same episode: "You are the great knowledge, the great illusion, the great insight, the great memory, and [also] the great delusion, the great Goddess (*mahādevī*), the great Demoness (*mahāsurī*)" (1.58). To say that Devī is Mahāmāyā is thus to affirm that she is indeed Goddess, but it is also to affirm that she transcends the conventional distinction between *devas* and *asuras*.[8]

The second conceptual formulation that prior usage bequeaths to the *Devī Māhātmya* is the equation of *māyā* with *prakṛti*, the primordial matter that evolves into the manifest universe. It was in the philosophical school of Sāṃkhya that *prakṛti* received its classical development as one of the two fundamental principles of the universe, the other being *puruṣa* (spirit). This atheistic dualism had, however, been adapted to theistic philosophical needs long before the *Devī Māhātmya* was composed. In particular, that watershed of theistic speculation, the *Śvetāśvatara Upaniṣad,* had formulated the crucial issues in an illuminating way. Having explained the distinction between the Lord and the individual soul, the text then related them both to *māyā*:

> The Vedas, the sacrifices, the ceremonies, the acts of devotion, the past, the future, and what the Vedas declare—all this does the Lord (*māyin,* the possessor of *māyā*) pour forth out of this [i.e., the creator god, Brahmā], and in it is the other [the individual soul] confined by *māyā.* Know *māyā* to be *prakṛti,* and the possessor of *māyā* to be the great Lord. This whole world is pervaded by beings that are part of him (4.9–10)

It would be risky to rely on a narrow interpretation of such philosophically pregnant concepts as *māyā* and *prakṛti.*[9] Nonetheless, the *Devī Māhātmya* is inclined to favor their identification in a way that is reminiscent of the *Śvetāśvatara.* Thus, in the first episode Mahāmāyā is addressed in hymns with the affirmation, "You are the *prakṛti* of all, manifesting the triad of constituent strands (*guṇas*)" (1.59) and, later on, with the confession, "You are the supreme, original, untransformed *prakṛti*" (4.6). On the basis of such passages it seems safe to say that the *Devī Māhātmya* has shifted the focus of the Sāṃkhya school and the *Śvetāśvatara Upaniṣad* by understanding *prakṛti* not as the material shroud or possession of spirit but as itself supremely divine, as Devī herself.

By way of summarizing these various implications of the designation "Mahāmāyā," let us consider the myth recounted in this first episode. As part of his introduction to Devī, the sage declares: "The yogic slumber (*yoganidrā*) of the lord of the worlds, Viṣṇu, is [this same] Mahāmāyā, and through her is this world being deluded" (1.41). Such a declaration enables him to move directly to the myth, which involves Viṣṇu, *yoganidrā,* and the *asuras* Madhu and Kaiṭabha. But in order to appreciate the unique features of the *Devī Māhātmya*'s version, we must ascertain the resonance of this particular myth at the time the *Devī Māhātmya* was written.

Throughout the *Mahābhārata,* the Madhu-Kaiṭabha myth is associated, virtually without exception, with the figure of Viṣṇu. The myth is recounted in full on several occasions, and Viṣṇu's epithet *madhusūdana,* "slayer of Madhu," occurs in the epic more than two hundred times. The classical version of the myth can be summarized as follows.[10] It is the time of *pralaya,* the state of dissolution that occurs at the end of a cosmic cycle. All that exists is the universal ocean. On the ocean, Lord Viṣṇu sleeps, lying on his serpent, Śeṣa, who is coiled into the shape of a couch. While Viṣṇu sleeps, two *asuras* named Madhu and Kaiṭabha arise from the wax in his ear and, puffed up with pride and egotism, begin to assail the god Brahmā, who is seated on the lotus that grows from Viṣṇu's navel. Brahmā awakens Viṣṇu by shaking the lotus, whereupon Viṣṇu engages the two demons in battle, sometimes physically, sometimes in a contest of wits. Given that nothing but ocean exists, Madhu and Kaiṭabha think they have outwitted Viṣṇu by asking to be slain in a dry place. But Viṣṇu raises his thighs and kills the demons on them. From the fat of the two *asuras*, which then permeated the waters, the earth was created.

In the *Devī Māhātmya*'s retelling of this thoroughly Vaiṣṇava myth are several crucial modifications. Although the setting is exactly the same, Viṣṇu is described as having entered into *yoganidrā*, the twilight slumber of tranquillity, a term not used in the epic. The demons begin their assault upon Brahmā, who again endeavors to awaken Viṣṇu. He does so here, however, not by shaking the lotus but by invoking Devī, who is addressed as Yoganidrā, that is, as the personification of the state of sleep into which Viṣṇu has entered. The climax of the invocation reads:

> Whatever and wherever anything exists, whether it be real or unreal, O [you] who have everything as your very soul, of all that, you are the power (*śakti*); how then can you be [adequately] praised? By you the creator of the world, the protector of the world, who [also] consumes the world, is [here] brought under the influence of sleep (*nidrā*); who here is capable of praising you? Since Viṣṇu, Śiva, and I have been made to assume bodily form by you, who could have the capacity of [adequately] praising you? May you, praised in this fashion, Devī, with your superior powers confuse these two unassailable *asuras*, Madhu and Kaiṭabha, and may the imperishable Lord of the world be quickly awakened, and may his alertness be used to slay these two great *asuras*. (1.63–67)

Devī then accedes to Brahmā's request by withdrawing from Viṣṇu's various limbs, Viṣṇu awakens, and the *asuras* are dispatched, as in the earlier versions.

Several conclusions seem to follow from this account. First, the *Devī Māhātmya* clearly suggests that it is solely through the grace, the gracious withdrawal, of Devī that Viṣṇu can fulfill his familiar duty of slaying the *asuras*. In fact, it is only through this grace that he can act at all. And if this is true of Lord Viṣṇu, the implication is that each of us human beings is similarly indebted to her.[11] Second, Devī is held to be the primary ontological reality. From her the gods explicitly derive their bodily form, and from her, as well, all material existence proceeds. This is evident both from the prior affirmation that Devī is *prakṛti* and from the suggestion that it is the substance of the *asuras* that comes to form the earth—for Devī is, we have noted, the great *asurī*. One might go so far as to say that whatever *is* is Devī. Finally, the text reveals the paradoxical action of Devī Mahāmāyā. It suggests, on the one hand, that it is she who deludes the two self-important demons into thinking they can outwit the divine. But, on the other hand, it is also she who shows how, through the frustration of their egotistical desires and their apparent death, those same demons come to participate in a divine plan far larger than themselves—indeed, in the cosmic process of creation. Devī is both the great deluder and the one who redeems the victims of her magic tricks by incorporating them into the life divine.

The event from the second episode that is of interest to us may be dealt with more briefly. This is the point at which the text, having established Devī's cosmic status, turns to an account of her career on earth. It is apparent from the outset that the event precipitating that career is the severe dislocation of the mundane equilibrium. The second episode thus begins:

> Once upon a time, a battle between the gods (*devas*) and *asuras* raged for a full hundred years, when [the buffalo-demon] Mahiṣa was leader of the *asuras* and Indra [was leader] of the gods. The gods' army was conquered there by the mighty *asuras*, and having conquered all the gods, the *asura* Mahiṣa became lord (literally, "Mahiṣa became Indra"). (2.1–2)

Faced with this quandary, the remnants of the *devas*' army seek out Śiva and Viṣṇu and describe the course of events. There follows the famous account of Devī's origin as a force on earth:

> Having listened to the words of the gods, Viṣṇu and Śiva became angry, with furrowed brows and twisted faces. Then from the face of Viṣṇu, filled with rage, came forth a great fiery splendor (*tejas*) [and also from the faces] of Brahmā and Śiva. And from the bodies of Indra and the other gods came forth a great fiery splendor, and it became unified in one place. An exceedingly fiery mass like a flaming mountain did the gods see there, filling the firmament with flames. That peerless splendor, born of the bodies of all the gods, unified, and pervading the three worlds with her splendor, became a woman. (2.8–12)

Our text then recounts how this woman—who is, of course, Devī—received her various limbs and weapons from different gods and how, thus constituted, she proceeded to vanquish Mahiṣa and his hordes (see figure 3).

From the perspective of our concern with Devī's relation to specific male deities, two comments are in order. First, whereas there is justification for saying that Devī is here conceptualized as subordinate to the gods—because she is derivative from, and indebted to, each of them—it can also be argued that the reverse is true. It is she who succeeds in restoring equilibrium on earth, a feat that the gods, both individually and collectively, had been unable to accomplish. Moreover, it is clear that, despite having been derived from the gods, Devī is subsequently understood to be a continuing, independent salvific presence in the world. Thus, at the end of this episode she consents to bring relief to those who will call upon her in future calamities. Moreover, the episode concludes not by having her dissipate into the bodies of the gods but by stating simply, yet suggestively, "She vanished" (4.30–33).

Figure 3. A modern rendition of Devī as the slayer of the buffalo-demon Mahiṣa. Dipin Bose, *Mahiṣāsura Mardinī*, 1957, tempera on paper. Courtesy National Gallery of Modern Art, New Delhi.

Second, we must note the conceptual model that the *Devī Māhātmya* employs here in describing Devī. The first episode in the text established her primacy in the cosmic context. Now the second endeavors to demonstrate not only that Devī also has an earthly career but that she is the supreme ruler of earthly creatures. To portray Devī in this role, the *Devī Māhātmya* draws on a classical Indian model, that of the king as described in a classic text, *The Laws of Manu.* As part of his vision of social order, Manu, the ascribed author, begins his account of the king as follows:

> When this world was without a king and people ran about in all directions out of fear, the Lord emitted a king in order to guard this entire (realm), taking

> lasting elements from Indra, the Wind, Yama, the Sun, Fire, Varuṇa, the Moon, and (Kubera) the Lord of Wealth. Because a king is made from particles of these lords of the gods, therefore he surpasses all living beings in brilliant energy [*tejas*], and like the Sun, he burns eyes and hearts, and no one on earth is able even to look at him. . . . In order to make justice succeed, he takes all forms again and again, taking into consideration realistically what is to be done, (his) power, and the time and place. The lotus goddess of Good Fortune resides in his favour, victory in his aggression, and death in his anger; for he is made of the brilliant energy of all (the gods).[12]

The conclusion that this model of secular power underlies the *Devī Māhātmya*'s vision of Devī's earthly origin seems inescapable. That such a model is utterly appropriate seems equally obvious, for only one whose power, in the world's own terms, is unrivaled can cope with the great disturber of the mundane equilibrium, Mahiṣa. The *Devī Māhātmya* thus affirms that the effective agent on earth, as in the cosmos, is not masculine but feminine, not king but queen.

Finally, we must examine the *Devī Māhātmya*'s use of the term *śakti*, "power," with regard to Devī, particularly in the third episode. As we have already seen, the *Devī Māhātmya* understands *śakti* as a singular and universal phenomenon—as a phenomenon that Devī simply *is.*[13] But in addition, it understands *śakti*s as plural and particular phenomena, as something that each individual deity *has.* This latter conceptualization emerges in the course of Devī's martial engagement with the *asura*s Śumbha and Niśumbha. When Śumbha, incensed at the destruction of two of his generals, sends forth his legions against Devī, she multiplies her own forces:

> At that very moment, O king, in order to destroy the enemies of the gods, and for the sake of the well-being of the supreme gods, very valorous and powerful *śakti*s, having sprung forth from the bodies of Brahmā, Śiva, Skanda, Viṣṇu, and Indra, [and] having the form of each [of them], approached Devī (*caṇḍikā*). Whatever form, ornament, and mount a particular god possessed, with that very form did his *śakti* go forth to fight the *asura*s. (8.11–13)

The text then describes how seven *śakti*s emerged from seven gods, each possessing the distinctive iconographic features of its source. These *śakti*s are named Brahmāṇī, Māheśvarī, Kaumārī, Vaiṣṇavī, Vārāhī, Nārasiṃhī, and Aindrī.[14] Together with another figure whom we shall consider in a moment, they are referred to collectively in the ensuing combat as "the Mothers."

Four features of this passage and its consequent development deserve our attention. First, it is tempting to conclude that the text views each god as having a consort who is called a *śakti* and is a form of Devī. But closer examination reveals quite a different situation. In fact, the *Devī Māhātmya* is careful to avoid using language that would imply that the *śakti*s are consorts of their respective gods. This is evident from the fact that, in the mythology current at the time that the *Devī Māhātmya* was composed, two of the gods who here put forth *śakti*s—Indra and Śiva (Maheśvara)—were already acknowledged to have consorts. Indra's spouse has been known since Rig Vedic times as Indrāṇī or Śacī, while Śiva's spouse is referred to throughout the *Mahābhārata* as Umā or Pārvatī. Indra's spouse has never before been designated by the word *aindrī*, however, and Umā is called *māheśvarī* on only one known occasion (*Mahābhārata* 14.43.14). Consequently, when the *Devī Māhātmya* calls Indra's *śakti* Aindrī, "the one related to Indra," and Śiva's *śakti* Māheśvarī, "the one related to Maheśvara," it apparently wishes to make clear that a god's *śakti* is not the same as any previously recognized consort of his.[15] A *śakti* does not have the merely formal and external relation of a consort with her god. Rather, she is far more fundamental, more internal, to his identity, for she is in fact his power *(śakti)*.

Second, it is clear that although the polarity of Śiva and Śakti is well known in later Śākta and tantric circles, the *Devī Māhātmya* shows no preference for Śiva when discussing Devī as *śakti*. The only special attention paid to Śiva at this juncture is that, after their emergence, the *śakti*s are said to gather around him (8.21). However, no particular importance is attached to this fact.

Third, an even more striking contrast with later views emerges from the fact that the *Devī Māhātmya* does not recognize that a *śakti* is feminine and that its possessor or vehicle is masculine—for Devī herself possesses a *śakti*. Immediately after the previously named *śakti*s have gathered around Śiva, the text declares: "Then from the body of Devī came forth the very frightening *śakti* of Caṇḍikā (Devī), gruesome and yelping [like] a hundred jackals" (8.22). In the subsequent combat, this *śakti* is treated as kindred to the other *śakti*s, as one of the Mothers.

Finally, for all this proliferation of forms of Devī, and for all the involvement of some of them with male deities, our text never loses sight of the fact that Devī is the primary reality and that her agency is the only effective one. This is indicated at the very end of the episode, where the text sets the stage for the final dramatic encounter by reducing the combatants to the bare minimum. The demon Śumbha has accused Devī of false pride and haughtiness, for in the foregoing encounters she has relied not on her own strength but on that of others. At this point, Devī proclaims her relation to the apparently heterogeneous forms of the Goddess: "I alone exist here in the world; what second, other than I, is there? O wicked one, behold these my hierophanies (or "extraordinary powers": *vibhūtayaḥ*) entering [back] into me" (10.3). The text continues: "Thereupon, all the goddesses, led by Brahmāṇī, went to their resting place in the body of Devī; then there was just Devī (*ambikā*) alone" (10.4). Subsequently, Devī throws down the gauntlet for the final combat: "When I was established here in many forms, it was by means of my extraordinary power. That has now been withdrawn by me. I stand utterly alone. May you be resolute in combat" (10.5).

Our text thus concludes as it began, with the assertion that there is but one truly ultimate reality and that it is feminine; with the indication that this reality takes on different forms, to which the ignorant impute independent and permanent existence but which the wise recognize as grounded in Devī; and with the demonstration that this reality is related to male deities, as to all that exists, not externally but internally—not as consort, but as *śakti.*

FOUR CROSSCURRENTS INVOLVING DEVĪ

Quite apart from the conceptual structure of the *Devī Māhātmya,* there is a historical dimension to the synthesis it accomplishes, and this, too, contributes to the diverse emphases that the later tradition places on this classical text of Devī. We may here glance briefly at four distinct strands that appear to feed into the *Devī Māhātmya*'s synthetic vision of Devī.

First, scholars are virtually unanimous in the opinion that the basic impulse behind the worship of the Goddess in India is of non-Aryan, non-Sanskritic origin. For all its brilliance in incorporating diverse Sanskrit motifs into its vision of Devī, the *Devī Māhātmya,* too, seems to support this view. Thus, for instance, the most common designation of Devī in this text (other than the word *devī* itself) is *caṇḍikā,* which probably means "the violent and impetuous one" but which is used throughout as a proper name. Although feminine forms of the adjective *caṇḍa* exist in earlier texts, never prior to the *Devī Māhātmya* does the word *caṇḍikā* appear in Sanskrit.[16] Since the *Devī Māhātmya* attests to the existence of a cult of Devī (see 12. 1–12), it seems sensible that we should look for the historical origin of her worship in non-Sanskritic circles, in the worship of a deity known as Caṇḍikā.

Second, although the *Devī Māhātmya* does not understand Devī to be the consort of Śiva, there is some evidence that her worship and her identity are intertwined with those of Śiva. After Caṇḍikā, the second most frequent name for Devī in the *Devī Māhātmya* is Ambikā, a name associated in late Vedic texts with the nascent figure of Rudra-Śiva.[17] In addition, there is the intriguing fact that the destruction of Mahiṣa, which the *Devī Māhātmya* and subsequent Purāṇic literature clearly ascribe to Devī, had previously been recounted in the *Mahābhārata,* where it appears as the crowning event in the epic's first account of the birth and early career of Skanda.[18] Skanda is, of course, known throughout the Purāṇas as the offspring of Śiva and Umā, yet the *Mahābhārata* takes a somewhat different tack. Its account is extraordinarily complicated—largely because at this juncture Skanda is a new figure in Sanskrit mythology, one whose genealogy is unclear—but also enormously suggestive. Throughout the account, Agni's claims to the paternity of Skanda predominate over those of Śiva. At the same time, it is immediately after Śiva's claims are introduced (3.220) that the narrative reaches its climax by telling of Mahiṣa's defeat at the hands of Skanda. Moreover, although the identity of Skanda's rightful mother is never clearly determined, embryonic "Goddess motifs" abound. One candidate for motherhood is a horde of ogresses euphemistically called "the Mothers," in addition to which are several momentary appearances by a goddess named Śakti. One cannot help but feel that, at least mythologically and perhaps liturgically as well, Devī's identity emerges out of a matrix in which Śiva, Skanda, and Agni also figure prominently.[19]

Third, as we have seen, the *Devī Māhātmya* incorporates the familiar Vaiṣṇava myth of Madhu and Kaiṭabha and conceptualizes the Goddess in a way that resembles Manu's conceptualization of the king. There are also further indications of historical interaction between Vaiṣṇavism and the worship of Devī. The regal imagery of the second episode, for instance, has a distinctly Vaiṣṇava aura to it, and the way in which the Goddess enumerates her future appearances at the end of chapter 11 is strongly reminiscent of the *Bhagavad Gītā*'s teaching of the Lord's incarnations *(avatāras)*.[20] Further, we learn from the critical edition of the *Mahābhārata* that, just prior to the *Bhagavad Gītā*, a number of manuscripts insert one of the earliest Sanskrit hymns to the Goddess, known as the *Durgā Stotra*.[21] This insertion would seem to reflect the redactors' sense that there is a natural connection between Krishna and Devī. Similarly, there has been an ongoing, but usually only implicit, relationship between the *Bhagavad Gītā* and the *Devī Māhātmya*, evidenced by the fact that the seven hundred verses of the former appear to have been the model for giving the *Devī Māhātmya* the very popular alternative title *Durgā Saptaśatī*, "Seven Hundred (Verses) to Durgā."[22]

Finally, the *Devī Māhātmya* provides further evidence for the relation that Charlotte Vaudeville has perceived between Devī and Krishna Gopāla, for references to the myth of Śumbha and Niśumbha are found earlier only in Krishnaite documents.[23] In the *Harivaṃśa*'s account of Krishna's childhood, Viṣṇu descends to hell (*pātāla*) to solicit the aid of the goddess Nidrā. He proposes a plan for his birth and that of the goddess to Devakī and Yaśodā, and then foretells the future course of events. Among other things he predicts that this goddess will slay the demons Śumbha and Niśumbha (47.49).[24] Later (65.51) the text asserts that she has, in fact, slain them. This connection between a Śumbha-Niśumbha-Goddess myth and the Krishna Gopāla cycle is evidently more than a product of chance, for reference to such a myth also occurs in the Krishna story told in the *Viṣṇu Purāṇa* (5.1.81) and in Bhāsa's *Bālacarita* (2.20–25).[25] Vaudeville has argued persuasively that the tales about Krishna Gopāla originated as a cycle of hero stories among the non-Aryan castes of North India, who were predominantly worshipers of Devī.[26] The implications for our understanding of the *Devī Māhātmya* would thus seem clear. What we have in the Śumbha-Niśumbha myth is a fragment of the mythology of Devī as it was current among certain North Indian peoples who came to know the heroic exploits of Krishna Gopāla. Just as those exploits went on to receive sophisticated religious elaboration in the manifold expressions of Krishna *bhakti,* so, too, did the Śumbha-Niśumbha-Goddess story become integrated with other mythological motifs and receive *its* elaboration in such texts as the *Devī Māhātmya.*

INTERPRETING THE DEVĪ MĀHĀTMYA

Given, then, that the *Devī Māhātmya* accomplishes a conceptually rich synthesis of diverse religious strands, what ramifications has this vision had for Hindu religious life in later centuries? Is it possible to understand the consequences of the text's existence as readily as we have identified the elements that fed into it? If so, what are they?

Our answers to these questions must be a good deal more fragmentary and tentative than we might wish, in part because a comprehensive history of Devī's worship—toward which this volume is a contribution—has yet to be written, and in part because the hermeneutical questions involved in understanding the relation between texts and religious life in India are so complex. To conclude this essay, let me identify four different angles from which the later tradition has engaged the *Devī Māhātmya.* Although each has sought to bring the text into a conversation with quite different features of Hindu life, together they provide a fair indication of the range of Devī's presence in Indian lives, past and present.

First, if we constitute a phenomenology of the *Devī Māhātmya* in the narrowest sense, by asking what it is that people do with the words of the text, the answer is simple. They recite them. This could, of course, be said of most religious compositions in India, which have tended to live orally and in performance, rather than constituting the written basis for commentary and exegesis. But the *Devī Māhātmya* is one of the extreme cases of this oral emphasis, for its words have been understood to embody a unique and eternal power, which is released solely through the proper ritual preparation and verbatim recitation of the words. It is mantra in almost exactly the same way that the *Rig Veda* is mantra. It is the form of the words, as opposed to their content, that commands attention. The chief concern of commentators has therefore been the precise enumeration of verses and the exact specification of the ritual activity that should attend their recitation. Today, and for centuries past, the *Devī Māhātmya* has been regarded as an extraordinarily potent mantra. Professional reciters abound, and recitation of the text is thought to be effective in accomplishing a great range of goals, usually worldly ones—from passing an examination to ending a family quarrel—sought by the individual who purchases the services of the reciter. In a devotional context, recitation is also understood to be pleasing to Devī in one or another of her many guises. It thus forms part of both private and public worship in a great many ways, whether the particular theology be Tantric monism or the modified dualism of *bhakti.*[27]

Second, while the *Devī Māhātmya* remains chiefly a recited text, its mantras also have "meaning of another sort, for together they constitute one of the principal scriptural delineations of the goddess. The text is to be *understood* as well as *chanted,* and consequently in the editions available in the . . . bazaar the Sanskrit stanzas are given together with their . . . [vernacular] translation."[28] The oral and performative life of religious words has only very recently begun to command scholarly attention: exploration of the complex relationship between the recitation of a text and the understanding that a reciter (or a reciter's patron) has of that text has scarcely begun. With regard to the *Devī Māhātmya,* the crucial work to date is that of Cynthia Humes, whose interviews with reciters and devotees lend great subtlety to our understanding of Devī and her worship.[29] We know now, for instance, that recitation of the *Devī Māhātmya* in Sanskrit is dominated by men, whereas women usually recite vernacular translations.[30] This in turn tends to produce interesting devotional convergences between recitation of the *Devī Māhātmya* and folk songs, a traditional form of women's religious expression. Similarly, with regard to contemporary interpretations of the story, Humes documents a widespread consensus between men and women that Devī is more mother than warrior and that she may even be married, judgments that clearly downplay certain elements of the narrative. As Humes also reports, both men and women agree that, while Devī shares characteristics such as creativity, power, and maternity with human women, she is not to be understood as a role model for humans—although a few women informants demur on this point.

Third, recent anthropological study has demonstrated that text-based ideas about Devī are woven into popular practice in complex, nonlinear ways. Akos Östör, for instance, is deliberately concerned not to privilege texts in his analysis of life in a Bengali town. And yet he discovers a striking and close correspondence between the categories villagers use to understand their everyday experience, particularly during the great annual Durgā Pūjā festival, and the categories employed in the popular understanding of the *Devī Māhātmya.*[31] The story of Devī is quite unself-consciously woven into the very fabric of the social order and of daily behavior. Similarly, both Alf Hiltebeitel, drawing on texts and fieldwork in Tamilnadu, and William Sax, in his recent study of Goddess pilgrimage in the Himalayas, have explored how different regional traditions rework basic aspects of Devī's mythology in the light of local approaches to politics, social order, gender relations, and ritual practice.[32] As the anthropological record is beginning to show, while the story of the Goddess and her buffalo antagonist is known throughout the subcontinent, its contemporary significance and its bearing on local culture are always a function of particular historical events, often in the distant past. In anthropological terms, to speak of Devī as a generic Hindu deity is therefore often problematic, for her identity is always strongly colored by local custom.

Finally, given that Devī's identity is so intimately interconnected with the myths about her, it comes as no surprise that psychoanalytic theory, with its attention to dreams and myths, has figured in several contemporary interpretations of the Hindu Goddess. With this broadening of disciplinary perspectives, however, it becomes still more difficult to offer generalized interpretations of Devī and her worship. For instance, the Indian psychoanalyst Sudhir Kakar has argued that the mythology of Devī provides "the 'hegemonic narrative' of Hindu culture as far as male development is concerned" and that "certain forms of the maternal-feminine may be more central in Indian myths and psyche than in their Western counterparts."[33] More recently, Stanley Kurtz has gone much further, arguing that the dynamics of Indian child-rearing practices call for a radical reshaping of psychoanalytic concepts. The theology of the-one-and-the-many as it emerges in Hindu conceptions of Devī finds a social parallel in the practice of joint mothering, and Freud's Oedipus complex must give way in the Indian context to what Kurtz calls "the Durgā Complex."[34] To evaluate such an argument would take us well beyond the scope of this essay. But it serves as a fitting reminder of the varied ways that Devī has seized the human imagination, whether devotional or academic, for millennia in India and now in many other places throughout the world.

NOTES

1. See F. E. Pargiter, trans., *The Mārkaṇḍeya Purāṇa* (Calcutta: The Asiatic Society, 1888–1904), pp. viii–xiii; and V. V. Mirashi, "A Lower Limit for the Date of the *Devī Māhātmya*," *Purāṇa* 6, no. 1 (1964): 181–84.

2. See Louis Renou, *L'Hindouisme: Les textes, les doctrines, l'histoire* (Paris: Presses Universitaires de France, 1958), p. 67; and P. V. Kane, *History of Dharmaśāstra*, 5 vols. (Poona: Bhandarkar Oriental Research Institute, 1930–62), 5:154–87, esp. pp. 154–56, 171–72. See also Pratapchandra Ghosha, *Durga Puja, with Notes and Illustrations* (Calcutta: Hindoo Patriot Press, 1871), pp. 20, 39.

3. H. H. Wilson, *Works*, ed. R. Rost, vol. 1 (London: Trübner, 1862), p. 68.

4. As Shrivatsa Goswami pointed out to me, Juan Roger Riviere is in error when he claims, in "European Translations of Purāṇic Texts" (*Purāṇa* 5, no. 2 [1963]: 243–50), that this translation of the *Devī Māhātmya* is the first European translation of a Purāṇic text. The first such translation is in fact from the *Bhāgavata Purāṇa*: Daniel H. H. Ingalls alludes to it in his foreword to Milton Singer, ed., *Krishna: Myths, Rites, and Attitudes* (Honolulu: East-West Center Press, 1966), p. viii. The full reference is: *Bagavadam ou Doctrine Divine, Ouvrage Indien, canonique; sur l'Être Suprême, les Dieux, les Géans, les hommes, les diverses parties de l'Univers, &c.*, traduit du Sanskrit

d'après une version tamoule, par Méridas Poullé, un Malabare Chrétien (Paris: Foucher d'Obsonville, 1788).

5. For full documentation of this point, see my *Devī-Māhātmya: The Crystallization of the Goddess Tradition* (Delhi and Columbia, Mo.: Motilal Banarsidass and South Asia Books, 1985; hereafter cited as *Crystallization*), pp. 51–52.

6. Since there are neither capital letters nor articles in Sanskrit, whereas English employs both, the translation of *devī* as "the Goddess" can be misleading. In English, when we wish to speak of ultimate reality as masculine—of God with a capital "G"— we automatically omit the article: "Praise be to God." But it sounds odd to say, "Praise be to Goddess"; the language wants us to say, "Praise be to *the* Goddess" or "to *a* goddess." The *Devī Māhātmya* would not allow such a qualification—not only on grammatical grounds but also, as we shall see, on theological ones: Devī is not one goddess among others, but Goddess Supreme. In this essay I shall force Sanskrit to bear the brunt of a compromise by employing the term "Devī," with a capital. In the long run, however, we speakers of English ought to accustom ourselves to such phrases as "Praise be to Goddess"—an idea that has been richly elaborated in recent feminist scholarship and practice.

7. The crux of the merchant's dilemma is that, although abysmal abuse at the hands of his family prompted his retreat to the forest, he now finds that he yearns for news of them. Hence the sage's opening statement. I will follow here the numbering of verses adopted in my recent English translation, *Encountering the Goddess: A Translation of the Devī-Māhātmya and a Study of Its Interpretation* (Albany: State University of New York Press, 1991). For the original Sanskrit, see *Durgā-saptaśatī, saptaṭīkā-samvalitā*, ed. Harikṛṣṇaśarma (1916; repr. Delhi and Baroda: Butala and Company, 1984).

8. In the light of the interpretation of the *Devī Māhātmya*'s first episode that I will shortly offer, one could argue that one reason why Mahāmāyā has such power over the *asuras* is that, in a sense, she *is* the *asuras*.

9. The same Sanskrit word, *māyā*, has, for example, been extensively explored in the philosophical discussions of the Vedānta school.

10. This reconstruction of the myth is based on a consideration of all the epic variants. For a full translation of one particular version, see J. A. B. van Buitenen, trans., *The Mahābhārata* [Books 1–5], 3 vols. (Chicago: University of Chicago Press, 1974–78), 2:611–12 (*Mbh.* 3.194.8–30).

11. See, for instance, 5.15, where Devī is said to "abide in all creatures in the form of sleep (*nidrā*)."

12. Wendy Doniger, trans., with Brian K. Smith, *The Laws of Manu* (London: Penguin Books, 1991), 7.3–6, 10–11 (p. 128).

13. See 1.63, a portion of Brahmā's invocation of Devī quoted above. See also 5.18, 11.8, and 11.10.

14. The seven gods from whom they emerge are, respectively: Brahmā, Śiva, Skanda (Kumāra), Viṣṇu, Varāha (Viṣṇu's boar incarnation), Narasiṃha (Viṣṇu's man-lion incarnation), and Indra.

15. As further evidence for this interpretation, we might note that the *Devī Māhātmya* never employs the name Umā and that it uses the name Pārvatī on only three occasions, never with emphasis.

16. This assertion, made tentatively by Pargiter in his translation of the *Mārkaṇḍeya Purāṇa* (p. xii), has been confirmed by my own inquiries into the Vedic and epic literature.

17. See, for example, *Yajur Veda* 1.8.6; *Śatapatha Brāhmaṇa* 2.6.2.13–14.

18. This account, to which the balance of this paragraph refers, occurs at *Mahābhārata* 3.207–21 (see van Buitenen's translation, 2:638–61). The epic preserves a second account of Skanda's birth (9.43–45), but this does not include the Mahiṣa story. Moreover, the "Goddess motifs" that we are about to take note of are also much less in evidence there.

19. Although the post-Vedic figure of Agni was clearly of limited cultic significance by the time the *Devī Māhātmya* was composed, it is worth noting a certain homology between Devī and Agni—beyond what we might expect by virtue of Agni's relation to Śiva—in the conceptualization of the divine as "the flaming one" (see Wendy Doniger O'Flaherty, *Asceticism and Eroticism in the Mythology of Śiva* [London: Oxford University Press, 1973], pp. 90–100). One finds, for instance, a plurality of mothers attributed to Agni as far back as *Rig Veda* 10.5.5. (See also the material discussed in my *Crystallization*, pp. 313–30, esp. pp. 316–17.) One of the distinctive forms of Devī in the *Devī Māhātmya* is Kālī, a name that also appears in *Muṇḍaka Upaniṣad* 1.2.4 to designate one of Agni's seven quivering tongues. Likewise, Devī's names Śrī and Lakṣmī are intertwined with the figure of Agni in an appendix (*khila*) to the *Rig Veda* known as the *Śrī Sūkta* (see J. Scheftelowitz, ed., *Die Apokryphen des Ṛgveda* [Breslau: M. and H. Marcus, 1906], and J. Scheftelowitz, "Śrī Sūkta," *Zeitschrift für die Deutschen Morgenländischen Gesellschaft* 75 [1921]: 37–50). Another of the *Devī Māhātmya*'s common epithets for Devī is Durgā, a name that contains a play on words: Devī is the great protectress from worldly adversity (*durga*), and at the same time she is herself unassailable and hard to approach (*durgā*) (see 4.10, 4.16, 5.10, 9.29, and 11.23). A similar play on words can be found in earlier texts: *Taittirīya Āraṇyaka* 10.1 quotes *Rig Veda* 1.99, a one-verse hymn to Agni that praises him for leading us through difficulties (*durgāṇi*) and then declares: "In her who has the color of Agni, flaming with ascetic power (*tapas*), the offspring of Virocana, who delights in the fruits of [one's] actions, in the goddess Durgā do I take refuge; O one of great speed, [well] do you navigate. Hail [to you]!" In the *sūtra* literature, this same Vedic hymn to Agni comes to be known as the *Durgā Sāvitrī* (see, for example, *Viṣṇu Dharmasūtra* 56.9, and *Baudhāyana Dharmaśāstra* 4.3.8; see also the quotation of *Rig Veda* 1.99 in the *Rātrī Khila* in Scheftelowitz, ed., *Die Apokryphen*, pp. 110–12).

20. The appendix to the *Devī Māhātmya* known as the *Prādhānika Rahasya* goes so far as to characterize the text as an account of "the *avatāra*s of Caṇḍikā" (see my *Encountering the Goddess*, p. 185). Although this appendix is a somewhat later composition, such a phrase attests to the ongoing interplay between Vaiṣṇava and Goddess-oriented conceptualizations of divinity. For more on the issues raised in this paragraph, see *Encountering the Goddess*, pp. 24–27.

21. For a translation of this hymn, see *Crystallization*, pp. 272–75.

22. The fact that the *Devī Māhātmya* actually has somewhat fewer than six hundred verses creates a fascinating dilemma for later interpreters, as I discuss in *Encountering the Goddess* (pp. 27, 31, 139–40, 162). The relationship between Devī and royalty, both human and divine, is a significant, but as yet inadequately understood, phenomenon. For important foundational studies, see Madeleine Biardeau, *Autour*

de la Déesse hindoue (Paris: Editions de l'Ecole Pratique des Hautes Etudes en Sciences Sociales, 1981); the essays in *Puruṣārtha,* vol. 5; Sanjukta Gupta and Richard Gombrich, "Kings, Power and the Goddess," *South Asia Research* 6, no. 2 (1986): 123–38; J. C. Heesterman, *The Inner Conflict of Tradition: Essays in Indian Ritual, Kingship, and Society* (Chicago: University of Chicago Press, 1985); and Alf Hiltebeitel and Thomas J. Hopkins, "Indus Valley Religion," in Mircea Eliade, ed., *The Encyclopedia of Religion* (New York: Macmillan, 1986) 7:215–23.

23. See, for example, Vaudeville's "Krishna Gopāla, Rādhā, and the Great Goddess," in *The Divine Consort,* ed. Hawley and Wulff, pp. 1–12.

24. References are to the critical edition of the *Harivaṃśa,* ed. P. L. Vaidya, 2 vols. (Poona: Bhandarkar Oriental Research Institute, 1969, 1971).

25. *Viṣṇu Purāṇa* (Bombay: Oriental Press, 1889), readily available in H. H. Wilson's English translation (see vols. 6–10 of his *Works,* which have been frequently reprinted); and *Bālacarita* (Delhi: Munshiram Manoharlal, 1959), available in English in A. C. Woolner and L. Sarup, trans., *Thirteen Trivandrum Plays Attributed to Bhāsa* (London: Oxford University Press–Humphrey Milford, 1930–31). See also *Devī Māhātmya* 11.38–51, where Devī, describing five of her future appearances, announces that when two new demons, also named Śumbha and Niśumbha, have arisen, she will be born "in the house of the cowherd Nanda, in the womb of Yaśodā" in order to slay them.

26. See Vaudeville's "Aspects du mythe de *Kṛṣṇa-Gopāla* dans l'Inde ancienne," in *Mélanges d'Indianisme à la mémoire de Louis Renou* (Paris: Éditions de Boccard, 1968), pp. 737–61; and "The Cowherd God in Ancient India," in *Pastoralists and Nomads in South Asia,* ed. Lawrence Saadia Leshnik and Günther-Dietz Sontheimer (Wiesbaden: Otto Harrassowitz, 1975), pp. 92–116.

27. In *Encountering the Goddess,* pp. 159–69, I present two case studies demonstrating this variety. The issues addressed in this paragraph are discussed at much greater length in the second half of that volume, particularly on pp. 99–117.

28. Lawrence Babb, *The Divine Hierarchy: Popular Hinduism in Central India* (New York: Columbia University Press, 1975), p. 218; my italics.

29. See Humes's "The Text and Temple of the Great Goddess: The *Devī-Māhātmya* and the Vindhyācal Temple of Mirzapur" (Ph.D. diss., University of Iowa, 1990). See also her "Glorifying the Great Goddess or Great Woman? Women's Experience in Ritual Recitation of the *Devī-Māhātmya,*" in *Women and Goddess Traditions,* ed. Karen King (Minneapolis: Fortress Press, forthcoming), on which the balance of this paragraph is based, as well as Humes's chapter in this book. On the performative dimension of religious texts more generally, see William A. Graham, *Beyond the Written Word: Oral Aspects of Scripture in the History of Religion* (New York: Cambridge University Press, 1987).

30. This raises the interesting question of whether recitation of a vernacular translation possesses the same mantric power as recitation in Sanskrit. When I put this to one of my colleagues and informants, A. N. Jani, in July 1991, asking whether recitation of my English translation of the *Devī Māhātmya* would be likely to produce consequences comparable to recitation of the Sanskrit original, he replied with characteristic empiricism: "Let us see!"

31. See Östör's *The Play of the Gods* (Chicago: University of Chicago Press, 1980), as well as my discussion of his analysis in *Encountering the Goddess,* pp. 154–56.

32. See Alf Hiltebeitel, *The Cult of Draupadī*, 2 vols. (Chicago: University of Chicago Press, 1988, 1991); and William S. Sax, *Mountain Goddess: Gender and Politics in a Himalayan Pilgrimage* (New York: Oxford University Press, 1991).

33. Sudhir Kakar, *Intimate Relations: Exploring Indian Sexuality* (Chicago: University of Chicago Press, 1989), pp. 131–32.

34. See Stanley N. Kurtz, *All the Mothers Are One: Hindu India and the Cultural Reshaping of Psychoanalysis* (New York: Columbia University Press, 1992), chap. 5. Kurtz calls the pre-Oedipal stage in Hindu culture "the Ek-Hi Phase," the phrase *ek hī* meaning "just one," that is, Just One Mother. "The Durgā Complex" is the title of chap. 6.

VINDHYAVĀSINĪ
Local Goddess yet Great Goddess

Cynthia Ann Humes

The village known as Vindhyachal, literally "Vindhya mountain," sits midway between Allahabad and Banaras where the Vindhya mountain range touches the southern shores of the holy Ganges. This bustling pilgrimage town has grown up around the ancient temple complex devoted to Vindhyavāsinī, "the goddess who dwells in the Vindhyas."

If you ask her devotees who Vindhyavāsinī is and why she is famous, nearly all will respond with a variant of her best-known myth, about how she saved the baby Krishna from being killed by his wicked uncle, king Kaṃsa. Kaṃsa learned he was destined to die by the hand of his cousin Devakī's child. When Viṣṇu incarnated himself as Krishna, he exhorted Yoganidrā ("Yogic Sleep," or she who causes such somnolence), who is also Mahāmāyā ("Great Delusionary Power"), to cast her spell on Kaṃsa and his forces and to take birth herself of the cowherd couple Nanda and Yaśodā. With the aid of the Goddess's delusionary power, Devakī's husband, Vasudeva, carried Krishna undiscovered to Nanda's home and returned with the divine girl-child. When Kaṃsa learned that Devakī had given birth, he rushed there, grabbed the baby by her foot, and sought to dash her head against a stone, but she slipped from his hand. Assuming her eight-armed form, she announced that Kaṃsa's slayer had been born. She then flew off to Vindhyachal, where she became known as Vindhyachal Nivāsinī or Vindhyavāsinī—"she who dwells in the Vindhya mountains" (see figure 4).

One prominent aspect of this account gives expression to a feature of Vindhyavāsinī that seems to be historically true. The myth suggests that she had an independent force and identity before she became incorporated into the legend and worship of Krishna, and that her power could be mobilized to support the ongoing evolution of Hindu religion. Indeed, many scholars accept on various grounds that Vindhyavāsinī is among the more ancient of

Figure 4. Vindhyavāsinī, goddess of Vindhyachal, as she is described in Tantric literature. Drawing by Rita DasGupta, 1995, ink drawing.

Hindu goddesses. She and her cult are believed to have contributed importantly to the rise of a Hindu theology of the Great Goddess. As R. C. Hazra explains, in the early centuries of the common era, when local female deities grew in prominence, "to give these new goddesses a position in the Śākta pantheon, they had to be connected either with Umā [Śiva's spouse] or with Vindhyavāsinī (or Yogamāyā)"—a phenomenon that has been confirmed by J. N. Tiwari and others.[1]

The power of Umā (or Pārvatī) to assimilate other, local goddesses and thereby draw them into a larger Śākta network is relatively well known. As Satī, for example, Umā became enraged by the insult to her husband, Śiva, at her father Dakṣa's sacrifice and committed self-immolation. Grieving, Śiva danced angrily with her lifeless body over his shoulder, and parts of her body fell to the earth, spawning a host of regional goddesses. But as another myth reveals, Vindhyavāsinī sometimes retained her independence and was not subsumed to Umā. Kauśikī is the dark goddess who is formed from the *kośa* or "sheath" of black skin that was sloughed off when Umā assumed a golden complexion. The virgin Kauśikī then rushed to the Vindhyas to slay the demon brothers Śumbha and Niśumbha. Although she is thus absorbed into Umā's mythology, Vindhyavāsinī acts separately and is thus held apart from an identity determined by marriage to Śiva.

Interpreting all goddesses as incarnations of Umā was acceptable to those who primarily worshiped Śiva. Those who preferred Viṣṇu or an independent goddess, however, found it more appealing or useful to understand all goddesses as incarnations of the great power behind/of Viṣṇu. Moreover—a third alternative—Vindhyavāsinī's diverse mythological associations made her a highly effective means of absorbing others. Her mythology not only linked her to a wide region but connected her to other goddesses, and to Viṣṇu, Indra, and the pastoral deity Krishna. Unlike Umā, her power was not controlled or diminished by a more powerful husband. Vindhyavāsinī was thus capable of providing the nuclear origin for a cult of the unmarried, virgin Great Goddess, who was understood as the single Ādiśakti, the world's primeval power. Vindhyavāsinī's modern devotees still maintain that she is Ādiśakti and say that Umā is but an incarnation of this power. Thus, as Umā claims to absorb Vindhyavāsinī, so Vindhyavāsinī claims to absorb Umā.

Some of the most influential ancient scriptural references to a single Great Goddess (Mahādevī), who responds to devotees' personal appeals by manifesting herself in other forms, refer to Vindhyavāsinī's mythology. The ancient hymns incorporated into Sanskrit epic literature, especially the *Mahābhārata* and the *Harivaṃśa,* by the sixth century C.E. all describe Mahādevī as either "dwelling in the Vindhyas" or as the goddess who becomes incarnate to aid Viṣṇu. These same works mention peripheral groups who routinely offered this mountain goddess liquor and sacrifices of animals and humans, thereby suggesting her origins among tribal peoples. She was closely connected with nature and was believed to exist within the actual region: she literally "dwelt in the mountains." Just as the Vindhya mountain range is a large one, extending from the west to east coasts across middle India, so was her region of dominance and immanence perceived to be vast. Thus the goddess of the Vindhyas, originally a native and "non-Sanskritic" deity, was incorporated into early Brahmanical written traditions. Well-known mythological threads from various Sanskrit texts were woven into her worship, which served in turn to spread her worship beyond the Vindhyas.

Vindhyavāsinī's association with motifs of absorption and identification helps to explain how she could be consistently linked with her local context—mountain-dwelling societies and their often "unorthodox" traditions—yet at the same time be understood as possessing the monistic characteristics of Mahādevī. This fusion of so-called "little" and "great" traditions is readily visible to anyone who visits Vindhyavāsinī's temple today.

A PILGRIMAGE TO THE VINDHYACHAL TEMPLE

What is it like to be a pilgrim in Vindhyavāsinī's temple? Imagine you have come on one of the days special to the goddess, as most pilgrims do. You will probably have arrived by one of the many hot, dusty, bumpy buses that inch along the roadways at a punishing forty kilometers per hour. They are packed with other pilgrims, who jam the aisles and lean out the windows. As you follow the flow of brilliantly colored crowds along the road, you soon enter a maze of narrow village lanes. A myriad of shops line three sides of the temple for many city blocks. These small stores are usually the outermost rooms of Vindhyachal homes: nearly all citizens wealthy enough to own a dwelling in the vicinity of the temple participate in the commercial opportunities afforded them by the hundreds of thousands of pilgrims who wend their way past their homes every year along Vindhyachal's sinuous paths. Shops in Brahmin homes may sell ritual accouterments; others peddle metal utensils, vegetables, fruits, sweets, beauty items, childrens' toys, cloth, dry goods, milk products, and more, the goods varying according to the shopkeeper's caste. Merchants raucously call out to you to buy sweets, coconuts, flowers, incense, and little red squares of cloth to offer to the goddess and thereby to ensure her favor. Once you have chosen, bargained for, and bundled up the offering, you arrive at the top of a crest, where a crude, black stone image of the goddess is housed in a tiny and otherwise unremarkable plain stone edifice, now surrounded by a multitude of shrines appended over the years. By the time you actually reach the steps of the temple, you have learned from your neighbors that you will probably have to wait for some time to earn Vindhyavāsinī's *darśan*—often thirty minutes or more, and during the semiannual nine-day Navarātra festivals sacred to the Goddess, from two to six hours or even longer.

It is considered preferable for pilgrims to leave some gift at the feet of every idol they worship. Since there are numerous images in the Vindhyachal temple complex, pilgrims are advised by the "money vendors" strategically located adjacent to the temple to prepare for this duty by trading their paper money, at a 10 percent loss, for heavy pocketfuls of coins. Slipping your shoes off near the stairs of the temple—or for a small fee wisely giving them over to a shopkeeper's protection—you merge into the great ill-shapen "line" and walk barefoot into a large hall adjacent to the goddess's main shrine (see figure 5). This open-air pavilion was constructed by the king of Vijayanagara in the last century, and in the mid-1980s temple priests sponsored the inscription on its high marble walls of the sixth-century Sanskrit *Devī Māhātmya,* or "Glorification of the Goddess," already familiar to readers of this book. The text is best known locally as the *Durgā Saptaśatī,* the "Seven Hundred [Mantras] of Durgā," and the pavilion is now named *Saptaśatī Bhavanam* ("*Saptaśatī*'s Abode"). Looking up, you gaze at the text; looking forward, you see a dozen men sitting cross-legged facing the temple and reciting the text in a low drone. These religious specialists are called pandits, from the Sanskrit *paṇḍita,* "learned." Seated patiently on their mats of holy *kuśa* grass, wearing cotton *dhotī*s dyed an auspicious yellow, and surrounded by ritual paraphernalia (a brass or silver pot of purifying Ganges water, incense, conch shells, flowers, sweets, and stacks of books), these pandits spend their days reciting religious texts such as the *Devī Māhātmya,* chanting efficacious mantras in Sanskrit (the "perfect language" of the gods), and performing marriage ceremonies and other rituals for interested pilgrims.

Affluent-looking pilgrims unaccompanied by a family priest are usually approached several times on the temple grounds and sometimes even at the bus stop or along the paths by Brahmin pilgrim guides of Vindhyachal known as *paṇḍā*s (also a variant of the word *paṇḍita*).[2] Despite the similarity in their titles, you will soon learn that *paṇḍā*s are quite different from *paṇḍita*s. Whereas pandits rarely demean themselves by pursuing customers, guides often aggressively try to convince pilgrims that without their professional help in performing religious worship the trip to Vindhyachal will be less fruitful. Guides offer ritual, not spiritual, advice, explaining where to go, who to see, what is best to offer at each site, and how to offer it. They may even accompany customers throughout their trips, especially if the pilgrim wishes to perform the popular *trikoṇa yātrā,* or "triangle pilgrimage," that links this temple with two other goddess sites in the wider "sacred field of the Vindhyas," the Vindhyakṣetra (see figure 6). Your guide will earn his keep not only by leading the way and providing a running commentary on

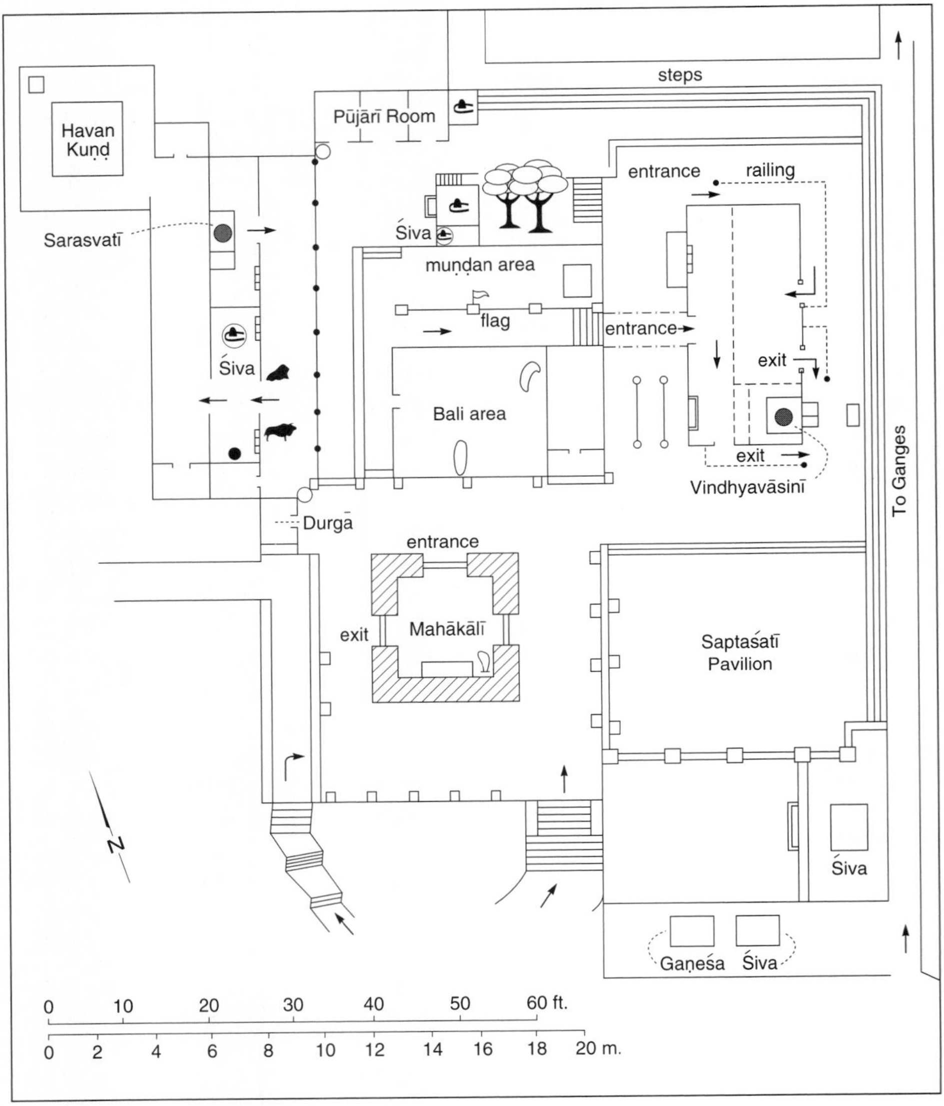

Figure 5. The Vindhyavāsinī temple complex. Diagram by Donald J. Saltarelli, Jr.

the "glory" of each site visited but also by shielding you from overly aggressive beggars and the tireless appeals of temple priests.

In return for their assistance, these guides expect some economic reward, whether it be clothing, food, cash, or all three. Some of the bolder guides vigorously berate customers even while inside the temple if they do not provide sufficient remuneration for their services. But you needn't be

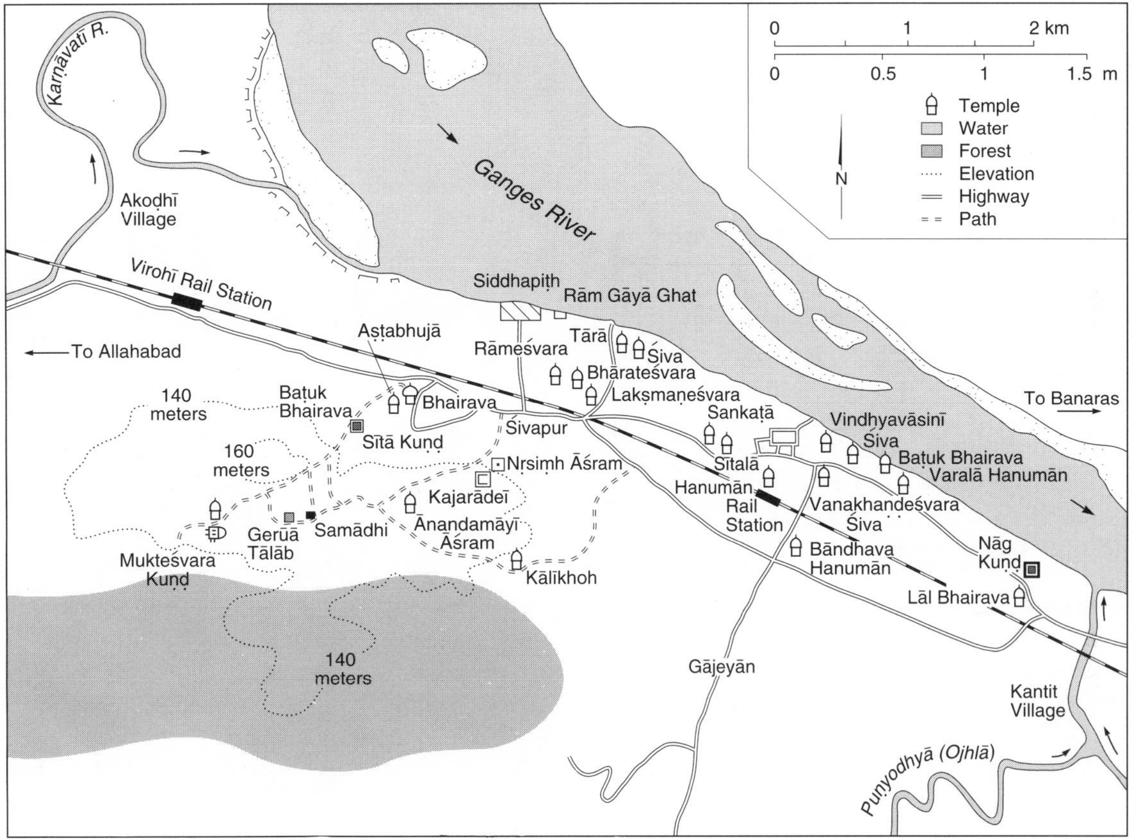

Figure 6. Vindhyakṣetra, the "sacred field of the Vindhyas." Diagram by Donald J. Saltarelli, Jr.

too intimidated: as in most commercial transactions in India, guides expect their patrons to bargain. As for the pandits, they generally prefer to work with guides—who first convince their clients to request specialized ritual services and then refer them to "their" pandit (who will split the reward with the guide according to a predetermined percentage). Some of the most memorable events you experience at Vindhyachal may well be connected with the unpleasantness of the goddess's worship in its manifestation as a business. Foreigners may feel this especially, but many Indian Hindus do as well.

Indeed, as you follow the line away from the pandits and their recitations, you are continually interrupted by demands for money. Having positioned themselves on the marble floors in places where they deliberately obstruct traffic, bored drummers beat single-handedly without any noticeable rhythm, holding one palm outstretched. Noting that the drummers sometimes get attention by actually striking pilgrims with their sticks or holding onto their clothing, you flip down one of the small coins you have purchased and pass by unharmed. Equally brazen are the hordes of young local girls who perch like rows of crows atop temple walls and flap fans to cool those waiting in the humid heat to see the goddess. Realizing again that often they "accidentally" hit pilgrims on the head with their fans (giggling knowingly to one another) if no coin is surrendered, you hand over a few paise and try to enjoy the rush of air they propel over your head.

Now you are quite near: looking down into a small pit immediately adjacent to Vindhyavāsinī's shrine, you can see several animal sacrificers in a bloody ritual arena ornamented by a waist-high statue of a lion. These muscled men lean against the entrance, holding their menacing swords at their sides, attentively scanning the crowds, and, with fingers still sticky and flaked with blood, beckoning devotees to come forward and offer costly, but tasty, sacrifices of goats and chickens to the goddess in her manifestation as the bloodthirsty Kālī. Barbers to your left sit amidst mounds of black hair, resting on their heels with legs folded like accordions, ever on the lookout for parents with young children in need of a ritual haircut (*muṇḍan*). Usually one or two mendicants attend the many small shrines of Śiva in the temple environs; they will walk up to you in line and smile pleasantly, palm open. These dusty, near-naked men offer to bless you with Śiva's sacred ash or, if you're game, with a touch of the writhing cobra some wear as a necklace in emulation of Śiva. For just ten paise, why not?

After being jostled for what seems like ages, listening to and sometimes joining in the popular folk songs that well up spontaneously like waves from the surging crowds, you finally reach the doors of the small shrine. Excitedly, you reach up to the lintel and touch the feet of the Lord of Obstacles guarding her doors—the elephant-headed Gaṇeśa—signaling that at last your goal is nearly attained. Bending through the low doorway, you touch the litter-strewn but hallowed floor and raise your now-sanctified fingertips to your forehead. Then, standing wedged between other squirming devotees, you crane your neck past your neighbor to gain your first sidelong glimpse of the Goddess. She stands in a brass enclosure that protects her from the milling throng.

Pressed forward by the crowd, you extend your hands through the bars and give one of the priests tending the goddess your bundle of overpriced goods together with some cash. The priest cracks your coconut on the stone at her feet and tosses your money into a corner. After the cloth, flowers, and candies are proffered at her feet for an instant, you receive most of the items back—if, that is, the priests working that day are conscientious or you are accompanied by a protective guide. If you are lucky, you will actually be able to take a moment to look at the black, birdlike face of the goddess, who wears a red sari. Adorned with a large silver nose-ring and encircled by dozens of flower wreaths, she stands upon a small black lion. Most important, you seek to gaze into her wide silver eyes so that she may gaze back into yours: this is *darśan*.[3] But soon, and without warning, you are grabbed by a strong bare-chested priest working like a barroom bouncer to control the crowds. Your head is forced down and you are hurled through the tiny exit, where in bewilderment you stand up shaking and rack your brain trying to process such intense sensory input—did the goddess see me?

Indeed, the senses can easily become dazed during a temple visit on a busy day. Your vision is assailed by the sight of such unfamiliar and chaotic activities; your hearing by the shameless begging, pounding drums, reverberating brass bells, shrieking *shehnāī* reed instruments, and the many background layers of voices trilling like a wild raga accompanied by the drone of ritual mantras; your nose by the heady odor of cheap incense, thick stormclouds of *ghī,* and your neighbor's sweat; and your body by the thousands of flies, the constant pressing of the crowds, and the mixture of sticky rotting coconut milk, dirt, flowers, and Ganges water that tenaciously pastes your bare feet to the floor at each step. It was always quite easy for me to determine which pilgrims had never before been to Vindhyachal just by gauging the level of shock and disorientation visible on their faces. They gawk open-mouthed and wide-eyed, particularly after having been ejected like cannonballs from the dark, humid recesses of the suffocating temple.

Now that you have seen Vindhyavāsinī, you may wish to perform the triangle *yātrā* and visit the two other sites where the goddess is believed to be established in other forms: Kālīkhoh ("Kālī's cave") and Aṣṭabhujā, the "eight-armed" goddess (see figure 7). In the early to mid-nineteenth century, the popularity of this *yātrā* led to the establishment of other worship sites to Kālī and Sarasvatī, and eventually, small temples immediately

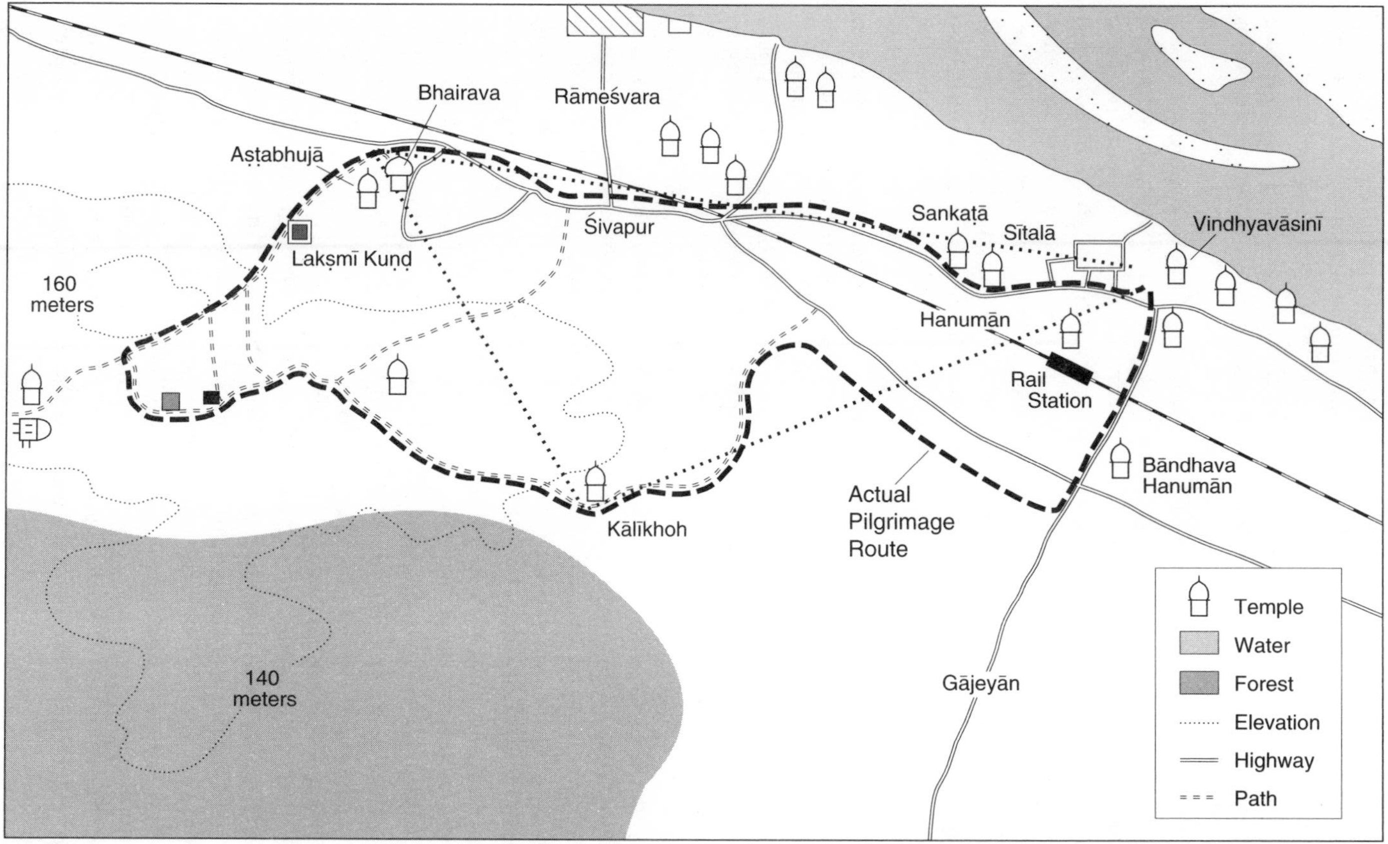

Figure 7. The triangle *yātrā*. Diagram by Donald J. Saltarelli, Jr.

adjacent to the Vindhyavāsinī shrine, which are also arranged in a triangular format. Visiting these three—the "short" or "easy" (*laghu*) triangle *yātrā*—is said by some to satisfy the same requirements as completing the longer journey. But these ancillary temples were clearly established for commercial reasons—to attract the pilgrim trade—and rigorous devotees believe that only the original pilgrimage offers the full vision of the Great Goddess in her three forms.

It seems that at every step on one's visit to the Vindhyachal temple there is someone to pay and something to purchase. Here the business of religion is intricately subdivided, with pilgrims milked for every possible paisa throughout. That this religious site has commercial dimensions is not unique; from early times, Hindu temples have functioned as economic centers. As at many North Indian temples, the right to prosper from ritual acts performed for pilgrims is the hereditary "property" of the guides and the pandits they authorize. In a sense, the Goddess's blessings are believed to be open for purchase. Guides claim that pilgrims' visits will be more fruitful as a result of their intervention, since they are able to gain access to her power more fully than could pilgrims; similarly, pandits have skills in the recitation of mantras that elude the layperson. But guides and pandits must attract pilgrims to the temple in the first place; selling their product requires them to advertise the special qualities of the goddess and promote her intercession. This they do in a variety of ways, particularly by describing her "glory" (*māhātmya*), which is believed to be best expressed in Sanskrit texts.

Certain texts are held to be more conducive than others to promoting the vision of Vindhyavāsinī that the guides and other religious officiants wish to evoke. The theology taught by their ancestors, which previously brought pilgrims to the complex, is no longer thought to be as appropriate or marketable as it once was. Instead, new interpretations are regarded as more effective, and folk traditions remain significant only for particular cores of rural clientele. Yet all guides make at least passing reference to the *Vindhya Māhātmya,* which is the *sthala-māhātmya* ("glorification of the sacred site") of Vindhyachal. Bookstalls sell cheap abridged versions that highlight the major sites found today in Vindhyakṣetra. These pamphlets do not describe the major events as they are recounted in that text, however. The portions chosen are largely those that confirm the vision of the Goddess found in that pan-Indian paean to the generic Great Goddess, the *Devī Māhātmya,* the text displayed in the temple's entrance hall, and whose recitation the guides urge their clients to sponsor. Quotes from the *Devī Māhātmya* are included in the pamphlets to confirm the authenticity of the *sthala-māhātmya*'s claims about each site.

The theology of the goddess that the guides routinely offer their customers today is heavily dependent on the *Devī Māhātmya* and its subtexts, not on the *Vindhya Māhātmya.* This is not an evolution from simple to complex, however. The explanation of ultimate reality found in the early-nineteenth-century *Vindhya Māhātmya* is quite sophisticated, whereas the *Devī Māhātmya* is in fact more vague in its philosophy, allowing for greater diversity of interpretation. The local text posits a unity of all goddesses by affirming Vindhyavāsinī as the ultimate power, the qualityless *brahman* that submits itself to a process of self-qualification. All other goddesses are understood as portions or manifestations of her, as are all gods and all the universe. She exists in transcendent and proximate form within Vindhyakṣetra, which is thus the most powerful and sacred area in all the worlds. The *Vindhya Māhātmya* thus betrays a preference for a specific philosophy of the Goddess as understood within the Vindhyavāsinī mythological framework and insists on the supremacy of the Vindhya region as a sacred space where the Goddess is immediately accessible. By contrast, the *Devī Māhātmya* offers another way to express the identity of all Hindu goddesses. It describes a single, transcendent Great Goddess, generically conceived and independent of a particular region, "who possesses most of the classical characteristics of ultimate reality as understood in the Hindu tradition" and who subsumes all "particular goddesses under her as partial manifestations of her," including the "Dweller in the Vindhyas" (Vindhyācala Nivāsinī) mentioned briefly in its eleventh chapter.[4]

At Vindhyachal, there has thus been a shift away from understanding Vindhyavāsinī as an immediate, site-specific form of Mahādevī. Instead, priests promote her identity as the generic Ādiśakti—the single, transcendent primeval power extolled in the *Devī Māhātmya.* Concomitant with this development, many religious officiants now insist on a theology that forbids or radically deemphasizes incarnations, mythologies, and rituals that are now viewed as inappropriately "regional" or "heretical," or, sadly, "misunderstood"—although these used to be readily accepted as appropriate to Vindhyavāsinī's cult when she was still understood in a mythological and sectarian fashion. In part, this shift reflects the concern of the guides and pandits to universalize her appeal: by downplaying her specificities and appropriating a more universalistic glorification that also allows for a variety of interpretations, they hope to increase the number of her potential adherents—their potential customers. I believe that financial considerations are a major reason why most of the *Vindhya Māhātmya* is ignored, whereas the *Devī Māhātmya* is inscribed in temple walls, recited by pandits, and quoted by guides.

COMPETING GLORIFICATIONS OF VINDHYAVĀSINĪ

In approximately two thousand verses, the *Vindhya Māhātmya* details the glory of Vindhyavāsinī and her sacred domain of Vindhyakṣetra. The text intersects with the context of the temple and its cult in a number of ways. First, like many other *sthala-māhātmyas*, this text serves as a sourcebook for the Brahmins who work at Vindhyachal in that it legitimates and aggrandizes worship at various sites and festivals for which they should be hired. In addition, a few of its most popular tales are still related to curious pilgrim clients. Second, as a source of theology the *Vindhya Māhātmya* explains the nature of Vindhyavāsinī and her relations to the myriad deities who have come to dwell near her. Third, for devotees, its elaborate description of the area stresses its distinctiveness and highlights the local concentration of the Goddess's transcendent activity. The text provides a means to envision the sacred sphere underlying the phenomenal realm and speaks of the other avatars the Goddess assumes in response to the appeals of distraught devotees. Fourth, the *Vindhya Māhātmya* includes specific instructions for Tantrics, those who practice a spiritual discipline (*sādhana*) that they believe can empower them to attain any material or spiritual desire. It explains procedures that bestow on them supernatural powers (*siddhi*) and tells how to construct a *yantra.* A *yantra* is a "'device' for harnessing the mind in meditation or worship . . . a diagram, usually of geometric interlocking triangles and circles" that in some way represents the cosmos.[5] The *yantra* is created either by physical movement through Vindhyakṣetra or by embedding the sites it contains within oneself. Thereby the Tantric may experience directly the Goddess who, immanent in all, is yet especially focused within this sacred land. Ultimately, she *is* Vindhyakṣetra, and the Tantric may in this way become her. Finally, the text functions as a historical document. To some degree it is a historical description—idealized, to be sure—of the area and its goddess as they would have appeared during the early 1800s.

The *Devī Māhātmya* offers a very different theological vision of Vindhyavāsinī: it sees her as one among various incarnations of a generically conceived Great Goddess. Nor does there appear to be much connection between that text and the land of Vindhyakṣetra; almost none of the sites that occupy the attention of the *Vindhya Māhātmya* are mentioned, and indeed the pan-Indian text seems to deny, or at the very least ignore, the primacy of the Vindhya region. Yet these potential limitations have not impeded the conviction that the *Devī Māhātmya* gives a more "accurate" vision of the Goddess and her abode than does the *Vindhya Māhātmya.* Why? Why do Vindhyavāsinī's caretakers prefer the *Devī Māhātmya* over the *Vindhya Māhātmya,* and what impact does this preference have on conceptions of Vindhyavāsinī and her cult?

Hindu deities are believed to enjoy listening to generous praise: reciting the "glory" of a god or goddess is one way to get divine attention and favor. *Sthala-māhātmyas* are often chanted aloud to please the resident deity, and Brahmins are paid for this service. Thus *sthala-māhātmyas* may "spring up" at potentially lucrative sites, both to legitimate the site as a glorious place and to add another service occupation to the pilgrimage economy. At Vindhyachal, however, not only is the *Vindhya Māhātmya* not recited in its entirety but, for reasons I will explain, it is deliberately kept obscure.

To some degree, guides continue, albeit perfunctorily and selectively, to tell the "glorification" (*māhātmya*) of Vindhyachal to their pilgrim clients. In this restricted sense, the *Vindhya Māhātmya* still acts as a pilgrimage priest's "primer." And many guides appear to know the text well. But the abridged vernacular pamphlets rarely encode more than the most basic features found in chapters 26 through 31, which styles itself the core or "short" (*laghu*) *Vindhya Māhātmya* and tells about the triadic *yantra* of temples, the worship of the three goddesses, and the defeat of Śumbha and Niśumbha. The detailed theology of Vindhyavāsinī contained in the text is not utilized.

The *Vindhya Māhātmya* explains that the Goddess bestows both liberation (*mokṣa*) and material enjoyment (*bhoga*). Ultimate reality is revealed as One; the single Great Goddess is *brahman,* the absolute, devoid of qualities. *Brahman* "gives rise" to "undistinguished" or "unseparated" material nature (*prakṛti*). This unified *prakṛti* then separates into the three constitutive qualities of the universe called *guṇa*s, literally "strands"—*sattva, rajas, tamas*—and the interaction of the *guṇa*s constantly causes creation. The Goddess is known simultaneously as Nārāyaṇī, the Greatest, and the Eternal, without whose *śakti* no creation is possible, even by the gods. Thus, as *brahman,* she is One, beyond attributes, and none can see her. It is only as she exists in manifest forms of *prakṛti* that people see her as Śivā, for instance—any female aspect of Śiva—or as Sarasvatī. This view of ultimate reality specifically rejects a bipolar Śākta theology of *śakti* and *puruṣa,* an eternal dualism of matter and spirit, but it does affirm *śakti* as the power underlying and constituting ultimate reality itself.

The Goddess's self-transformation into the phenomenal world in fact follows the *satkāryavāda* philosophy that effects preexist in their cause. The world is an effect that is an actual transformation (*pariṇāma*) of the underlying substratum; thus the world is not mere appearance (*vivarta*). The "short" *Vindhya Māhātmya,* which begins in chapter 26, accordingly explains how the goddess manifests herself within the land and in specific incarnations to protect the world and her devotees. Field research has confirmed that among the philosophically inclined, the most common interpretation of Vindhyavāsinī offered by devotees was this monistic *satkāryavāda* view affirming that the world is the actual transformation of its underlying substratum. In this sense, the philosophy of the Goddess found in the *Vindhya Māhātmya* is continuous to this day. In dozens of chapters, the text further explains at length how all deities, including Viṣṇu and Śiva, adore Vindhyavāsinī as the supreme, and how some were able to vanquish various demons through her power, while others saw the establishment of sacred bathing spots in their own honor within Vindhyakṣetra. Indeed, it seems the area is studded at every step with sites of worship holy to all manner of gods, goddesses, and yogis.

The text's elaborate description of literally hundreds of sites stresses Vindhyachal's distinctiveness and highlights the "localness" and immediacy of Vindhyavāsinī's divine activity. The glorification facilitates visualization of sacred Vindhyakṣetra; pilgrims are encouraged to witness each site in person through the divine lens provided by the text. To perform a pilgrimage there is to participate in Vindhyavāsinī's sacred abode. But this pilgrimage has changed, at least on a phenomenal level, over time. Today, many of the sites are no longer maintained, and the vernacular précis of the *Vindhya Māhātmya* omit most of the sites that occupied the greatest attention in the text, although all preserve the pilgrimage to the triad of goddess temples. Guides explain that the *Devī Māhātmya* is the best text available anywhere in India for the practice of devotion to the Goddess and that people should glorify the Great Goddess enshrined at Vindhyachal with that preeminent text rather than one preoccupied with specific local incarnations. Change at Vindhyachal thus attests first to the success of efforts to unify regional goddesses as incarnations of a single transgeographical Great Goddess, and second to the prominent rise of the *Devī Māhātmya* as the *bhakti* text par excellence for those who worship her. Third, although the *sthala-māhātmya* could serve as a visualization tool for devotees, because it remains unpublished in its entirety it does not serve this function today for any significant numbers of devotees outside of the Vindhyachal region itself.

Vindhya Māhātmya 27.3 introduces another name for ultimate reality conceived as *brahman* and power: Mahālakṣmī ("Great Lakṣmī"). Mahālakṣmī exists within Vindhyakṣetra in the form of a *yantra,* the base of which is a triangle superimposed over *brahman,* which is conceived as existing in a center point (*bindu*). At each corner, Vindhyavāsinī has transformed herself into three *mahādevīs* ("Great Goddesses") who are distinguished by the primacy of one of the *guṇas*: Mahāsarasvatī by the quality of *sattva,* or goodness; Mahākālī by *tamas,* or darkness; and Mahālakṣmī by *rajas,* or activity. Each Great Goddess then incarnates herself into other manifestations. Mahāsarasvatī becomes Aṣṭabhujā Devī; Mahākālī as Kālīkhoh Devī resides at "Kālī's cave"; and Mahālakṣmī is Vindhyavāsinī. The following diagram outlines the transformations.

The Unmanifest Vindhyavāsinī in the Point (*bindu*)
Parabrahman/Ādiśakti/Mahālakṣmī

↓

Transformation into Undifferentiated *Prakṛti*
Three-*guṇa* Vindhyavāsinī

↓

Transcendent Forms of Vindhyavāsinī		
Mahākālī (*tamas*)	Mahālakṣmī (*rajas*)	Mahāsarasvatī (*sattva*)
↓	↓	↓
Manifest Forms of Each of the Three Transcendent Mahādevīs		
Mahākālī	Mahālakṣmī	Mahāsarasvatī
as	as	as
Kālīkhoh Devī	Vindhyavāsinī Devī	Aṣṭabhujā Devī

The triangle *yātrā* is a tour of the triad of temples housing the three manifest forms of the goddess. The earliest historical reference to this pilgrimage appears in a journal entry written by the pilgrim Enugula Veeraswamy in 1830.[6] Nearly one-third of today's pilgrims perform it, because they believe to gain a complete vision of the Goddess, one must see her in all three aspects.[7] However, if pilgrims can visit only one of the three temples, they visit the Vindhyachal temple, where Vindhyavāsinī dwells. They do so because they believe the ultimate reality, conceived as *brahman* and power, exists most intensely at this shrine. At Vindhyachal the Great Goddess Mahālakṣmī—the unmanifest central point (*bindu*)—manifests herself in increasingly material forms, first in a state of three-*guṇa* potentiality, next in transcendent yet unembodied forms, and finally in manifest form as Vindhyavāsinī, whose earthly name is interpreted by some (in a play on words) to reflect her ultimate nature as the "Dweller in the Point": Binduvāsinī.[8]

The play on words between Vindhyavāsinī as a manifest goddess to be adored and Binduvāsinī as the unmanifest Goddess to be contemplated is paralleled by a pun pointing to the conception of Vindhyakṣetra as both a pilgrimage field to be seen and a Tantric mechanism to be exploited. In ethnographic interviews pilgrims often mentioned that the triangle *yātrā* is actually a powerful triangle *yantra.* Three chapters, comprising half of the "short" *Vindhya Māhātmya,* explain the Tantric activities that must be performed at each of the three goddess shrines if the adept intends to construct this huge *yantra* and properly worship the goddess of the Vindhyas. In contrast, the text requires thirty-six chapters to describe adequately the "glory" of the sacred area. For the devotee, the text must provide not just a glimpse of the divine play at Vindhyakṣetra, but a sustained vision of celestial glory on earth.

The Tantric adept can ritually construct the triangle *yantra* through the proper use of visualization, movement, and mantra. This method emphasizes correct ritual preparation, including cleansing rituals, "root" mantras, prayers, and invocations to the goddesses dwelling within the Vindhyachal *yantra.* To establish the *yantra* is to place the macrocosm within oneself, and doing so can yield mundane benefits, spiritual and magical powers (*siddhi*), and/or enlightenment (*mokṣa*).

Figure 8. The triangle *yantra*. Diagram by Donald J. Saltarelli, Jr.

Chapter 27 elaborates the *yantra* of Mahālakṣmī. At the center the Great Goddess Vindhyavāsinī dwells in the form of a point (*bindu*) as the unmanifest absolute (see figure 8). The *bindu* is enclosed by a triangle pointing downward. At the corners, Mahālakṣmī dwells in the east, Mahāsarasvatī in the west, and Mahākālī in the south. Two interlocking triangles enclose the inner triangle. At the corners, six *śakti*s are established, none of whom are popularly known today. These two triangles are then surrounded by three groupings of lotus petals, each separated by circles. The first set of petals contains eight mothers, who are paired with eight Bhairavas. Sixteen *devī*s surround the mothers in a second set of petals, and these goddesses are protected by eight guardians of the directions who stand amidst the eight pairs. The guardians of the directions are in turn assisted by twenty-four protective *śakti*s. Finally, at the four city gates that complete the *yantra,* Gaṇeśa, Kumāra, Puṣpadanta, and Vikaratana stand guard, while four deities bestow *siddhi* and success on practitioners: Ānanda Bhairava at the east gate, Siddhinātha at the west, Kapāla Bhairava at the south, and Ruru at the north. *Yoginī*s stand outside on all sides, protecting the sanctity of the entire *yantra.* Thus, hundreds of deities are believed to be embedded in and between the petals, triangles, and circles. By traveling to these places in particular patterns while performing the requisite rites and chanting the proper mantras, adepts can construct the Vindhyachal *yantra* for themselves, and thereby conjure up its power.

Although the *Vindhya Māhātmya* describes this *yantra* in amazing detail, most modern-day Vindhyachal devotees seek only to trace the innermost triangle, that formed by Mahālakṣmī, Mahāsarasvatī, and Mahākālī. In all likelihood, many of the deities embedded in the petals and points never had shrines that existed in the conventional, phenomenal sense. But according to Tantric adherents they truly exist there, and thus the ritual reconstruction of the *yantra* is possible today. The triangle *yantra* is within but beyond the physical place; it constitutes a subtle sacred realm far more "real" than what we can see with our limited, ordinary vision.

Krishna Mohan Mishra, a priest who decorates the image of Vindhyavāsinī Devī and is renowned for his spiritual powers, explains that the triangle *yātrā* and triangle *yantra* are both external and internal. Through intense religious devotion and practice with a guru who relied on the *Vindhya Māhātmya,* he has learned where each of the deities of the *yantra* is located in Vindhyakṣetra on the exoteric level. But Tantrics like Mishra also know how to "do" the triangle *yātrā* and *yantra* on an inner level, without any physical movement. He performs both the pilgrimage and the diagram internally by the practice of *nyāsa,* the embedding of the deities within his own body, using the requisite mantras and visualizations that are described in detail in the *Vindhya Māhātmya.*

In this Tantric vision, since *yantra*s are abodes constructed by and for the Goddess to inhabit, and since the Goddess is believed to dwell forever within the *yantra,* all of the pilgrimage sites of the triangle *yātrā* are themselves the Goddess. The sight (*darśan*) of them reveals the unfolding of the magnificent deity into phenomenal reality, her actual transformation into the world, thus physically demonstrating the precise theology of the *Vindhya Māhātmya.* The Tantric application of the text remains constant to this day, then—on a very superficial level for the many pilgrims who travel between the three major shrines, but on a profound level for the select few. Tantrics believe that the esoteric knowledge preserved in the text is privileged information; the most "sacred space" of Vindhyachal should be restricted to the properly initiated. The *Vindhya Māhātmya* itself repeatedly states that its wisdom is the most secret of Tantras and should be taught only to the initiated.

When I asked hundreds of pilgrims and non-Vindhyachal pandits questions about Vindhyavāsinī's mythology, the *Vindhya Māhātmya* itself was not once quoted to me. In answer to questions about the triangle *yātrā,* however, they often referred to the vernacular pamphlet descriptions based on the Sanskrit text. Their comments were always made in the context of portraying the pilgrimage as *yantra,* but they added no further data from the *sthalamāhātmya* on the three primary sites or on Tantric activities. If they did refer to any Sanskrit text concerning the three primary sites, it was invariably the pan-Indian *Devī Māhātmya.* Specifically, they recited the two verses that mention the Great Goddess's intent to take birth again to destroy Śumbha and Niśumbha and then dwell in Vindhyachal, or they drew on an appendix to the text called the "Secret Pertaining to Primordial Matters" (*Prādhānika Rahasya*). Its typology is similar to that found in the *Vindhya Māhātmya* and may well have influenced its theology. The *Prādhānika Rahasya* describes the Great Goddess as ultimately one but as evolving into two other great goddesses. Mahālakṣmī, constituted of the three *guṇas*, assumed another form as Mahākālī by means of pure *tamas,* then a second *sattva* form as Mahāsarasvatī. All three forms of *mahādevīs* produced sets of male-female twins at Mahālakṣmī's request, who eventually helped to create the universe. In other portions of the appendix's twenty-nine verses, the mother of the world, Mahālakṣmī, is described as both formless and possessed of form.

The *Vindhya Māhātmya* thus differs from the *Devī Māhātmya* and its appendix in four major ways. First, the *Vindhya Māhātmya* depicts Vindhyavāsinī not as one among many expressions of the Great Goddess but as the most transcendent form of Mahālakṣmī. Second, Vindhyavāsinī/Mahālakṣmī in manifest form as Vindhyavāsinī is composed primarily of *rajas.*[9] Third, in ultimate form she is extolled in terms resonant within Advaita tradition: *brahman, bindu,* and so on. Finally, although the *Devī Māhātmya*'s *aṅgas* do explain how to envision various goddesses, as well as detailing certain practices concerning the text's recitation, the *Vindhya Māhātmya* is far more explicit about the worship of the Goddess. Furthermore, unlike the *Devī Māhātmya,* it specifically enjoins that Tantric and Smārta methods be employed to conjure and honor her as the power within and beyond all.

The two *māhātmyas* also treat the Śumbha and Niśumbha myth quite differently. The *Devī Māhātmya* devotes six of its thirteen chapters (5–10) to the story of Śumbha and Niśumbha's defeat, but without once mentioning Vindhyavāsinī or Krishna. Moreover, the location of the battle is said to be the Himalaya mountains. The eleventh chapter opens with the gods singing a lengthy hymn of praise to the victorious Goddess. Pleased, she offers them a boon, whereupon they ask for the pacification of all miseries and the destruction of their enemies. In response, she graciously promises to incarnate herself in the future whenever demons arise, beginning thus:

> When the twenty-eighth era in the Vaivasvat Manu interval has come,
> Two more great demons, also [named] Śumbha and Niśumbha, will be born.
> Then, born in the house of the cowherd Nanda, appearing from the womb of
> Yaśodā,
> I will slay these two, dwelling on the Vindhya mountain.
>
> (11.37–38)

In this slaying of a second demonic pair named Śumbha and Niśumbha, it is made explicit that the goddess who will defeat them will be the substitute sister of Krishna—Vindhyavāsinī, born of Nanda—and that the location of their battle will be the Vindhya mountains.

The *Devī Māhātmya* describes the defeat of Śumbha and Niśumbha sometimes as a fait accompli (5.10; 12.34–35) and sometimes as a future event (11.37–38). When I asked eighty reciters of the Sanskrit text about the identity of these "other" two demons, nearly all looked at their books as if for the first time and made faltering comments such as, "That is odd, I never noticed that before," "I am not sure," or "It must be an elaboration of the third episode" (namely, the destruction of Śumbha and Niśumbha). Many expressed confusion and dismay that their text was so vague on important points, especially the Goddess's rebirth during the Vaivasvat age to destroy the two demons, or how the three goddesses at Vindhyachal relate to each other and which came first to the mountains. Several reciters said that there are many eras, during which numerous events are repeated, such as the killing of Śumbha and Niśumbha, so "other" Śumbha and Niśumbha pairs have been (and will continue to be) killed. This interpretation allows for the defeat of the twin demons independent of a Krishnaite context, as well as explaining variations as to how and where they are killed.

In a near reversal of the *Devī Māhātmya,* the *Vindhya Māhātmya* describes Krishna's birth and his connection with Vindhyavāsinī in some detail, after which the Goddess's future destruction of the twin demons is predicted (chapter 26). The earliest battle, taking place in the Himalayas, is later dispensed with in just a few verses (31.4–6), and the rest of that chapter describes at length the second battle in the Vindhyas. In the first battle, Mahāmāyā became manifest in the Himalaya mountains, slew the twin demons, and then predicted that the demons would take birth again during the twenty-eighth interval of the Kali age. She advised the gods to come to Vindhyakṣetra when the two threatened again, since that is where she would have gone after taking birth in Nanda's home. Thirty-seven verses then recount the Goddess's second destruction of the two *within* Vindhyakṣetra. The *Vindhya Māhātmya*'s description seems to suggest three incarnations of the Goddess: she is first born of Nanda and helps Krishna; then she appears in the Himalayas and kills the twins; finally, she is born of Nanda again—now to destroy the demons, but in the Vindhyas.

Scholars have concluded that the Śumbha-Niśumbha myth is a fragment of Great Goddess mythology that was current among North Indian peoples who only later came to know of the heroism of Krishna Gopāla. Further, texts predating the *Devī Māhātmya* set the myth within the Vindhyas, and the goddess who destroyed the demons was the regional but great goddess Vindhyavāsinī.[10] The *Vindhya Māhātmya* follows a similar approach to the regional myth even as it retains some of the *Devī Māhātmya*'s temporal ambiguities. Its primary claim is that the destroyer of the twins is the goddess of a specific place—the Vindhyas—and is ever rooted there. The task of connecting Krishna's birth with the defeat of Śumbha and Niśumbha is accomplished haphazardly in the *Vindhya Māhātmya,* appearing almost as an afterthought. The *Devī Māhātmya* removed the battle site to the Himalayan mountain range, a more "civilized," universalist arena, known well and controlled by "orthodox" Hindu deities. Its brief mention of the next birth of the goddess in Nanda's home vitiates regional claims to Vindhyavāsinī's supremacy and immediacy by demoting her to the status of a secondary manifestation of the Goddess. In contrast, the *Vindhya Māhātmya* takes great pains to deemphasize the "earlier" defeat in the Himalayas, and by severing the connection with Krishna Gopāla by the intervention of five chapters elevates the independent local tradition instead.

Today, rather than the local text, which betrays a distinct preference for the Vindhyavāsinī tradition, guides and pandits emphasize the universalist nature of the Goddess instead. This seems to reflect a redefinition of how the Goddess is viewed at Vindhyachal. In their claim to universalization, her Brahmin caretakers lay greater stress on nonmythological elements and the nonsectarian worship of a single, transcendent Great Goddess of all India, rather than the proximate, geographically embedded Goddess dwelling in the Vindhyas.

It is unclear whether the *Vindhya Māhātmya* was ever popularly recited in its entirety. However, evidence shows that, at least in the form of oral lore, much of the text was explained to pilgrims. The "short" *Vindhya Māhātmya* details the triangle *yātrā,* myths of the major sites, and specific ways to worship the three goddesses. Selected segments from this section of the text are almost always told to pilgrims today, and they form the lion's share of the material for the brief pamphlets sold as the essence of the *Vindhya Māhātmya.* Further, in his 1830 journal Enugula Veeraswamy recorded the same myths from the "short" *Vindhya Māhātmya* that are told today. During Veeraswamy's stay in "Vindhya Vasini Kshetram," he visited only the Vindhyavāsinī shrine, but his guide told him about all three major sites:

> Three Shaktis are said to be manifest here. They are Maya Bhoga, Maya, and Kali. Bhogamaya is said to reside near the town and receive the raja naivedyams. "Yogamaya" also called "Ashtabhuji" is said to reside on the mountain 4 miles from here. Kali is said to reside on one side nearby here. All the sacrifices are made before Kali; *Puraschargnas* are performed before Yogamaya whereas Rajopachara is made for the worship of Bhogamaya.[11]

Thus, as early as 1830 each goddess received different offerings in accord with her essential nature as determined by *guṇa*s: Kālī, dominated by *tamas,* prefers animal sacrifices; Aṣṭabhujā, dominated by *sattva,* enjoys the pure recitation of mantras (*puraścarana*); and Vindhyavāsinī receives sumptuous "royal" offerings (*rājopacāra*), reflecting *rajas.* In addition, a man "from the Ganges" described to Veeraswamy the "Vindhya Vasini Mahatmyam," which extoled the merits of Rama Gaya, a local river site where one makes offerings to ancestors, as well as confirming that "Vindhya Vasini Ksetram" grants release to pilgrims. The text also asserted its own prominence by noting its mention in various Purāṇas.

All the above cohere with the text of the *Vindhya Māhātmya* itself and with the manner in which Vindhyavāsinī is understood today. But Veeraswamy also related stories that conflict with modern interpretations. He wrote:

> Yogamaya born of Yasoda escaped from Kamsa and is said to reside on this mountain. The celestials then prayed to her to destroy the rakshasas (demons) who had escaped destruction by Lord Krishna. She therefore took shape as Mahakali and reduced the burden of Earth. Thereafter she desired to join her Lord Sambamurti; she therefore became a *Bhogashakti* giving up her "Ugraswarupa" or *fierce manifestation.*[12]

This passage assumes that Aṣṭabhujā Devī appeared first; it is she who escaped from Kaṃsa. Kālīkhoh Devī was formed next by Yogamāyā and slew various demons. Yogamāyā and Mahākālī are unmarried, whereas the third manifestation, Vindhyavāsinī, is wedded to Lord "Sambamurti" (Śiva) and quite literally pacified or "tamed" by marriage to him. When I asked guides about this entry, they unanimously denied the veracity of all these elements: Vindhyavāsinī is the primordial manifestation and is unwed, they insisted. Yet what Veeraswamy heard from the "man from the Ganges" is indeed found in the *Vindhya Māhātmya.*

On the one hand, the unmanifest Great Goddess is depicted as transcendent and unmarried, clearly superior to the male gods who are merely her devotees and remain dependent on her invigorating power (*śakti*) to perform even the simplest task. On the planes of transformation, too, the consort relationship to male deities is deemphasized; only goddesses born from her lowliest transformations are married, and all of the three *mahādevī*s manifest at Vindhyachal are portrayed as unmarried throughout most of the *Vindhya Māhātmya.* On the other hand, in the prayers to the *mahādevī*s beginning at 27.10 and in the Tantric sections on the triangle *yantra,* they are directly linked to male deities, although to varying degrees. With regard to the specific incarnation of Vindhyavāsinī/Mahālakṣmī, verse 27.10 extols her as Maheśvarī, while verse 30.16 lauds her thus: "O Mahāmāyā, she who is dear to Hara, wife of Śiva in the form of Durgā, bestower of desires, queen of the gods—homage, homage, O Mahālakṣmī." Here she is clearly married to Śiva. As for Kālīkhoh Devī and Aṣṭabhujā Devī, however, they remain unmarried but are affiliated with male deities through their epithets and qualities. Kālīkhoh Devī is called Bhairavī and Śivā (the feminine forms of Bhairava and Śiva) but is seated either on Garuḍa (normally Viṣṇu's vehicle) or on the elephant Airāvata (normally Indra's vehicle). Aṣṭabhujā Devī is Vāc ("Speech"), who creates, sustains, and destroys the world as Sarasvatī, claiming for herself the roles of the male Hindu trinity—Brahmā, Viṣṇu, and Śiva. Thus, Veeraswamy's account is clearly supported in the *Vindhya Māhātmya*. And yet such visions of the Goddess and her manifestations are not promoted today.

For instance, it is no longer taught, or even generally understood, that Vindhyavāsinī is wed to Śiva, on any level. I asked 115 pilgrims and priests, "Is Vindhyavāsinī married? If so, to whom?" These were the results:

Do not know	41
She is ever virgin	59
Married, but do not know to whom	7
Married to Viṣṇu	2
Married to Śiva	1
Śākta dualist interpretation	1
As the ultimate she is unmarried, but when manifest she is Mahālakṣmi and is married to Viṣṇu	2
As the ultimate she is unmarried, but when manifest she is Mahālakṣmi and is married to Śiva	2

Thus, we see that a once complex understanding of the goddess and her relations to deities of the Hindu pantheon, which was preserved in local traditions glorifying her, has become radically simplified by efforts to universalize the Goddess, uprooting her from a proximate, immediate, and localized immanence and supplying her with a more lofty and dislocated transcendence.

THE TRIUMPH OF THE DEVĪ MĀHĀTMYA

Despite the fact that many guides whom I knew quite well could gain easy access to copies of the *Vindhya Māhātmya,* and although I had heard of this work from the very first day I visited Vindhyachal in August 1987, it was not until November 1989, after appealing to a renowned religious figure of Banaras (who had no connection with the Vindhyachal temple), that I was able to procure a photocopy of a manuscript. Guides kept telling me that "soon" they would show it to me, but our cordial relations notwithstanding, none let me have even a glimpse. Now that I have read it, I realize there are many reasons why it was in their best interests to keep it obscure.

What are these guides afraid of? Why has there been such a concerted effort on the part of her Brahmin caretakers to distance the goddess Vindhyavāsinī from the highly developed theology that the *Vindhya Māhātmya* offers? Pamphlets written by guides that are intended to popularize the worship of Vindhyavāsinī and prove her orthodoxy specifically omit—and some even outright discredit or refute—"Tantric" interpretations of Vindhyavāsinī, although all say the triangle *yātrā* is a "powerful *yantra*." Other authors take pains to discredit any rumors to the effect that Vindhyavāsinī was not the first or preeminent deity to govern the area. This they do not by quoting the *Vindhya Māhātmya*—the obvious text—but by resorting to the *Prādhānika Rahasya* of the *Devī Māhātmya*. There, Mahālakṣmī is accorded supremacy and therefore must be "first," but this would seem to be a roundabout way of vindicating Vindhyavāsinī. To "Sanskritizing," "sanitizing" guides, the *Vindhya Māhātmya* is an inconvenient reminder of an overly developed regionalist theology; and for those favorably inclined toward Tantra, the text contains information best kept hidden from the uninitiated.

What, then, does the history of the *Vindhya Māhātmya* tell us about the nature of religious activities at Vindhyachal today? Most obvious is the fact that an increasing disparity exists between the "text" of the *Vindhya Māhātmya* and the "text" of the Vindhyakṣetra. Historical accounts mention many *liṅgas*, tanks, and temples described in the text but that have since disappeared. This suggests that the nineteenth-century text's "sacred map" used to correspond much more closely than it now does to Vindhyachal's actual, phenomenal sites and activities. Today, this map survives merely as an ideal construction. There has been a gradual disintegration of the vivid sacred reality that was once considered to be the direct transformation of the goddess herself into phenomenal Vindhyakṣetra.

It would seem that a contributing cause to this decreasing correspondence is economic incentive—or disincentive. Because the rights to work at the sites are divided on a daily rather than a site-specific or perennial basis, no single family feels responsible for temple upkeep, nor have several committees formed since the 1950s to address this problem succeeded in maintaining temples properly. Smaller, less lucrative temples consequently fall into disrepair. Of late, however, guides have begun to repair dilapidated sites and to attract people by inscribing verses from the *Vindhya Māhātmya* on the temple walls. Such projects parallel a trend to legitimize shrines by etching the Sanskrit (and hence sacred) word into stone. But this hardly amounts to an effort to restore the Vindhyakṣetra of the *Vindhya Māhātmya*. Only lucrative sites that may create new job opportunities for a younger generation of severely underemployed Brahmin men are chosen for refurbishing.

Many devotees retain the conviction that Vindhyachal is indeed home to the Great Goddess, but, in their view, the text that most accurately "describes" the scenery of Vindhyachal is the *Devī Māhātmya*. Of course, such a position also eliminates the need to preserve shrines specific to the *sthalamāhātmya* that are not mentioned in the *Devī Māhātmya*. The tank known as Tārakeśvara Kuṇḍ is an interesting case in point. The demon Tāraka, a devotee of Śiva, established a *liṅga* and tank called Tārakeśvara Kuṇḍ. Although the *Vindhya Māhātmya* devotes twelve of its forty chapters to describing the battles and shrines that lend this Śaivite bathing pond its glory, Tārakeśvara Kuṇḍ is conspicuous by its absence in pilgrimage practice today. I did not meet a single pilgrim who had visited it (and I interviewed hundreds). Pamphlets include only a few verses about it, and even the village named for the site is now pronounced Tarakāpur, the long vowel having shifted to the third syllable. The etymology popular today links the village to the demoness Tarakā, defeated by Rāma, rather than to Tāraka, the demon devotee of Śiva.

A further case of change illustrates the power of politics. By the late nineteenth century the great temple of Kālīkhoh had deteriorated into a tumbledown condition. Kālīkhoh was the central temple of the so-called Thugs ("deceivers") who supposedly for centuries murdered naive travelers and subsequently dedicated a portion of their loot to Kālī at Vindhyachal.[13] As Stewart N. Gordon has convincingly shown, however, the "Thugs" were neither a bizarre religious cult nor any kind of homogeneous group. Those labeled Thugs were teams of marauding soldiers from various regions who stole and killed not out of religious compulsion but from economic and political motives.[14] Their superiors ordered them to extort cash needed for purchasing weapons and paying mercenaries who would do battle with the British. The sole link to religion consisted in their efforts to win the blessings of Vindhyavāsinī, who as the greatest regional Goddess was believed able to bestow the authority to rule on those whom she chose. After the British successfully stigmatized these groups by attributing to them unorthodox activities, they proceeded to wipe them out in the 1830s, whereupon all devotees at Vindhyachal temples became suspect, particularly if they were from warrior castes.

Now on the defensive, the guides took great pains to prove their orthodoxy and their faithful cooperation with the British. Tantric practices, animal sacrifice, and the elevation of the regional power and authority of the goddess all came to be increasingly discredited by those who wished to justify religious practices in Vindhyakṣetra by aligning them with progressive social values. Opting for practices and beliefs that reflected the "improved" standards was not, however, a knee-jerk reaction to the British. Many Hindus believed that the most authentic interpretation of Vindhyavāsinī was as a Vedicized, vegetarian, and universalist goddess, a view pleasing to her increasingly "sophisticated" pilgrim clientele who took to the now safer and improved roads in pursuit of her blessing.

These examples underscore the fact that guides are subject to the vicissitudes of theological orthodoxy, human greed, and governmental meddling. Today, brief pamphlets quote only short, innocuous portions of the Sanskrit *Vindhya Māhātmya*, even while drawing on its sacred authority. Because the most influential priests at Vindhyachal today actively promote a single, "correct" view of Vindhyavāsinī as a monistic, vegetarian, and non-Tantric goddess, those portions of the *Vindhya Māhātmya* that identify her as the wife of Śiva and those that present Tantric elaborations of the triangle *yantra* and methods to gain *siddhi* are simply no longer mentioned. Priests and pamphlets alike describe only the most easily accepted—and most remunerative—practices. On both descriptive and theological levels, then, the *Vindhya Māhātmya* does not reflect the way in which Vindhyakṣetra and its deities are understood today.

Why have this universalist theology and its accompanying practices, such as recitation of the *Devī Māhātmya,* become so widely accepted, and therefore so lucrative? Perhaps in part the changes in theology mirror shifts in pilgrims' personal sense of self—specifically, from a specific and local sense of self to a more cosmopolitan identity, a move from immanence to transcendence. The Vindhyachal temple offers one of the most visceral, immanent, and intense pilgrimage experiences for which one could hope, and it is frequented by both rural and urban patrons. Yet despite the intensity and particularity of temple practices, interviews revealed that those who were educated, regardless of their background, tended to perceive the Goddess in a universalist sense. And urban devotees who traveled great distances to reach Vindhyachal, whether educated or not, evinced a combined respect for her immediacy as well as her station as the Great Goddess of all India. When they explained why she was famous, they referred to her being Ādiśakti and the goddess of all the worlds. In contrast, less educated people from local rural areas, while recognizing her as the Great Goddess, tended to offer comments that laid greater stress upon her regional and geographical character: she was the "village deity," she ruled the area, she lived right there, she was the specific goddess who had aided their ancestors, and so forth. Having grown up in nearby lands and therefore within or near Vindhyakṣetra, they both affirmed and exalted Vindhyavāsinī's regional identification. Those whose sense of self remained rooted in an immanent, localized existence thus tended to support the *Vindhya Māhātmya*'s insistence that the center of the universe is ever in Vindhyakṣetra—that the sacred space is right there, and specifically there.

Perhaps priests have discovered that the world of many of their pilgrim clients is larger than the Vindhya range nowadays, and that these clients bring with them a broader range of issues and identities that they seek to integrate into themselves as they worship. To furnish them with a means to make sense of their world, priests have constructed a correspondingly extended framework to describe the goddess at Vindhyachal. This more universal goddess can assure pilgrims that they are worshiping the goddess of the dominant group, not a backward superstition left over from an unenlightened past. The local goddess is deemphasized and relocated—and she is only resurrected when small groups of rural neighbors come to practice their "antiquated," but tolerated, habits.

This outcome likewise accords with India's development as a modern, secular state. It also dovetails with the recent rise in politicized religiosity that goes by the name of Hindu fundamentalism. Here, too, universalist identities promote national unity. As particularism is pushed out of the public arena and regionalism decried, truth is relativized so that competing visions can be seen as equally valid. A dogma of alternatives is thereby embraced. Thus it is that the ambiguous, albeit pan-Indian, text is exalted above the regional and sectarian. To gain enough support for their livelihood, the priests have had to give up local claims to truth, even those backed by elaborate philosophical justifications, and instead adopt a more tolerant, less definite attitude, except in those cases where the elites of society have reached a consensus.

When asked to evaluate the increasing dissonance between ideal and real maps of Vindhyakṣetra, some informants explained that the glory of the Goddess and her sacred domain must be understood in terms of "layers" and gradual evolution and devolution. In each age, they said, the truths of the *Vindhya Māhātmya* are reenacted by the Goddess—but differently. Vindhyakṣetra today preserves references to some of these incarnations, and any changes there are a necessary condition of our existing in time. Only the Great Goddess dwelling at the timeless center (*bindu*) remains unchanging. Vindhyavāsinī is the transcendent ultimate, she who is beyond human history, but in her manifest state she kindly transforms herself and moves within and throughout human history. In this sense, her "glory" is in constant transition—because she is, as well.

NOTES

1. R. C. Hazra, *Studies in the Upapurāṇas,* vol. 2, *Śākta and Non-sectarian Upapurāṇas* (Calcutta: Sanskrit College, 1963), p. 30. See also, for example, J. N. Tiwari, *Goddess Cults in Ancient India* (Delhi: Sundeep Prakashan, 1985), pp. 89–90; and Charlotte Vaudeville, "Krishna Gopāla, Rādhā, and the Great Goddess," in *The Divine Consort,* ed. Hawley and Wulff, pp. 6–9.

2. I translate *paṇḍā* as "guide" throughout this essay, whereas I render *paṇḍita* in a semi-anglicized form, "pandit."

3. The icon is believed to be an image of Kauśikī, often defined as "she of the sheath" (*kośa*). But the term *kauśika* also means "owl," a fact that is taken to support the common belief that Vindhyavāsinī flew like a bird to her new home. The goddess has four arms: three hands bear a conch shell, a discus, and a mace, and the fourth displays the *abhayā mudrā,* a gesture of fearlessness. In an interview conducted on October 18, 1989, Krishna Mohan Mishra, a Vindhyachal priest who specializes in icon decoration, added further detail. The goddess is adorned by a necklace of 108 skulls. On her right side is a dancing Gaṇeśa atop his mouse vehicle, who appears to hold sweets, the Vedas, and an ax. On her left side a *yoginī* ("goddess or mistress of yoga") sits on an elephant howdah with a fan. Vindhyavāsinī's nose has some small cracks, as do her feet, but there are no chipped parts.

4. David Kinsley, *Hindu Goddesses: Visions of the Divine Feminine in the Hindu Religious Tradition* (Berkeley: University of California Press, 1986), p. 132.

5. Diana L. Eck, *Banaras, City of Light* (New York: Alfred A. Knopf, 1982), p. 378.

6. Sri P. Sitapati, ed. and trans., *Enugula Veeraswamy's Journal* (Hyderabad: Andhra Pradesh Government Oriental Manuscripts Library and Research Institute, 1973).

7. Eighty out of 257 interviewed had performed the triangle pilgrimage. In addition to taking *darśan* of Vindhyavāsinī, eight others had visited Aṣṭabhujā, and one had gone to Kālīkhoh.

8. One guide explained that "Binduvāsinī" Devī is the primordial deity whose entire temple used to be merely a flat stone, understood to be a simple point; she was later called "Vindhyavāsinī" Devī by those who, being unfamiliar with her transcendent nature, identified her by her place of residence (Munna Prasad Pandey, interview, September 23, 1987).

9. Some of the devotees with whom I spoke quoted portions of the *Prādhānika Rahasya* to refute the understanding perpetuated by local guides and pandits that Vindhyavāsinī is dominated by the *rajas guṇa.* They argued that at Vindhyachal the Great Goddess is Mahālakṣmī and therefore must be *triguṇā* (consisting of all three *guṇas*) even at the manifest level. For a closer examination of the *Prādhānika Rahasya,* see Thomas B. Coburn, *Encountering the Goddess: A Translation of the Devī-Māhātmya and a Study of Its Interpretation* (Albany: State University of New York Press, 1991), pp. 109–15.

10. Thomas B. Coburn, *Devī-Māhātmya: The Crystallization of the Goddess Tradition* (Delhi and Columbia, Mo.: Motilal Banarsidass and South Asia Books, 1985), p. 247.

11. Sitapati, ed. and trans., *Enugula Veeraswamy's Journal,* p. 84.

12. Ibid., pp. 84–85.

13. Interestingly, both the word *thug* and the term *loot* are derived from Hindi, the former from *ṭhag,* meaning one who cheats or deceives, the latter from the verb *lūṭnā,* meaning "to plunder."

14. See Stewart N. Gordon, "Scarf and Sword: Thugs, Marauders, and State-Formation in 18th-Century Malwa," *Indian Economic and Social History Review* 6, no. 4 (1969): 403–29. See also Cynthia A. Humes, "Rājās, Thugs, and Mafiosos: Religion and Politics in the Worship of Vindhyavāsinī," in *Render unto Caesar: Religion and Politics in Cross-cultural Perspective,* ed. Sabrina Petra Ramet and Donald J. Treadgold (Washington, D.C.: American University Press, 1995), pp. 219–47.

KĀLĪ
Blood and Death Out of Place

David R. Kinsley

> She is dark as soot, always living in the cremation ground. Her eyes are pink, her hair disheveled, her body gaunt and fearful. In her left hand she holds a cup filled with wine and meat, and in her right hand she holds a freshly cut human head. She smiles and eats rotten meat. She is decked with ornaments, is naked, and is absorbed in drinking. Having conceived the deity in this way, one should propitiate her in the cremation ground. The householder will worship her at home, at dead of night, having partaken of fish, meat, and wine and being naked.[1]

So is described the fearful goddess Kālī, "the black one." Though most popular today in Bengal, she has been known in Hindu religious texts for more than fifteen hundred years and has been worshiped at one time or another throughout the Indian subcontinent. This essay on Kālī does two things. First, and necessarily briefly, it summarizes her most common appearances and roles. Second, it attempts to make sense of Kālī within the context of the Hindu religious tradition.

DANGER AND DISRUPTION IN THE MYTHOLOGY OF KĀLĪ

Although Kālī is sometimes said to be beautiful, and contemporary lithographs sometimes portray her as almost cherubic, Hindu texts referring to the goddess are nearly unanimous in describing her as terrible in appearance and as offensive and destructive in her habits.[2] Her hair is disheveled, her eyes red and fierce, she has fangs and a long lolling tongue, her lips are often smeared with blood, her breasts are long and pendulous, her stomach is sunken, and her figure is generally gaunt. She is naked but for several characteristic ornaments: a necklace of skulls or freshly cut heads, a girdle of severed arms, and infant corpses as earrings. She is usually said to have four arms. In her upper left hand she holds a bloodied cleaver, in her lower left, a freshly cut human head; her upper right hand makes the sign "fear not," and her lower right hand, the sign of one who confers boons.

Her habits and associations reinforce her awful appearance. Her two favorite dwelling places are battlefields and cremation grounds. On the battlefield she is usually said to carry a skull-topped staff, to howl ferociously, and to consume her enemies by eating their flesh and drinking their blood. In the cremation ground she is described as surrounded by snakes, jackals, and ghosts and is often found sitting on a corpse. Unlike most other Hindu deities, she does not have an animal vehicle but instead rides a *preta,* a ghost. And although Kālī's temples today may be found in the midst of cities and towns, earlier literature describes her temples as being located on the fringes of civilization, in the woods or near cremation grounds.[3] Kālī also has a long history of association with criminals and is notorious for having been the patron goddess of the murderous Thugs.[4] Finally, her appetite for blood is well attested. She is often said to drink blood, both on and off the battlefield, and at her temples she regularly receives animal sacrifices.

In the mythology of Kālī we find her associated primarily with three other Hindu deities: Durgā, Pārvatī, and Śiva. In each case Kālī's destructive habits and fearsome nature persist.

Two of Kālī's most famous deeds are recounted in the myth of the goddess Durgā's destruction of the demons Śumbha and Niśumbha. In the *Devī Māhātmya* version of this myth, Kālī is born when two demon generals, Caṇḍa and Muṇḍa, are sent to taunt and attack Durgā. Durgā loses her composure, grows furious, and from her darkened brow springs Kālī. She howls loudly, wades into the demon army crushing and eating her enemies, and finally decapitates Caṇḍa and Muṇḍa. Later in the battle she is summoned by Durgā to kill the demon Raktabīja ("Drop of Blood"). This demon has the magical ability to recreate himself every time a drop of his blood touches the ground. Thus, when Durgā wounds him she only makes her situation more desperate, and soon the battlefield is filled with Raktabījas. Kālī then rescues Durgā by swallowing the swarm of blood-born demons and sucking the blood from the original Raktabīja until he falls lifeless.[5] In these myths Kālī seems to be Durgā's embodied fury, appearing when Durgā loses control or is confronted with a formidable task.

Kālī plays a similar role in her association with the goddess Pārvatī. In general, Pārvatī is a benign goddess, but from time to time she manifests destructive aspects. When she does, Kālī is often brought into being. In the *Liṅga Purāṇa* Pārvatī is requested by Śiva to slay the demon Dāruka, who has been granted the boon that he can be killed only by a woman. Pārvatī is then described as entering Śiva's body and remaking herself from the poison in his throat. She reemerges as Kālī, of terrible appearance, and with the help of beings who include *piśāca*s, flesh-eating spirits, she begins to attack

Dāruka and his hosts. However, owing to her frenzy the universe itself is threatened with destruction and is saved only by Śiva's intervention.[6] Kālī is depicted in a similar way elsewhere in the same Purāṇa. When Śiva sets out with his army to destroy the demons of the three cities, Kālī is mentioned as accompanying him. She is said to whirl a trident, to be adorned with skulls, to be intoxicated from drinking the blood of demons, to have her eyes half-closed in drunkenness, and to wear an elephant hide. She is also, however, praised as the daughter of Himalaya, thus being clearly identified with Pārvatī. It would seem that in the process of Pārvatī's gearing up for war, Kālī has appeared as Pārvatī's wrath personified, her alter ego, as it were. [7]

In the *Vāmana Purāṇa* Pārvatī is called Kālī because of her dark complexion. When Pārvatī hears Śiva use this name, she takes offense and does austerities to rid herself of her dark skin. After she succeeds in this, she is renamed Gaurī, the golden one. Her dark sheath, however, is transformed into the furious battle queen Kauśikī, who subsequently creates Kālī herself in her fury. So again, although there is an intermediary goddess, Kauśikī, Kālī is shown to play the role of Pārvatī's dark, negative, violent nature.[8]

The myth of the creation of the *daśamahāvidyās*, the ten awesome manifestations of the great Goddess, casts Kālī in a similar role. The story is told that once upon a time the sage Dakṣa decided to undertake a great sacrifice. He invited all the gods except Śiva, excluding him because of his antisocial behavior. Śiva was not offended, but his wife Satī was. Becoming enraged at this social insult, she filled the ten directions with furious forms, the first of which was Kālī. Śiva, thus terrified, agreed to let Satī attend the festivities.[9]

In her association with the god Śiva, Kālī's tendency toward wildness and disorder, although sometimes tamed or softened by him, persists, and at times she incites Śiva himself to dangerous, destructive behavior. In South India there is a tradition that tells of a dance contest between the two. After the defeat of Śumbha and Niśumbha, Kālī took up residence in a forest, along with her retinue of fierce companions, and proceeded to terrorize the surrounding area. A devotee of Śiva living in that area became distracted from his practice of austerities and petitioned Śiva to rid the forest of the violent goddess. When Śiva appeared, Kālī threatened him, claiming the area as her own. Śiva challenged her to a dance contest and defeated her when she was unable (or unwilling) to match his energetic *tāṇḍava* dance.[10]

Although Kālī is said in this tradition to have been defeated and forced by Śiva to control her disruptive habits, we find very few images and myths depicting a becalmed, docile Kālī.[11] Instead, we find references or images that show Śiva and Kālī in situations in which either or both behave in disruptive ways, inciting each other, or in which Kālī's wild activity dominates an inactive, sometimes dead, Śiva.[12]

The former type of relationship is seen when the two are described as dancing together in such a way that they threaten cosmic order. In

Bhavabhūti's *Mālatīmādhava* the divine pair are said to dance wildly near the goddess's temple, which is located near a cremation ground. Their dance is so chaotic that it threatens to destroy the world. Pārvatī is described as standing nearby, frightened.[13] Here the scenario is not that of a dance contest but one of a frenzied, cataclysmic dance in which the two deities complement each other, mutually reinforcing their madness and destructive habits. This image is common in Bengali devotional hymns addressed to Kālī:

> Crazy is my Father, crazy my Mother,
> And I, their son, am crazy too!
> Shyama [the dark one, an epithet of Kālī] is my Mother's name.
> My Father strikes His cheeks and makes a hollow sound:
> *Ba-ba-boom! Ba-ba-boom!*
> And my Mother, drunk and reeling,
> Falls across my Father's body!
> Shyama's streaming tresses hang in vast disorder;
> Bees are swarming numberless
> About Her crimson Lotus Feet.
> Listen, as She dances, how Her anklets ring![14]

In iconographic representations of Kālī and Śiva, Kālī nearly always dominates the pair. She is usually shown standing or dancing on Śiva's prone body (figure 9), and when they are depicted in sexual intercourse, she is on top, straddling him. Although in the myth of the dance contest Śiva is said to have tamed Kālī, it seems clear that he never finally subdued her. She is most popularly represented as a being who is uncontrollable and is more apt to provoke Śiva to dangerous activity than to submit to his control.

In general, then, we may say that Kālī is a goddess who threatens stability and order. Although she may be said to serve order in her role as the slayer of demons, more often than not she becomes so frenzied on the battlefield, usually becoming drunk on the blood of her victims, that she herself begins to destroy the world that she is supposed to protect. Even in the service of the gods, then, she is ultimately dangerous and tends to get out of control. In her association with other goddesses she appears to represent their embodied wrath and fury—a frightening, dangerous dimension of the divine feminine that is released when these goddesses become enraged or are called upon to take part in war and killing. In her relation to Śiva she appears to play a role opposite to that of Pārvatī. Pārvatī calms Śiva, counterbalancing his antisocial or destructive tendencies. It is she who brings Śiva within the sphere of domesticity and who, with her soft glances, urges him to soften the destructive aspects of his *tāṇḍava* dance.[15] Kālī is Śiva's "other" wife, as it were, provoking him and encouraging him in his mad, antisocial, often disruptive habits. It is never Kālī who tames Śiva but Śiva who must

Figure 9. The goddess Kālī dancing on Śiva. Contemporary lithograph.

becalm Kālī. Her association with criminals reinforces her dangerous role vis-à-vis society. She is at home outside the moral order and thus seems unbound by that order.

In nearly every respect Kālī would appear to be a classic example of a demoness whose blessing is realized only by her absence. To her devotees, however, she is the highest manifestation of the divine and is approached as "mother." To understand the meaning of Kālī, we must discover ways in which she might express truths that "fit" the Hindu vision of reality and look for ways in which she allows her devotees redemptive participation in those truths.

CHAOS, ORDER, AND TRANSCENDENCE

In seeking to understand the meaning of Kālī for Hindus we should naturally start with hints from the Hindu tradition itself. In medieval Hinduism the Goddess is often said to be the embodiment of *māyā, prakṛti,* and *śakti.*[16] As a manifestation of the Goddess, Kālī may be understood to express the nature of these realities, or the truths inherent in these ideas.

The term *māyā* is typically associated with various Vedāntic schools, in which it means primarily superimposition grounded in ignorance. In Purāṇic texts, however, *māyā* is more often described in terms of egocentricity (*ahaṃkāra*), the magical quality of creation, the very fabric of existence itself. *Māyā* lends to reality a mysterious and unpredictable quality that sometimes borders on the destructive. Egos, big and small, divine and human, in their self-importance and pique at real or imagined insults, set the whirligig of both mythological and human events spinning, often seemingly out of control. The world as humans live in it, and the world of the gods, too, may be seen to be grounded in ego duels that threaten cosmic and human order. Kālī's wild appearance and behavior suggest, perhaps, the darker aspects of reality as *māyā*. She is the great bewitcher, embodying dramatically the inherent threat of *māyā* to the civilized order.

Kālī hints at meanings implicit in *prakṛti* and *śakti,* too. *Prakṛti* is also the created order, the "natural" order, consisting of three qualities: purity (*sattva*), energy (*rajas*), and lethargy (*tamas*). Together these threads (*guṇas*) constitute the fabric of the material world, the fabric of embodied existence. The inherent tendency of *prakṛti* is to specify and individualize, to assume grosser and more concrete manifestations, to serve its own ends of self-perpetuation. *Prakṛti* is usually considered smothering with respect to human spirituality.[17] It binds the religious sojourner in a deterministic mesh from which escape is difficult.[18] *Prakṛti* is lush and teeming and is difficult to control. So is Kālī. She perhaps represents *prakṛti* uncontrolled. She is growth, decay, death, and rebirth completely unrefined.

She is *śakti,* too, I think, from the same perspective. *Śakti,* usually translated by such terms as "power" and "might," is often personified as a goddess. As *śakti,* various Hindu goddesses represent the tendency of the divine to action rather than inaction, the tendency to display and to play. Kālī is that tendency in the raw, as it were, power out of control, or power in imbalance with stasis. In what is possibly her most popular and well-known iconographic image, Kālī is represented as dancing on her consort, Śiva, who lies still beneath her feet. She dominates the primordial tension between detached calm and frenetic display in such a way that creative action becomes threatening and dangerous.

Other things are clear in the mythology and imagery of Kālī. She is almost always associated with blood and death, and it is difficult to imagine two more polluting realities in the context of the purity-minded culture of Hinduism. As such, Kālī is a very dangerous being. She vividly and dramatically thrusts upon the observer things that he or she would rather not think about. Within the civilized order of Hinduism, the order of dharma, of course, blood and death are acknowledged. It is impossible not to acknowledge their existence in human life. They are acknowledged, however, within the context of a highly ritualized, patterned, and complex social structure that takes great pains to handle them in "safe" ways, usually through rituals of purification. For those inevitable bloody and deathly events in the human life cycle there are rituals (called *saṃskāra*s, "refinements") that allow individuals to pass in an orderly way through times when contact with blood and death is unavoidable. The dharmic order is not naive and has incorporated into its refined version of human existence the recognition of these human inevitabilities.

But the Hindu *saṃskāra*s are patterned on wishful thinking. Blood and death have a way of cropping up unexpectedly, fortuitously, tragically, and dangerously. The death of an infant, or blood spilt in any accidental and tragic circumstance, is an affront and a threat to the neat vision of the order of dharma. The periodic flow of menstrual blood or the death of an aged and beloved old woman (whose husband has cooperatively died before her) is manageable within the normal order of human events. But a hemorrhage, the uncontrolled flow of blood, and untimely death are unmanageable. They are out of place and dangerous in the context of civilized order.[19] Yet they can never be avoided with certainty, no matter how well protected one thinks one is.

Kālī, at least in part, may indicate one way in which the Hindu tradition has sought to come to terms with the built-in shortcomings of its own refined view of the world. It would be nice if the system worked in every case, but it clearly does not, and it is perhaps best—and even redemptive—to recognize that it does not. Reflecting on the ways in which people must negate certain realities in their attempts to create social order, Mary Douglas writes:

> Whenever a strict pattern of purity is imposed on our lives it is either highly uncomfortable or it leads into contradiction if closely followed, or it leads to hypocrisy. That which is negated is not thereby removed. The rest of life, which does not tidily fit the accepted categories, is still there and demands attention. The body, as we have tried to show, provides the basic scheme for all symbolism. There is hardly any pollution which does not have some primary physiological reference. As life is in the body it cannot be rejected outright. And as life must be affirmed, the most complete philosophies . . . must find some ultimate way of affirming that which has been rejected.[20]

Kālī puts the order of dharma in perspective, or perhaps puts it in its place, by reminding the Hindu that certain aspects of reality are untameable, unpurifiable, unpredictable, and always threatening to society's feeble attempts to order what is essentially disorderly: life itself.

To her devotees Kālī is known as the divine mother. In the light of what I have said, I would suggest that she is mother to her devotees because she gives birth to a wider vision of reality than the one embodied in the order of dharma. The dharmic order is insufficient and restricting without a context—without a frame, as it were. Kālī frames that order, putting it in a compelling context. As the alternative to the order of dharma, as *māyā, prakṛti,* and *śakti* out of control, as death and blood out of place, Kālī makes that order attractive indeed.

Yet the wider vision that she presents may be understood in a more positive way as well. The Hindu religious tradition consistently affirms a reality that transcends the social order. From the perspective of *mokṣa,* final release from the endless round of births and deaths, the order of dharma is seen as a contingent good, a realm that must finally be left behind in the quest for ultimate good. Standing outside the dharmic order, indeed threatening it, Kālī may be viewed as she who beckons humans to seek a wider, more redemptive vision of their destiny.

Depending upon where one is in one's spiritual pilgrimage, then, Kālī has the power either to send one scuttling back to the womb of dharma or to provoke one to cross over the threshold to *mokṣa.* In either role she might be understood as the mother who gives her children shelter.

NOTES

1. The *dhyānamantra* of *Śmaśānakālī* in Kṛṣṇānanda Āgamavāgīśa, *Tantrasāra,* 2 vols. (Calcutta: Basumatī Sāhitya Mandir, 1934), 1:374.

2. For an example of one of the exceptions, see the *Karpūrādi Stotra,* which describes her as young and beautiful (verse 1) and says that she has a gently smiling face (verse 18).

3. *Mānasāra Śilpaśāstra* 9.289 says that Kālī's temples should be built far from inhabited areas, near cremation grounds, or near the dwellings of Caṇḍālas (outcastes who handle corpses).

4. Kālī is associated with thieves as early as the *Bhāgavata Purāṇa* (ca. 10th century C.E.). See 5.9.12–20.

5. *Devī Māhātmya,* chaps. 7 and 8.

6. *Liṅga Purāṇa* 1.106.

7. Ibid., 1.72.66–68.

8. *Vāmana Purāṇa,* chaps. 25–29. In several late versions of the *Rāmāyaṇa* Kālī appears in her familiar role. On his return from Laṅkā, where he has just vanquished the mighty ten-headed Rāvaṇa, Rāma is confronted with an even more terrifying foe—a thousand-headed Rāvaṇa. When Rāma is unable to defeat this monster, his wife, Sītā, assumes the form of Kālī and handily slays the new menace. However, becoming drunk on the demon's blood, she begins to dance wildly and threatens to destroy the world, whereupon Śiva is summoned to stop her rampaging. The story is told in the *Adbhūta Rāmāyaṇa* (a Kashmiri Śākta text), in Sāralā Dāsa's Oriya *Rāmāyaṇa,* and in the Bengali *Jaiminibhārata.* See Narendra Nath Bhattacharyya, *History of the Śākta Religion* (New Delhi: Munshiram Manoharlal, 1974), p. 149.

9. Summarized in Sir John Woodroffe [Arthur Avalon], ed., *Principles of Tantra: The Tantratattva of Śrīyukta Śiva Candra Vidyārṇava Bhaṭṭācārya Mahodaya* (Madras: Ganesh and Co., 1960), pp. 208–13. See also *Skanda Purāṇa* 5.82.1–21, where Kālī is born when Satī, angry at Dakṣa's insult to Śiva, rubs her nose in a fit of wrath. I am grateful to Phyllis Granoff for calling my attention to this reference.

10. C. Sivaramamurti, *Nataraja in Art, Thought and Literature* (New Delhi: National Museum, 1974), pp. 378–79, 384. See also M. A. Dorai Rangaswamy, *The Religion and Philosophy of Tēvāram* (Madras: University of Madras, 1958), 1:442, 444–45; and R. K. Das, *Temples of Tamilnad* (Bombay: Bharatiya Vidya Bhavan, 1964), p. 195.

11. Some renditions of Śiva's dance, in which the entire Hindu patheon is shown as spectators or musicians, do include Kālī standing passively by. See, for example, the painting at the Śiva temple at Ettumanur, 16th century, and the scene from a 17th-century temple at TripRayār, Kerala, in Sivaramamurti, *Nataraja,* figs. 150 and 152, pp. 282 and 284, respectively. In both scenarios Kālī rides a *preta* and her appearance is unchanged. It should perhaps be pointed out that the gaunt old woman who is so frequently shown attending upon Śiva while he dances, usually playing with a pair of cymbals, is not Kālī, as is sometimes supposed, but the devotee Kāraikkālammaiyār, a famous saint who renounced her beauty in devotion to Śiva (p. 353).

12. That Śiva should have to resort to his *tāṇḍava* dance to defeat Kālī suggests the theme of Kālī's inciting Śiva to destructive activity. Śiva's *tāṇḍava* dance is typically performed at the end of the cosmic age to destroy the universe. Descriptions of the *tāṇḍava* dance often dwell on its destructive nature. The chaotic dancing of Śiva, who wields a broken battle-ax, must be tempered by the soft glances of Pārvatī (Sivaramamurti, *Nataraja,* p. 138). In this aspect of his dance Śiva tends to get out of control, and in the legend of the dance contest with Kālī, it is she who provokes him to it.

13. M. R. Kale, ed. and trans., *Bhavabhūti's Mālatīmādhava, with the Commentary of Jagaddhara,* 3d ed. (Delhi: Motilal Banarsidass, 1967), pp. 44–48.

14. "M.," *Gospel of Śri Ramakrishna,* trans. Swami Nikhilananda (New York: Ramakrishna-Vivekananda Center, 1942), p. 961.

15. The theme of Pārvatī's acting as a restraining influence on Śiva is mentioned by Glenn E. Yocum, "The Goddess in a Tamil Śaiva Devotional Text, Māṇikkavācakar's *Tiruvācakam*," *Journal of the American Academy of Religion* 45, no. 1, supplement (1977): K372.

16. See, for example, the *Devī Māhātmya,* where she is called *mahāmāyā* (1.2.40–42, 45, 58, 73), *prakṛti* (1.59, 5.7), and *śakti* (1.63, 5.18); and the *Devī Bhāgavata,* passim.

17. The practice of classical yoga aims precisely at disentangling the aspirant from the mesh of *prakṛti* by reversing *prakṛti*'s natural evolution. Yoga is the devolution of matter, as it were, in which *prakṛti* is tamed and stilled.

18. The *Devī Bhāgavata,* while identifying Mahādevī with *prakṛti* throughout, does not hesitate to affirm the binding nature of *praktṛti.*

19. In *Purity and Danger: An Analysis of Concepts of Pollution and Taboo* (Baltimore: Penguin Books, 1970), Mary Douglas locates taboo in the idea of dirt out of place. In a sense Kālī may be regarded as taboo, a dangerous being out of place in the civilized sphere.

20. Ibid., p. 193.

ŚRĪ
Giver of Fortune, Bestower of Grace

Vasudha Narayanan

According to a story well known in the Śrī Vaiṣṇava community of South India, a young man approached Vedānta Deśika, a thirteenth-century theologian, and sought financial help to enable him to conduct his wedding. Vedānta Deśika, a devotee of Viṣṇu and the goddess Śrī, was apparently quite poor himself. But to help the young man in front of him, he composed a work known as the "Prayer to Śrī" (*Śrī Stuti*). As soon as Deśika sang his words in praise of Śrī, it is said, coins of gold rained down around the young man. Deśika's sense of detachment was so great, the story goes, that he walked away without even looking at the coins.[1]

A similar story is told about the eighth-century philosopher Śaṅkara. Śaṅkara, an ascetic, was begging for his daily food when he encountered a poor woman. This woman was ashamed that she had nothing except a small berry to give him. Śaṅkara, it is said, was so moved by her poverty that he sang a hymn to Śrī that is known today as the "Prayer to Honor the [Goddess] Who Showers Gold" (*Kanaka Dhārā Stotra*). The penniless woman was now blessed with earthly good fortune, which the goddess Śrī showered on her.[2]

These tales are striking in that they portray Śrī not just as the giver of wealth—the immediate objective in both cases—but also as one who bestows a salvific grace sought by poets and philosophers. In his introduction to Deśika's *Śrī Stuti,* the editor comments: "If one meditates and recites this poem, one will get wealth, progeny, and all good fortune through the Mother's grace. This prayer also shows the path to get the wealth that can never be destroyed: the wealth of liberation (*mokṣa*)."[3] Śrī is thus worshiped as the goddess who grants worldly prosperity as well as liberation from the cycle of life and death.

Śrī, more popularly known as Lakṣmī, is perhaps the best-known goddess in the Hindu and Jain traditions. Her portrait, which depicts her standing or seated atop a resplendent lotus, graces millions of homes, shops, and businesses (see figure 10). Majestic on her red lotus, holding lotuses in her hand, she is said to bestow wealth and salvific grace just by glancing at a person. Her left hand points to the ground; in Hindu iconography this is the *varadā,* or "boon-giving," gesture. Pictures on calendars often show her giving wealth to her devotees, a shower of gold coins flowing from her right hand.

Yet Śrī's existence as an independent goddess is only half the picture. While she indeed appears by herself in many calendar-art illustrations and has her own shrine in many temples, she is also portrayed both in temples and in theological treatises as Viṣṇu's inseparable consort—as icons that depict Śrī as dwelling on the chest of Viṣṇu attest. A certain tension would thus seem to exist between her autonomy, on the one hand, and her close relationship with Viṣṇu, on the other, and it is this apparent tension that the first part of this essay will explore. We can then go on to investigate a few of Śrī's many additional personalities, as manifested in local temples throughout the South Indian states of Tamilnadu and Andhra Pradesh.

Śrī has a long history. She first appears in the great *Śrī Sūkta* ("Hymn to Śrī") that was probably added to the *Rig Veda* sometime between 1000 and 500 B.C.E. There she is praised in the two roles to which we have already drawn attention: as the wife of Viṣṇu and as the beneficent one who dwells on the lotus flower. Yet it is in the Purāṇas, where she is extolled in quite a number of hymns, that she emerges with a distinct personality. A roughly parallel development can be seen in sculpture and architecture. Images of Śrī first appear around the third century B.C.E. in sculptures found at Kausambi, in North India, and on coins issued during the reign of the Gupta dynasty, around the fourth century C.E. Separate shrines to Lakṣmī within the precincts of Viṣṇu temples may have been built as early as the seventh century; we do know that they were definitely in existence by the tenth century. Such shrines were particularly popular in the temples built or managed by the Śrī Vaiṣṇava community of South India.

ŚRĪ IN EARLY ŚRĪ VAIṢṆAVA LITERATURE

Among the devotees of Viṣṇu in South India the most influential group, both historically and in theological terms, has been the Śrī Vaiṣṇavas. The community, which crystallized in the wake of the eleventh-century preceptor Rāmānuja, looked to Sanskrit scripture and to the songs of the Tamil saints (*ālvār*s) for the basis of its theology. The sect's name is significant, for it makes reference not only to Viṣṇu but also to his consort, Śrī. Śrī Vaiṣṇavas distinguish themselves from other Vaiṣṇava groups by insisting that the

Figure 10. Śrī standing on a lotus. Polychrome calendar-art depiction by "Krishna." Madurai: Palan Patippakam, 1991.

intimate bond between these two is crucial to the life of faith and the logic of salvation: without Śrī there is no deliverance.

Śrī Vaiṣṇavas accept Vedic and *smṛti* literature written in Sanskrit (the former ascribed to divine revelation, the latter to human acuity), as well as the Tamil songs of the *āḻvār*s, as sacred texts; they also accept the authority of certain texts collectively known as the Pāñcarātra. In some of these texts, especially one possibly composed around the eighth or ninth century C.E. called the *Lakṣmī Tantra,* the goddess Śrī is glorified as a uniquely powerful deity. "It is she who creates . . . it is she who protects the three worlds. . . . And at the very end . . . she will dissolve [within herself] what has been created."[4] Śrī is thus portrayed as the supreme being who both creates the universe and subsumes it into herself.

During the formative years of the Śrī Vaiṣṇava community (in the tenth and eleventh centuries), early teachers such as Yāmuna, Kūrattāḻvāṉ, and Parāśara Bhaṭṭar wrote a number of hymns (*stotra*s) in praise of Śrī, petitioning her grace.[5] The main themes that emerge from these hymns are the inseparability of Śrī and Viṣṇu and their mutual love, which is evident in the process by which the creation of the universe itself takes place. Even in these early poems, however, the disciples of Rāmānuja downplay some of Śrī's powers, especially her role in the process of creation, which is so conspicuous in the *Lakṣmī Tantra.* For example, Rāmānuja's disciple Kūrattāḻvāṉ opens his "Hymn to Śrī" with the following verse:

> Glancing at Śrī's face, heeding her every wish,
> Hari [Viṣṇu] creates, destroys, and protects the worlds.
> He gives heaven and hell, and the highest state.
> United with her in his pleasure, he creates all;
> For without Śrī, this play [of creation]
> Brings him no joy—
>   May that Śrī grant us happiness.
>
> (*Śrī Stava,* verse 1)

Viṣṇu's wishes conform to those of Śrī; without her happiness, he takes no enjoyment in his divine play, his *līlā.* The celebration and display of Viṣṇu's glory brings him pleasure only when he shares it with his beloved consort. Thus Śrī is of critical importance in making the world come to be what it is. Yet it is clearly Viṣṇu who creates the universe, which he then shares with his spouse: Śrī is not herself the creative power behind the universe, as the *Lakṣmī Tantra* would have it. We see this, for example, in a poem composed by Kūrattāḻvāṉ's son Parāśara Bhaṭṭar, in which he describes the relation between the male and female divinities. According to the poem, Viṣṇu creates the universe as Śrī watches, this creation making manifest Viṣṇu's hidden splendor:

O Lord who fulfills desires!
Like a peacock
shaking loose its brilliant feathers
and holding them high in front of a hen,
by your wish
you spread out
the expanse of souls and matter
    that are [hidden and] one with your body
    during the time of dissolution,
and playfully display your glory
    before the eyes of Śrī.

(*Śrī Raṅgarāja Stava* 2.44)

With an ease like that of a peacock displaying his plumage, Viṣṇu shakes loose creation from matter so subtle that it seems to be one with his body. The cosmos is a manifestation of Viṣṇu's splendor, and he playfully displays it in Śrī's presence. There is, of course, an underlying erotic note in this verse, for the peacock usually dances in full glory to attract the hen. Creation, then, is understood in Śrī Vaiṣṇava literature as forming part of the love play between Viṣṇu and Śrī. This divine playfulness finds expression in the creation of the worlds as well as in the passion (*sṛṅgāra*) that Śrī and Viṣṇu share. However, it is still Viṣṇu who is responsible for the creation process, not Śrī. This emphasis on the male divinity stands in contrast to statements often made in Tantra literature glorifying Śrī—and yet these statements, too, are quoted with approval by Śrī Vaiṣṇavas.

While Śrī Vaiṣṇavas agree that the relationship between Śrī and Viṣṇu is an inseparable one, they differ among themselves in the way they construe it. All Śrī Vaiṣṇavas consider Śrī to be a mediator between human beings and Viṣṇu in the matter of salvation, but the community is split on the issue of her equality to Viṣṇu. The controversy came to a head between the thirteenth and fifteenth centuries. Vedānta Deśika (1268–1368) believed Śrī to be coequal and coeval with Viṣṇu and capable of saving human beings on her own. Others, following the teachings of Piḷḷai Lōkācārya (also thirteenth century), believed that although Śrī was a goddess, she was neither equal to nor coeval with Viṣṇu. For them, she has no independent salvific power of her own but instead plays a supporting role in salvation by interceding with Viṣṇu on behalf of human beings.

Significant in this connection is the conception of Śrī held by the theologian Vedānta Deśika, whose views are representative of that portion of the Śrī Vaiṣṇava community who call themselves Vaṭakalais. Deśika's attitude toward Śrī finds expression in his many theological texts, commentaries, and prayers written in Sanskrit, Tamil, or Maṇipravāḷa (a hybrid of Tamil and Sanskrit). These writings reveal that, for Deśika, Śrī is the great mediator between God and the human soul. She has her own particular nature, which can be distinguished from that of Viṣṇu, in that she is auspiciousness itself. At the same time, though, she is inseparably bound to him. In Deśika's analysis, Śrī's uniquely salvific power derives from the concomitance of these two roles: she possesses a certain distinctness and yet a distinct inseparability. As we shall see, these two roles are symbolized by Śrī's associations with the lotus, on the one hand, and, on the other, with the breast of Viṣṇu. Both are present, for example, in a verse addressed to Viṣṇu that Śrī Vaiṣṇavas recite every day:

> O you on whose breast
> dwells the lady of the flower
> saying: "I cannot move away from him
> even for a second!"[6]

But it is primarily Śrī's role as the mother and mediator that preoccupies Deśika.

ŚRĪ AS THE MEDIATOR

Let us listen, then, to the following verses of Deśika:

> O incomparably glorious Śrī, who grants auspiciousness to everything that is auspicious! You grace the breast of Viṣṇu with your radiance . . . you are the protector of those who seek your refuge . . . and I, who am without any other refuge, now surrender myself to you.
>
> O Mother who resides on the lotus, hearken to my plea! I babble like a child; with your grace (*prasāda*) make the Lord who is your beloved listen to my [petition].[7]

Śrī is mother, just as Viṣṇu is father, a point to which Deśika often returns: "O Goddess, you are my mother; the lord with auspicious qualities is my father."[8] According to Deśika, it is the special province of the mother to be gracious, to forgive. When human devotees stray from the right path, Śrī's role then becomes crucial, for she is the one who can mediate between the errant child and the just father.

Viṣṇu, too, is innately gracious, but his is an initial, prevenient grace, which Deśika designates *kṛpā*. It is a grace common to all human beings—the quality in human nature that enables every person to seek refuge with Viṣṇu and thus become his devotee. There is also, however, a further and more specific salvific grace, which Deśika calls *prasāda*—that action of divine self-extension whereby an individual can achieve release (*mokṣa*) from the confining conditions of humanity. Out of consideration for justice—and it is a father's duty to dispense justice—Viṣṇu cannot offer this act of generosity indiscriminately: too much wrongdoing has taken place in the world. For him *kṛpā* and *prasāda* are distinct, and justice prevents the latter from being a reflex of the former. As a father might wish he had some pretext for ignoring the misdeeds of his children, so Viṣṇu longs for a reason to ignore human infractions against the divine order. But without some such excuse, even the smallest sign of faith, he cannot rightly act.[9]

According to the Śrī Vaiṣṇava teachers, however, a mother's nature is different from a father's. In a family it is often the mother who mediates between the children and the father, for the simple reason that she is not so rigidly bound by considerations of justice and order. Deśika expresses this idea in relation to Śrī, the archetypal mother, by saying that in her nature no distinction exists between *kṛpā* and *prasāda:* she is always, pervasively, immediately gracious, always ready to save.[10] The lord relents only if he is solicited for help; with a prayer his *prasāda* is available. But Śrī forgives voluntarily; she needs no reason. Śrī thus becomes the primary refuge of all who err: not only is it preferable to turn to her, but it is necessary. As Deśika, quoting Śaunaka, states: "The person who craves to reach the Lord should, out of necessity, seek the protection of Lakṣmī. It does not suffice to seek refuge with the Lord."[11] For she is that aspect of the Godhead that forgives as a matter of course, whose essence is unqualified grace.

The importance of all this for the devotee becomes clear in Deśika's *Cillarai Rahasyaṅkaḷ* ("Minor Secrets"):

> The mother who is the owner (*śeṣī*) of all except the Supreme Owner (*sarvaśeṣī*), whose nature is such that her grace is unmixed with any anger and is showered on all, does not spare any effort to make the punishing Lord pleased with those who have committed several faults. She cools the heat of his anger, which arises because he is the father. Bhaṭṭar said, "O Mother! When your Lord gets angry with a man as a father does with his son, you ask, 'What is this? Who is not at fault in this world?' and make him forget the offenses; . . . therefore you are indeed my mother!" Thus she unites one with his auspicious feet and brings the Lord to the state of saying [as the poet Periyāḻvār put it], "Even if the Lady of the lotus [Śrī] finds fault with the devotee, I would say that MY devotee can do no wrong; why, if he does, then *that* act would be right.". . . We pray to her to be the mediator, for the Lord punishes.[12]

Śrī, by contrast, never punishes.[13] Indeed, her salvific potential is implicit in her very name. Deśika derives the name Śrī in six different ways, each having to do with her graciousness:

śrīyate: she who is resorted to
śrayate: she who resorts [to the Lord]
śṛṇoti: she who listens [to humans]
śrāvayati: she who makes [the Lord] listen
śṛṇāti: she who removes [past karma, the faults and hindrances that stand in devotee's way]
śrinati: she who makes [humans] perfect [for *mokṣa*][14]

In his commentaries on the *dvaya* mantra, Deśika goes on to explain how these various meanings are integrated in Śrī's personality. The most important of all mantras for Śrī Vaiṣṇavas, the *dvaya* mantra is the object of repeated meditation and the focus of several theological treatises. In it the word Śrī occurs twice, and in commenting on the first of these Deśika draws in most of the meanings we have just listed above:

> In the first line [of the *dvaya* mantra] the word Śrī indicates the wonder of her maternal affection toward her subjects and the wonder of her love for her husband; she is the mother because she is the refuge of all human beings and the rightful wife of the Lord. She seeks refuge with the Lord. She listens to the petitions of the devotee and makes the Lord listen. She takes away the faults [of the devotee]. Through her grace [Tamil: *aruḷ*] she makes wisdom and other qualities rise [in the devotee]. These are the meanings of the name *śrī* denoted by scripture.[15]

As wife to Viṣṇu, then, and as mother to humans, Śrī is by her very nature a mediator. This mediational role overarches both her principal iconographic forms—as a jewel on the breast of Viṣṇu and as the independent nurturer who stands or sits upon a lotus.

ŚRĪ AND THE LOTUS: HER AUSPICIOUSNESS

One of the most striking features of the iconography of Śrī is her persistent association with the lotus. She is said to dwell on the lotus or, indeed, in a "forest of lotuses," and lotuses are all about her.[16] She shares their hue and, in particular, their fragrance, for the scent of the lotus is as inseparable from its source as is Śrī's grace from Śrī herself, and as constant.[17] It is a perception evidently too basic to have required comment, on the part either of Deśika or of other Śrī Vaiṣṇava theologians, that the association between Śrī and the lotus consists in the fact that both are pure forms of auspiciousness (*kalyāṇa, maṅgala*). To a large extent these theologians simply rely on scripture to establish the tie. As Deśika puts it: "The auspicious lotus is to be seen as an important example of auspiciousness; . . . this is stated in scripture: verses in the *Viṣṇu Smṛti* and other works make it clear."[18] This theme is echoed by several Śrī Vaiṣṇava theologians even today.

Although Śrī is all-pervasive, latent in everything, she manifests herself only in auspicious places, of which the lotus itself is the great exemplar. In a brief verse Deśika says that because Śrī has the quality of pervasion she can be said to be everywhere, and everything is her body. He adds, however, that her own auspicious form is in the Lord.[19] This note of qualification indicates that Śrī should not be understood as the immanent pole of divinity, with Viṣṇu as the transcendent pole. The purity of her auspiciousness sets her apart from creation as such: she is not simply *prakṛti* ("nature"), as in the

Tantric view. Deśika is well aware that she is hailed as *prakṛti* in the text that recites her thousand names, the *Lakṣmī Sahasranāma.* But he interprets the reference as meaning "she who participates in the creation of *prakṛti,*" a point he argues by analogy to another of her names, *vidyā,* knowledge, which he alleges really means "the one who grants knowledge."[20] Similarly, she is not only the fulfillment of all desires but the one who fulfills them. As Deśika says: "She fulfills all desires of all people. She is noble (*ārya*); she gives prosperity; she is filled with good thoughts; she gives righteousness, pleasure, wealth, and liberation (*dharma-kāma-artha-mokṣa-dā*)."[21] These last are the four aims or ends of human life, and the fact that Śrī grants the fourth, liberation from the encumbering conditions of life itself, along with the rest is especially significant. It indicates how far her auspiciousness extends, namely, utterly beyond the realm of this world: "She gives the highest state (*parinirvāṇa*) . . . she helps one cross the cycle of life, and death. . . . O Śrī, you give one knowledge of the sacrifices, the great knowledge, the secret knowledge, knowledge of the self, and through these you give their fruit . . . liberation."[22]

The word *śrī* means "auspicious," and the idea that Śrī's auspiciousness is self-caused leads us to yet another nuance involved in depicting Śrī on the lotus, for this image shows her existing on her own, rather than as a part of Viṣṇu. It affirms her distinct personality and her existence as a goddess who is the source of auspiciousness and glory. This understanding of Śrī distinguishes the Śrī Vaiṣṇava position from that of other sects. Deśika categorically affirms—with the backing of scriptural authority—what Śrī is *not.* She is not insentient matter (any form of *prakṛti*) nor is she merely a personification of Viṣṇu's grace (*dayā*).[23] Deśika argues that Śrī has a distinct personality, that she is the perfect consort of Viṣṇu, equal to him in every way and subservient to him only because she herself wills it so. "Scripture affirms that [the Lord and Śrī] are a couple," says Deśika, "and it is not [ours] to ask why."[24]

The question then arises: does the worship of Śrī—a distinct person—compromise the exclusiveness of the Śrī Vaiṣṇavas' devotion? They answer that it does not. One way to understand how this is possible is to consider another of the dominant Śrī Vaiṣṇava images for Śrī.

ŚRĪ ON VIṢṆU'S BREAST: DISTINCT BUT INSEPARABLE

The lotus, as we have seen, is a symbol of Śrī's separate identity. But there is another image that poets, artists, and theologians alike have associated with Śrī, one that calls attention to quite a different facet of her character. Śrī abides on the breast of Viṣṇu, adorning it (see figure 11). When Deśika speaks of this image, he is thinking of the inseparable connection (*apṛthak siddhi*) that binds them to one another: he describes Śrī as "eternally united"

Figure 11. Śrī on the breast of Viṣṇu. From the jacket of M. S. Subbulakshmi, "Bhaja Govindam and Vishnusahasranamam," Odeon Records, The Gramophone Company of India, Ltd.

with Viṣṇu.[25] Thus, even when the Lord incarnated himself as a celibate young man—as the dwarf Vāmana—Śrī was hidden on his breast. Referring to the simple cloth that Brahmins wear on their upper body, Deśika says that in this instance, "The Lord covered his breast with a shawl to hide Śrī, who is inseparable from him."[26] In commenting on a verse from the *Bhagavad Gītā,* he pays close attention to the phrase "take refuge in me alone." Marshaling twenty-five verses from elsewhere in scripture that testify to Śrī's eternal connection with Viṣṇu, Deśika concludes that the words "me alone" cannot refer solely to Viṣṇu but must include Śrī as well.[27] Elsewhere, in discussing the word "alone," he comments:

> Some say that the word *eka* [alone] refers to the singleness of the refuge. [But we say] that Śrī is always with him as an attribute, just as his qualities are inseparable from his form. She is the goddess of all and the beloved one of the Lord; with him she protects devotees as his partner in dharma. Even though scripture says that the cause of the universe is one, it is implied that other requisites [like souls and matter] exist as the Lord's attributes. Similarly, Śrī is also implied. . . . The Lord is the single means to the goal, but his qualities always exist with him. And so it is seen by those who have the eyes of scripture that the Lord is always with his wife. When one says "light" or "the object that is the source of light," the connection of one with the other is always implied; similarly, when either of the two [the Lord or Śrī] is mentioned, the other is always included.[28]

In this passage Deśika is carrying forward Rāmānuja's theological method. Rāmānuja held that *brahman,* ultimate reality, is qualified by souls and matter (*cit* and *acit*) but that this does not falsify the unity of reality or its encompassing nature, since souls and matter are its attributes (*viśiṣṭya*). Here, Deśika characterizes Śrī as an "attribute" of the Lord, and just as Rāmānuja had insisted that *brahman,* souls, and matter are inseparable, so does Deśika argue in the case of Śrī.[29] All this does not, however, imply that, for Deśika, Śrī's status is essentially the same as that of sentient souls. On the contrary, she, like her mate, is the owner of the universe (*śeṣī*), whereas sentient souls are owned (*śeṣa*). She is no more separable from him than are the sun's rays from the sun itself in the eye of the perceiver. Deśika, quoting Kūrattāḻvāṉ's *Śrī Stava,* argues that Viṣṇu and Śrī—who are inseparable—together create, rule, and sustain the universe.[30] It is this inseparability that allows one to speak of the "oneness" of the deity.

So inextricably entwined are Śrī and Viṣṇu that Deśika is unwilling even to frown upon those who worship Śrī as if she were a divinity separate from her husband:

> Those whose goal is only liberation and who worship with no ulterior motive, worship Śrī in union [with Viṣṇu, i.e., as portrayed on the breast of Viṣṇu] or as the one enjoyed by the Lord [portrayed at his side]. Those who desire

> worldly benefits worship her separately. But there is no impropriety . . . for she is our mother, and in all forms, her being this wife of Viṣṇu is an established fact.[31]

More desirable, however, is not to forget the connection, which Śrī's position on Viṣṇu's breast so vividly symbolizes.

ŚRĪ'S MANIFESTATIONS IN ŚRĪ VAIṢṆAVA TEMPLES

Even though Śrī Vaiṣṇava theological texts emphasize the inseparability of Śrī and Viṣṇu, a sense of her autonomy and her several personalities emerges from the myths and legends that surround the many Śrī Vaiṣṇava temples found throughout South India. The Śrī Vaiṣṇava community considers 106 temples dedicated to Viṣṇu and Śrī to be especially sacred, temples that are important because the *ālvār*s, the Tamil poet-saints, sang about them.[32]

All Śrī Vaiṣṇava temples have separate shrines for Viṣṇu and Śrī. These shrines house two kinds of consecrated images: a primary, immovable image and a smaller image used during festival processions. Śrī has a large separate shrine of her own in Śrī Vaiṣṇava temples and several festivals are celebrated exclusively for her (see figure 12). It is important to note that, in the shrine of Viṣṇu, Śrī is always represented as residing on his chest. Sometimes the primary image of Viṣṇu is accompanied by an additional image of Śrī—who is shown at his feet (if he is reclining) or by his side—while the processional image of Viṣṇu housed in this chamber is always accompanied by images of his consorts, Śrī and Bhū (the earth goddess). Thus, Viṣṇu is never worshiped alone; he is always with Śrī. Śrī, however, is alone in her shrine, without her consort as a companion. In other words, it seems clear that Viṣṇu can be worshiped only in conjunction with Śrī, whereas Śrī can be, and is, worshiped alone.

If a spatial separation thus exists between the shrines in a Śrī Vaiṣṇava temple, the myths surrounding the temple and the holy land it is built on frequently speak of a temporal separation between Śrī and Viṣṇu, as well. These stories are found in texts called *sthala-māhātmya*s that glorify a particular temple or place. Abridged versions of such stories, which are framed within the context of a conversation between a mythical seer (*ṛṣi*) and his wife or between various deities, are frequently reprinted in pamphlets sold outside the temples. Although these stories have their origins in local legends or folktales, they have taken on a form that makes them masquerade as Purāṇas, thereby exemplifying the process often called Sanskritization.

At the beginning of these local stories, Śrī, who is so intimately bound up with Viṣṇu in theological writings, is frequently separated from him, their reunion usually taking place at the site where the temple is now located. This interplay of union and separation is illustrated in the literature

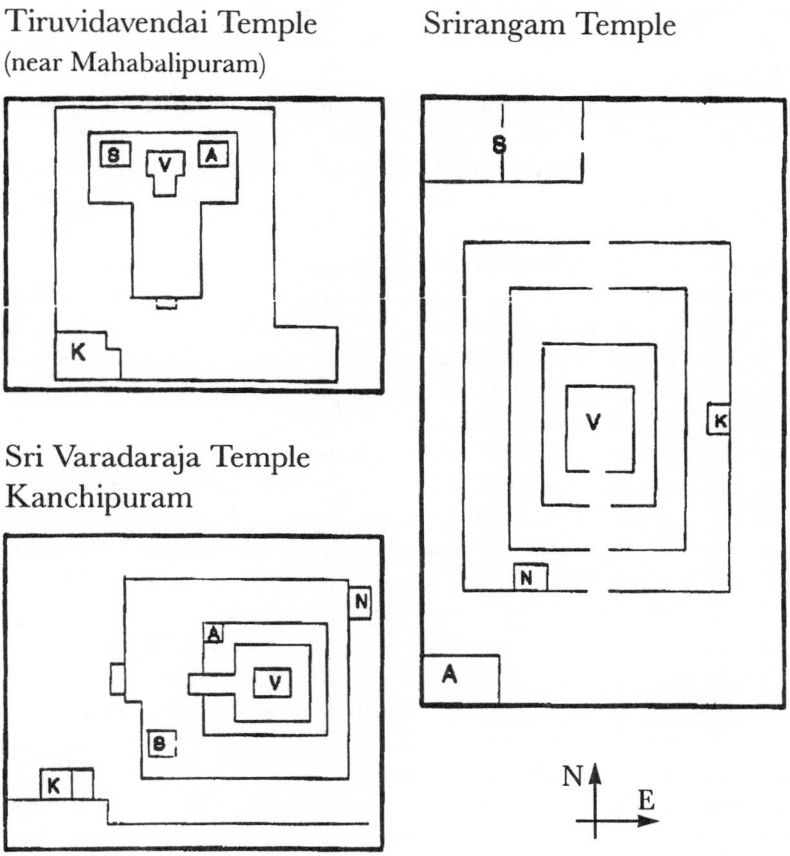

Figure 12. The position of the shrine to Śrī in three Śrī Vaiṣṇava temple complexes. S: shrine for Śrī; V: shrine for Viṣṇu; A: shrine for Āṇṭāl; N: shrine for poet-saint Nammāḻvār; K: temple kitchen. Diagram by Vasudha Narayanan.

concerning the temple at Tirumala-Tirupati (Tiruvēṅkaṭam, in Tamil literature). At the same time, Nammāḻvār, often considered the greatest of the Tamil poet-saints, sings about the inseparability of Śrī and Viṣṇu in this very temple, in a verse so fundamental that it is recited by Śrī Vaiṣṇavas everywhere as part of their daily liturgy. In fact, we have already quoted this salutation to Viṣṇu:

> O you on whose breast
> dwells the lady of the flower
> saying: "I cannot move away from him
> even for a second!"
>
> (*Tiruvāymoḻi* 6.10.10)

As the verse indicates, at this temple Śrī is represented on the breast of Viṣṇu, just as she is at all Śrī Vaiṣṇava temples. Moreover, at Tirumala-Tirupati Viṣṇu is known by the special name "Śrī-nivāsa" ("he on whom Śrī abides"), and, as if to underscore their connection, there is no separate shrine for Śrī within the temple complex itself. Nonetheless, a temple to Śrī does exist nearby, in the foothills of the mountain range on which the Viṣṇu temple is located.

In the famous story that tells how all this came to be, Śrī is portrayed as coming down to earth after a quarrel with Viṣṇu. She settles down in the city of Kolhapur, in the modern state of Maharashtra. Viṣṇu then follows her to earth, where he meets Padmāvatī, the adopted daughter of a local king. In a story that is reminiscent of the *Rāmāyaṇa*'s account of King Janaka's finding Sītā, we are told that Padmāvatī had apparently been found on land that was being ploughed in preparation for a sacrifice. Padmāvatī grows up and meets Viṣṇu, a meeting that takes place in what has traditionally been considered a "romantic" setting by Tamil-speaking people. Viṣṇu, in the guise of a young man, is chasing an elephant, and in a forest blooming with flowers he meets Padmāvatī. A marriage is negotiated, and Viṣṇu prepares to get the funds required to mount a grand wedding. After various trials and tribulations, Viṣṇu borrows large sums of money from Kubera, the heavenly treasurer, to advance as a dowry and thereby win the hand of Padmāvatī. In the legend, Padmāvatī is not specifically identified with the goddess Śrī; instead, she is represented as an incarnation of a sort of shadow goddess known as Vedavatī. But at the time of the wedding itself Śrī, who has been residing in the city of Kolhapur, is brought to Viṣṇu, at which point she replaces Padmāvatī in the story. Thus she is united with Viṣṇu once again.[33]

The story is curious in several respects. It seems initially to say that Padmāvatī is not Śrī; rather, she is an incarnation of a lesser-known divine being called Vedavatī. But the finding of a young girl on freshly ploughed ground reminds one of the story of Sītā, who is definitely considered to be an incarnation of Śrī. Furthermore, the name Padmāvatī, which associates the princess with the lotus (*padma*), also suggests that we should identify her with Śrī. Nevertheless, in the story the identification of Śrī with Padmāvatī is questioned. Padmāvatī is considered to be the daughter of Ākāśa Rājā, the local king, and when Viṣṇu is courting her, Śrī is still far off in Kolhapur. It takes Śiva and Brahmā to reunite her with Viṣṇu just before he gets married to Padmāvatī. At that point Śrī happily resumes her existence on Viṣṇu's breast, whereupon Viṣṇu's marriage to Padmāvatī is celebrated.

In worship, however, it does not all come out so neatly, and it is much harder to maintain a distinction between Śrī and Padmāvatī. The temple dedicated to Padmāvatī, located in Tiruchanur at the foot of the Tirumala-Tirupati hills, is quite simply understood to be Śrī's temple. Overall, then, one senses a great ambiguity in the various ways in which Śrī has been identified with Padmāvatī, the local goddess, to a large extent because several local and regional legends have coalesced with Purāṇic stories in Sanskrit that are known much more widely than the legends specific to particular temple sites. The same ambiguity can be seen in stories connected with other Śrī Vaiṣṇava temples, as well.

The story of Padmāvatī connected with the temple at Tirumala-Tirupati, which highlights a separation between Viṣṇu and Śrī, is echoed in many local legends. Many texts that glorify a particular sacred spot portray Śrī as having moved from heaven to earth to dwell at that place. She then grows up as a local girl, Viṣṇu follows her to earth, and they are eventually reunited. In the story recounted about Nācciyār Kōil ("The Temple of the Goddess") near Kumbakonam, in Tamilnadu, Śrī is said to have come to earth to protect human beings. A holy man called Medhāvi finds her in the form of a baby under a *vañjuḷa* (*aśoka*) tree and therefore calls her Vañjuḷavalli. She is raised as his daughter. Viṣṇu sends out his emanations in search of her, and eventually all of them meet in Nācciyār Kōil, also called Tirunaraiyur.[34] It is here that Viṣṇu reveals himself as the supreme being to Medhāvi and is reunited with Śrī. She thus remains eternally in his presence—but Medhāvi nonetheless requests that in this temple Śrī (known as *nācciyār,* "goddess" or "lady") should have the leading role in all rituals and festivals. The temple itself is known by her name, and the story explains the ritual situation rather neatly.

These legends obviously seek to link a local story to the broader Sanskrit Purāṇic tradition. Śrī Vaiṣṇava temple stories usually have three or four layers. The opening layer explains why the site of the temple is sacred and describes how Viṣṇu manifested himself to a divine being or holy person. A second layer then recounts a local legend about a young girl who later marries the deity. These young girls are frequently said to have been "found" somewhere and to have been born in a miraculous manner; in other words, they are not the product of ordinary human birth. They are raised by kings or holy men, usually in a patriarchal situation, and are given a local name, which means that they are not generically known as Śrī at any of these temples. At Tirupati (Tiruchanur), for example, the goddess is known only as Padmāvatī; at Nācciyār Kōil she is called Vañjuḷavalli; at Koiladi, Indirā Devi; at Tēreḻuntūr, Ceṅkamalavalli; and so on.[35] In many, but not all, versions of the story, these young girls are identified with Śrī, who is said to have left heaven on some pretext or other. In a few cases—as in the stories of a Muslim princess and a Malayali princess, who are described as being in love with the deity who resides in the temple at Srirangam—the human personalities are left relatively intact.[36]

Then there is a third layer in the story, which talks of a visit by an *āḻvār* and explains how he or she was graced with a vision of the lord enshrined in that temple. Finally, one occasionally finds a fourth layer, which mirrors the third by speaking of a visit to the temple site by a Śrī Vaiṣṇava teacher—one of the figures who, after the eleventh century C.E., succeeded the *āḻvār*s as the primary vessels of authority in the community. The effect of the whole, in which the four layers are sometimes compressed, is to join local legends and the "standard" Purāṇic story by introducing the notion of a temporary separation between Viṣṇu and Śrī, a concept that is untenable to Śrī Vaiṣṇava theologians. The reunion of the divine couple mitigates that offense, while at the same time revitalizing the sacredness of the place in question. And the motif of visits by *āḻvār*s and preceptors both integrates local sites into a regional network and validates the authenticity of each specific place, each of which promulgates its particular version of the unifying goddess, Śrī.

ŚRĪ IN TEMPLE RITUAL

The divine separations that we encounter in temple legends are also acted out in annual rituals performed in the major Śrī Vaiṣṇava temples. One such ritual is called the "Festival of Romantic Quarrels" (*praṇaya kalaha utsava*) and is described in many Pāñcarātra texts.[37] This festival, which takes place in the spring at the Srirangam temple, depicts a lovers' quarrel between Viṣṇu and Śrī.[38] The ritual image of the Lord is taken out during the day—presumably so that he can enjoy some time without his wife constantly watching over his shoulder. When the Lord comes back that evening, he finds the doors of the temple locked. He comes in through an alternate entrance, only to find Śrī waiting there, furious. She confronts him, wanting to know where he has been all day, and a quarrel ensues. Special cantors known as *araiyar*s assume the role of Śrī in this quarrel, while the temple priests sing on behalf of Viṣṇu, each group standing by its respective image to communicate the messages of the deities to each other. Viṣṇu claims that he was out hunting all day and has now brought flowers (*pārijāta*) for his wife. Incensed, Śrī asks him to leave: she says she is not falling for *that* line again. The cantors sing and act out a number of verses from the *āḻvār*s' works in which the poets express their anger against the Lord. But then Nammāḻvār (one of the Tamil poet-saints) appears on the scene and persuades Śrī to abandon her wrath. The divine pair are thus reconciled, whereupon they exchange garlands of flowers as a token of their love for each other.

It is difficult to offer a single, consistent interpretation of this curious ritual. At the same time, it is the very multivalency of its symbols that makes the drama so rich in meaning. The classical Śrī Vaiṣṇava position has been summed up by S. Venkataraman: "Thus Nammāḻvār establishes his role as a teacher."[39] This is obviously true, in that Nammāḻvār does indeed come into the narrative and manages to reconcile the two divinities by what he says. But there is a subtler, more significant dimension as well. According to the Śrī Vaiṣṇavas, Nammāḻvār is able to effect this reconciliation because he understands that divine justice (as represented by Viṣṇu) and divine grace (as represented by Śrī) are inextricably interrelated, to the point that they are inseparable. The story conveys their inseparability: Śrī cannot long continue to reject Viṣṇu.

In another approach to this ritual, Śrī is taken to represent a human soul; and she does indeed behave here as if she were one of the classical heroines of secular Tamil literature: a woman deserted by her lover. According to tradition, the lesson to be learned is that human beings should not become resentful when they notice that God takes an interest not only in them but in others around them—often showering blessings that could stir up envy.

Finally, there is a third possible interpretation. Śrī—and the human soul—are reconciled to the Lord by the words of Nammāḻvār, which are said to contain salvific wisdom.[40] At the simplest level of the story, Śrī experiences the human emotion of jealousy, and she vents her anger at the supposed waywardness of her husband. This interpretation suggests the existence of some local legend that was later synthesized with the stories of Śrī.

As to the status of Śrī in relation to Viṣṇu, almost every ritual that is performed for Viṣṇu in the central chamber of Śrī Vaiṣṇava temples is also performed in the parallel universe of Śrī's shrine—but the rituals dedicated to Śrī are sometimes shortened versions of those that honor Viṣṇu. For instance, when the "Festival of Recitation" is conducted for Lord Raṅganātha (Viṣṇu) at the Srirangam temple, it lasts ten days. Immediately after it is completed, the same festival is celebrated for Śrī, in front of her shrine, but this time it lasts only five days. Although it is possible that the festivals were once of equal duration, this is no longer the case. Some rituals, however, such as those connected with Navarātrī (the Festival of Nine Nights), are celebrated primarily for Śrī. And in still other rituals, like Vasantotsava (the "Celebration of Spring"), Śrī and Viṣṇu participate equally. In the temple rituals at Srirangam, says Parāśara Bhaṭṭar, Viṣṇu and Śrī play with flowers, adorning themselves with fresh blossoms, celebrating the vibrancy of spring and the creation of life. In some respects Śrī has the edge: when she playfully uses the crook of Viṣṇu's elbow as her pillow, the marks of her braid are imprinted on his arm.[41]

Overall, then, we sense a rough equality in the number and type of rituals conducted for Viṣṇu and Śrī. Still, in Srirangam and many other Śrī Vaiṣṇava centers the celebrations for Śrī are confined within the precincts of the temple, whereas Viṣṇu is allowed to travel outside. Thus, in Srirangam, Śrī is popularly called *paṭi-tāṇṭāta-patnī*, "the wife who does not step outside the threshold [of the temple]." In the Śrī Vaiṣṇava community as a whole, however, no consistency exists on this point: in other temples, such as those at Tiruchanur and Tirupati, Śrī is taken in procession through the streets of the town during festivals.[42] Yet this is the exception, for usually when the festival image of Śrī is taken from her shrine, the procession remains within the lanes encompassed by the temple walls. This cloistered atmosphere may reflect male attitudes toward women that form part of Hindu tradition—attitudes that prescribe certain restrictions for women.[43]

In sum, temple stories and the rituals celebrated on behalf of Śrī clearly differ in their emphasis from theological writings that speak about her inseparability from Viṣṇu. The stories about Śrī blend local legends and Purāṇic myths, pulling together diverse strands of folklore and theology. In them we find both temporal and spatial separation (albeit followed by reunion). Similarly, both the spatial arrangements in Śrī Vaiṣṇava temples and certain of the rituals performed there underscore Śrī's autonomy and independent identity. Undeniably, however, other rituals curtail her activity in a way that harmonizes with stories in which she is portrayed as a wife who dutifully stays indoors while her husband attends to the world. All in all, in both theological writings and rituals concerning Śrī there appears to be a certain core that remains constant, while at the same time some flexibility is preserved through verbal, visual, and ritual commentaries.

This flexibility has allowed for the increasing popularity of a new manifestation of Śrī, as well as new developments in the patterns of her worship, since the 1960s. Around 1970 a leading Śrī Vaiṣṇava theologian published a prayer addressed to the "Eight Lakṣmīs," the *Aṣṭa Lakṣmī Stotram*, and in the early 1980s an audiocassette containing both this song and the "Thousand Names of Lakṣmī" became very popular.[44] The eight Lakṣmīs are viewed as manifestations of Śrī, and some of them represent her powers. In this poem we see Śrī as primeval (*ādilakṣmī*), as the goddess of grain (*dhānyalakṣmī*), as being fearless and instilling fearlessness in her devotees (*dhairyalakṣmī*), as one who is worshiped by elephants (*gajalakṣmī*), as giving progeny through her favor (*santānalakṣmī*), as being victorious and making her devotees so (*vijayalakṣmī*), and as bestowing knowledge and wealth (*vidyālakṣmī* and *dhanalakṣmī*). Although these attributes of Śrī can all be found in traditional literature, along with at least a dozen others, the emergence of these eight in precisely this combination is, as far as I can discern, quite new. According to traditional prayers, Śrī possesses eight "perfections" (which are not enumerated), which she grants to her devotees. But the list in the prayer to the eight Lakṣmīs contains names like "Primeval Lakṣmī" and "Lakṣmī Worshiped by Elephants" that do not fit the earlier notion of the eight perfections.

These eight forms of Lakṣmī are now widely worshiped both by Śrī Vaiṣṇava and other Hindu communities in South India. In 1974, not long after the prayer to the eight Lakṣmīs gained popularity, a large temple called Aṣṭa Lakṣmī Kōil ("Temple of the Eight Lakṣmīs") was built in Madras, on the shores of the Bay of Bengal. This temple does not contain the traditional separate shrines for Viṣṇu and Śrī. Rather, there are eight small shrines, arranged clockwise in a circle, one for each of the eight Lakṣmīs, and then a ninth shrine, in which we find Viṣṇu and Śrī together, sharing the same space. The effect is to cast Viṣṇu in the role of consort to Śrī Lakṣmī, rather than the other way around, as has been traditional. This is quite remarkable: I know of no other temple in which Śrī has been given such utter prominence. Although this temple is not exclusively Śrī Vaiṣṇava—it is in fact "ecumenical" in that it was built with the blessings of three sectarian Hindu movements (the Advaita tradition of Śaṅkarācārya, and the Śrī Vaiṣṇava and Madhva communities)—it has become popular among Śrī Vaiṣṇava women, many of whom go to worship there. In addition, traditional silver articles used in home worship, as well as decorative jars (*kumbha*), now appear with the eight manifestations of Lakṣmī molded on their sides. While the traditional jars, tumblers, and cups used for worship have been around for centuries, as far as I can see, silver implements worked into the form of the eight Lakṣmīs have come into existence only in the last twenty years or so. Booklets, popular manuals of prayer, ritual worship, and above all a burgeoning audiocassette market are also popularizing devotion to the eight Lakṣmīs, along with more established forms of veneration for the generic Śrī. Such pamphlets and manuals are sold in little shops outside temples in larger cities throughout Tamilnadu.

If it were not such an inappropriate phrase in this context (given Śrī Vaiṣṇava attitudes toward the drink), I would be tempted to say that we are seeing here old wine in new bottles. And the worship of Śrī, either alone, in tandem with Viṣṇu, or in her new "eight forms," has never been more widespread. It is difficult to say exactly what is responsible for this new upsurge of interest in the worship of the most familiar form of the Goddess in South India. The new momentum would seem to have something to do with the rise of goddesses such as Santoṣi Mā and Vaiṣṇo Devī elsewhere on the subcontinent. Closer to home, in Tamilnadu itself, it may well be connected to what seems to be a general rise in the popularity of manifestations of the Goddess, as exemplified by a rejuvenation of the cults of Karumāriamman and others. But whatever is powering this new interest in goddesses of various kinds, the devotees of Śrī clearly feel that she deserves this attention—because, as one might say, she has it all. And not only does she have it, but she gives it away to all who worship her: good fortune in this life, and liberation in the next.

NOTES

1. The editor of Vedānta Deśika's magnum opus, "The Essence of the Three Secrets" (*Rahasyatrayasāram*), narrates this story in his introduction to the book: see *Rahasyatrayasāram* (hereafter *RTS*), ed. Śrī Rāmatēcikācāryar Svāmi, 2 vols. (Kumbakonam: Oppiliyappaṉ Sanniti, 1961), 1:24.

2. This story is usually found in the prefaces to the printed versions of Śaṅkara's prayer to Śrī. My source is the appendix called "Garland of Prayers" (*Stotramālā*) in a popular Sanskrit and Tamil prayer manual, *Sakala Kāriya Sittiyum Śrīmatrāmāyaṇamum,* ed. Sri Ubhaya Vendanta C. R. Srinivasa (Ayyangar, Madras: The Little Flower Company, n.d.), p. 60.

3. Introduction to the *Śrī Stuti* in *Śrī Tēcika Stotramālā* (hereafter *STS*), ed. Śrī Rāmatēcikācāryar, 2 vols. (Kumbakonam: Oppiliyappan Sanniti, 1970), 2:689. Indic terms cited in this essay (other than titles of works) are Sanskrit, except as otherwise indicated.

4. *Lakṣmī Tantra: A Pāñcarātra Text,* trans. Sanjukta Gupta (Leiden: E. J. Brill, 1972), p. 5 (1.39–40).

5. Around the tenth century, Yāmuna, the first Śrī Vaiṣṇava teacher, wrote a short work called "Four Verses" (*Catuḥślokī*). In his "Hymn of Surrender" (*Śaraṇāgatigadya*), Rāmānuja ritually surrenders himself to Śrī before he submits himself to Viṣṇu. Kūrattāḻvāṉ, (11th century), Rāmānuja's companion and scribe, composed a longer poem called "Hymn to Śrī" (*Śrī Stava*) in honor of the goddess, and his son Parāśara Bhaṭṭar wrote the "Treatise on the Attributes of Sri" (*Śrīguṇaratnakośa*). These hymns are recited regularly as part of both temple and home worship by members of the Śrī Vaiṣṇava community.

6. *Tiruvāymoḻi,* in *Nālayira Tivyap Pirapantam,* ed. P. P. Aṇṇaṅkarācāriyar (Madras: V. N. Tēvanātaṉ, 1971), p. 522 (6.10.10). All translations are my own.

7. *Śrī Stuti,* verse 1, in *STS,* 2:691; *Śrī Devanāyaka Pañcasat,* verse 4, in *STS,* 1:422.

8. *Śrī Stuti,* verse 23, in *STS,* 2:722.

9. This matter is discussed in greater detail in my doctoral dissertation: see V. Rajagopalan [Narayanan], "The Śrī Vaiṣṇava Understanding of *Bhakti* and *Prapatti*" (Ph.D. diss., University of Bombay, 1978), pp. 435–37.

10. Vedānta Deśika, *Catuḥślokībhāṣyam* (hereafter *CSB*), in *Catuḥślokībhāṣyam, Stotraratnabhāṣyam, Gadyatrayabhāṣyañca,* ed. Chettaloor V. Srivatsankacharyar (Madras: Venkatesa Agraharam, 1968), p. 14.

11. *RTS,* 2: 16, 183.

12. *Rahasya Ratnāvaḷi Hrutayam,* in *Cillarai Rahasyaṅkaḷ* (hereafter *CR*), ed. Śrī Rāmatēcikācāryar, 2 vols. (Kumbakonam: Oppaliyappaṉ Sanniti, 1972), 1:107–8.

13. See *CSB,* p. 12.

14. *RTS,* 2:180. See also *CSB,* p. 3, following *Āhirbudhnya Saṁhitā* 21.8.

15. *Rahasyatraya Culakam Tvayātikāram,* in *CR,* 1:234–35.

16. *Śrī Stuti,* verse 4, quoted by Deśika in his *Śaraṇāgatigadyabhāṣyam* (hereafter *SGB*), p. 132. See also Rāmānuja's *Śaraṇāgatigadya,* verse 1.

17. *Śrī Sūkta,* verse 9, quoted in *SGB,* p. 131. See also *CR,* 1:49.

18. *SGB,* p. 132.

19. *CSB,* p. 16. Śrī Vaiṣṇavas observe a theoretical distinction between the Lord's personal form (*divyamaṅgalavigraha*) and his all-pervasive form, in which the whole universe is contained in his body (*divyātmaśarīra*). Deśika makes it clear that Śrī, too, has a personal form, which resides in the Lord, and an all-pervasive manifestation, in which the universe forms her—and the Lord's—body. Śrī's equality with Viṣṇu and the insistence that she is the perfect consort in every way are thus reiterated.

20. *CSB,* p. 4.

21. From the *Lakṣmī Sahasranāma* ("The Thousand Names of Lakṣmī"), quoted in Deśika, *Rahasya Ratnāvaḷi Hruyatam,* in *CR,* 1:106.

22. *CR,* 1:105–6.

23. See *CSB,* pp. 4–8.

24. *CSB,* p. 5.

25. *RTS,* 1:37; Deśika is here drawing on *Rāmāyaṇa* 6.114–15.

26. *RTS,* 2:186.

27. *RTS,* 1:36–38; the verse quoted is *Bhagavad Gītā* 18.66.

28. *RTS,* 2:258–61. This sentiment is also expressed at *RTS,* 2:20.

29. See Rāmānuja, *Vedārtha Saṃgraha,* in *Śrīmad Rāmānuja Granthamālā,* ed. P. B. Aṇṇaṅgarācāriar (Kāñcī: V. N. Tēvanātaṉ, 1974), pp. 20–21.

30. *Śrī Stava,* verse 1, quoted by Deśika in *RTS,* 2:18.

31. Ibid.

32. Technically, they recognize 108 temples as sacred, but two of these are not on earth: the mythical ocean of milk and the supreme heaven, both of which are deemed to be abodes of Viṣṇu and Śrī. Materials on the legends and rituals connected with Śrī were obtained from visits to over sixty-five Śrī Vaiṣṇava temples in South India between 1975 and 1993.

33. This story appears in several versions. See, for example, P. Sitapati, *Sri Venkateswara: The Lord of the Seven Hills, Tirupati* (Bombay: Bharatiya Vidya Bhavan, 1977), pp. 128–37, esp. p. 135. See also T. K. T. Viraraghavacharya, *History of Tirupati* (Tirupati: Tirumala-Tirupati Devasthanams, 1977), pp. 23–24.

34. In Pāñcarātra theology Viṣṇu is said to have four "emanations" or "manifestations" (*vyūhas*). Vāsudeva, the initial manifestation, is portrayed iconographically as Viṣṇu sleeping on the ocean of milk. From Vāsudeva arise Saṅkarṣaṇa, Pradyumna, and Aniruddha, each of whom is responsible for certain aspects of creation and preservation.

35. Girls born in any village in the states of Tamilnadu, Karnataka, and Andhra Pradesh are frequently named after the goddess enshrined there. This practice is continued even if the inhabitants migrate to other places: girls born into families whose ancestors hail from a particular village will still be given the name of that village's goddess as a formal, "ritual" name, used whenever sacraments are performed. Failure to follow this naming practice, it is thought, may incur the wrath, or at least the displeasure, of the deity.

36. On the story of the Muslim consort (Tamil: *tulukka nācciyār*), see my article "*Arcāvatāra*: On Earth, as He Is in Heaven," in *Gods of Flesh, Gods of Stone: The Embodiment of Divinity in India,* ed. Norman Cutler, Joanne Waghorne, and Vasudha Narayanan (Chambersburg, Pa.: Anima Books, 1985), pp. 56–57.

37. For a complete account of these citations, see H. Daniel Smith, "Festivals in Pāñcarātra Literature," in *Religious Festivals in South India and Sri Lanka,* ed. Guy Welbon and Glenn Yocum (New Delhi: Manohar, 1982), p. 37.

38. This drama is enacted on the ninth night of the recitation of the *Tiruvāymoḻi* during the "Festival of Recitation" in Alvar Tirunagari, the birthplace of the poet Nammāḻvār. In Srirangam it is conducted during the month of Citra, but without the participation of the cantors called *araiyars*. In other places the drama receives rather more perfunctory treatment. It is still read aloud in Tirumokkur, and it used

to be acted out in Tirumaliruncolai. See S. Venkataraman, *Araiyar Cēvai* (Madras: Tamilputtakālayam, 1985), p. 84. For a partial analysis of this festival as it is celebrated in Srirangam, see Paul Younger, "Ten Days of Wandering and Romance with Lord Raṅkanātan̲: The Paṅkun̲i Festival in Śrīraṅkam Temple, South India," *Modern Asian Studies* 16, no. 4 (1982): 623–56.

39. Venkataraman, *Araiyar Cēvai,* p. 91.

40. A fourth interpretation is possible, one that would involve role reversals: Śrī portrays the Lord, while Viṣṇu assumes the role of a wayward human being. However, this interpretation is inconsistent with other elements of the ritual, such as the scene in which the Lord places his feet on Śrī's head.

41. See the *Śrī Raṅgarāja Stava,* ed. P. B. Aṇṇāṅgarācāriar (Kāñcī: n.p., 1974), pt. 1, p. 39, and verse 108.

42. See D. Ramaswami Ayyangar's introduction to the *Stotras of Vedānta Deśika (Stotrāṇi)* (Bombay: Sri Vendanta Desika Sampradaya Sabha, 1973), p. "O."

43. These attitudes were more or less prevalent at different times and were particularly applicable to the higher castes. However, many women donated their wealth to temples and instituted rituals—activities that reflect a certain sense of financial independence on their part. Statements about male attitudes toward women therefore must be made with certain qualifications. It seems safe to say that while some men—especially those who espoused the generally negative views that Manu, the first-century lawgiver, held about women—believed that women should lead a somewhat restricted life, these beliefs were not always translated into practice.

44. *Śrī Aṣṭa Lakṣmī Stottiram,* composed by Śrī U. Ve. Vidvān Mukkūr Śrīnivāsavaradācāriyar Svāmikaḷ. No publication information is provided in this little pamphlet, which was given to me in 1970, but I have not been able to find this prayer in major compendia of popular prayers published earlier than 1970.

RĀDHĀ
Consort and Conqueror of Krishna

Donna M. Wulff

In Western works that make reference to Rādhā, she is often described as a simple cowherd woman (*gopī*) who becomes the favorite of the god Krishna.[1] Such an understanding may derive from the Sanskrit Purāṇas, which depict Krishna in his amorous relations with an entire group of women from the cowherd community of Vraja (Hindi: Braj), in which he grew up.[2] Beginning with the twelfth-century *Gītagovinda* of Jayadeva, however, and continuing through a succession of song lyrics in Bengali, Brajabuli, and Hindi, poets have celebrated Krishna's love with one of these women in particular, Rādhā, and in their songs she is clearly no mere mortal.[3]

To be sure, Rādhā's roots appear to have been humble. Available evidence points to a possible literary or performative origin, perhaps in the songs of the Ābhīrs, a cattle-herding community of North India, and our earliest sources—a succession of stray verses in Sanskrit, Prakrit, and Apabhraṃśa from about the third century C.E. that celebrate her love with Krishna—are not explicitly devotional.[4] Nonetheless, her association with him, established throughout much of the subcontinent by the close of the first millennium, soon came to have religious significance. From the *Gītagovinda* onward, we have abundant evidence from various quarters that Rādhā was perceived and worshiped by Vaiṣṇava devotees as Krishna's divine consort (see figure 13).

But the notion of consort may likewise be misleading. One who understands the term to imply subordination will find Rādhā's portrayal in text and performance alike surprising. First, poetic and theological treatises represent her as Krishna's coequal partner, interpreting her nature and status by means of central Hindu concepts dating back to ancient times. Second, unlike such figures as Pārvatī, the mountain-born wife of Śiva, and Śrī/Lakṣmī, Viṣṇu's gracious spouse, Rādhā is usually considered to be

Figure 13. Rādhā and Krishna taking shelter from the rain. *Varṣa Vihāra,* Pahari Hills, Garhwal, ca. 1770–80. Ross-Coomaraswamy Collection, Museum of Fine Arts, Boston.

Krishna's mistress rather than his wife.[5] Finally, Sanskrit and vernacular plays and medieval poetry still sung in dramatic performances show her to be an audacious mistress, emerging triumphant again and again through her cleverness and that of her friends, through her strength of character, and, most important, through the steadfastness and power of her love.

The present essay looks briefly at claims made about Rādhā's metaphysical status by the major communities that worship her. It focuses specifically, however, on her representation in poetry, song, and drama. We shall explore Rādhā's devotional significance by looking at her portrayal in two contrasting dramatic forms: on the one hand, a pair of sophisticated Sanskrit dramas that have been cherished largely by being read by devotees, individually as well as in small groups, and, on the other, a popular, highly dramatic musical form that has been performed by troupes to audiences of several hundred or more throughout greater Bengal and even beyond.[6] The two plays were composed by Caitanya's disciple Rūpa Gosvāmī, who lived and wrote in Vṛndāvana (Hindi: Vrindaban or Brindavan) during the first half of the sixteenth century; the musical form, known as *padāvalī kīrtan* or simply *kīrtan,* was developed by generations of Caitanya's followers starting from roughly the same time. Although the two forms are very different, they reveal an essentially common Rādhā, one who inspires devotees by the strength of her feeling.

The terms *prakṛti* (earthly nature) and *māyā* (the imaginative creativity of illusion), both grammatically feminine, have long been predicated of Rādhā, as they have of other Indian goddesses.[7] Yet it is another feminine term—*śakti* (divine energy, creative power)—that has been used most often by those who seek to define her metaphysical nature. For example, in their theological treatises, Rūpa and Jīva Gosvāmī, who represent one influential sect of her worshipers, the Bengali or Gauḍīya Vaiṣṇavas, assert that Krishna has a threefold divine energy (*śakti*).[8] The highest and most essential (*svarūpā*) of these aspects is his blissful energy, his *hlādinī śakti,* which is Rādhā.[9] In their understanding, then, far from being a lowly cowherd woman, Rādhā is an essential and exalted part of the godhead.

As evidence of Rādhā's divinity, however, it is not enough to find statements exalting her in the treatises of Vaiṣṇava theologians. Rūpa's and Jīva's identification of Rādhā as Krishna's *hlādinī śakti,* for example, has little or no relevance in most people's religious lives. Even if the concept is known to certain people in a community, it is unlikely to figure in their devotional practice or experience. To show that such views have prevailed more generally, we must widen our focus to include forms with a broader reach. Accordingly, here we move out not just to Rūpa's plays but also to the dramatic performances of *padāvalī kīrtan* so as to sample the rich evidence for Rādhā's divine nature and her central place in Vaiṣṇava devotion. Although Rūpa's Sanskrit plays have been far less accessible than *padāvalī kīrtan,* the elements they share with *kīrtan* suggest a common narrative tradition with considerable religious power.

RĀDHĀ IN THE PLAYS OF RŪPA GOSVĀMĪ

According to Vaiṣṇava tradition, Rūpa's two full-length dramas were originally conceived as a single work. The first of these, the *Vidagdhamādhava,* is a lengthy, episodic play in seven acts that concerns the vicissitudes of Rādhā's and Krishna's love in the pastoral setting of Vṛndāvana. Unlike Jayadeva in his *Gītagovinda,* Rūpa gives Rādhā a specific rival in the person of Candrāvalī. He introduces further dramatic tension in the figures of Rādhā's husband, Abhimanyu, and his mother, Jaṭilā, who investigate rumors of Rādhā's love affair with Krishna. The sequel to the *Vidagdhamādhava,* the *Lalitamādhava,* is an even longer and more diffuse play in ten acts that begins in the same idyllic Vṛndāvana, depicts the pathos that afflicts the cowherd community in the wake of Krishna's departure for Mathurā, and finally moves to Krishna's royal capital at Dvārakā. There, Satyabhāmā—the beautiful new arrival whom Rūpa shows to be none other than Rādhā—poses a threat to Krishna's chief queen, Rukmiṇī—in reality Candrāvalī—until the climactic revelation and subsequent harmonious resolution.

In his widely known theory of *bhaktirasa* ("moods of devotion"), Rūpa delineates five primary modes (*bhāvas*) through which the devotee may relate to Krishna: *śānta,* contemplative adoration; *dāsya,* humble servitude; *sakhya,* intimate companionship; *vātsalya,* parental affection; and *mādhurya,* erotic passion. Only in the first of these is Krishna conceived as a transcendent deity; in the remaining four, the devotee is to meditate on him as the darling child and beguiling youth brought up in a community of cowherds. If one comes to Rūpa's plays with some knowledge of his general theory, which centers almost exclusively upon Krishna, one will naturally expect them to illustrate these five modes of relating to the Lord. One may well be initially perplexed, then, by the plays themselves. First, although the various *bhāvas* are indeed represented in them, it is not these but the successive phases in the love of Rādhā and Krishna that provide the major structuring principle. Furthermore, there are numerous indications throughout the dramas that Rādhā's significance for Rūpa goes far beyond that of a model of devotion. In what follows, we shall review this evidence as we explore Rūpa's vision of Rādhā and her relation to Krishna. The intricacy of the arguments reflects the learned style of the plays; however, the wider significance of Rūpa's vision is confirmed by its congruence with the composite picture that emerges in performances of *padāvalī kīrtan.*

Rādhā as Model of Devotion

There is no disputing the fact that Rādhā is for Rūpa an ideal devotee. Indeed, it is hardly possible to speak of Rādhā in his dramas without speaking of her love for Krishna. In a telling verse (*VM* 3.49) in which she is described as his ornament, an image that seems unambiguously to subordinate her to him, she is also said to be herself rendered beautiful by her love. Moreover, throughout the plays it is the explicitly devotional quality of this love, together with its remarkable intensity, that elicits repeated comment. Generally voiced by the main secondary characters—especially Paurṇamāsī, the venerable go-between who personifies the night of the full moon, her granddaughter and companion, Nāndīmukhī, and Vṛndā, the goddess of the forest—these comments serve to communicate Rūpa's religious views and emotions to the audience or reader.

Throughout the two dramas, Rādhā's love expresses itself spontaneously in religious modes that possess considerable significance with respect to devotion. A charming verse contrasts her incessant preoccupation with Krishna, whom she at first endeavors in vain to forget, with the transitory states attained by sages and yogis via their arduous efforts:

> Seeking to meditate for a moment upon Krishna,
> The sage wrests his mind from the objects of sense;
> This child draws her mind away from him
> To fix it on mere worldly things.
> The yogi yearns for a tiny flash of Krishna in his heart;
> Look—this foolish girl strives to banish him from hers!
> (*VM* 2.17)

Here, Rūpa implicitly contrasts two religious ideals, that of passionate devotion (*rāgānugā bhakti*) and that of the ascetic renunciation of passion (yoga, *sannyāsa*). Although Rādhā has attained to the single-minded concentration on Krishna that is sought by (Vaiṣṇava) ascetics, she has done so, paradoxically, not through dispassion but through passion. Moreover, she has achieved this blessed state naturally, without conscious effort.

The obverse of Rādhā's single-minded concentration on Krishna is her utter obliviousness to the world: her friend Lalitā notes with astonishment this sublime condition as she accompanies to a tryst the distracted Rādhā, who has put all her ornaments on wrong.[10] The image of a female yogi is similarly evoked by a tender scene toward the end of the second act of the *Vidagdhamādhava* in which Rādhā's intense desire to see Krishna culminates in a supreme effort to make him appear before her eyes through the force of meditation (*praṇidhāna*).

Further indications of the intensity and devotional quality of Rādhā's love are the numerous passages in both dramas in which she expresses her inability to live if she cannot meet Krishna (*VM* 3.12, for example, or *LM* 3.27–28). At the end of the second act of the *Vidagdhamādhava,* as she contemplates suicide because Krishna has rejected her, she asks her friend Viśākhā to allow her body to remain in Vṛndāvana with her vinelike arm on the trunk of the *tamāla* tree.[11] Early in the next act, when Paurṇamāsī, wishing to elicit an expression of Rādhā's love, deliberately misleads her into thinking that Krishna has refused to meet her, she expresses a similar aspiration: that she might die and be reborn as a bee so that she can hover around Krishna's garland of wildflowers, wholly intent upon his redolent face (*VM* 3.16). Classical Sanskrit dramas abound in examples of pining heroines who express the desire to take their own lives. Here, however, the motif gains new significance, for Rādhā's utterances are indicative of a profound religious devotion that extends even beyond death.

Separation in the *Vidagdhamādhava* is always relatively short-lived, and Rādhā's morbid fantasies never materialize. But Krishna's departure for Mathurā in the third act of the *Lalitamādhava* proves to be too much for her to bear.[12] After giving expression to her extreme grief with such poignancy that Paurṇamāsī declares the entire world to be plunged into a vast ocean of pathos without so much as an island (*LM* 3.23), the disconsolate Rādhā, at the urging of her friends, begins a desperate search.[13] In her obsession with Krishna, she longs for anything that has had contact with him. His necklace of *guñjā* berries becomes a companion in her misery: having graced Krishna's chest as has she herself, it too is now abandoned to roll in despair on the ground (*LM* 3.37). Even Rādhā's former rival, Candrāvalī, is eagerly but vainly sought by her. All else having failed, Rādhā takes refuge in the dark waters of the Yamunā, which resemble Krishna's black limbs, and a voice from the heavens announces that she has pierced the orb of the sun.[14] Apparent death here is merely a change of form, and it is in the guise of the lovely Satyabhāmā that Rādhā is subsequently reunited with Krishna in the heart of Dvārakā, his fastness in western India—a new Vṛndāvana. Evidently, Rūpa could not tolerate the separation brought about by Krishna's departure from Vṛndāvana any more than could Rādhā.

Rādhā's role as model devotee is indicated even more clearly by her responses to the name of Krishna. Even before her first meeting with him, she betrays unmistakable emotion whenever her friends mention him by name, as they do deliberately. It is in this connection that Rūpa reveals most unambiguously the intimate relation between Rādhā's emotion and the experience of ardent Vaiṣṇava devotees. When Nāndīmukhī describes Rādhā's *pūrvarāga,* the first blossoming of her love, by enumerating the effects of Krishna's name on her (*VM* 1.14.30–31), Paurṇamāsī deems Rādhā's response fitting and eloquently expresses her own feelings in the following oft-quoted verse:

Dancing on the tip of your tongue,
they make you long for myriads of mouths,
Alighting in the hollow of your ear,
they make you wish for ears in plentitude,
And when they reach the doorway to your heart,
they still the turbulence of all the senses:
"Krish-na"—just two syllables—
yet how much nectar do they not contain?
(*VM* 1.15)

On the strength of Paurṇamāsī's endorsement, Rādhā's response is explicitly established as an ideal for Vaiṣṇava devotion. That Rādhā also relates more actively to this name of her beloved is indicated by a punning verse in which her friend Viśākhā describes her as constantly uttering the name Krishna (*VM* 2.38). Rūpa thus links Rādhā with Krishna devotees not only on the level of emotion but in the realm of ritual as well, for the repeated utterance or singing of Krishna's name has been a central element in Gauḍīya Vaiṣṇava practice, both individual and communal, at least since the time of Caitanya.[15]

Rādhā as Object of Devotion

The foregoing illustrations of Rādhā's devotion to Krishna, in which Rādhā is clearly portrayed as the ideal devotee, represent only part of the picture. In the first place, for virtually every instance that I have cited, one can find a parallel passage attesting to Krishna's fervent devotion to her. We have observed that Rādhā's single-minded concentration on Krishna is expressed in terms drawn from descriptions of yogic practice; Krishna, too, is on more than one occasion compared to a yogi, for he thinks incessantly upon Rādhā, losing sleep and renouncing all other enjoyments as long as he is deprived of her company.[16] Corresponding to Rādhā's reiterated expression of her utter inability to live without Krishna is a passage in which Krishna likewise acknowledges that he cannot live even for an instant without her (*VM* 3.22). And just as Viśākhā, addressing Rādhā, refers to Krishna as "the lord of your life" (*te jīvitapati, VM* 2.48) so Krishna calls Rādhā a life-giving herb, later confessing to her, "You are my life, O Rādhā!" (*VM* 2.46.1; 5.31).[17] Such parallel expressions of emotion clearly have profound metaphysical implications, to which we shall shortly return.

The intense preoccupation of Rādhā and Krishna with each other is indicated by another set of parallel passages that contain similar metaphysical overtones. So obsessed with Krishna does Rādhā become that she sees him everywhere. When she thus mistakes a black *tamāla* tree for her dark lover, Viśākhā asks her how it is that the three worlds have become Krishna for her.[18] Krishna poses the analogous question for himself as he eagerly awaits Rādhā at their point of rendezvous: "Rādhā appears before me on every side; how is it that for me the three worlds have become Rādhā?" (*VM* 5.18). Rūpa seems to have been especially taken with this mode of indicating Krishna's infatuation, for on two additional occasions he has other characters make virtually the same observation about Krishna's "delusion" (*VM* 3.18; 6.23.20–21). Moreover, it is not only Rādhā in her obsession with Krishna who is explicitly termed "mad" but also Krishna in his unbridled passion for her. At one point, as Krishna is rushing headlong to meet her, Krishna's companion Madhumaṅgala, steadying him, asserts that he has been "maddened (*unmādita*) by an evil spell [uttered] by the wicked *gopī*s" (*VM* 6.14.3–4).

Rādhā's devotion to Krishna at times assumes worshipful forms, such that she is aptly called his worshiper (*ārādhikā*).[19] Similarly, certain of Krishna's words and actions are clearly intended to suggest modes of adoration. In their first full meeting, for example, Krishna expresses the desire to be in the nectar of Rādhā's favor (*VM* 3.43.3), using the word *prasāda,* "grace," a term that has strong religious connotations. Lalitā's reply, that he may obtain Rādhā's favor by serving her (*sevā*), is likewise significant, for *sevā* is the usual Vaiṣṇava term for service to the Lord.[20] Krishna is more than willing: the verse he utters in response enumerates the ways in which he proposes to adorn and minister to her (*VM* 3.44). Later in the play, when Krishna tries to appease Rādhā after he has spent the night with Candrāvalī, he indicates his penitence by making obeisance again and again, his peacock-feather headdress touching the dust (*VM* 4.46; see figure 14). Still later, seeing his own worshipful gestures replicated in the world of nature, he describes to Rādhā an expanse of lotuses rippled by the breeze as "doing *āratī* to your smiling face."[21]

Even in the case of the most explicitly devotional element in Rādhā's relation to Krishna—her response to his name—there are remarkably close parallels. In the sixth act of the *Vidagdhamādhava,* when Madhumaṅgala promises to bring Rādhā, who is hiding, to Krishna but gives him instead a leaf inscribed with the two syllables of her name, Krishna expresses his utter delight at this gift, in a verse that is strongly reminiscent of Paurṇamāsī's rapturous words about *his* name (*VM* 6.24). Paurṇamāsī herself, shortly after uttering the verse exclaiming over Krishna's name, speaks of Rādhā's with no less enthusiasm as she proposes to entice Krishna with its auspicious syllables (*VM* 1.16.6–7). In the light of Paurṇamāsī's devotion to Rādhā, which is made explicit, as we shall see below, at numerous points in the dramas, this passage may reasonably be construed as signifying that Rādhā's name is sweet not only to Krishna but also to Paurṇamāsī, and thus to Vaiṣṇava devotees as a whole.

The view of Rādhā as figuring in the dramas solely or even primarily as the ideal embodiment of devotion to Krishna is challenged not only by Krishna's equal degree of devotion to her but also by a second body

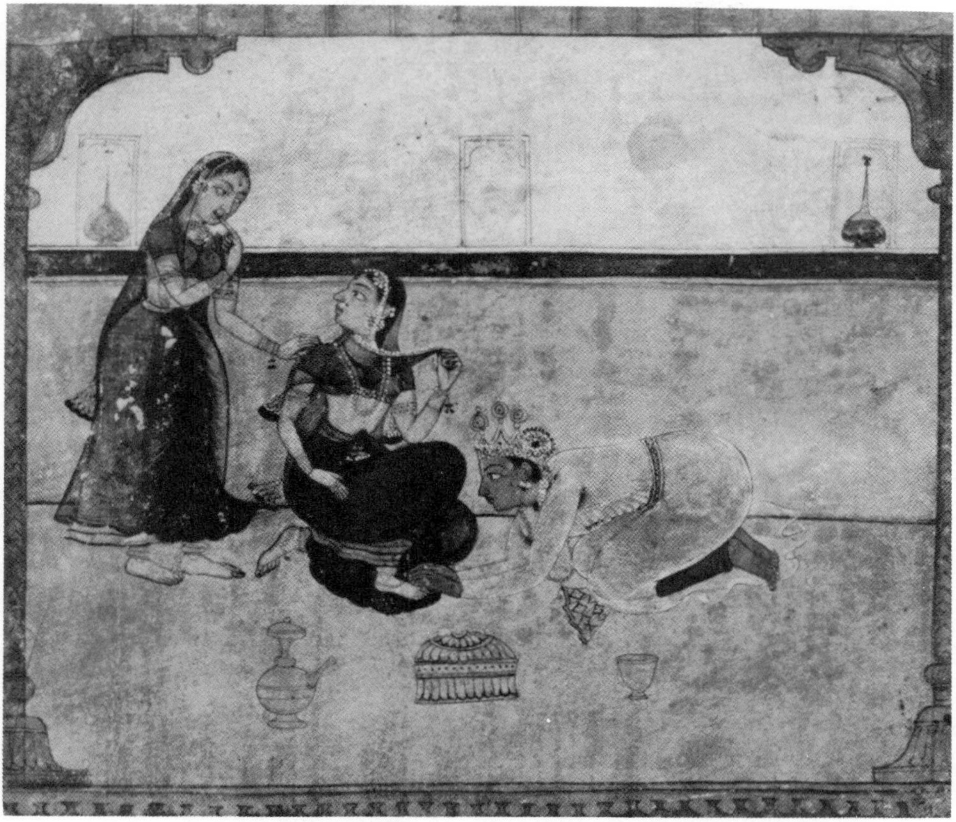

Figure 14. Krishna kneeling to take dust off Rādhā's feet. Detached illustration from a manuscript of subimperial Mughul style, ca. 1610–20. Ross Collection, Museum of Fine Arts, Boston.

of evidence: the attitudes expressed by such secondary characters as Paurṇamāsī and Vṛndā, whose responses to Rādhā as well as to Krishna exhibit strong devotional elements. In the introductory scene in Act I of the *Vidagdhamādhava,* Nāndīmukhī expresses envy of Paurṇamāsī's grandson Madhumaṅgala, who is privileged to enjoy Krishna's constant company. Paurṇamāsī's reply indicates that Nāndīmukhī's task—namely, to increase Rādhā's passion for Krishna—is no less a privilege, for Rādhā, Paurṇamāsī confesses, means everything to her (*VM* 1.14.25). In a later conversation with Madhumaṅgala and Vṛndā, Paurṇamāsī reaffirms her deep love for Rādhā, comparing her feeling in its spontaneity and lack of ulterior motive with Rādhā's love for Krishna (*VM* 5.2.10–5.4.4).

The devotional significance of Rādhā for Paurṇamāsī, and by extension for the devotee who sees or reads this drama, is likewise evident from Paurṇamāsī's words of gratitude to Krishna at the end of the final act. When Abhimanyu is persuaded not to take Rādhā to Mathurā, Paurṇamāsī exclaims with considerable relief that she has been spared the pain of separation from Rādhā (*rādhikāviśleṣavedanā, VM* 7.59.3). Her statement and the threatened separation that it reflects constitute a reversal of the situation of the *gopīs* depicted in the *Bhāgavata Purāṇa* and the *Lalitamādhava,* in which it is Krishna who is taken to Mathurā and the *gopīs* who experience the anguish of separation.

Paurṇamāsī is not the only secondary character in the drama who expresses emotions toward Rādhā that are more commonly directed toward Krishna. In a beautiful verse uttered in amazement in the final act of the *Vidagdhamādhava,* Vṛndā juxtaposes Rādhā's youth with her maturity in love, exhibiting a parental tenderness (*vātsalya*) toward Rādhā that is reminiscent of Yaśodā's maternal affection for Krishna:

Just yesterday she was playing in the dust,
  her ears newly pierced,
Her hair, barely as long as a cow's ear,
  tied with a colored thread;
Oh, where has this Rādhā learned such proficiency
  in the ways of love
That she has conquered the unconquerable!
(*VM* 7.44)

In the *Lalitamādhava,* Yaśodā herself expresses *vātsalya* toward Rādhā, whom she terms *vatsā laghvī,* "my dear little child," comparing her to Krishna in the delight that seeing her gives. Paurṇamāsī replies that all the inhabitants of Gokula feel a comparable delight (*LM* 1.42.15–19).

Vātsalya is not the only mode of devotion to Krishna specified in Rūpa's theory that is also exemplified by certain characters in their relations to Rādhā. Both *sakhya* and *dāsya,* friendship and servitude, are likewise directed toward Rādhā as well as toward Krishna. Indeed, although Krishna's fellow cowherds and his humorous companion Madhumaṅgala demonstrate *sakhya* toward him, this mode is most fully represented by the love for her of Rādhā's two close friends, Lalitā and Viśākhā. In addition to promoting her love affair with Krishna, they elicit the expression of her deepest feelings, as well as portraying externally, through their conflicting advice, aspects of her inner struggle. Their tender concern for her well-being is manifest especially at times of crisis, when her anguish leads to loss of consciousness and seems to threaten her very life (for example, *LM* 3.18; 3.33.1–2). The strength of Lalitā's affection is revealed most fully in her expressions of grief at the loss of Rādhā: her distress is in fact comparable to Rādhā's own agony at Krishna's departure (*LM* 3.54.23–28; cf. *LM* 6.36).

Although Rūpa gives considerable attention to the *sakhīs* (girlfriends, especially of Rādhā) in his *Ujjvalanīlamaṇi,* he speaks of *sakhya* in his *Bhaktirasāmṛtasindhu* exclusively in relation to Krishna. This is a puzzling fact, given the examples that we have just surveyed, as well as Rūpa's theoretical exposition of *dāsya.* In *Bhaktirasāmṛtasindhu* 3.2, he identifies three kinds of servants: those devoted to Krishna and his beloved women, those devoted to one of these women, and those who serve Krishna alone. When Satyabhāmā-Rādhā arrives in Dvārakā, she is entrusted to the care of Navavṛndā, who is requested to serve her, a duty that is said to be conducive to the welfare of all (*LM* 6.20). Lalitā's all-consuming desire in her separation from Rādhā and Krishna is also to serve Rādhā and to fan the two of them when they are together (*LM* 6.41). Both Navavṛndā's assignment and Lalitā's yearning for servitude anticipate the attitude of the youthful maidservant (*mañjarī*) of subsequent Vaiṣṇava tradition who attends Rādhā and Krishna in their lovemaking. Thus, both the prominent role of Rādhā's girlfriends and the emerging figure of the maidservant in Rūpa's dramas qualify, through their primary relation to Rādhā, the virtually exclusive emphasis on Krishna represented by his theory of *bhaktirasa.*

Krishna as a Model of Devotion

We have seen that Rādhā does indeed serve as a model of devotion to Krishna, but that her significance is not exhausted by this role, for she is also an object of the devotion both of Krishna and of certain important secondary characters. That the roles of model and object need not be mutually exclusive is clear from the fact that Krishna himself periodically serves as a model for the devotee. He several times expresses wonder at Rādhā's great love, most memorably on one occasion to Madhumaṅgala as he tearfully overhears Rādhā's declaration to her friends of her unwavering devotion (*VM* 2.47.1). Moreover, after he is taken from Vṛndāvana, he repeatedly proclaims his preference for its qualities and inhabitants over those of any other realm.

The most remarkable demonstration of this preference, which is clearly Rūpa's as well, is Krishna's response to a play depicting his encounter with Rādhā in Vṛndāvana that is staged for him in Mathurā at Nārada's direction by a heavenly troupe of actors, in order to keep him from becoming disconsolate. Krishna's attraction to the actor playing the role of Mādhava, the Krishna of Vṛndāvana, is so strong that he utterly forgets who he is and has to be constrained from rushing headlong toward the stage to embrace his alter ego. As he watches the play unfold, he voices the desire to become a *gopī* in order that he might participate in the love sports, and he later muses over the fact that the play afforded him the same bliss as did the experiences it represented (*LM* 4.32.68–69).[22] In each of these reactions, it becomes clear that not only Rādhā but Krishna too is a model for human devotees: in this respect they have a surprisingly parallel status.

Earthly yet Sublime: The Nature of Rādhā's Love

We have observed the devotional quality of Rādhā's love for Krishna as well as the wonder that it evokes in him. To appreciate more fully her significance for Vaiṣṇava devotion, we must now look more closely at the nature of her love.

Although Rūpa in his *Ujjvalanīlamaṇi* emphasizes the uniqueness of Rādhā's love, its expression in his dramas reveals certain characteristically human qualities. Among these are her hesitancy to show her feelings even to her two close friends, her shyness, especially in her early encounters with Krishna, and the unmistakably human apprehension that she will be found unworthy of his affection. Early in their courtship she is still sufficiently respectful to be initially horrified at Lalitā's suggestion that she play a joke on Krishna (*VM* 3.34.7–10), and only later does she herself take the initiative in such teasing by hiding from him (*VM* 6.23.3–5; *VM* 7.36).

Likewise identifiably human are Rādhā's inner conflicts, which Rūpa portrays with admirable sensitivity. As her passion grows, she is torn between her love for Krishna and her dharma as a married woman (*VM* 1.34; *VM* 3.18; cf. *LM* 2.25). Subsequently, in response to his unfaithfulness, she comes to know the anguish of *māna,* often weakly translated as "pique," in which pride and jealous anger struggle in her heart against the intense desire for reconciliation.[23] Suddenly bereft of her company when she is in this latter state, Krishna reflects on her conflicting moods in the following poignant verse:

> Now assuming a steadfast pose,
> now showing signs of wavering,
> One moment uttering scornful sounds,
> the next, words of eagerness,
> Now with a look of innocence,
> now with a glance bewitching
> Rādhikā is split in two
> swayed now by anger, now by love.
> (*VM* 4.51)

Rādhā's warm humanness, evident throughout Rūpa's dramas, renders her eminently accessible to Vaiṣṇava devotees. Yet the plays themselves, as well as Rūpa's theory, also point in numerous ways to her transcendence. The remarkable intensity of her love makes it an object of perpetual wonder to those around her; she is by turns called foolish and mad (*VM* 2.0.11; 6.8.44). Her agonized frenzy at Krishna's departure for Mathurā Rūpa calls *divyonmāda,* "divine madness."[24] Rādhā herself, as well as those who observe her, describes her state as fundamentally incomprehensible.

Two other terms applied to Rādhā's love in the *Vidagdhamādhava* are *sahaja* and *svābhāvika,* both of which mean "natural."[25] Rādhā's spontaneity is clearly of paramount important for Rūpa. Her relative lack of conventional restraint allows her to be far more intimate with Krishna than her more docile rival. In his *Ujjvalanīlamaṇi,* Rūpa designates Candrāvalī's love by the term *ghṛtasneha,* love that is like clarified butter, and he repeatedly refers to the respect (*ādara*) that is its chief characteristic. Rādhā's love, by contrast, is called *madhusneha,* love that is like honey; instead of respect, it is characterized by a sense of possessing the beloved (*madīyatva*).[26] Its bold, playful ways and their effect on Krishna can best be seen in two successive verses from the final act of the *Vidagdhamādhava:*

> Words of protest filled with passion,
> Gestures of resistance lacking force,
> Frowns transmuted into smiles,
> Crying dry of tears—friend,
> Though Rādhā seeks to hide her feelings,
> Each attempt betrays her heart's
> Deep love for demon Mura's slayer.
>
> Bold employ of teeth and nails
> By one experienced in love sports:
> Rādhā's show of opposition
> Gives Hari immeasurable delight.
>
> (*VM* 7.38–39)

Unlike Candrāvalī, whose deferential reserve indicates greater awareness of Krishna's lordly majesty (*aiśvarya*) and constrains him to show similar courtesy toward her, Rādhā responds primarily to Krishna's sweet charm (*mādhurya*), and their more intimate love affords him the greater delight.

In addition to the wonder repeatedly evinced at her incomparable love, Rādhā's transcendence is indicated by certain adjectives and other expressions found throughout the dramas. Krishna calls her *jagadapūrvā,* "unprecented in the world" (*VM* 1.31.68), and her qualities are elsewhere termed *lokottara,* "extraordinary" or "transcendent" (*VM* 1.13; 3.21.19). Greatness in general is predicated of her by means of two synonymous terms, *mahiman* and *māhātmya* (*VM* 2.31.4; 3.12.1; *LM* 3.55), while her cosmic significance is strongly suggested by certain passages in the *Lalitamādhava* in which the effects of her actions, like Krishna's, are said to extend to the entire universe.[27] Finally, taking full advantage of the fact that the word *rādhā* designates a constellation, Rūpa several times puns on her name in a way that again hints at her cosmic stature (*VM* 1.31.58–59; 4.11; 5.29; 6.2.29–31; *LM* 2.22).

The metaphysical implications of the devotional parallels that we have noted earlier should by now have become clear. Just as Rādhā's demented state, in which she sees Krishna everywhere, perceiving nothing else in the three worlds, is a metaphysically accurate apprehension of reality—for Krishna, the Lord, is the reality behind everything in the universe—so the "deluding" effects of his parallel bewitchment may be taken as veridical if Rādhā is recognized as his *śakti,* who, with him, pervades the whole world. The conviction of Rādhā and Krishna that each is the life of the other may correspondingly be interpreted as hinting at their metaphysical equality as well as affirming their intimate interdependence. We have observed that both Rūpa and his nephew Jīva assert in their theological treatises that Rādhā is the *hlādinī śakti* of Krishna, his "blissful potency." Rūpa further states explicitly that Rādhā should be worshipped, indeed that her worship is as important as that of Krishna himself.[28]

Thus, metaphysically Rādhā is understood as consubstantial and coeternal with Krishna; moreover, in at least one important respect she is superior to him. Not only is her exclusive devotion to Krishna unique in Vraja; it is even declared to surpass Krishna's love for her. Just as the proud scholar Uddhava in the *Bhāgavata Purāṇa* comes to acknowledge the superiority of the *gopī*s' love for Krishna to his own more arid religious realization, so Krishna himself in Rūpa's dramas pays wondering homage to Rādhā's love. That love in fact wins a double victory, for it not only exceeds his but wholly captivates him, the "invincible" Lord to whom is subject the entire universe. As much as her love itself, the paradox of Rādhā's inexplicable power over Krishna repeatedly evokes astonishment and delight.

That it is in her love that Rādhā surpasses Krishna is highly significant. It is this love, rather than Krishna or Rādhā alone, that is relished by the other characters in the dramas, certain of whom are clearly model devotees. In the final act of the *Vidagdhamādhava,* Vṛndā exclaims to Paurṇamāsī:

What supreme enjoyment arises
    when Krishna and Rādhā are united!
Who could cease to tell of that
    quintessence of erotic mood
Save one speechless utterly
    with ecstasy?

(*VM* 7.2)

Through her great love, made manifest in songs, in poems, in vernacular plays, and in dramas such as Rūpa's, Rādhā affords Vaiṣṇava devotees a means of access to Krishna. She is necessary not because the Lord is conceived as unapproachable (as is often the case in religious traditions in which a mediator plays a prominent role), for it is not Krishna's majestic otherness (*aiśvarya*) that is paramount for Gauḍīya Vaiṣṇavas but rather his exquisite sweetness (*mādhurya*). Something quite different is clearly at work here. Rādhā is necessary because love requires two, because sweetness needs "another" to taste it.[29]

There are several indications in Rūpa's works that love itself is what is absolute. Its experience by the devotee is valued above all else; in the plays the importance of manifesting the mutual passion of Rādhā and Krishna outweighs all other considerations, even the pain that temporary deception may cause them. Furthermore, expressions used to designate Rādhā's emotion, such as *durūha* or *durvibodha,* "difficult to fathom" or "incomprehensible," are reminiscent of terms earlier applied to *ātman* or *brahman,* the "self" or the absolute referred to throughout the Upaniṣads and discussed in much subsequent Indian philosophy. It is significant that the absolute for Rūpa is not a metaphysical principle but an emotion; it with such love, and not with *brahman,* that unity is sought. Rādhā, as love embodied, is thus the supreme avenue of religious realization.

The love of Rādhā and Krishna is a subtle interplay of freedom and commitment, spontaneity and constancy. If we envision these poles as opposite ends of a continuum, we may place Krishna nearer the freedom end and Rādhā nearer that of commitment. Yet each partakes to some degree of the other's predominant quality. Rādhā's love as it emerges in Rūpa's dramas incorporates elements of freedom in two ways. It is at least outwardly *parakīyā,* love free from the constraints of marriage, for she is wed to Abhimanyu in the *Vidagdhamādhava* and her love affair with Krishna in the *Lalitamādhava* must be concealed from his ever vigilant queen.[30] Moreover, as we have observed, her love shows spontaneity in its intimacy and its lack of deference. Nevertheless, its complete steadfastness puts it closer to the opposite pole.

Krishna, in contrast, exhibits almost total freedom. Although his irresistible attraction to Rādhā leads to an uncharacteristic single-mindedness, his love for her is never wholly exclusive. This perpetual fickleness on his part represents both the universality of divine love, which is as diffuse and varied as the many degrees to and ways in which he is loved, and his transcendence of all conventional boundaries.

Why should commitment in love be preferred over freedom? For the Vaiṣṇava, the highest religious ideal is the sweetness of perpetual relatedness to the divine, rather than the release from all bondage that the goal of *mokṣa* represents.[31] It is thus not surprising that Rūpa accords highest praise to Rādhā's love. If steadfast love is what is ultimate, then Rādhā—its supreme embodiment—can have no rival.

RĀDHĀ IN PADĀVALĪ KĪRTAN

So far we have been coming to know Rādhā through the medium of Sanskrit—and a highly stylized Sanskrit at that—but by far the greatest body of material that we have about her is written in the vernacular languages of North India. Especially significant are the medieval song lyrics (*padas*) composed on the Rādhā-Krishna theme in Hindi, Bengali, and an artificial hybrid language combining the two, Brajabuli. Although most of these songs date from the fourteenth through the seventeenth centuries, those in Bengali and Brajabuli in particular continue to be sung today, especially in West Bengal, in a complex but widespread form of devotional performance. Because its structuring elements are the lyrical songs known as *padas*, this musical form is called *padāvalī kīrtan.* Its two broad themes are the love of Rādhā and Krishna and the life of the ecstatic mystic Caitanya. Episodes (*pālās*) depicting the first of these themes paint a somewhat different and more widely disseminated portrait of Rādhā than the one presented in Rūpa's Sanskrit plays.[32]

A *kīrtan* troupe typically consists of a lead singer, who may be either male or female, several supporting singers, who are usually of the same sex as the lead singer, and two or sometimes three male drummers who play on both ends of elongated, barrel-shaped drums suspended from straps around their necks. In a performance, the lead singer and his or her troupe stage a kind of musical drama—containing elements of dance—that centers on a single devotional theme. For some three or four hours, to the nearly constant background rhythm of drums and small brass hand cymbals, the lead singer spins out a narrative, punctuating the story at intervals with songs based on the medieval lyric poems called *padāvalī.* The performance area, often located in the center of an audience of devotees who sit on the floor in a circular arrangement, is bare of scenery. The only props used are the lead singer's shawl, which is sometimes pulled over the head to resemble a sari, and perhaps the garland of flowers with which a lead singer is often honored.

Even operating within these spare means, however, a skilled singer can create a powerful drama through effective timing, the expressive power of such musical elements as variations in tempo and dynamic level, the subtle or expansive use of gesture, and the visual and kinesthetic reinforcement of aurally perceived rhythms provided by dance. It is mainly the lead singer who tells and enacts the story, but the supporting singers also use gesture as they echo the lines of the lead performer in antiphonal fashion. With their highly trained fingers the drummers beat out intricate patterns—every bit as complex as those of the major classical traditions—on the two leather heads of their slender drums, amplifying these at intervals by sharply articulated vocal sounds. These include the elaborate syllabic patterns (*bols*) that are used in learning the various musical meters, as well as such exclamations as "*haiya*"—sounds apparently drawn from boatmen's songs. In addition to their strong hand and arm movements and the dramatic swinging of their heads, the drummers often dance vigorously with the lead singer during the songs, with the supporting singers, most of whom keep time with hand cymbals, sometimes joining in the dance as well.

Kīrtan singers portray Rādhā entangled in a web of emotional relationships in which her love for Krishna unfolds, and the successive phases of her love for him provide the themes of some of the most popular episodes enacted in *kīrtan.* These episodes include a range of occasions on which the two are united, as well as various situations of separation. But it is in the episodes of separation that Rādhā's nature is most fully revealed.

We have seen that *kīrtan* is a powerful medium for conveying and evoking emotions. An expressive singer is able to move an audience of devotees profoundly, gathering them up in the deep love of the other characters toward Rādhā, as well as in Rādhā's own agony and longing.[33] Accordingly, as we look at episodes representing Rādhā in each of the four types of separation identified in Rūpa's theory, we shall focus both on Rādhā's expressions of her own emotions and on the emotional responses of other characters in the drama to her. As we do so, we shall discern a number of basic similarities to her depiction in Rūpa's plays, as well as ways in which the tradition of vernacular performance has given her a stronger, far less restrained voice.

As in the case of the Sanskrit dramas we have surveyed, Rūpa Gosvāmī's theological writings once again provide us with a helpful structure. In his *Bhaktirasāmṛtasindhu,* Rūpa describes four modes of separation that figure in erotic love. For each of these modes, I give first a rough English approximation, then the Sanskrit term, and finally a fuller and more precise English description:

1. Infatuation (*pūrvarāga*), Rādhā's and Krishna's erotic yearning that precedes their first full union;
2. Pique (*māna*), Rādhā's mixed emotions—including anger, jealousy, hurt, and deep longing—that follow upon each revelation of Krishna's betrayal;
3. Bewilderment (*premavaicittya*), Rādhā's temporary delusion, caused by the depth of her love, in which she thinks Krishna has left her when he is right in front of her eyes; and
4. Abandonment (*pravāsa*), Rādhā's anguished state when Krishna has in fact left her forever to fulfill his mission of slaying the demon-king Kaṃsa.

We meet three of these in particular—infatuation, pique, and abandonment—in modern Bengali *padāvalī* performances, and it is not entirely accidental that we do, for these rubrics were used to classify the medieval poems in the numerous Vaiṣṇava anthologies from which the leaders of *kīrtan* troupes draw in constructing their *pālās*. The more classically trained lead singers in fact quote regularly from Rūpa's Sanskrit treatises. All singers of *kīrtan,* in attempting to provide for their audiences as full a depiction as possible of the love between Rādhā and Krishna, quite naturally take up each mode—and take them up repeatedly.

Infatuation: Pūrvarāga

Through poems and performances that portray Rādhā's response to hearing the sound of Krishna's flute, seeing his picture, or glimpsing him from afar or in the company of her elders, the poets and singers of *kīrtan* convey the tender feelings of a young girl in love for the first time. The threshold on which she stands is represented at times by an internal conflict, at times by an alternation between the boldness of girlhood and the modesty of womanhood. Her friends and the elders of the community are perplexed by her bizarre behavior: she sighs repeatedly, moves about restlessly, suddenly takes off her jewels only to put them on again, and looks again and again at a nearby grove of *kadamba* trees.[34] In verses describing the later stages of infatuation, she confides in her friends, expressing her intense inner conflict, for the irresistible attraction that she feels for Krishna threatens her standing as a respectable married woman bound by the strictures of dharma.

Krishna, too, is deeply affected by his first sight of Rādhā, and verses in which he describes her beauty reveal his infatuation with her. Far from being a powerful deity in relation to her, he is depicted as a lovelorn youth pining for another glimpse of his beloved. Her friends, who come to him as messengers, take advantage of Krishna's lovesick condition to make explicit comparisons between the two lovers—always, of course, at Krishna's expense. In a series of theological paradoxes, they highlight the wonder of Rādhā's inexplicable power over the Lord of the universe:

> You charm the whole world, it's true,
> But Rādhā's charm captivates you.
> The worlds pay you homage, it's true,
> But a mere glimpse of Rādhā and your heart is lost.
> Your songs and your flute attract the three worlds,
> But Rādhā's words put all these to flight.
> You pervade the world with fragrance, it's true,
> But our Rādhā's perfume steals away your heart.[35]

In addition to conveying the emotions of the two chief characters in the unfolding drama, the lead performer expresses the responses of Rādhā's friends to her lovelorn condition. In a song based on a famous poem attributed to Caṇḍidās, for example, the lines of commentary termed *ākhar,* which alternate with those of the original poem, meditate with deep feeling upon Rādhā's state. The author utilizes the classical comparison of the woman in love to a *yoginī,* a woman adept in the techniques of yogic meditation. The poem opens by asking what deep pain is afflicting Rādhā and goes on to describe her strange behavior: she sits alone and does not hear anything people say to her; she stares intently at the dark clouds; she refuses to eat; and she wears a brick-red sari, the color of the garments worn by ascetics but also, by deliberate ambiguity, the color of a wedding sari.[36]

Quite a new perspective is furnished by the commentary lines that amplify and interpret the lines of the original poem in performance. In addition to translating the medieval Bengali of Caṇḍidās into a more modern idiom, these lines, clearly spoken by someone who cares deeply for Rādhā, most probably one of her intimate friends, respond to her condition with tender concern. At a moment of particular musical intensity, we hear her friend's cry of anguish in response to the poet's revelation that Rādhā is refusing food:

> Oh, alas, I die to consider:
> How long can she live
> If she won't eat or drink?[37]

Although the words come from her friend, the mode of devotional love is *vātsalya,* a parental and specifically maternal concern for Rādhā's wellbeing. This element of emotional response in the commentary is an extension of the original poem; through it the lead singer invites the audience to participate imaginatively and emotionally in the story.

Pique: Māna

The remarkable subtlety and complexity of the emotions presented in *kīrtan* is nowhere better illustrated than in episodes representing Rādhā's sulking anger when Krishna seems to have deserted her. There are two such episodes, "The Offended Heroine" (*Khaṇḍitā*), in which Rādhā gradually detects on her lover's body the signs of his infidelity, and "The Lovers' Quarrel" (*Kalahāntaritā*), in which Rādhā's friends convey messages back and forth between the estranged lovers, who, though hurt and angry, nevertheless yearn to be reunited.

The episode of the offended heroine takes place at dawn. Krishna, his body bearing the marks of the night's lovemaking with another woman, usually Rādhā's chief rival, Candrāvalī, arrives at the grove in which Rādhā has spent the night waiting in vain for him. Rādhā at first fails to recognize him, mistaking him in his sandal-paste-besmeared condition for his fair-skinned elder brother, Balarāma. Her friend Lalitā, however, soon figures out who he is. Wishing to do her duty in welcoming him, because he is Rādhā's beloved, but fearing Rādhā's displeasure should she be too friendly, she offers him a seat just outside their bower. Krishna, however, fails to comprehend the significance of the liminal place that has been assigned to him. Relieved to be accepted into their company, he abandons the stance of abject apology with which he has resolved to approach them. Rādhā, still in the dark about the identity of her visitor, greets him politely and inquires about Balarāma's mother. Krishna, hurt because Rādhā has not recognized him, now reveals his identity, and Rādhā lapses into a stunned silence.

During the remainder of the *pāla,* the lead singer uses various means to express Rādhā's ambivalence. Angry and deeply hurt, she still longs to forgive Krishna and take him back. At times she is sarcastic; at others she voices her hurt and resentment, for example by enumerating all the preparations that she had made for Krishna's arrival throughout the long night. Little by little she recognizes the signs of his night's enjoyment, but Krishna denies her accusations, alleging that he has merely been worshiping the goddess Gaurī. Finally, when Rādhā vents her anger directly, Krishna falls at her feet and begs for pardon. But then, just when she decides to relent, Candrāvalī's messenger arrives and demands that Krishna return Candrāvalī's anklet. Rādhā is furious and leaves without forgiving Krishna.

The sequel to "The Offended Heroine" is "The Lovers' Quarrel," in which Rādhā's friends serve as messengers, attempting to bring about a reconciliation between the estranged lovers. Their role is more complex, however, and at least to a Westerner aspects of it are somewhat puzzling. They question Rādhā about her reasons for rejecting Krishna, eliciting expressions of sorrow and regret from her and deliberately intensifying those emotions. They reproach her mercilessly, causing her to weep piteously because of what she has done. Even the lead singer appears perplexed: noting how pale she has become, he asks whether her friends should make her cry any longer. Yet he goes on to offer a religious explanation: the more she cries, the more distinct is the possibility that she will be reunited with Krishna, just as the devotee who cries out of longing for Krishna will surely attain him.

Such an interpretation appears to presuppose that Rādhā represents the devotee, whose love for Krishna must be increased and purified. Yet, somewhat surprisingly, Rādhā's messenger Brindā is equally assiduous in fanning the flames of Krishna's remorse and tells him that he, too, will have to cry for a long time before he can be reunited with Rādhā. Both of them are made to see what they have lost, both experience intense anguish, and both are suitably contrite. Rādhā's friends play a crucial role throughout the episode in developing and making manifest the emotions of Rādhā and Krishna, thus involving the audience both cognitively and emotionally in the divine drama. It is clear from the performances that it is not simply toward Krishna that the devotee's emotions are directed, as one might infer from Rūpa's theory, but rather toward Rādhā as well.

Bewilderment: Premavaicittya

In contrast to the other three forms of love in separation—infatuation, pique, and abandonment—no tradition of performances exists on the theme of Rādhā's bewilderment. There are, however, striking verses on this theme in the anthologies of medieval Vaiṣṇava songs, and this form of separation is portrayed in the fifth act of Rūpa's *Vidagdhamādhava*. An especially lovely verse illustrating Rādhā's paradoxical experience of separation in the very lap of love is attributed to the poet Govindadāsa:

> When they had made love
> she lay in his arms in the *kunja* grove.
> Suddenly she called his name
> and wept—as if she burned in the fire of
> separation.
>   The gold was in her *anchal*
>   but she looked afar for it!
> Where has he gone? Where has my love gone?
> O why has he left me alone?
> And she writhed on the ground in despair,
> only her pain kept her from fainting.
> Krishna was astonished
> and could not speak.
>
> Taking her beloved friend by the hand,
> Govinda-dāsa led her softly away.[38]

Here, too, it is evident that Rādhā, along with Krishna, is the object of intense devotional emotion: Krishna himself serves as a model for the wonder that the devotee should feel at the depth of Rādhā's love.

Abandonment: Pravāsa

Among the most intense *kīrtan* performances are those that portray the cowherd village of Vraja, where Krishna has grown up, in the wake of his departure for the city of Mathurā, where he must fulfill his destiny by slaying the demon-king Kaṃsa. The convergence of the feelings of all those whom he has left behind renders performances on this theme especially powerful, and it is not surprising that "Abandonment" (*Māthur*), the episode depicting that moment, is the one most frequently sung during rituals commemorating the dead. *Kīrtan* was until fairly recently a mandatory element in such rituals, not only for Vaiṣṇavas but for devotees of Śiva, Kālī, and Durgā, and indeed for all Bengali Hindus as well.

Renderings of *Māthur* provide a focus and an outlet for grief. As the lead performer sings and enacts the anguish of Krishna's foster parents, his close friends, his beloved Rādhā, and indeed *all* the women of the village, devotees weep openly, sometimes uncontrollably. As we have seen in the other forms of love in separation, moreover, the devotee's emotions are here directed by the secondary characters and by the lead singer not simply toward Krishna but toward Rādhā as well. Here, too, devotees are not merely striving to emulate Rādhā; rather, they find maternal feelings toward her evoked within them in response to the extremity of her suffering.

Both in Rūpa's dramas and in *kīrtan,* the vicissitudes of Rādhā's and Krishna's love, and especially Krishna's infidelity, cause Rādhā to come repeatedly into conflict with Krishna. In Rūpa's plays, based in part on the conventions of the classical Sanskrit theater, Rādhā maintains her attitude of restraint in all such scenes. In *kīrtan,* however, she is capable of using the direct, earthy language of a village woman to abuse her unfaithful lover. Her modes of conquest thus move from captivation and wonder in Rūpa's plays to humiliation and verbal defeat in *kīrtan.* So thoroughly does she shame him in a rendering of "The Lovers' Quarrel" by one famous performer, Nanda Kishor Das, that the singer himself actually expresses pity for the abject Krishna. Because of his great love for Rādhā, she and her friends are able in such situations to defeat and humiliate the Lord of the universe himself.

CONCLUDING REFLECTIONS

In our survey of certain poems, songs, narration, and dialogue found in *kīrtan* performances, we have seen that the emotions portrayed are subtle and varied. As we noted in the case of Rūpa's plays, the theory of devotional aesthetics (*bhaktirasa*) articulated by Rūpa Gosvāmī provides a convenient, indeed an essential, starting point for interpreting these performances. Yet in one significant respect that theory does not fit the *kīrtan* performances we have considered. According to Rūpa's *Bhaktirasāmṛtasindhu,* the focus of the devotee's emotions should clearly be Krishna, not Rādhā. *Vātsalya bhāva,* for example, is tender parental affection for him. Yet we have seen that *kīrtan* troupes present Rādhā as an equally important object of the devotee's emotions, including *vātsalya bhāva,* and—quite remarkably—we find the same dual focus in Rūpa's own dramas. This evidence points to a disparity between a more orthodox theory of Vaiṣṇava devotional aesthetics deriving largely from the Krishna-centric *Bhāgavata Purāṇa* and a more popular literary and dramatic tradition that has flourished in greater Bengal as well as in Braj, in which devotional emotion is directed toward a divine-human couple, rather than a single male deity. Moreover, as their relationship is played out in the earthly arena, the balance of power often tilts toward Rādhā.

Within lived Vaiṣṇava religion, therefore, especially in Bengal, Rādhā looms far greater in relation to Krishna than most Sanskrit treatises on the subject would lead us to expect. Her divinity, however, is not primarily an elevated status, a position that transcends the merely human by means of ontological difference. Her divine nature lies rather in an exaltation and transfiguration of some of the most basic and archetypal of human emotions. Indeed, two of her most important designations, *mahābhāva* ("great feeling") and *premabhakti* ("the devotion of selfless love"), point not to metaphysical qualities but rather to the intensity and purity of her love. Accordingly, her devotees do not typically relate to Rādhā by petitioning her for earthly favors, or even—at least primarily—by prayer, but by becoming absorbed in the unfolding, minutely detailed story of her love for her Lord.[39]

Finally, there is the fascinating question of Rādhā's relation to real women in real societies, in Bengal and elsewhere. To what extent have her strength as a woman and her audacity toward her lover served as a model for women, especially in their relationships with their husbands? Preliminary findings in my research in West Bengal indicate that one cannot get at this issue directly: when asked whether they aspired to be like Rādhā, most of the Bengali women I interviewed responded that they could never be like her, for Rādhā is a goddess, whereas they are mere mortals. However, the pervasiveness of the Rādhā-Krishna theme in Bengali culture down to the present day, which is evident especially in popular love songs, suggests that her influence on Bengali society, though subtle, has been both profound and enduring. Rādhā may not command literal imitation in Bengal, but her profile as the ideal lover—and also as the ideal devotee—establishes a standard against which all human behavior may be measured.

NOTES

1. See, for example, W. G. Archer, *The Loves of Krishna in Indian Painting and Poetry* (London: George Allen and Unwin, 1957), in which he describes Rādhā as "the loveliest of all the cowgirls" (p. 72).

2. The Purāṇic sources include the *Viṣṇu Purāṇa* (ca. 5th century C.E.) and the widely influential *Bhāgavata Purāṇa* (ca. 8th century C.E.), as well as the *Harivaṃśa* (ca. 3d century C.E.). Although Rādhā does not appear by name in any of these, she has often been identified with Krishna's unnamed favorite who appears in the *Bhāgavata Purāṇa* (10.29–33).

3. For a discussion of Rādhā in the medieval Hindi poetry of Sūr Dās, see John S. Hawley, *Sūr Dās: Poet, Singer, Saint* (Seattle: University of Washington Press, 1984), chap. 3.

4. See Barbara S. Miller, "Rādhā: Consort of Kṛṣṇa's Vernal Passion," *Journal of the American Oriental Society* 95, no. 4 (1975):655–71.

5. On Pārvatī, see Wendy Doniger O'Flaherty, "The Shifting Balance of Power in the Marriage of Śiva and Pārvatī," in *The Divine Consort,* ed. Hawley and Wulff, pp. 129–43. Rādhā's status as Krishna's mistress has caused difficulties for Vaiṣṇava theologians, who have risen to the occasion by arguing for the superiority of *parakīyā* love—love for another's wife—over *svakīyā* love—love within the legal constraints of

marriage—without ever contradicting the view put forth in *Bhāgavata Purāṇa* 10.33 that such love is not to be taken as a model for society.

6. Troupes have also performed in towns and cities not in Bengal—such as Brindavan and Banaras—where large numbers of Bengalis live. For more on the two Sanskrit dramas, see my *Drama as a Mode of Religious Realization: The Vidagdhamādhava of Rūpa Gosvāmī* (Chico, Calif.: Scholars Press, 1984), pp. 5–6.

7. See, for example, C. Mackenzie Brown, "The Theology of Rādhā in the Purāṇas," in *The Divine Consort,* ed. Hawley and Wulff, pp. 57–71.

8. The term *Bengali Vaiṣṇavas* is misleading, for this sect has a sizable presence in such pilgrimage centers as Brindavan and Banaras, and its influence extends throughout much of eastern India.

9. The theory of Krishna's threefold *śakti* is set forth in Jīva Gosvāmī's *Bhagavat Sandarbha.* See S. K. De, *Early History of the Vaiṣṇava Faith and Movement in Bengal,* 2d. ed. (Calcutta: K. L. Mukhopadhyay, 1961), pp. 277–85.

10. See *VM* 6.21. The last word of this verse, *jagadvismṛtam,* "the world forgotten," succinctly expresses a central goal of yoga: total obliviousness to the mundane realm.

11. *VM* 2.47. The *tamāla* is black, like Krishna, and is thus closely associated with him. Rādhā's wish presupposes the conventional imagery of classical Sanskrit poetry, in which the (feminine) creeper and the (masculine) tree around which it is entwined represent the loving couple.

12. Rūpa was clearly wrestling in the *Lalitamādhava* with a difficult theological problem posed by the *Bhāgavata* account: How was it possible for Krishna to leave the *gopīs*, and especially Rādhā, seemingly without regret? Did he have no notion of the grief that he would cause, or was he utterly heartless? And would he, too, not be consumed by grief?

13. The classical model for this motif is Purūravas's anguished search for the nymph Urvaśī, as represented, for example, in Kālidāsa's *Vikramorvaśīyam.* The *gopīs*' search for Krishna when he disappears from their midst as narrated in the *rāsa* chapters of the *Bhāgavata Purāṇa* (10.30–31) is also clearly in the background.

14. The parallel with one traditional account of Caitanya's death in the ocean at Puri is striking; he, too, is said to have entered the water because its waves appeared to him to be Krishna's dark form.

15. See the list of practices found in Rūpa's *Bhaktirasāmṛtasindhu* (hereafter *BRS*) 1.2.25–27, especially the discussion of "limbs" (*aṅgas*) 32–34: *gīta, saṅkīrtana* (in particular the first of its three subtypes, *nāmakīrtana*), and *japa.* See also Norvin J. Hein, "Caitanya's Ecstasies and the Theology of the Name," in *Hinduism: New Essays in the History of Religions,* ed. Bardwell L. Smith (Leiden: E. J. Brill, 1976), pp. 15–32.

16. *VM* 3.4; 3.8.14–15; 5.14; and cf. 2.24. *Ekāgratā,* concentration on a single point, is a fundamental element of yoga.

17. The terms *jīvitapati* and the virtually synonymous *prāṇanātha* are reminiscent of several of the names of Viṣṇu enumerated, for example, at *Mahābhārata* 13.149, notably *jīvana, prāṇa, prāṇada,* and *prāṇabhṛt.* See Jan Gonda, *Aspects of Early Viṣṇuism,* 2d ed. (Delhi: Motilal Banarsidass, 1969), p. 18. In the *Vidagdhamādhava,* however, such terms assume a new significance, for the context is not a metaphysical one but an emotional one of love and longing.

18. *VM* 6.8.44. Viśākhā here calls Rādhā *premodbhrānte,* "you who are mad with love." Paradoxically, it is this "demented" condition that allows her to perceive metaphysical truth.

19. *LM* 2.33.3; the designation is obviously a pun on her name, the diminutive of which is Rādhikā.

20. In *LM* 7.16, Navavṛndā contrasts the worship of Krishna with flowers and incense with the *sevā* of the *gopī*s, which consists of the play (*līlā*) of sidelong glances and embraces.

21. *VM* 5.41. *Āratī* is a graceful form of worship that is performed by waving a tray of oil lamps in circular patterns.

22. In expressing his desire to become a *gopī* (*LM* 4.19), Krishna uses the word *sārūpya,* "identity of form," a term used in the Purāṇas to designate a kind of liberation (*mokṣa*).

23. In Rūpa's *Ujjvalanīlamaṇi* (hereafter *UNM*), *māna* is one of the four types of separation (*UNM* 15, *śṛṅgārabhedaprakaraṇam,* pp. 526–48 of the Kāvyamālā edition) (hereafter KM): *The Ujjvalanīlamaṇi by Shrī Rūpagoswāmī,* with the commentaries of Jīvagoswāmī and Vishvanātha Chakravarty, edited by Durgāprasād and Wāsudev Laxman, 2d ed, *Kāvyamālā* no. 95 (Bombay: Nirṇaya Sāgar Press, 1932).

24. See *UNM* 14, *sthāyibhāvaprakaraṇam,* p. 483 of KM.

25. For the use of the term *sahaja* among *sahajiyā* Vaiṣṇavas, see Edward C. Dimock, Jr., *The Place of the Hidden Moon: Erotic Mysticism in the Vaiṣṇava-sahajiyā Cult of Bengal* (Chicago: University of Chicago Press, 1966), pp. 35–36, 42, 117–19.

26. *UNM* 14, *sthāyibhāvaprakaraṇam,* pp. 428–33 of KM.

27. The Sanskrit idiom is "the three worlds" (*tribhuvana, LM* 4.12; *trilokī, LM* 2.8.21–22).

28. Rūpa, *Saṃkṣiptabhāgavatāmṛta* 2.1; 2.43–44. On Rādhā as Krishna's *hlādinī śakti,* see De, *Early History of the Vaiṣṇava Faith,* pp. 279–81.

29. The metaphor of tasting is central to *rasa* theory: one of the basic meanings of *rasa* is "flavor," and aesthetic experience is referred to in works on poetics as *rasāsvāda,* "tasting *rasa.*"

30. On the theological debate over whether the love of Rādhā and Krishna is *svakīyā rati* (married love) or *parakīyā rati* (extramarital love), see De, *Early History of the Vaiṣṇava Faith,* pp. 204–6, 348–51; and Dimock, *Place of the Hidden Moon,* pp. 200–214. Noteworthy in this connection is the tenth act of the *Lalitamādhava,* in which Rādhā is married to Krishna in a grand ceremony of reunion.

31. Rūpa explicitly contrasts these two religious ideals at several points in his theoretical writings. See, for example, *BRS* 1.4, in which he asserts that *bhakti* (active, interactive devotion) is incomparably superior to *mokṣa* or *mukti* (release from the endless cycle of death and rebirth).

32. The term *pālā* refers to a *kīrtan* performance, a three- to four-hour exposition and elaboration of a given theme. It also refers, however, to the episode or "play" itself, a generally accepted story line that is independent of any given rendering. Although the term *play* is in fact the closest English equivalent, it is somewhat misleading, for these are dramatic musical renderings with elements of dance, not fully staged plays. In 1980 there were an estimated 250 *kīrtan* troupes in West Bengal alone.

33. These portrayals raise the intriguing question of the extent to which Rādhā has served as a social as well as a religious model for women. This issue is a central focus of my current research on forms of devotional performance in West Bengal.

34. The *kadamba,* a tree with a dark trunk and spiky yellow flowers, evokes the image of Krishna's dark body clothed in a yellow loincloth.

35. Nanda Kishor Das, in a performance of the episode of "Śrī Krishna's Infatuation" (*Śrī Kṛṣṇer Pūrvarāg*).

36. A. K. Ramanujan, personal communication.

37. My translation of the entire poem, as well as of the song text, including the intertextual lines of commentary, can be found in my "Internal Interpretation: The *Ākhar* Lines in Performances of *Padāvalī Kīrtan,*" in *Contacts between Cultures,* vol. 2, *South Asia,* ed. K. I. Koppedrayer (Queenston, Ont.: Edwin Mellen Press, 1992), pp. 317–24.

38. Edward C. Dimock, Jr., and Denise Levertov, trans., *In Praise of Krishna: Songs from the Bengali* (New York: Doubleday, 1967), p. 23. The *anchal* (Bengali or Hindi: *āñcal*) is the end of a sari, usually worn over the head or the shoulders; it is also used to tie up money and often (at least in Bengal) keys. I differ somewhat from Dimock in my interpretation of *premavaicittya*: whereas he sees it at least in part as "the realization that separation is not far off" (p. xix), I see it as the paradoxical *experience* of separation in a situation of utter intimacy. See my *Drama as a Mode of Religious Realization,* p. 152 and p. 248, n. 14.

39. Rādhā thus contrasts sharply with the Virgin Mary, to whom prayers are offered in order that she might intercede with her son on the worshiper's behalf. See Marina Warner, *Alone of All Her Sex: The Myth and the Cult of the Virgin Mary* (New York: Alfred A. Knopf, 1976), esp. chap. 19.

PART TWO

Goddesses Who Mother and Possess

GAṄGĀ
The Goddess Ganges in Hindu Sacred Geography

Diana L. Eck

O Mother Gaṅgā, may your water,
    abundant blessing of the world,
    treasure of Lord Śiva, playful Lord of all the earth,
    essence of the scriptures and
    embodied goodness of the gods,
May your water, sublime wine of immortality,
Sooth our troubled souls.[1]

The pursuit of the Goddess in the Hindu tradition leads one to the bank of the river that Hindus revere as Mother—Gaṅgā Mātā, Mother Ganges. Here the mythology of the Hindu tradition and the sacred topography of the land of India flow inseparably together. The Gaṅgā is both goddess and river. She is claimed as the consort of Śiva and Viṣṇu alike. Her waters are said to be the liquid embodiment of *śakti* as well as the sustaining immortal fluid (*amṛta*) of mother's milk. And her *avataraṇa,* her "descent" to earth, brings both her power and her nurturance to incarnation on the plains of India.

Along her entire length the Gaṅgā is sacred, and just as a temple or a holy city might be circumambulated, so is this entire river circumambulated by a few hardy pilgrims who walk her length from the source to the sea and back again on the other shore. Many *tīrtha*s, sacred "crossings," pilgrimage places, mark her course: Gangotri, her source in the Himalayas; Hardwar, also known as Gaṅgādvārā, "Door of the Ganges," where she breaks out of the mountains into the plains of North India; Prayag, where she joins the Yamuna River as well as the mythical underground Sarasvati; Banaras (Kāśī), the city of Śiva, where she makes a long sweep to the north as if pointing to her Himalayan source; and, finally, Ganga Sagara, where the river meets the sea in the Bay of Bengal.

All along the river, and especially at her great *tīrtha*s, devout Hindus bathe in the Gaṅgā, taking the waters cupped in their hands and pouring them back into the river as offerings to the *pitṛ*s and the *deva*s (see figure 15). They present in the river, as in the sanctum of a temple, offerings of flowers. On great occasions they ford the river in boats, shouting, "Gaṅgā Mātā kī jai!" ("Victory to Mother Ganges!") and trailing garlands of flowers hundreds of feet long to adorn the neck of this Goddess River. They return to their homes, perhaps hundreds of miles away, carrying vessels of her water. And they come again that distance to bring the ashes of their dead to her care.

The *māhātmya*s ("praises") of the Gaṅgā, which are found in the Sanskrit epics and Purāṇas, extol the greatness of the river and describe her many glories. On the most mundane level, the chanting of her name alone is said to relieve poverty, banish bad dreams, and vouchsafe perpetual protection from the falling dung of flying crows.[2] On a more exalted plane, *mokṣa* itself is said to result from bathing in the waters of the Gaṅgā or being cremated on her banks.[3] This is especially the case in the Kali Yuga, our present degenerate era, when the traditional means of gaining release have become too difficult for ordinary people.[4] The Gaṅgā, it is said, is supreme among rivers, as Kāśī is supreme among holy cities and the Himalayas are supreme among mountains.

The Gaṅgā as goddess is more than a single river. She functions in India as the archetype of sacred waters. Other rivers are said to be like the Gaṅgā, others are said even to be the Gaṅgā (such as the River Kaveri, the "Gaṅgā" of South India).[5] But the Gaṅgā remains the paradigmatic sacred river to which they are likened. The River Gaṅgā is not confined to the course she takes across the plains of North India but participates in that spatial transposition that is so typical of Hindu sacred topography, pervading the sacred waters of all India's great rivers.[6]

If a person elsewhere in India cannot go to the Gaṅgā, going to another sacred stream *is* going to the Gaṅgā. There are said to be seven rivers of such great sanctity: Gaṅgā, Yamuna, Godavari, Sarasvati, Narmada, Sindhu, and Kaveri. If such rivers as these are out of reach, one might simply go to the nearest stream. In fact, in every temple and home the Gaṅgā is called to be present in the waters used in ritual, either by mixing those waters with a few drops of Gaṅgā water or by uttering the name and *mantra*s of the Gaṅgā to invoke her presence. The Gaṅgā is the quintessence and source of all sacred waters, and indeed of all waters everywhere.

Not only is the Gaṅgā said to be present in other rivers, but others are also present in her. By bathing in this one river, one bathes in all rivers. As a contemporary Indian author writes, "When a pilgrim dives into the sacred waters of the Gaṅgā, he feels the thrill of plunging into the waters of all the rivers of India."[7] The *māhātmya*s claim that the Gaṅgā concentrates in her

Figure 15. Bathers in the Ganges during the festival of Makarasaṃkrānti in Banaras.

waters some thirty-five million *tīrtha*s. More simply, it is said that every wave of the river is a *tīrtha.*[8]

There are few things on which Hindu India, diverse as it is, speaks with one voice as clearly as it does on Gaṅgā Mātā. She carries an immense cultural and religious significance for Hindus, no matter what part of the subcontinent they call home, no matter what their sectarian leaning might be. As one Hindi author writes, "Even the most hardened atheist of a Hindu will find his heart full of feelings he has never felt before the first time he reaches the bank of the Gaṅgā."[9]

Some of those "feelings" were eloquently expressed by Jawaharlal Nehru, who was at the most westernized end of the modern spectrum of Indian life and who loved the Gaṅgā deeply:

> My desire to have a handful of my ashes thrown into the Gaṅgā at Allahabad has no religious significance, so far as I am concerned. I have no religious

> sentiment in the matter. I have been attached to the Gaṅgā and the Jumna rivers in Allahabad ever since my childhood and, as I have grown older, this attachment has also grown. I have watched their varying moods as the seasons changed, and have often thought of the history and myth and tradition and song and story that have become attached to them through the long ages and become part of their flowing waters. The Gaṅgā, especially, is the river of India, beloved of her people, round which are intertwined her racial memories, her hopes and fears, her songs of triumph, her victories and her defeats. She has been a symbol of India's age-long culture and civilization, ever-changing, ever-flowing, and yet ever the same Gaṅgā. She reminds me of the snow-covered peaks and the deep valleys of the Himalayas, which I have loved so much, and of the rich and vast plains below, where my life and work have been cast.[10]

It is in part the province of scholars to see and uncover those affirmations that have been explicitly denied. As one who considered himself thoroughly secular, Nehru denied that the Gaṅgā had any "religious" significance for him—presumably meaning "supernatural" significance. His attachment to the river and his desire to have his ashes thrown into it was, on the contrary, as natural and organic as his love for the land of India. In this, one might say, he was thoroughly Hindu, and his affirmation of the land, its waters, its mountains, was a thoroughly Hindu religious affirmation. For the natural *is* the religious. Although the river has attracted abundant myth and *māhātmya,* it is the river itself, nothing "supernatural" ascribed to it, that has been so significant for Hindus. The river does not stand for, or point toward, anything greater, beyond itself; it is part of a living sacred geography that Hindus hold in common. It is with certain presuppositions about that common geography that Hindus, even such as Nehru, behold the Gaṅgā. The Gaṅgā is one goddess we cannot consider apart from the land in which she flows and the pattern of symbols that this land embodies.

LIVING LAND

Leaving the river for a moment, let us look at some of the mythic images of the cosmos in which the Gaṅgā moves. One of the most striking aspects of the multitude of Hindu cosmogonic myths is the organic, biological vision that they express. The completed universe is imagined as a living organism, a vast ecosystem, in which each part is inextricably related to the life of the whole. And the whole is indeed alive: it is in constant process and movement, growing and decaying. There is no such thing as objectified "nature" or lifeless "elements," for everything belongs to the living pattern of the whole.

One well-known image is that of the sacrifice of the primal giant Puruṣa, a cosmogonic event in which each part of this macrocosmic being became an element of the natural world.[11] From his feet came this earth; from his torso the *antarīkṣa,* the mid-region of the sky, extending as far up as the blue extends; and from his head came the heavens above the sky. More particularly, from his eye came the sun; from his mind, the moon; from his mouth, the gods Indra and Agni; from his breath, the winds.

Another image is that of the Golden Embryo, Hiraṇyagarbha, called in the Rig Veda the "firstborn of creation," the egg or embryo that contained within it all the vast and particular life of this cosmos.[12] When it had incubated for a long time, it split open; the top half became heaven; the bottom, earth; and the space between, the mid-region of the sky. The outer membrane became the mountains; the inner membrane, the clouds and mists; the veins of the egg, the rivers; the interior waters, the oceans. Every atom of the universe came from the life of that embryo. In a later myth, the egg is replaced by Viṣṇu, reclining asleep on the cosmic waters, containing within his body the whole of the universe in unmanifest form. When the time is ripe, the lotus springs from his navel, unfolds, and gives birth to Brahmā, the agent of creation.[13]

These are images of a biological worldview, grounded in the Vedas, strengthened by the indigenous *yakṣa* and *nāga* traditions, and persisting still in the Hindu mythic imagination. It is a view in which the universe, and by extension the land of India, is alive with interconnections and meanings and is likened to a living organism. There is no nature "worship" here, but a sacramental natural ontology. In an excellent essay, Betty Heimann writes: "In India the veneration of Nature has never been discarded as outdated and primitive. On the contrary, primitivity is here appreciated in its productive ambiguity and inexhaustible potentialities. Nature cult is the fundament of the earliest forms of Indian religions and remains the basis of even the highest and most exalted speculations of Indian philosophy."[14]

In this organic ontological vision, the term *symbol,* if we are to use it at all, describes the vehicle of movement from meaning to meaning. Symbols enable one to follow certain strands of the complex interrelatedness of the whole, up and down, back and forth, from heaven to earth, from place to place. Poets use the image of the loom: the universe is woven on the loom, as it were, by two maidens, Night and Day, who lay and draw the threads.[15] Gārgī asks the sage Yājñavalkya, "What is the warp and woof on which this all is woven?"[16] For this "All" is a woven fabric. One may follow any thread, horizontally or vertically, seeing it slightly differently in one woven context and then another. One thread runs along the warp from the sun above to the fire here below, to the eye of the sacrificial horse, to the human eye, to the Yamuna River, to the subtle channel called *piṅgalā* within the body-cosmos. Another thread runs from the Moon above, to the Soma that dwells as waters in the vault of the heaven and as plants on earth, to the earthly waters, to the human mind, to the River Gaṅgā, to the subtle channel called *iḍā* within the body-cosmos.[17]

In a sense, everything is a symbol in that it leads into the living web of relationships that constitutes the whole, for symbols do not live alone but in a pattern of meaning shaped by other symbols. But here the symbol does not, as in some Western interpretations, point beyond itself to some other reality. The Holy is constituent of the life and fullness of the whole. The symbolic referent in this organic ontology is not the Holy, but the Whole, which each symbol, each thread, helps to constitute.

Just as the cosmos is a biological whole, so on the microcosmic level the land of India is pictured as an organic whole, a full sacred geography. The living landscape is dense with significance. Each village has its *grāmadevatā,* the lord of its place. The sacred literature is full of *māhātmyas* of place: the Naimiṣa forest, the Gaṅgā, Yamuna, and Godavari rivers, the Himalaya and Vindhya mountains. Such places have been affirmed to have particularly strong strands of connection to the macrocosm. They are called *tīrtha*s, a word that originally meant "ford" or "crossing place" and has come to mean a "spiritual ford," a place of pilgrimage.

The earth, like the macrocosmic Puruṣa, is a body, both in its wholeness and its diversity. In the *Mahābhārata* it is put this way:

> Just as certain parts of the body are called clean, so are certain parts of the earth and certain waters called holy.[18]

Those "certain parts" of earth that give ready access to the heavens are *tīrtha*s. They are thresholds, doorways upward, where one's prayers are more quickly heard, one's desires more readily fulfilled, one's rituals bound to bring more abundant blessings. And it is precisely because these doorways were opened by some hierophany, some *avatāra,* that they are *tīrtha*s for human beings. *Avatāra* and *tīrtha,* both coming from the root *tṛ,* "to cross over," are the dynamics of movements along the warp of the cosmic loom: crossing down and crossing up.

There are thousands of *tīrtha*s in India, some well known through the whole land and some of but local prominence. The great *tīrtha* cycles include the seven sacred cities (*saptapurī*); the four divine abodes (*cār dhām*), one at each compass point; and the "seats" (*pīṭha*s) of the goddess, each corresponding to a part of the body of the goddess Satī.[19] The whole of India adds up to a body-cosmos.

Pilgrims circumambulate the whole of India as a sacred land, visiting the *dhām* at each compass point, marking with their feet the perimeter of the whole, bringing sands from the southern tip of India at Ramesvaram to place in the Gaṅgā when they arrive, and returning with Gaṅgā water to sprinkle the *liṅga* at Ramesvaram. This network of *tīrtha*s constitutes the very bones of India as a cultural unit. Considering its long history, India has had but a few hours of political and administrative unity. Its unity as a nation, however, has been firmly constituted by the sacred geography it has held in common and revered: its mountains, forests, rivers, hilltop shrines, and sacred cities. It is no surprise, then, that the national anthem of Nehru's independent India is a litany of the great place-names of her sacred geography. This hymn expresses a Hindu view of the living land that is as old as India itself.

LIVING WATERS

India's rivers have been the life-giving arteries of this living land. The waters of this earthly realm, the rivers and oceans that course through, surround, and support the continents, have, in the Hindu view, their counterparts in heaven, above the vaulted blue of the sky. In the beginnings, they were set free to run upon the earth by the gods themselves. The seers of the *Rig Veda* envisioned the connection in this way:

> Forth from the midst of the flood they flow,
> The sea, their leader, purifying, never-sleeping,
> Indra, the thunderer, the bull, dug out their channels.
> Here may these goddess waters bless me!
>
> Waters that flow from heaven,
> Or spring from the dug earth, or meander freely,
> All of which, bright and pure, head for the ocean,
> Here may these goddess waters bless me!
>
> In whose midst King Varuṇa moves,
> Observing men's truth and falsehood,
> Nectar they are, and bright and pure,
> Here may these goddess waters bless me!
>
> In which King Varuṇa, in which Soma, in which all the gods
> Became drunk with strength,
> In which Agni Vaiśvānara entered,
> Here may these goddess waters bless me![20]

The waters are identified here as divine, as goddesses set free from their heavenly source by Indra, who dug their channels. They are rivers of blessing and purification. Elsewhere in the *Rig Veda* the seven rivers are said to be set free when Vṛtra is slain.[21] There are the great Sindhu, now called the Indus; the Sarasvati, a river that since Vedic times is said to have disappeared; and the five rivers of the Punjab. Since then, the names of the seven have changed, and the Gaṅgā has become their leader, but the tradition of seven divine rivers has persisted.[22]

The poet seers of the Vedas launched a tradition of praise for the blessing and purifying energy of the "goddess waters" that continued for more than two thousand years, through the many Purāṇic *māhātmyas* and *stotras* to the great poetic hymns to the Gaṅgā, such as Jagannātha's "Gaṅgā Laharī." It is particularly the life, the movement, the activity of the waters of the Gaṅgā that has attracted poets and devotees through the ages. Hers are not the motionless waters of the precreation seas, but running, energetic waters of life. The traditional etymology of Gaṅgā derives the name from the verb *gam,* "to go."[23] Her hymns constantly emphasize the running, flowing, energetic movement of her waters, and they do so at times with elaborate alliteration and onomatopoeia, as in this line from the famous "Gaṅgā Laharī"; *marullīlā-lolallaharī-lulitāmbhoja-paṭala.* (May your running waters . . . "covered with lotuses that rock in your waves and roll playfully in the wind" . . . weaken the web of my earthly life.)[24]

It is running water that is the chief agent of purification in the complex Hindu scheme of purity and pollution. Water absorbs pollution, but when it is running, it carries pollution away as well. It is in part because they are "never-sleeping" that these goddess waters bring purification. The Gaṅgā *māhātmyas* proclaim her purifying powers in elaborate detail: even to be touched by a breeze bearing a tiny droplet of Gaṅgā water will erase the sins of lifetimes in an instant!

AVATARAṆA

Each year as the hot and dry season reaches its peak in May and early June, Hindus celebrate the descent of the Gaṅgā from heaven to earth in anticipation of the monsoon rains. The day is Gaṅgā Daśaharā, the tenth day of the bright fortnight of the month of Jyeṣṭha. It is called the "birthday" of the Gaṅgā, and on that day her banks are crowded with bathers. A dip in the Gaṅgā "destroys ten [sins]" (*daśahara*) or ten lifetimes of sins; but as festival manuals confirm, even those far from the Gaṅgā may gain similar benefits from bathing in whatever "Gaṅgā" is near at hand.[25]

The descent—*avataraṇa*—of heavenly waters to earth is an ancient theme with many variations in Hindu mythology. In one of the great Vedic myths, Indra, who has pillared apart heaven and earth and established the sky between them, engages in combat with the great serpent Vṛtra, who has coiled around the vault of heaven and closed up the celestial waters.[26] The waters stored in the vault of heaven are often identified with *soma,* the nectar of the gods and the strengthening elixir of immortality. In defeating Vṛtra, Indra sets free these divine waters for the nourishment of the earth.

In the many Vaiṣṇava versions of the myth, the river is called Viṣṇupadī, after its origin in Viṣṇupada ("the celestial realm of Viṣṇu" or "the foot of Viṣṇu"). Viṣṇu, who in the *Rig Veda* was Indra's helper in releasing the nectarous waters, is here the primary cause of their descent to earth. In taking his famous three strides, Viṣṇu, the dwarf-turned-giant, stretched through and took possession of the threefold universe. With his third stride he is said to have pierced the vault of heaven with his toe and released the heavenly waters.[27] Through this opening in the shell of the universe, the Gaṅgā, which had hitherto flowed around the cosmic egg, flowed into the heavens, landing first in Indra's heaven, where she was caught by the steady polestar Dhruva. From there she ran down the sky to the moon as the Milky Way, and from the moon to the realm of Brahmā situated just above Mount Meru, rimmed by the peaks of the eight directions and forming the calyx of the lotus of this world. From Meru, the river split into four parts and ran out upon the various lotus-petal continents. One branch, the Alakanandā, flowed into Bhāratavarṣa (India) as the Gaṅgā.[28]

In the most celebrated myth of the Gaṅgā's descent to earth, it is Śiva whose role is predominant. The story, which is told in the *Rāmāyaṇa,* the *Mahābhārata,* and in many Purāṇas, is too long to recount here.[29] What is significant for our understanding of the goddess Gaṅgā, however, is that the Gaṅgā fell from heaven in order to revive the sixty thousand sons of King Sagara, burned to ashes by the scorching heat of the glance of the sage Kapila, whose meditation they had rudely disturbed. It was Bhagīratha whose rigorous ascetic discipline finally won the favor of Gaṅgā. She agreed to come to earth, but was certain that the earth would shatter under the force of her fall. Śiva promised to catch her on his head and tame her in the thicket of his ascetic's hair before releasing her to flow upon the earth. Thus did the Gaṅgā fall, winding her way through Śiva's hair and out upon the plains of India, where Bhagīratha took charge of her and led her to the sea. From there she reached the netherworld and became the saving funereal waters for the sons of Sagara.

According to some accounts, the Gaṅgā split into seven streams as she emerged from the hair of Śiva, three flowing to the east, three to the west, and the Bhāgīrathī to the south. This tradition recalls the seven rivers of the Vedic hymns and reminds us that the Gaṅgā in essence waters the whole earth. Indeed, when Bhagīratha brought the Gaṅgā to earth, her waters not only restored the ashes of the dead but also replenished the ocean, which had been swallowed by the sage Agastya.[30]

It is because the Gaṅgā descended in her *avataraṇa* that she is a place of ascent as a *tīrtha.* She, as *triloka-patha-gaminī,* "flowing in the three worlds," has crossed over from heaven to earth to the netherworld and has thus become a place of crossing for human beings, both the living and the dead. As she quickened the ashes of the sons of Sagara, so will she quicken the ashes of all the dead. Thus it is that the story of the Gaṅgā *avataraṇa* is read at *śrāddha* ceremonies, that Gaṅgā water is used in *śrāddha* and *tarpaṇa* rites, and that the place where the Gaṅgā skirts the Mahāśmaśāna, the "Great Cremation Ground" of holy Banaras, has made that place the best place to die in all of India. For the dead, the Gaṅgā has the epithet *svarga-sopana-saraṇī,* "the flowing staircase to heaven." There is no theme more pervasive in Gaṅgā hymnody than the yearning for the lap of the Gaṅgā at the time of death. The popular "Gaṇgāṣṭakam," for instance, begins with the following verse:

O Mother! Cowife of Pārvatī! Necklace adorning the worlds!
Banner rising to heaven!
I ask that I may take leave of this body on your banks,
drinking your water, rolling in your waves,
remembering your name, bestowing my gaze upon you![31]

LIQUID CONSORT

The mythology of the *Devī Bhāgavata* and *Brahmavaivarta Purāṇa*s relates the Gaṅgā closely to Viṣṇu and more specifically to Krishna as one of the forms of the female *prakṛti,* "nature," or in some instances as one of the forms of Rādhā herself.[32] In one instance, the Gaṅgā in human form, sitting with great adoration next to Krishna, arouses the jealously of Rādhā, who threatens to drink her up. Gaṅgā immediately disappears, taking refuge inside the foot of Krishna. The earth is then distressed by the draught that results from Gaṅgā's disappearance. It is only when the gods supplicate Rādhā and calm her jealousy that Gaṅgā emerges from the foot of Krishna and flows forth again.[33]

In another myth, the three cowives of Viṣṇu—Gaṅgā, Sarasvatī, and Lakṣmī—quarrel among themselves over the attentions of their common husband. Both Sarasvatī and Gaṅgā curse one another to become rivers on earth and to bear the burden of human sins. At this point, Viṣṇu intervenes and specifies that in their lives as rivers Sarasvatī will become the wife of Brahmā and Gaṅgā will become the wife of Śiva. Lakṣmī, who had done nothing but try to mediate in the quarrel, will become the sacred *tulasī* plant and will remain his wife.[34] Gaṅgā and Sarasvatī, however, lament so loudly that Viṣṇu finally agrees that while they go their separate ways they will remain, in essence, with him.

If Gaṅgā is a cowife of Viṣṇu and a form of Rādhā, it is clear that her relationship to the Lord is intimate, so much so, in fact, that she flows out of his very body. And as Krishna and Rādhā share one body, so do they mingle in the waters of the Gaṅgā. One striking account tells of the full harvest moon of the autumn month of Kārttika. All the gods have assembled and watch in awe as Krishna and Rādhā dance. As Śiva sings rapturous songs, they all fall into a swoon, and when they come to their senses, the magic circle of Rādhā's and Krishna's dance has become a sea of water. The two have liquified to become the waters of the Gaṅgā.[35]

LIQUID ŚAKTI

From the Śaiva point of view, it is Śiva whose relationship with Gaṅgā is most prominent and most intimate. If she is consort of Hari, so is the *śakti* of Śiva; if she flows from the foot of Viṣṇu, so she meanders in Śiva's hair.

Śiva as Gaṅgādhara, "Bearer of the Gaṅgā," is commonly depicted wearing the Gaṅgā in his hair, either as the mermaid who clings to the crescent moon in his topknot or as the stream of water spurting up like a geyser. The Gaṅgā, therefore, is Śiva's constant companion, making his tangled ascetic's locks her way station on her perpetual fall from heaven to earth. Her *avataraṇa* is a continuing process, not a single event; each wave of the Gaṅgā falls upon Śiva before reaching the earth. In agreeing to bear the Gaṅgā, Śiva involved himself in a relationship rather than a simple project.

So close is the relationship of Gaṅgā and Śiva that she is called his wife and is occasionally depicted in sculpture approaching him as a bride.[36] Naturally, as cowife and rival, she arouses the jealousy of Pārvatī, much as she does that of Rādhā. Gaṅgā, born of Himalaya, the Mountain, and his wife Menā is in fact Pārvatī's sister; but she is also Pārvatī's rival. Pārvatī's jealousy became a favorite theme of both poets and artists. The poet Jagannātha, for instance, writes:

Who here can speak the greatness of your gracious form,
which vanquishes our worldly fears
    by its mere beholding,
which Śiva ever holds upon his head,
    despite the strong entreaties of the Mountain's daughter
    who grows faint with envy.[37]

Śiva is called Umā-Gaṅgā-patīśvara, "Husband and Lord of Umā (Pārvatī) and Gaṅgā," and is depicted as such by artists, who show Gaṅgā clinging to his hair and a frowning Pārvatī turning her face away in jealousy.[38]

In the *Skanda Purāṇa* Śiva, speaking to Viṣṇu, resolves the issue by identifying Gaṅgā with Pārvatī as the female aspect of the Divine, however construed:

> As Gaurī (Pārvatī) is, so is the Gaṅgā. Therefore, whoever worships Gaurī properly also worships the Gaṅgā.
>
> And as I am, so are you, O Viṣṇu. And as you are, so am I. And as Umā (Pārvatī) is, so is the Gaṅgā. The form is not different.
>
> And whoever says that there is some difference between Viṣṇu and Rudra, between Śrī and Gaurī, or between the Gaṅgā and Gaurī is a very foolish person.[39]

The Gaṅgā embodies the Supreme Sadā-Śiva's active energy or *śakti*. *Śakti* is that life energy, conceived as female, through which the qualityless, ineffable Sadā-Śiva manifests himself in the world. This *śakti* can be apprehended, praised, and loved. She can even be touched in this, her liquid form. A contemporary Hindi religious writer speaks of the Gaṅgā as the "liquid image" (*mūrti*) of Parabrahma, Paramātmā.[40] Kālidāsa, in the *Kumārasambhava,* calls her *śambhor ambumayi-mūrti:* Śiva's water-form.[41] It is a female form, flowing out upon the earth for the blessing of all. Says the *māhātmya* from the *Skanda Purāṇa:*

> She, the Gaṅgā, is my supreme image, having the form of water, the very essence of Śiva's soul. She is nature (*prakṛti*) supreme and the basis of countless universes.
>
> For the protection of the world do I playfully uphold the Gaṅgā, who is mother of the world, the supreme Brahman's very embodiment.[42]

As this "embodiment" the Gaṅgā makes Śiva's activity in the world possible. Śiva-in-action is indeed *śakti,* the energy that creates and nourishes all the manifest universe. Without this energy, that One is unnameable, qualityless, and without expansion. *Śakti* bodies forth the living cosmos, and the Gaṅgā is liquid *śakti.* Her fall from heaven to the head of Śiva is repeated countless times daily in the simple ritual act of pouring water upon the Śiva *liṅga.* The unutterable incandescence of the *liṅga* of fire is joined with the torrential energy of the celestial waters. Without the Gaṅgā, Śiva would remain the scorching, brilliant *liṅga* of fire; without Śiva, the Gaṅgā would flood the earth.[43] Bearing her on his head, Śiva became the vehicle for the Gaṅgā's fall. But if Śiva is a vehicle for the Gaṅgā, she is also a vehicle for Śiva: for it is through her liquid *śakti* that Śiva is able to enter into the world as an active agent of salvation. As Skanda explains to Agastya in one of the Gaṅgā *māhātmya*s:

> O Agasyta, one should not be amazed at the notion that the Gaṅgā is really Śakti, for is she not the supreme energy of the eternal Śiva, which has taken the form of water?[44]

The Śiva we speak of here, however, is not Rudra-Śiva but the One called Sadā-Śiva, who includes and transcends Brahmā, Viṣṇu, and Rudra-Śiva. The Gaṅgā as the liquid *śakti* of this Supreme Śiva embodies all these gods, just as in another context she is said to embody Krishna and Rādhā together. The opening stanza of one hymn makes this clear:

> Oṃ. Praise be to the auspicious Gaṅgā, gift of Śiva, O praise! Praise be to her who is Viṣṇu embodied, the very image of Brahmā, O praise!
>
> Praise to her who is the form of Rudra, Śaṅkara, the embodiment of all gods, the embodiment of healing, O praise![45]

Likewise, the opening stanza of the "Gaṅgā Laharī" calls her the "essence of the scriptures and embodied goodness of the gods."[46]

MOTHER GAṄGĀ

It is significant that Gaṅgā is the embodied "goodness" of the gods, for hers is an energy perpetually praised as good. Her destructive force is utterly purified and calmed in the hair of Śiva. As she flows out upon the plains, she is Mother, and she is the perfect dream-mother: embracing, nourishing, and forgiving, without a trace of anger. In India, where virtually every manifestation of female divinity is tinged with ambiguity, it is noteworthy that this river, which possesses such tremendous potential for destruction, is acclaimed in such unambiguous terms.

The image of rivers as mothers is ancient and widespread. The Vedic poets say, for instance, that when Indra released the waters of heaven, they ran out upon the earth like mother cows to suckle their young, like milk cows rich in milk.[47] The poets beg of the rivers, "Like longing mothers, give to us here on earth the most blessed nectar that you have!"[48] When the cow-rivers run upon the earth they are pregnant with the sun; they are also called the mothers of Agni, fire.

The Gaṅgā inherits her mothering capacities from those ancient waters. It is she who accepts from Agni the burning seed of Śiva and becomes the mother of the war god, Skanda.[49] Elsewhere, as the wife of Śantanu, she is the mother of the eight Vasus and of the hero-sage Bhīṣma. When Bhīṣma finally dies in the great battle of the *Mahābhārata,* she rises in human form from the river, weeping as bitterly as any mother.[50]

The waters of the Gaṅgā are the drink of life. As the gods drink *soma* for life, so do humans drink Gaṅgā water. It is as nourishing as mother's milk, and indeed the *Mahābhārata* compares human thirst for her waters to that of hungry children thirsting for their mothers' milk.[51]

It is as Mother Gaṅgā that this river is most universally known to Hindus, and, like a mother, the Gaṅgā can be trusted to render unconditional love to her children. Even those utterly unfit for salvation by Brahmanical standards will be embraced and saved by the Gaṅgā.

In India today the most widely known hymn to the Gaṅgā is the "Gaṅgā Laharī" of the seventeenth-century poet Jagannātha, whose patrons were the Mughal emperor Shāh Jahān and his son, the *littérateur* prince Dārā Shikoh. The poet was outcasted by his Brahmin subcaste because of his long love affair with a Muslim woman at court. According to legend, Jagannātha went to Banaras to try to restore his status by proving himself acceptable to Brahmins there, but he was unsuccessful. As the story goes, he sat with his beloved atop the fifty-two steps of Pañcagaṅgā Ghāṭ and, with each of the fifty-two verses he composed, the river rose one step. At the conclusion of the hymn, the waters touched the feet of the poet and his beloved, purified them, embraced them, and carried them away.[52]

In the "Gaṅgā Laharī" Jagannātha addresses the river as Mother, the one who will love and claim the child rejected by everyone else. He is so despicable that he is shunned even by outcastes; he is criticized even by madmen; he is so filthy with sin that all the *tīrtha*s hang their heads in shame at their inability to cleanse him. There are plenty of gods who will care for the good, but who except the Gaṅgā will care for the wicked?[53] He approaches the Gaṅgā with complete trust and faith:

I come to you as a child to his mother.
I come as an orphan
    to you, moist with love.
I come without refuge
    to you, giver of sacred rest.
I come a fallen man
    to you, uplifter of all.
I come undone by disease
    to you, the perfect physician.
I come, my heart dry with thirst,
    to you, ocean of sweet wine.
Do with me whatever you will.[54]

Above all, it is mercy and compassion that flow out from the foot of Viṣṇu or from the hair of Śiva in the form of this mothering river. It nourishes the land and all its creatures, living and dying. The hymns repeatedly affirm that this river is intended as a vehicle of mercy:

> This Gaṅgā was sent out for the salvation of the world by Śambhu, Lord of lords, filled with the sweet wine of compassion.
>
> Śaṅkara, having squeezed out the essence of *yoga* and the Upaniṣads, created this excellent river because of his mercy for all creatures.[55]

In earlier ages and better times *mokṣa* could be had only by means of meditation (*dhyāna*), austerities (*tapas*), or ritual sacrifice (*yajña*). But now, it is said, in this Kali Yuga, these are no longer viable. Only the Gaṅgā can bring the blessings of salvation.[56]

THE RIVER

The Gaṅgā's history in the Hindu mythological tradition is long and rich. Here we have only pointed to some of its various facets. As a celestial stream flowing upon the earth she has her mythic origins in the world of the Vedas. As the tradition developed, she wound her way into the myth and ritual of Vaiṣṇavas and Śaivas alike. She is hardly the best-known consort of either Viṣṇu or Śiva, but she has acquired the position of consort to both of them, something no other goddess can claim. Even Brahmā keeps close company with her, carrying the river in his water pot.

The river's accumulation of mythological traditions demonstrates the distinctive persistence of natural geographical symbols in India. For the Gaṅgā is most certainly not loved and worshiped because she is spouse of Śiva, cowife of Pārvatī, consort of Viṣṇu, or the liquified Rādhā-Krishna. Rather, she has attracted this mythology over the years precisely because *she* is worshiped and loved. Here one sees the difference between the organic myth or symbol and the narrative one. For the Gaṅgā's significance as a symbol is not exhaustively narrative. First, she is a river that flows with waters of life in a vibrant universe. Narrative myths come and go in history. They may shape the cosmos and convey meaning for many generations, and then they may gradually lose their hold upon the imagination and finally be forgotten. But the river remains, even when the stories are no longer repeated. The river flows on, bringing life and conveying the living tradition, even to those of this age for whom everything else is demythologized.

In the Hindu tradition, any place can become the sacred abode of the gods, if the proper rites are performed. When a temple is consecrated and its image installed, the great rites of *pratiṣṭhā* serve to call the presence of the divine to that place. With any image fashioned of wood or stone or rudely crafted of clay, rites of invitation (*āvahana*) are observed at the beginning of worship, inviting the deity to be present, and rites of dismissal (*visarjana*) are observed at worship's end, giving the deity leave to go. With the worship of the Gaṅgā no such rites are ever observed. This river is no ordinary image in which the divine has come to dwell. She is celestial—unmediated and immediate. Whatever is holy, whatever is merciful, whatever is utterly auspicious is already there.

NOTES

1. Jagannātha, *Gaṅgā Laharī* (Varanasi: Ṭhākur Prasād and Sons, n.d.), verse 1. Translations from this work and from the Vedic and Sanskrit sources are my own.
2. *Skanda Purāṇa,* Kāśī Khaṇḍa 27.22 (Calcutta: Gurumaṇḍala Granthamālāya no. 20, 1961), vol. 4. The Kāśī Khaṇḍa will hereafter be cited as KK.
3. KK 27.30, 37, 105, and 134.
4. KK 27.18; 28.27–29.
5. For a discussion of the way in which the Gaṅgā is an all-India agent of Sanskritization, see M. N. Srinivas, *Religion and Society among the Coorgs of South India* (London: Oxford University Press, 1952), p. 214. Srinivas discusses the sanctity of the Kāverī and, in an appendix, recounts the Kāverī's myth of origin.
6. For a discussion of what I have termed "spatial transposition," see my *Banaras, City of Light* (New York: Alfred A. Knopf, 1982), pp. 39–42, 283–94.
7. Raj Bali Pandey, *Varanasi: The Heart of Hinduism* (Varanasi: Orient Publishers, 1969), p. 30.
8. Rāmpratāp Tripāṭhī, *Purāṇõ mẽ Gaṅgā* (Prayāg: Hindī Sāhitya Sammelan, 1952), p. *jha.*
9. Ibid., p. *ga.*
10. From Jawaharlal Nehru's will and testament, quoted in Eric Newby and Raghubir Singh, *Gaṅgā: Sacred River of India* (Hong Kong: Perennial Press, 1974), p. 9.
11. *Rig Veda* 10.90.
12. See *Rig Veda* 10.82 and 10.121.

13. See, for example, *Kūrma Purāṇa* 1.9. *Bhāgavata Purāṇa* 2.5.6 and *Mārkaṇḍeya Purāṇa* 45–47 also contain accessible accounts of the transformation of the Hiraṇya-garbha motif.

14. Betty Heimann, *Facets of Indian Thought* (London: George Allen and Unwin, 1964), p. 107, in the essay entitled "Indian Metaphysics." I am also deeply indebted to another essay in this posthumous collection, "India's Biology," in which Heimann develops the notion of a biological worldview.

15. See, for example, *Atharva Veda* 10.7 and *Rig Veda* 10.130.

16. *Bṛhadāraṇyaka Upaniṣad* 3.6 and 3.8.

17. The esoteric symbolism of the two rivers is elaborated by Heinrich von Stietencron in his work *Gaṅgā und Yamunā* (Wiesbaden: Otto Harrassowitz, 1972). He deals primarily with the river goddesses as they appear to the right and left of medieval temple entrances in northern India.

18. *Mahābhārata* 13.111.16.

19. "Ayodhyā, Mathurā, Māyā (Hardwar), Kāśī, Kāñcī, Avantikā (Ujjain), and the city of Dvārāvatī (Dvārakā)—these seven give *mokṣa*." This verse describing the *saptapurī* is found in many Purāṇas and is known to practically every literate Brahmin. The four divine abodes are Purī in the east, Rameśvaram in the south, Dvārakā in the west, and Badrināth in the north. On the *pīṭha*s, see D. C. Sircar, *The Śākta Pīṭhas* (1948; repr. Delhi: Motilal Banarsidass, 1973).

20. *Rig Veda* 7.49.

21. The seven are mentioned repeatedly as a group. See, for example, *Rig Veda* 1.32.12, 1.34.8, 2.12.12, and 4.28.1. *Rig Veda* 10.75 mentions the Gaṅgā, but she does not figure among the seven.

22. These seven rivers are the Gaṅgā, Yamunā, Godāvarī, Sarasvatī, Narmadā, Kāverī, and Sindhu.

23. Amarasiṃha, *Amarakośa* (Varanasi: Chowkhamba Sanskrit Series no. 198, 1970).

24. Jagannātha, *Gaṅgā Laharī*, verse 20.

25. Rāmpratāp Trīpaṭhī, *Hinduõ ke Vrat, Parva, aur Tyauhār* (Allahabad: Lokbhāratī Prakāśan, 1971), p. 86.

26. See W. Norman Brown, "The Creation Myth of the Rig Veda," *Journal of the American Oriental Society* 62, no. 2 (1942): 85–98. See also, for example, *Rig Veda* 1.32, 2.12.

27. *Bhāgavata Purāṇa* 5.17; *Devī Bhāgavata Purāṇa* 8.7. Sculpture depicts this myth as well. C. Sivaramamurti, in *Gaṅgā* (New Delhi: Orient Longman, 1976), includes two plates from twelfth-century Mysore in which Brahmā is shown pouring the Gaṅgā from his water pot upon Vāmana-Viṣṇu's upraised foot.

28. *Kūrma Purāṇa* 1.44; *Brahmavaivarta Purāṇa,* Kṛṣṇajanma Khaṇḍa 34; *Bhāgavata Purāṇa* 5.17; *Viṣṇu Purāṇa* 2.2.8.

29. For versions of the story, see *Rāmāyaṇa* 1:38–44; *Mahābhārata* 3.104–8; *Bhāgavata Purāṇa* 9.8–9; *Brahmavaivarta Purāṇa,* Prakṛti Khaṇḍa 10; *Devī Bhāgavata Purāṇa* 9.11; and KK 30. K. Damodaran Nambiar lists many others in "The Nārada Purāṇa: A Critical Study," *Purāṇa* 15, no. 2, supplement (1973): 1–56. In several accounts of the *avataraṇa* it is Krishna to whom appeal is made by Bhagīratha.

30. The *Mahābhārata* account of the *avataraṇa,* for instance, immediately follows the story of Agastya's swallowing the ocean.

31. "Śrī Gaṅgāṣṭaka," verse 1, in *Nityakarma Vidhi tathā Devapūjā Paddhati* (Varanasi: Ṭhākurdās Surekā Cairitī Phaṇḍ, 1966).

32. See C. Mackenzie Brown, *God as Mother: A Feminine Theology in India* (Hartford, Vt.: Claude Stark and Company, 1974), pp. 161–67.

33. *Brahmavaivarta Purāṇa,* Prakṛti Khaṇḍa 11; *Devī Bhāgavata Purāṇa* 9.13.

34. *Brahmavaivarta Purāṇa,* Prakṛti Khaṇḍa 6; *Devī Bhāgavata Purāṇa* 9.6.

35. *Brahmavaivarta Purāṇa,* Prakṛti Khaṇḍa 10; *Devī Bhāgavata Purāṇa* 9.12.

36. Sivaramamurti, *Gaṅgā,* fig. 6.

37. Jagannāṭha, *Gaṅgā Laharī,* verse 12.

38. Sivaramamurti, *Gaṅgā,* pp. 21–24, figs. 7 and 8.

39. KK 27.182–84.

40. Tripāṭhī, *Hinduõ ke Vrat,* p. 95.

41. Kālidāsa, *Kumārasambhava* 10.26.

42. KK 27.8–9.

43. For other elaborations of the *agni-soma* polarity and resolution, see Wendy Doniger O'Flaherty, *Asceticism and Eroticism in the Mythology of Śiva* (London: Oxford University Press, 1973), pp. 286–92.

44. KK 28.84.

45. KK 27.157–58.

46. Jagannātha, *Gaṅgā Laharī,* verse 1, quoted at the start of this essay.

47. *Rig Veda* 10.75.

48. *Rig Veda* 10.9.

49. O'Flaherty, *Asceticism and Eroticism,* pp. 93–110, describes the many myths of the birth and multiple mothers of Skanda.

50. *Mahābhārata* 1.95–100 describes her marriage to Śantanu and the birth of the Vasus and Bhīṣma. *Mahābhārata* 13.154.18–25 tells of Gaṅgā's lament at the death of Bhīṣma.

51. *Mahābhārata* 13.27.48–52.

52. The legend, which is well known, at least among the traditionally educated of Kāśī, has several variants. Lakshman Ramachandra Vaidya related something of Jagannātha's life and legend in his English introduction to the Sanskrit text of another of Jagannātha's poems, the *Bhāminī Vilāsa* (Bombay: Bhāratī Press, 1887).

53. These summarize some of the sentiments of *Gaṅgā Laharī,* verses 13, 28, 29, and 45.

54. *Gaṅgā Laharī,* verse 24.

55. KK 28, 84 and 88.

56. KK 27.19.

SARAṆYŪ / SAMJÑĀ
The Sun and the Shadow

Wendy Doniger

When I was asked to revise my contribution to the book of Indian goddesses, I found myself drawn back yet again to a figure who stands at the watershed both of the Indian goddess tradition and of my own association with that tradition: Saraṇyū.[1] Although it is useful to begin with a straightforward philological approach to establish our textual footing, following in the steps of the old boys, Bloomfield and Kuhn, it is now time for us to go on to raise questions of gender and race that did not concern them.

SARAṆYŪ IN THE VEDAS

The story of Saraṇyū, like most things Indian, begins *in nuce* in the *Rig Veda,* composed in Sanskrit in northwest India, c. 1200–1000 B.C.E. Since this text purposely conceals the story, it is helpful to have a brief summary of the plot before we try to decipher the riddling text:

> Tvaṣṭṛ ("the Fashioner," also named "the All-Maker," Viśvakarman) was the artisan of the gods. His daughter, Saraṇyū, married Vivasvant ("the Shining One"), the Sun, and gave birth to twins, Yama and Yamī. Then she put in her place a female of-the-same-kind (*savarṇā*), took on the form of a mare, and fled. The Sun took the form of a stallion, followed her, and coupled with her. From that were born the twin equine gods called the Aśvins.

Now, this is how the *Rig Veda* plays with the story:

> "Tvaṣṭṛ is giving a wedding for his daughter": people come together at this news. The mother of Yama, the wedded wife of the great Vivasvant, disappeared. They concealed the immortal woman from mortals. Making a female of-the-same-kind (*savarṇā*), they gave her to Vivasvant. What she became bore the twin equine gods, the Aśvins, and then she abandoned the two sets of twins—Saraṇyū.[2]

The cryptic form of the text is explained by Maurice Bloomfield's excellent suggestion that the passage "belongs to the class of Vedic literary endeavors which are styled in the Vedas themselves 'mystical utterances' (*brahmodya* or *brahmavādya*); it is a riddle or charade."[3] He gives as evidence the fact that no explanations are given for the hiding away of Saraṇyū, or who it was that bore the Aśvins; instead, a series of hints is presented and, at the end, her name, the answer to the riddle. As the later Indian tradition attempts to unlock the riddle of Saraṇyū, it draws upon many deep-seated, often conflicting, ideas about human and divine sexuality and masquerade.

In this first text, the female is explicitly an immortal, while her husband is a mortal (one of those from whom "they" hid her). Her name means something like "flowing," perhaps a hint of a connection with a river goddess and with the concept of impetuosity.[4] As Saraṇyū flows through Hindu mythology, the Purāṇic versions impart increasing degrees of intentionality and feeling to this person/force.[5] Saraṇyū's double is said to be of-the-same-kind (*savarṇā*), of the same sort, or type, or appearance, or of the same color or class, *varṇa*.[6] As we shall see, significant changes in this story arise out of the changing meaning of *varṇa*.

Bloomfield suggests that the double may be "a like one, *double entendre:* one like Saraṇyū in appearance, and like Vivasvant (the Sun) in character or caste . . . like Saraṇyū in appearance, i.e., her double, and also one who is suitable in her character to the mortal Vivasvant—more suitable than the divine Saraṇyū, we may perhaps understand."[7] This disparity results, in part, from the fact that the double woman is mortal, like the Sun, whereas Saraṇyū is immortal. The double produces no children, but Saraṇyū in her own persona produces a single, mortal child whose name (Yama) means "twin" and who is immediately referred to as one of a set of twins. At the same time, as the mare she produces the twin Aśvins, who are liminally immortal: they are half horse and half man, like the Greek Dioscuroi or the Roman Gemini; at first denied the privilege of sharing the elixir of immortality (*soma*), they eventually get it.

That Saraṇyū's husband and child are mortal is as clear as anything in this riddle. Yama is in many texts said to be the first mortal.[8] In other, closely related texts, the Sun is explicitly said to be a mortal, to have been born to die, in contrast with his seven immortal brothers.[9] These same texts also state that he was, even in the womb, inadvertently mutilated and consciously abandoned by his own mother. Thus, the theme of rejection by the mother can be traced back from Yama, rejected by his mother, to Vivasvant, Yama's father, who is rejected by *his* mother. And that same rejection is taken to explain why the Sun is deformed. The gods cut off his excess flesh and it became an elephant (or a human: there is a pun on *hastin,* "one with a trunk" and "one with a hand").[10] He is called Mārtāṇḍa ("dead in the egg" or "born of a dead egg"). Indeed, the daily rising and setting of the sun was seen by many cultures as the continual process of death and rebirth.

Though someone other than Saraṇyū herself makes the female of-the-same-kind, she herself abandons both the twin (Yama) and the equine twins; there are no other children. But Yāska, glossing the Vedic verses in his *Nirukta* (12.10) a few centuries later (c. 500 B.C.E.), adds another significant child:

> Tvaṣṭṛ's daughter Saraṇyū gave birth to twins from Vivasvant. Putting in her place another female, a female of-the-same-kind (*savarṇā*), taking on the form of a mare, she fled. Vivasvant, taking the corresponding form of a horse, followed her and coupled with her. From that were born the two Aśvins. Of the female of-the-same-kind Manu was born.

In the earlier text, "they" (the gods, we assume) substituted someone else for Saraṇyū, with or without her consent. Here she explicitly produces the substitute herself. This is a significant shift, which raises a question that we would do well to bear in mind throughout this inquiry: Who is the agent? Does the woman masquerade of her own will, or does someone else force her to do it? This also brings us to the critical question of points of view: Who *wants* this to happen? Who makes it happen?

Yama has, by the time of Yāska's *Nirukta,* explicitly become twins in the dual (*yamau*), and he has now been joined by another child, Manu, born of the female of-the-same-kind.[11] The mortality of Yama is closely related to the nature of his brother Manu, the ancestor of the human race. "Manu" means "the wise one," and Manu is the Indian Adam. Thus *mānava* ("descended from Manu") is a common word for "human" (which, in terms of the lexical meaning of Manu as "wise," might also be the Sanskrit equivalent of "Homo sapiens"). Although Manu is not mentioned in the riddle verse about Saraṇyū, the *Rig Veda* refers elsewhere to a Manu who is the father of the human race, identifying him in at least one passage (8.52.1) with a patronymic that makes him the son of Vivasvant. But Manu is also given the name (a matronymic?) of *sāvarṇi* or *sāvarṇya* (10.62.9 and 11)—the latter implying that, already in the *Rig Veda,* our ancestor was the son of the female of-the-same-kind or was himself someone of-the-same-kind.

That Saraṇyū and her double are regarded as the mothers of the two ancestors of the human race is even more significant a fact than might at first appear—for Saraṇyū and her double mark the dividing line between abstract goddesses who have children and anthropomorphic goddesses who do not. Before her, Aditi (the mother of the Sun, and of Indra) and Tvaṣṭṛ (her own father, and later said also to be the father of Indra) produce immortal children, as do Sky and Earth and a few other deities. But Saraṇyū is the first goddess to unite with a (mortal) god in order to give birth to children and, through her double, to human children. After Saraṇyū, many celestial nymphs (*apsaras*es) produce children with mortal men, and some goddesses give birth to divine children by themselves, through a kind of parthenogenesis (as Pārvatī gives birth to Gaṇeśa), but never anthropomorphically and never through sexual union with a god. There are stories in later texts explaining why the goddesses are all barren; their infertility is sometimes said to result from a curse uttered by Pārvatī.[12] But this is an afterthought, designed to account for what had already long been taken for granted, namely, that immortals, simply because they are immortal, do not have children; if you don't die, there is no need to reproduce yourself. Or, to put it the other way around, as the myth often does, if you have sex, you must have death. (This is also the message of the loss of Eden.) And, contrariwise, if you are immortal, you can't have sex (or, at least, procreative sex).

This explains why it is that, although Hindu gods and goddesses often marry—the *hieros gamos* is, after all, a major mythological theme—they do not usually procreate with their spouses. Instead, gods seduce mortal women, and celestial nymphs, rather than goddesses, seduce mortal men. The Saraṇyū myth marks the transition between these two patterns: mating with a liminal husband who is both a mortal and a god, she herself functions like the Vedic goddess Aditi and produces a god (Yama, god of the dead), while her double, functioning like one of the later celestial nymphs, produces a mortal (Manu, the founder of the human race).

The story of Saraṇyū and Manu is narrated in greater detail in the *Bṛhaddevatā,* a text composed some centuries after the *Nirukta:*

> Tvaṣṭṛ had twins, Saraṇyū and a three-headed son. He willingly gave Saraṇyū in marriage to Vivasvant, and Saraṇyū bore him Yama and Yamī, who were also twins. Out of her husband's sight (*parokṣam*), Saraṇyū created a female who looked like her (*sadṛśa*); tossing the couple of children (*mithunau*) to this female, she became a mare and went away. But in ignorance of this, Vivasvant begat Manu upon her, and Manu became a royal sage, who was like Vivasvant in his energy. Then Vivasvant became aware that Saraṇyū had departed in the form of a mare, and he went quickly after her, having become a horse. Saraṇyū, knowing that it was Vivasvant in the form of a horse, approached him for coupling (*maithuna*), and he mounted her. But in their haste the semen fell on the ground, and the mare smelled that semen because she desired to become pregnant. From that semen that was inhaled twins were born, the famous Aśvins.[13]

Now, just as the theme of maternal rejection is extended backwards from Yama to his father the Sun, so in this text twinhood is extended backwards from Yama to his mother Saraṇyū, whose twin brother has three heads where she has three forms. Moreover, Saraṇyū's twins are given twin nomenclatures: *yamau,* as in the earlier texts, but now also *mithunau,* literally "a couple," providing a pun for her own "coupling."

Saraṇyū's ambivalence toward her husband here splits the story into two contrasting sexual episodes. As a goddess, she leaves him (we are not told why); as a mare, she receives him. By conceiving through her nose rather than her genitals, the mare expresses the upward displacement of language (for surely these are talking horses): life and creativity spring from the head, not the loins. But she is also placing smell, the reliable animal criterion for the appropriate sexual partner, above vision, the flawed human (and, apparently, divine) criterion. Whereas vision made the Sun mistake the wrong female (created "out of his sight," *parokṣam*) for his wife, and made the mare at first mistake him for someone else, ultimately smell allows Saraṇyū the mare both to recognize her true mate and to conceive by him.

The statement that the Aśvins were conceived from the nose (*nāsāt*) may also have been inspired by a desire to account for their Vedic epithet of Nāsatyas, which Herman Lommel interprets as "Nose-beings," in harmony with the traditional Indian interpretation of the name.[14] "Nāsatya" is elsewhere said to mean "not false" (*na-a-satya,* literally, "not-not-true" or "not-not-real")—an interesting assertion in light of the fact that they are the "true" sons of Saraṇyū, in contrast with their not-equine, and not-immortal, brothers.[15]

SARAṆYŪ IN THE HARIVAṂŚA

In several later variants, the goddess is named not Saraṇyū but Saṃjñā, which means, significantly, "sign" or "image" or "name."[16] At the same time, Saṃjñā's surrogate is no longer said to be of the same kind or type but is rather her *chāyā,* her mirror image or shadow—a creature who is not exactly like her but is her opposite in terms either of inversion (the mirror image) or of color (the shadow). This is the version given in the *Harivaṃśa,* an appendix to the great epic, the *Mahābhārata,* composed in about the fifth century C.E.:

> Vivasvant was born of Kaśyapa and married Saṃjñā the daughter of Tvaṣṭṛ. She had beauty and youth and virtue, and she was not satisfied by the form of her husband, the greathearted one called "Dead-Egg." For the form of Dead-Egg, the Sun, was burnt by his own fiery glory in all his limbs, and so became unlovely. "Let him not be dead while he is still in the egg," his father, Kaśyapa, had said in love and ignorance, and so he became known as "Dead-Egg." But the Sun's fiery glory was constantly excessive, and with it he overheated the three worlds.
>
> The Sun produced a daughter and two sons: Manu and the twins Yama and Yamunā. But Saṃjñā, seeing that the form of the Sun had a dark color (*syāmavarṇa*), unable to bear it, transformed her own shadow (*chāyā*) of-the-same-kind (or color, *savarṇā*). Her own shadow became a Saṃjñā that was made of magic illusion. Saṃjñā said to the female of-the-same-kind, "I am go-

ing to my father's house; you stay here in my house. Treat my three children well, and do not tell this to my husband." The female of-the-same-kind replied, "Even if I am dragged by the hair, even if I am cursed, I will never tell your husband. Go wherever you like, goddess." Somewhat embarrassed, the wise woman went to her father's house. But her father reviled her and kept telling her, "Go back to your husband."

And so she took the form of a mare, concealing her form, and grazed in the land of the northern Kurus. But the Sun, thinking, "This is Saṃjñā," produced in the second Saṃjñā a son who was his equal. And because the Sun thought, "This one looks like (*sadṛśā*) the former Manu," his name was "Manu of-the-Same-Kind" (*savarṇa*). But the earthly (*pārthivī*) Saṃjñā gave extra affection to her own child and did not behave in the same way to the older children. Manu put up with her, but Yama could not put up with her. In his anger and childishness, and through the force of future destiny, Yama threatened Saṃjñā with his foot. Then the mother of-the-same-kind, who was very unhappy, cursed him in anger: "Let that foot of yours fall off."

But Yama, terrified by the curse and agitated by Saṃjñā's words, reported this to his father. "Turn back the curse!" he said to his father. "A mother should behave with affection (*sneha*) to all her children, but this one rejects us and is good to the younger one. I lifted my foot at her but I did not let it fall on her body. If I acted out of childishness or delusion, you should forgive that." The Sun said, "You must have had very good cause indeed if anger possessed you who know dharma and speak the truth. But I can't make your mother's words fail to come true. Worms will take flesh [from your foot] and go to the surface of the earth. Thus your mother's words will come true, and you will be protected from the blow of the curse."

Then the Sun said to Saṃjñā, "Why do you show excessive affection [to one] among your children when they are all equal?" She avoided this question and said nothing to the Sun, and he wanted to curse her to destroy her. Therefore she told everything to the Sun, and when the Sun heard this he became angry and went to Tvaṣṭṛ. Tvaṣṭṛ assuaged the Sun's anger and trimmed him on his lathe, removing his excessive fiery energy. Then he was much more handsome.

He saw his wife the mare, and, taking the form of a horse, he coupled with her by joining with her in her mouth, for she was struggling since she feared it might be another male. She vomited out that semen of the Sun from her nose, and two gods were born in her, the Aśvins, the healers. Then the Sun showed her his lovely form, and when she saw her husband she was satisfied.

But Yama was greatly tormented in his mind by his karma, and as the overlord of the ancestors, the king of dharma, he ruled over these creatures with dharma. And Manu of-the-Same-Kind will rule in the future during the era of Manu of-the-Same-Kind. His brother, Vivasvant's second son, became [the inauspicious] planet Śanaiścara ["slow-moving," Saturn]. Yamī, the younger of the two (twins), became the famous river, the Yamunā. (*Harivaṃśa* 8.1–48)

There are several significant developments in this expanded text. The double is still called the *savarṇā* (the female of-the-same-kind), as in the earlier versions, but she is also the *chāyā* (shadow or reflection) and *sadṛśā* (the look-alike). More important, there is real ambiguity now about the person whom the Shadow looks like, Saṃjñā or the Sun. Saṃjñā in this text perceives herself as literally of a different class from that of her husband. We have noted that *varṇa* may mean "kind" in the sense of mortal versus immortal and might therefore be translated as "class." Over the centuries, the word *varṇa* came primarily to denote "class" in a sociological rather than a purely morphological sense, reflecting the hardening of the lines between the social classes (called *varṇas*) and the increasingly overt racial overtones of "color" (also designated by *varṇa*). This shift in the meaning of *varṇa* may explain why the *savarṇā* ("same sort") of the Veda and Yāska becomes a *sadṛśā* ("look-alike") or a *chāyā* ("shadow") in the *Bṛhaddevatā* and the *Harivaṃśa*. The latter refers to the "dark color" of the Sun and the "same color" of the double woman, implying that Saṃjñā rejected the Sun because of his blackness and created an appropriately black mate for him (*chāyā* here perhaps indicating the dark shadow rather than the bright reflection)—someone who, being dark like him, was of-the-same-kind as he. The counter-intuitive idea that the sun is black seems to have occurred to several ancient Indo-Europeans, perhaps as a result of the black spots we see when we stare directly at the sun or of the sun's black color during its underworld journey, when it is night on earth. The *Harivaṃśa* implies that the sun gave himself a suntan: "He was burnt by his own fiery glory in all his limbs." In later texts, Yama is often described as a black man (with red eyes); in the *Amar Chitra Katha* comic, which we shall soon encounter, Yama is depicted as dark brown with thick red lips, like Al Jolson in blackface. Presumably, he inherits this color from his father. But there may be undertones of racism even in these early texts.

RACIST AND SEXIST IMPLICATIONS

But the more important meaning of *varṇa* in the story of Saṃjñā is "sort" in the sense of mortal versus immortal. Thus the *Harivaṃśa* refers to the shadow as "earthly" (*pārthivī*), belonging to the earth, in contrast with the other, the heavenly mother. The mortality and/or mutilation of the Sun (and, more significantly, of the sons of the Sun) is a pivotal point of the myth in all its variants. Some versions, such as the *Harivaṃśa* passage cited above, argue that Saṃjñā, herself a goddess, left the Sun because he was inadequate for her (mutilated and mortal, or black); some, such as the *Mārkaṇḍeya* passage to be cited below, that she left him because he was too glorious for her, a fact that resulted in his mutilation. The mare's motives are correspondingly reversed: in the *Bṛhaddevatā* she receives the stallion willingly, while in the *Harivaṃśa* she tries to avoid him. Whereas conception through the nose was taken in the *Bṛhaddevatā* as testimony that she *did* want to conceive by him and turned her face toward him as a willing human woman would, in the *Harivaṃśa* it is taken as testimony for just the opposite reaction, and she turns her face toward him (and her haunches away) as an unwilling mare would. In neither case does she present her hindquarters to him. And the reason that she avoids him in the *Harivaṃśa* is that, unlike him, she is (in this case, wrongly) suspicious of the identity of her sexual partner; she does not trust her eyes.

There is also a significant development in the nature of the mother of the human race: while Yāska and the *Bṛhaddevatā* explicitly state that Manu was the son not of the first wife, the true wife, but of the replica, the *Harivaṃśa* says that the first wife bore Manu (presumably Manu the son of Vivasvant, Vaivāsvata) and the twins. This text also says that the second wife, the double (no longer called Savarṇā), bore *another* Manu, a double of Manu, called Manu Sāvarṇi; the subsequent evolution of the text indicates that we are the descendants of the second Manu, not the first. Thus we are descended not only from a replicated mother (as we were even in the *Bṛhaddevatā*) but now from a replicated Manu, as well.

The name of the second Manu is a pun. The shadow of Saraṇyū is now called not only the *savarṇā* (the female of-the-same-kind), as in the earlier versions, but also the *chāyā* (shadow) and *sadṛśā* ("look-alike"). Therefore, Manu's usual epithet, "Of-the-Same-Kind" (*sāvarṇi*) is explicitly interpreted not with reference to her but in the sense of "Of-the-Same-Kind [as his brother]"—although we know that he is also, implicitly, "Born of the Female of-the-Same-Kind." In the earlier text, the epithet "Of-the-Same-Kind" was a matronymic, because Manu's mother was the double and there was no other Manu for him to resemble. But now that the epithet has also become descriptive of a sibling relationship, Manu himself is the double, and the other Manu is given the patronymic (Vaivāsvata) that was originally Manu's. Finally, since in this text Manu is given this epithet by the Sun—who, as usual, thinks that the double is the real Saṃjñā (both he and Yama refer to her as Yama's mother)—he cannot name her child, Manu, after a resembling mother, but he can name him after his resemblance to the previous child. Manu's epithet of Sāvarṇi thus reveals yet another punning meaning: he is the son of the woman of-the-same-kind as his father. This makes Manu not merely a double but a triple: he is of-the-same-kind as his replicated mother, his older brother (son of the true mother), and his (dark, mortal, lower-class) father.

Indeed, by changing the name of the mother from Saraṇyū to Saṃjñā, this text makes both the mothers of the human race unreal, for the name of the first wife means "the sign" or "the image" or "the name," and the name of the second wife means "the shadow." Saṃjñā is the Signifier. (Her name contains the verbal root *jñā*, cognate with the Greek *gnosis* and English *know.*) Since the word or name is the double of the thing or person, Saṃjñā is her own double from the start. And perhaps it is relevant to note here that *chāyā* is also used in Sanskrit to refer to a commentary on a text. Thus, if Saṃjñā is the text, Chāyā is the commentary; if Saṃjñā is the dream, Chāyā is the secondary elaboration. Yet it should be recalled that names and images in India are regarded as in many ways isomorphic with reality or even able to create reality.[17] This consideration not only distinguishes the Sanskrit term from its Greek and Latin cognates but gives greater force and meaning to the female who is "just" an image. Saṃjñā may even be a riddle term for Sandhyā, another name for the Dawn; the Doppelgänger woman is then evening twilight, and the sun has two wives.[18] The parallels between Saṃjñā and Sandhyā are striking, for each is the wife of the sun, ambivalent and incestuous.[19] Each also designates a linguistic symbol: just as "Saṃjñā" means "sign" or "image," so "Sandhyā" becomes the term for the "twilight speech" of later Hindi poetry, a speech marked by riddles, inversions, and paradoxes.

A feminist might well read this myth as a powerful astronomical image of male domination, inasmuch as the female images are regarded by the texts as mere reflections of the energy of their husband, the Sun. (Here it is relevant to recall that in both the Vedas and the Purāṇas, despite the fact that the Sun is mortal and Saṃjñā immortal, the Sun is worshiped and Saṃjñā is not.) And this interpretation is supported by other expressions of domination, as well. One manuscript of the *Harivaṃśa* inserts a short passage describing Saṃjñā's thoughts while she contemplates becoming a mare, thoughts about the nature of women's subordination to men:

> She became very worried, and thought, "To hell with this behavior of women." She kept blaming herself and her own womanhood: "No one should remain a woman, ever; to hell with this life with no independence. In her childhood, youth, and old age she is in danger from her father, husband, and sons, respectively.[20] It was stupid of me to abandon my husband's house; I did the wrong thing. Even though I have not been recognized, I have suffered now in my father's house, and there she is, the female of-the-same-kind, with all her desires fulfilled. I have lost my husband's house because of my naive stupidity, and it is no better here in my father's house."[21]

And with that, she decides to become a mare, perhaps because mares, unlike human women, are free—both to reject unwanted stallions and to indulge their unbridled sexuality.[22] This passage strikes a contemporary reader as a strange mix of a quasi-feminist perception of male persecution and a male chauvinist justification for that persecution, projected (by the male author of the text) into the mind of the victim (the woman). Yet the Sun is surely a most pathetic victimizer, and the real energy (perhaps even the real power) in all versions of the myth seems focused on the tricky females. If this myth is about victimization, then it is certainly equally, if not more, about subversion.

SARAṆYŪ IN THE MĀRKAṆḌEYA PURĀṆA

As the version of the Saraṇyū legend given in the *Mārkaṇḍeya Purāṇa* differs from the *Harivaṃśa* text only in certain details, it will be sufficient merely to note these differences rather than retell the whole myth. The *Mārkaṇḍeya* uses the story of Saṃjñā to introduce the *Devī Māhātmya,* one of the earliest, and still one of the most important, texts about the worship of the Goddess, Devī. This use of the story is a most significant move, for it comes at a moment when the dominant (male) Sanskrit tradition is just beginning to incorporate into its texts the corpus of stories about female divinities (a.k.a. goddesses), who had long been alive and well and living in the non-Sanskritic, vernacular traditions. In aid of this appropriation, the old Vedic myth—about a goddess, Saraṇyū, who was no longer worshiped even in the *Rig Veda* and a sun god who was worshiped both in the *Rig Veda* and at the time of the Purāṇas—serves as a bridge to, and perhaps a validation of, the new Purāṇic myth about a Goddess, Devī Mahīṣamārdinī, who enters the Sanskrit tradition in this text and is now widely worshiped.[23] For despite the fact that no known ritual (that is, no known worship) was dedicated to Saṃjñā/Saraṇyū, her myth is very important indeed, given that she is the ancestor of the human race. In the context of a Purāṇa that is so concerned with dynasties, this *Ur*-mother is clearly crucial.

The *Mārkaṇḍeya* tells the story of Saṃjñā/Saraṇyū twice.[24] In neither variant is anything said about the Sun's ugliness or dark color; instead, the *Mārkaṇḍeya Purāṇa* (74.8) tells us that Saṃjñā could hardly bear her husband's splendor (or semen: *tejas*) and that she also feared his anger. When her father threw her out of his house, she took the form of a mare, "not wanting the sun's heat, and frightened of his energy/semen" (74.23). That the word for "energy" (*tejas*) is also a word for "semen" is surely relevant: Saraṇyū in her anthropomorphic form avoids the Sun's "energy," while in her mare form she avoids the stallion's semen.

When the look-alike curses Yama, the curse is subtly different from that of the *Harivaṃśa,* for it makes explicit that it is the foot that is the object of the curse: "Since you threaten your father's wife with your foot, your foot will fall" (103.20), or "Your foot will fall to the earth" (74.29). In both *Mārkaṇḍeya* variants, the father, Vivasvant, also specifies that worms will take flesh from Yama's *foot* and fall to earth.

The pun or riddle about the foot ("Worms will take flesh and go to the surface of the earth; thus your mother's words will come true, and you will be protected from the blow of the curse"), as well as the mutilation that it so vividly describes, is a recurrent theme in this corpus. The Sanskrit curse and countercurse turn upon a double pun, for "foot" (*pada,* cognate with Latin *pes, pedes,* French *pied,* and English *foot*) has two other meanings that are relevant here. *Pada* also means "a quarter, a part" (that is, only one of the four assumed feet), so that the countercurse invokes a kind of implicit synecdoche, *pars pro toto:* Yama will lose not his whole body but only part of it, the part that the worms will take away. And *pada* also means a word or a line or measure of poetry (that is, only one of the four assumed quarters of a verse), a meaning that "foot" also has in English. Thus the trick of the part (*pada*) and of the word (*pada*) is what saves Yama's foot (*pada*).

The *Mārkaṇḍeya* prefaces one of its retellings of the story of Saṃjñā with a brief but stunning sequence:

> Saṃjñā was the daughter of Tvaṣṭṛ and the wife of Mārtāṇḍa, the Sun. He produced in her Manu, called Manu Vaivāsvata, since he was Vivasvant's son. But when the sun looked at her, Saṃjñā used to shut her eyes, and so the sun got angry and spoke sharply to Saṃjñā: "Since you always restrain (*saṃyamam*) your eyes when you see me, therefore you will bring forth a twin (*yama*) who will restrain (*saṃyamanam*) creatures." Then the goddess became agitated by terror, and her gaze flickered; and when he saw that her gaze darted about, he said to her again, "Since now your gaze darts about when you see me, therefore you will bring forth a daughter who will be a river that darts about." And so because of her husband's curse Yama and Yamunā were born in her. (*MP* 74.1–7)

Where Manu is named after his father, and is blessed, Yama is named after his mother, and is cursed; for he is named not after her name but after her evil deeds. The pun here is not on feet but on eyes. Indeed, in many texts about substitute sexual partners, the woman closes her eyes and her child is born blind; that is the fate of Dīrghatamas and Dhṛtarāṣṭra.[25] Here a pair of rather awkward puns on the actions of the mother's eyes (restraining and darting) makes Yama "the Restrainer" (one of his famous epithets), instead of lame. The injured eye here replaces the injured foot.

In both *Mārkaṇḍeya* variants, unlike the *Harivaṃśa,* the look-alike cleverly avoids calling herself a mother and merely claims, correctly, to be Yama's father's wife. But Yama suspects her, judging not by appearances (as his father does) but by actions. He says, "I do not think she can be my mother, for a mother does not behave badly even toward badly behaved sons" (see *MP* 103.22–32). His father, however, persists in referring to her as a mother, although he adds that he will modify the curse "because of his affection for his son." But finally, he, too, "realizes that the look-alike is not the true mother," even though, in this version, she does not break her promise to remain silent. And he says, "Surely you are not the mother of these [children]. You are some Saṃjñā or other who has come here. For how could a mother curse a son even among children with no good qualities?" (*MP* 103.27–32). In the other version, the Sun's words are given to Yama, who says, "Daddy, this great wonder was never seen by anyone, that a mother rejects her calf-love (*vātsalya*) for her son and gives him a curse. This woman does not act like a mother to me as Manu told me she did (to him); for a mother would not act with no good qualities even toward sons who had no good qualities" (*MP* 74.31–32). (In the *Amar Chitra Katha* comic book version of the myth, Yama says to his father, "Father, that woman is not our mother!" His father replies, "I agree. A son may change in his affections but a mother never ceases to care." And the Sun realizes, "The children are right. She must be an imposter.")

When the look-alike still avoids giving an answer, the Sun thinks about it and realizes the truth (*MP* 103.33). He summons the look-alike Saṃjñā and says, "Where has she gone?"—a question that seems to imply that he knows the look-alike is not the real Saṃjñā. But the look-alike nevertheless continues, at first, to say what Saṃjñā had told her to say: "I am Saṃjñā the daughter of Tvaṣṭṛ, your wife, and these are the children you begat in me." Subsequently (as in the *Harivaṃśa*), when he is about to curse her, she tells him all the details of what had happened (*MP* 74.33–35). In both variants, he goes to Tvaṣṭṛ, who puts him on the lathe and trims away his excessive energy, which he makes into weapons (as in the *Harivaṃśa*). Finally, the text tells us:

> Then Vivasvant's body was beautiful, and had no excessive fiery energy. He went to his wife, the mare, in the form of a stallion. But when she saw him approaching she feared it might be another male, and so she turned to face him, determined to protect her hindquarters. Their noses joined as they touched, and the seed of the Sun flowed from his two nostrils into the mare and came out of her mouth, and in that way the equine twin gods called the Aśvins were born.
>
> Moreover, as the seed stopped flowing (*retaso'ante*) a son named Revānta was born, mounted on a horse. Then the Sun showed her his own form, and when she saw that it was peaceful she was full of joy, and she took on her own form and was full of love, and he took her home. (*MP* 105.1–13)

And only after we are told what became of Manu the son of Vivasvant, Yama, Yamunā, the Aśvins, and Revānta, do we learn about the children of the shadow. The bard says, "Now learn from me the places assigned to the children of the shadow Saṃjñā: the firstborn son of the shadow was the equal of the eldest-born Manu, and so he obtained the name (*saṃjñā*) 'Of-the-Same-Kind' (*sāvarṇiki*)" (*MP* 75.35). It is striking, and surely no accident, that the name of the mother, Saṃjñā, is here used, finally, in its lexical sense of "name."

THE FATHER OF THE BRIDE

All three of these Purāṇic variants (the *Harivaṃśa* and the two *Mārkaṇḍeya* passages) give new prominence to an old, silent character: the father-in-law, Tvaṣṭṛ, who at first receives Saṃjñā when she flees from her husband, then forces her to leave his house, and finally mutilates her husband in order to make him acceptable to her. Tvaṣṭṛ is the artisan of the gods, the blacksmith, who is in many Indo-European mythologies crippled and consequently abandoned by his wife, or cuckolded; thus, in Greek mythology, Hephaestus's wife, Aphrodite, betrays him with Ares. Here it is Tvaṣṭṛ's son-in-law (Vivasvant) and his grandson (Yama) who are crippled and abandoned by their wife/mother, while his son (the three-headed Triśiras) is beheaded. This is an unhappy family: the Sun is rejected and mutilated by his mother; Yama is tormented by his karma; the female of-the-same-kind is miserable; and the first children are rejected by the first mother and mistreated by the foster mother. Only the child of-the-same-kind is not rejected: he alone is treated well by the mother of-the-same-kind.

The aggression of the bride's father against her husband in the Purāṇic corpus lends weight, retrospectively, to the possibly incestuous connection that some Indologists have seen between Tvaṣṭṛ and Saraṇyū in the Vedic corpus.[26] Adalbert Kuhn argues that "the anger of the gods regarding the wedding of the father and the daughter also explains why the gods hide Saraṇyū and slip a look-alike under Vivasvant."[27] The incestuous connection between Tvaṣṭṛ and Saraṇyū is further supported by the parallel between the story of Saraṇyū fleeing from the Sun in the form of a mare and the myth of Uṣas fleeing from her incestuous father, Prajāpati, in the form of a mare; he becomes a stallion, who mounts her; when she becomes a cow, he becomes a bull, and so forth, in order to produce various races of offspring.[28]

But if the theme of father-daughter incest is questionable, the theme of brother-sister incest appears here unmistakably. For Yama and Yamī commit incest in the Iranian tradition, and in the *Rig Veda* Yamī tries, in vain, to persuade Yama to go to bed with her.[29] The theme of the substitute mother (who rejects her husband because he is too far away from her, being mortal when she is immortal) is closely conflated with the theme of the resistant brother (who rejects his sister because she is too close to him, being his sibling).[30]

SARAṆYŪ: THE CLASSIC COMIC

Interesting bowdlerizations may be seen in the *Amar Chitra Katha* story of "Surya," which is "Retold from the Markandeya Purana" (see figure 16).[31] Here, the incestuous implications of the aggression of the bride's father against her husband in the Purāṇic corpus are veiled in the sanitized comic book version, but the presence of Saṃjñā's father remains pivotal. When Tvaṣṭṛ (here called Vishwakarma, from his Sanskrit epithet of Viśvakarman, "All-maker") kicks her out, he actually says, "I dote on you. But a woman's place is by her husband." Vishwakarma suggests that she marry Surya but asks her, "Think well. Are you sure you will be able to bear his brilliance in

Figure 16. Cover from "Sūrya" (Hindi edition), *Amar Chitra Katha* comic book no. 58, showing Sūrya and Saraṇyū. Bombay: India Book House, n.d.

all seasons?" To this she replies, veiling her face from him, "I am sure, father"—and she has a dreamy, sexy look in her eyes when she muses, "I was wondering how long I would be able to revel in Surya's warmth." One of the women who dress her for her wedding remarks, "Let me darken your eyes. You will need protection from his glances," whereupon another woman adds, "Glare, you mean." But Sanjna replies, "Need protection from Surya's glances? Me?"

When Manu grows up, we are told that "Surya and Sanjna were proud of him." Delighted, his father remarks, "He is brilliant!" to which his mother replies, "Like his father!" Thus the Sanskrit pun on *tejas* as "brilliance" or "semen" is given a third twist—"brilliance" in the contemporary sense of intellectual power. And the cosmic question of resemblance is reduced to the cliché compliment/complement of fathers and sons: "Chip off the old block." But Surya's brilliance reverts to its cosmic, solar meaning soon enough, when he says to his wife, "Come Sanjna, sit by me." Here, as usual, the *Amar Chitra Katha* editor bowdlerizes what was a more intimate sexual contact in the Sanskrit text: in place of the hot semen we have an invitation to sit nearby.

But even this contact is too much for Sanjna, and the text elaborates upon the theme of closing the eyes: "Sanjna, what's the matter?" "My lord! Why do you glare at me so! Lord! I cannot open my eyes." He says, "Sanjna! Look at me! I am your husband! Sanjna! Will you repel me?" "I am sorry, my lord." "Then listen carefully. Since you closed your eyes on me, the sustainer of all living beings, the son you bear now shall be Yama, the god of death." Since the pun on "restrain" is lost here, the curse makes no sense, except through an implicit connection between blindness and death.

But the sexual squeamishness of the *Amar Chitra Katha* cannot cope with the subsequent equine issue. Sanjna's only reason for turning into a mare is avoidance: "I cannot face Surya. I will turn myself into a mare. Then no one will find me." When Surya goes to Vishwakarma in search of her, Vishwakarma says, "I have divined that she turned herself into a mare." On the way to find her, they ask a passerby, "Have you seen a mare go by?" "Yes! A quaint one . . . by the river." Surya then says, "Why do you call it a quaint one?" "I speak the truth, sir. *This mare talks!*" To which Surya makes the wonderful reply, "It must be Sanjna." The talking horse is persuaded to resume her own form, and there is not a whisper about the mating of horses or the birth of the Aśvins.

The Shadow, like the Sun, is interpreted literally and naturalistically in the comic book; she is both a reflected image and a shadow. At first, the shadow is Sanjna's reflection in the water, which Sanjna draws out. But when Sanjna remarks, "You, Chhaya, are safe from the glare of Surya," Chhaya replies, "I shelter all who fear it"—a reference to the Shadow as shade, which is, on the literal level that this text favors, indeed safe from the sun. Chhaya is happy with Surya, although she thinks, "Poor Sanjna had to give up all this. Will she ever return? I must not forget that I am only Sanjna's shadow." Thus, in a single speech she expresses the banal, all-too-human materialism of the second wife and the reminder that she is merely a natural phenomenon, a shadow.

As in the Sanskrit text, she is a good mother only to her own children (two sons and a daughter): "But alas! She did not care for Sanjna's children in the same manner." This time we learn more about the stepdaughter, who is (as in the Sanskrit) cursed by Surya because of the sins of her true mother. But despite the generally naturalistic bent of this text, the stepdaughter's curse is not naturalistic (a darting river) but psychological (a fickle woman, more appropriate to the nature of both her mother and her stepmother): "You tremble before me? Then you shall bear a daughter too. And she, Yamuna, shall be as fickle as you." Now, as the Shadow beats Yamuna, Yamuna thinks, "How I wish I were motherless." Still the text tries to salvage Sanjna's good-motherhood, or at least her good-wifehood. The Shadow says to Surya, "I am Chhaya, the shadow of Sanjna. She did not want to leave you uncared for. So she sent me here instead." And when Sanjna turns back from mare into goddess, the first thing she says is, "My lord! How are our children?" to which he replies, "Manu, Yama and Yamuna will know a mother again."

And finally *everyone* is a good mother, in a finale reminiscent of the workings of the Greek tragedies in the hands of Melina Mercouri in "Never on Sunday." Sanjna says, "I shall never again wander away from home," and Surya adds, "Chhaya shall be forgiven and shall live with us." "So Surya and Sanjna went back to his abode in the skies and lived there in happiness with Chhaya and the children." And all the children, of both generations, are depicted in a final family snapshot. This text has traveled a long way from the Sanskrit corpus in which the tragic story of Saṃjñā and Manu attributes the origin of the human race to an abandoning mother.

SARAṆYŪ : KUNTĪ = YAMA : KARṆA

The theme of the abandoning mother, the wife of the sun, resurfaces in a transformation in a myth that is central to the *Mahābhārata:*

> The princess Kuntī was given the boon of invoking a god to give her a child, and she tried out her boon on the sun god, merely out of curiosity. The sun god split himself into two by his power of yoga, so that he came to her but still went on shining in the sky. As soon as Kuntī saw him, she begged him to go back, pointing out that she was still a child, but he insisted on having her, threatening that if she did not give in to him, he would burn to death "your foolish father, who does not know of your misconduct." Karṇa was born, but to conceal her own misdeeds, Kuntī threw the boy into the Horse River (*aśvanadyām*), lamenting, "Fortunate is the woman from whose breast you will drink. What dream will she have?" Then she returned to the palace, sick with sorrow and in fear of awakening her father. Karṇa was retrieved by a charioteer whose wife adopted him.
>
> Now Karṇa was born with golden armor and earrings grafted right onto his body. He always competed with Arjuna, who feared Karṇa's invincible armor.

> In order to help Arjuna, one day Indra [the father of Arjuna] came to Karṇa in disguise as a Brahmin and begged the armor from him. Indra suspected that the sun god had warned Karṇa that Indra would come in disguise, but Karṇa did not refuse the request, though he asked in return for a magic spear that Indra had. Then Karṇa said, "I will strip off the earrings and the armor and give them to you, but let me not look disgusting with my body flayed." Indra replied, "You will not look disgusting, and there will be no visible scar on your body. You will look like (*tadṛśa*) your father in glory (*tejas*) and in color (*varṇa*)" (3.294.32). Karṇa sliced the armor from his body, which was streaming with blood, along with the earrings, and gave them to Indra.[32]

The sun god forces himself upon Kuntī, in part by threatening to harm her father (an echo of the old incestuous connection between Saraṇyū and Tvaṣṭṛ). Karṇa's foster mother is first imagined by Kuntī, with envy, and subsequently described; the equine mother survives only the form of the "Horse River" that receives the child—a body of water not mentioned elsewhere in the epic, to my knowledge. And just as Sūrya is the only god who rapes Kuntī, so Karṇa is the only one of the Pāṇḍavas who is mutilated. His mutilation is, moreover, an inversion of Yama's mutilation: in the epic, which abounds in multiple fathers rather than multiple mothers, Karṇa and Arjuna have the same mother (Kuntī) but different fathers (the Sun and Indra), and one father (Indra) mutilates the son of the other father. In addition, Karṇa is restored to the condition of *looking like* his father in two respects essential to the myth of Saraṇyū: glory (or semen: *tejas*) and color (*varṇa*)—precisely the qualities for which Saraṇyū rejected Karṇa's father.

CONCLUSION

As anthropogonies, these stories are saying that the primeval children, our ancestors, were abandoned by their mother. And on the metaphysical level the myth of Saraṇyū/Saṃjñā seems to be saying that we, the descendants of Manu, are the children of the image—the children of *māyā,* not the children of the real thing.[33] These myths embody the Vedantic view that we are born into illusion, live in illusion, and can only know illusion. Clearly, this is a deeply religious story, not merely (or not even primarily) a story about men and women, or parents and children, or racial color. For, in addition to psychological questions regarding incest, stepmothers, rejected children, and unwanted husbands, as well as sociological questions about racial color, the Saraṇyū story raises theological questions about the origin of the human race and of human death, about appearance and reality, about the relationship between male and female divine powers, and about the nature of the relationship between humans and the divine. The metaphysical question of the origin of the human race is posed in the fate of Saraṇyū's second son, Manu, and the metaphysical question of death is posed in the mythology of Saraṇyū's first son, Yama. But that is yet another story, best left for another time.

NOTES

1. The tale of Saraṇyū/Saṃjñā is one that I have used variously in various books: I touched upon it in *Asceticism and Eroticism in the Mythology of Śiva* (London: Oxford University Press, 1973), pp. 276 and 292; translated it in *Hindu Myths* (Harmondsworth: Penguin Books, 1975), pp. 60–62 and 65–70; and analyzed it in *Women, Androgynes, and Other Mythical Beasts* (Chicago: University of Chicago Press, 1980), esp. pp. 174–85. Yet it still accuses me of not even having begun to plumb its depths, and draws me back to it.

2. *Rig Veda,* with the commentary of Sāyaṇa, 6 vols. (Benares: Chowkhamba Sanskrit Series no. 99, 1966), 10.17.1–2.

3. Maurice Bloomfield, "Contributions to the Veda III: The Marriage of Saraṇyū, Tvaṣṭṛ's Daughter," *Journal of the American Oriental Society* 15 (1893): 172–88, at p. 172.

4. See Stella Kramrisch, "Two: Its Significance in the Ṛgveda," in *Indological Studies in Honor of W. Norman Brown,* ed. Ernest Bender (New Haven: American Oriental Society, 1962), pp. 125–26.

5. David Shulman, personal communication, March 1993.

6. See Robert P. Goldman, "Mortal Man and Immortal Woman: An Interpretation of Three *Ākhyāna* Hymns of the Ṛgveda," *Journal of the Oriental Institute of Baroda* 18, no. 4 (1969): 274–303.

7. Bloomfield, "Marriage of Saraṇyū," pp. 172 and 188.

8. See, for instance, *Rig Veda* 10.14.2; *Atharva Veda,* with the commentary of Sāyaṇa (Hoshiarpur: Vishveshvaranand Vedic Research Institute, 1960), 18.3.13.

9. For example, see *Rig Veda* 10.72.8–9, and *Śatapatha Brāhmaṇa* (Benares: Chowkhamba Sanskrit Series no. 96, 1964), 3.1.3.3; see also O'Flaherty, *Women, Androgynes,* pp. 174–75.

10. *Śatapatha Brāhmaṇa* 3.1.3.4.

11. On the proliferation of twins, see Bruce Lincoln, *Myth, Cosmos, and Society* (Cambridge, Mass.: Harvard University Press, 1986), pp. 80–82.

12. See O'Flaherty, *Asceticism and Eroticism,* p. 303.

13. *Bṛhaddevatā* of Śaunaka (Cambridge, Mass.: Harvard University Press, 1904), 6.162–63, 7.1–6.

14. Herman Lommel, *Kleine Schriften* (Wiesbaden: Otto Harrassowitz, 1978), pp. 272–74.

15. Herman Güntert, in *Der Arische Weltkönig und Heiland* (Halle: Max Niemeyer, 1923), derives *nāsatya* from *nes,* "to save," and translates it as "savior."

16. In one verse (8.1) of the *Harivaṃśa* (critical edition; Poona: Bhandarkar Oriental Research Institute, 1969), she is called not Saraṇyū but Sureṇu.

17. See Wendy Doniger O'Flaherty, *Dreams, Illusion, and Other Realities* (Chicago: University of Chicago Press, 1984), pp. 1–18.

18. See Herman Lommel, "Vedische Einzelstudien," *Zeitschrift für die Deutschen Morgenländischen Gesellschaft* 99 (1949): 225–57, esp. pp. 243–57 (for Saraṇyū/Saṃjñā).

19. See Ananda K. Coomaraswamy, *The Darker Side of Dawn,* Smithsonian Miscellaneous Collections, vol. 94, no. 1 (Washington, D.C., 1935).

20. This is a satire on the famous verse in Manu (5.148): "In childhood a woman should be under her father's control, in youth under her husband's, and when her husband is dead, under her sons'. She should not have independence." See Wendy Doniger, trans., with Brian K. Smith, *The Laws of Manu* (London: Penguin Books, 1992), p. 115.

21. *Harivaṃśa,* a passage of four verses inserted after 8.14 in the critical edition.

22. See O'Flaherty, *Women, Androgynes,* pp. 149–238.

23. On the status of Saraṇyū in the *Rig Veda,* see ibid., pp. 149–65.

24. *Mārkaṇḍeya Purāṇa* (Bombay: Biblioteca Indica, 1890), chaps. 103–5 and 74–75.

25. On Dīrghatamas, see *Bṛhaddevatā* 4.21–25. Cf. also Sāyaṇa's commentary on *Rig Veda* 1.51.13; and *Mahābhārata* (critical edition; Poona: Bhandarkar Oriental Research Institute, 1933–69), 1.99. On Dhṛtarāṣṭra, see *Mahābhārata* 1.100.

26. Bloomfield, "Marriage of Saraṇyū," p. 181, citing Albrecht Weber, Adalbert Kuhn, and Henri Bergaigne.

27. Adalbert Kuhn, "Saraṇyū-'Erinnús," in *Zeitschrift für Vergleichende Sprachforschung,* vol. 1, ed. Theodor Aufrecht and Adalbert Kuhn (Berlin: F. Dümmler, 1852), pp. 439–70, at p. 448.

28. *Bṛhadāraṇyaka Upaniṣad* 1.4.1–6, in *One Hundred and Eight Upanishads,* ed. Wasudev Laxman Shastri Pansikar (Bombay: Nirnaya Sagara Press, 1913).

29. *Rig Veda* 10.10; see also Wendy Doniger O'Flaherty, *The Rig Veda* (Harmondsworth: Penguin Books, 1981), pp. 247–50.

30. See Goldman, "Mortal Man and Immortal Woman."

31. "Surya," retold by Mayah Balse, *Amar Chitra Katha* no. 58, ed. Anant Pai (Bombay: India Book Trust, n.d.).

32. See *Mahābhārata* 1.104, 3.290–94, and 5.138–42.

33. See Kramrisch, "Two: Its Significance in the Ṛgveda," pp. 112–15.

ŚERĀṄVĀLĪ
The Mother Who Possesses

Kathleen M. Erndl

Previous essays have introduced individual goddesses, their stories, images, and rituals. Here, we will take a somewhat different approach, focusing on a phenomenon that can be observed among many goddesses throughout India: the divine possession of a human vehicle.[1] As several other authors argue in this volume, although individual Hindu goddesses possess distinctive attributes, their identities also overlap to a considerable extent, and many—if not most—goddesses are, at least in some contexts, considered to be manifestations of the one Great Goddess, Devī. Similarly, goddesses tend to manifest themselves not in a single form but in multiple iconic forms, as well as in such natural phenomena as rocks, plants, rivers, mountains, and flames. This flexibility of identity and multiplication of form is nowhere more evident than in the phenomenon of divine possession.

Divine possession is the most dramatic way to encounter the Goddess experientially, and it also presents the greatest challenge to the Western worldview. It is one thing to read sacred texts about the Goddess or to view her images, to analyze the metaphors of the former or the aesthetic qualities of the latter. It is quite another to meet the Goddess face to face. By way of introduction, let me present two brief vignettes that encapsulate some of what I have experienced in my encounter with Goddess possession while doing fieldwork in northwest India and in trying to interpret it in a scholarly context back home.

The first incident took place in the Punjabi town of Mohali, a suburb of Chandigarh, in the winter of 1983. I was sitting on the floor in the home of a lower-middle-class family in the company of about fifty festively dressed people—women, men, and children. It was about two in the morning. We were attending a Devī *jagrātā*, an all-night ritual performance in which the Goddess is worshiped with devotional songs and stories of her exploits.

The performers, joined by the congregation, were singing a devotional song to the lively beat of a drum. The Goddess was present that night in the form of a flame that had been lit and consecrated, and then surrounded by offerings of fruit and flowers and placed on a platform at the front of the room. She was also present in the form of a sixteen-year-old girl called the "Little Mother," who was seated on another platform, next to the flame. The Goddess had entered her body and was "playing" within her. Her long black hair flew out from her face as though charged with electricity as her head whirled about in rhythmic circles. From time to time, members of the congregation would go up and make offerings to her.

I was tired and, frankly, a little bored, since I had seen all this before—and I found myself wishing that I had chosen to do research on something that took place at a more reasonable hour. Then for some reason I glanced at the woman sitting next to me. She was probably in her mid-fifties, plump, well-dressed, and matronly looking. I had not spoken with her, although earlier we had nodded to each other in greeting. Suddenly, the woman's head began to move from side to side, her eyes glazed over, and she started to shake. Standing up, she began to dance frenetically, her tightly bound hair loosening, then fanning out from her face. I was frozen with fear. The other people were moving away from her and pulling me along with them. Later—I do not remember how much later—she calmed down and sat quietly, but her eyes remained unfocused. I was left wondering whether this could happen to me.

The second event took place in Madison, Wisconsin, in November 1983. Having just returned from the field, I had presented a paper at the annual Conference on South Asia on the Devī *jagrātā* as a ritual performance. Although only a small portion of my presentation dealt with the phenomenon of Goddess possession, it was this part that evoked the most comment during the question-and-answer period. Afterward, a senior colleague asked me if I had ever believed that it really was the Goddess possessing those women. I answered impulsively, "Yes." Upon reflection I realized that it was the experience of observing possession, of coming face to face with this impressive manifestation of the Goddess's power (*śakti*), that brought home to me in a very concrete fashion the immediacy with which devotees experience the Goddess's presence. This in turn led me to take seriously the notion of the Goddess as an agent herself, rather than simply a symbol or projection.

Much scholarship on various kinds of spirit possession has assumed (usually tacitly) that the possessing entity is an epiphenomenon, that is, that it does not "really" exist. Anthropologist Manuel Moreno, however, has argued for what he calls a "processual" view of deities, as opposed to a "structural" view. The structural view sees deities as "disembodied symbols" of social realities and human relationships. The processual view, in contrast, accepts deities as effective agents, as personal beings who interact with humans. While acknowledging the value of structural analysis for illuminating aspects of social structure that are not readily apparent through observation, Moreno argues that such an analysis fails to take into consideration the dynamics of the interaction between deities and humans as Hindus themselves understand them.[2] His position is very close to my own: to understand the phenomenon of Goddess possession, one must treat the Goddess herself as an agent who interacts with both the person possessed and the devotees who worship her.

The word *her* at the end of the last sentence is deliberately ambiguous, for the devotees worship both the Goddess and the person who is possessed; both are Mātā. But the question still remains as to whether the Goddess and her human vehicle are completely separate entities, one of which temporarily "overtakes" the other, or whether they are in some sense in a relation of identity with each other, perhaps in a process of exchange or transformation. Here the line between human and divine becomes blurred (so much so that I was tempted to subtitle this essay "The Mother Who Is Possessed" rather than "The Mother Who Possesses"). Is it the human vehicle who becomes the sacred female by virtue of the infusion of *śakti*? Or is it the Goddess herself who "inhabits" the human vehicle as her chosen means of manifesting herself to her devotees? Of course, both are true, in much the same way as the "duck-rabbit" drawing is simultaneously both a duck and a rabbit, although only one at a time can be perceived. Also, one must know what to look for in order to see either one. A woman trembles, her eyes glazed, her hair disheveled. Some see a woman expressing her own power. Some see the Goddess herself. Others might see a psychological disorder or an outright fraud. It all depends on one's point of view. Here, my point of view will shift back and forth between that of the Goddess and that of her human vehicles, in keeping with the fluid nature of their complex relationship.

THE SEMANTICS AND DYNAMICS OF GODDESS POSSESSION

My area of study is northwest India, including the territories of Delhi and Chandigarh and the states of Punjab, Haryana, and much of Himachal Pradesh. While certain specifics of terminology and practice may be unique to this region, I believe that similar dynamics of Goddess possession can be found throughout India.[3] In northwest India, the worship of Devī is perhaps the most prevalent manner of religious expression among Hindus. The region boasts a multitude of pilgrimage sites associated with the Goddess, such as Vaishno Devi, Jvala Mukhi, and Chintpurni. Each of these houses a particular goddess who has her own personality, iconography, and cycle of stories, and who is simultaneously considered to be a manifestation of the one all-pervading divine force, *śakti*. When spoken of in general terms, as she often is, the Goddess is commonly called Śerāṅvālī, "Lion Rider" (a nickname of the demon-slaying Durgā) or simply Mātā, "Mother" (see figure 17). In her cult esoteric Tantric elements mingle with popular devotional worship (*bhakti*) and folk elements.

Although this lion-riding mother goddess has mythological and ritual affiliations with the great male deities Viṣṇu and Śiva, it is in her independent form that she is most often worshiped. That is, she is not seen as a consort deity, like Lakṣmī or Pārvatī, whose identity is linked with a male deity. Yet she is not completely different from such goddesses, for on some level all goddesses are one. One way to approach this complex issue is to view the various goddesses associated with Śerāṅvālī as functioning in an independent (as opposed to a consort) mode. It is this mode that most concerns us here, since the Goddess manifestations who typically operate independently—such as Vaiṣṇo Devī, Kālī, Jvālā Mukhī, and Santoṣī Mā—are the ones most likely to possess human vehicles. Although Punjabis and other people in northwest India are familiar with Lakṣmī and Pārvatī and do worship them on occasion, I have never heard them speak of these goddesses as possessing people.

The goddess Śerāṅvālī is both transcendent and immanent, her functions ranging from such cosmic concerns as the creation, preservation, and destruction of the universe to personal concerns—curing diseases, helping people in distress, and so on. She is the embodiment of *śakti*, the dynamic power of the universe. Implicit in the theology of this Goddess is a monism in which matter and spirit are not differentiated but rather form a continuity that is subsumed within *śakti*, the feminine creative principle. Whereas the Śaiva and Vaiṣṇava theologies both recognize *śakti* to be the active (feminine) aspect of the Divine, the complement to the inactive (masculine) aspect, the goddess-focused Śākta theology understands *śakti*, which is identified with the Great Goddess, to be the ultimate reality itself and the totality of all being. The general thrust of Śākta theology is to affirm the reality, power, and life force that pervades the material world. Matter itself, while always changing, is sacred and is not different from spirit. The Goddess is the totality of all existence; accordingly, as a reflection of the way things really are, she takes on both gentle (*saumya*) forms such as Vaiṣṇo Devī and fierce (*raudra*) forms such as Kālī. Creation and destruction, life and death, are two sides of the same reality. The Goddess encompasses both. Furthermore, the Goddess is not just a transcendent ideal but also an immanent presence in the lives of her devotees.

The Goddess is worshiped in various contexts and in various of her manifestations—at pilgrimage sites, in ritual performances, and at household shrines in forms such as stone, flame, and icon. The most dramatic way in which devotees experience the Goddess, though, is through her possession of human—and usually female—vehicles. This type of possession is not regarded as an affliction but rather as a sign of grace, as the Goddess's chosen

Figure 17. Serāṅvālī, the lion-riding goddess, accompanied by three cosmic forms of the Goddess—Mahākālī, Mahālakṣmī, and Mahāsarasvatī—issuing from the three stones enshrined at the Vaiṣṇo Devī temple. Polychrome poster-art depiction by Jain Picture Publication, Delhi, ca. 1990.

method of granting a sacred vision (*darśan*) to her devotees. While the concern of this essay is specifically divine possession within the Goddess cult, it is worth pointing out that many other kinds of spirit possession are prevalent in South Asia, such as unwanted possession by malevolent or mischievous spirits, ghosts, or ancestors (*bhūt-pret*). Susan Wadley, writing about Uttar Pradesh, John Stanley, writing about Maharashtra, and Gananath Obeyesekere, writing about Sri Lanka, all refer to differences between afflicting or evil spirits and invited or divine spirits.[4] Similarly, in northwest India possession by an evil spirit must be exorcised by force or appeasement, but possession by a benevolent deity such as Śerāṅvālī is usually encouraged and cultivated, even if not initially sought. Possession by an evil spirit is seen as an affliction or punishment; possession by the Goddess is seen as a gift, a sign of grace—a positive, albeit awesome and often troublesome, appearance.

But what exactly is possession? To describe this cross-cultural phenomenon, the following definition provides a good starting place: "any complete but temporary domination of a person's body, and the blotting out of that person's consciousness, by a distinct alien power of known or unknown origin."[5] Yet the word *possession* is inadequate except as a very rough gloss of what is actually a complex set of related phenomena. In Hindi and Punjabi certain phrases are used in the context of the Goddess cult to describe these phenomena, although the terminology naturally varies throughout India.

Two of the most common expressions are "wind form" (*pavan rūp*) and "playing" (Hindi: *khelnā*; Punjabi: *kheḍnā*). When a woman is possessed, the Goddess is said to take on a "wind form," enter her, and "play" within her. Her hair, no matter how tightly bound, is said to come undone and fly freely in response to the force of the wind (*pavan*). The state of possession is characterized by glazed eyes, a change in voice, and the whirling around of the head, with hair flying loose. Under normal circumstances, a respectable woman's hair is tied up and braided, not allowed to hang loose. In a discussion of hair symbolism among Hindu and Sikh Punjabis, Paul Hershman mentions that, among the contexts in which the expression *val khūle* ("loose hair") is used, we find "a woman possessed who in a trance whirls her head with her hair flying free."[6] In this instance, the Goddess is said to have taken on *pavan rūp*, "wind form."

Yet there are also times when the Goddess assumes her "wind form" without entering a human vehicle. In that sense, it is invisible yet perceptible. "Wind" is a subtle form that occupies an intermediate position between the unmanifest Goddess and a concrete manifestation. It is a form characterized by motion and breath that the Goddess takes on to move from one place to another or to display her power, but without becoming fully visible. For example, in several versions of the story of Queen Tārā, the charter myth for the all-night songfest (*jagrātā*) honoring the Goddess, the word *pavan* describes such a form: when King Harīcand's wakefulness prevents Tārā from attending the sweepers' *jagrātā*, Tārā prays to the Goddess, whereupon a cool breeze (*pavan, havā*) arises and puts the king to sleep. Likewise, a holy man who serves at a Durgā temple once told me that he had been called there by the Mother who had come to him in the form of "wind." Whenever he forgets to do some work, she again comes into his mind as "wind" to remind him. When this happens, he said, she enters his mind through the breath in his mouth, and he then sees her in his mind. This is not possession in the usual sense of the term.

Similarly, the expression "playing" is used variously. It can, for instance, refer to the wild and "playful" head and body movements of the person who is possessed. The Goddess is said to be "playing" in that person, as in the expression, "The Goddess plays in X," although sometimes the human vehicle is the agent, as in "X started playing." A slightly different but related use of "play" occurs in devotional songs that turn on the image of young girls (*kanyā, kaṅjak*), representative of the Goddess in her virgin aspect playing in the temple courtyard.[7] These songs represent the sweet and lovable aspect of the divine play, evoking *vātsalya bhāva* (parental love)—one of the principal modes of religious devotion (*bhakti*)—much as in the cult of the child Krishna. These expressions are tied in with general notions of divine play in the Hindu tradition.[8] Stories connected with the Goddess variously describe her actions as play (*khel*), drama or sport (*līlā*), and art or fabrication (*kalā*). These terms are used more or less interchangeably to suggest the Goddess's exuberant, but seemingly (to humans) purposeless, creativity. The word *possession* can thus provide only a rough and partial semantic equivalent for what is a fluid, multifaceted set of concepts.

The person possessed is called the *savārī*, "vehicle" (as in "she is the vehicle of Kālī"); *savārī* here designates the woman whom the Goddess, having assumed a particular form, rides on or inhabits and through whom she speaks. *Savārī* is also used to describe the Goddess herself: she is *savārī rūp*, "[one who has a] vehicle form," again referring to her action of "riding" or "mounting" a possessed person.

In reading about South Asia, one often gets the impression that possession, along with related ecstatic behavior, belongs to the "little tradition" and is thus largely confined to the lower castes and the poor and uneducated in rural areas. However, in my experience, the phenomenon of possession in the cult of Śerāṅvālī is widespread throughout the population. I have witnessed Goddess possession in both village and urban settings, among low and high castes (including Brahmins), the poor and the rich, the uneducated and the educated, Sikhs as well as Hindus. As far as gender is concerned, possession by the Goddess, though occurring in both sexes, is more frequent among women, while possession by a male deity such as Bābā Bālak Nāth is more common among men. At the same time, possession experiences vary considerably in their intensity, duration, and frequency. The degree of recognition, respect, and encouragement given to possession vehicles by other members of society is similarly quite variable.

Unplanned, uncontrolled possession occasionally occurs in a nonritual context. Although I have not directly observed this type of possession, I have heard reports of young girls "playing" for hours on end without warning. Such descriptions typically form part of the hagiographies of women who later achieved some control and regularity over their possession and have come to understand it in terms of the theology and religious practice of devotion to Devī. At the time of the initial possession, however, neither the vehicle nor others may have recognized (or accepted) that the possessing deity was the Goddess. Family members and others often suspect sorcery, insanity, or possession by a malevolent spirit, since these all exhibit similar symptoms.

Unplanned, uncontrolled possession may occur in devotees who participate in ritual activities such as a *jagrātā*, devotional singing, or pilgrimage. While the music is playing and the drums beating, someone may spontaneously start to shake, roll the head, or dance, as I described in the opening vignette of this essay. No one seems unduly surprised or disturbed when this happens, and in many cases it remains an isolated event in the person's life. However, such spontaneous possession experiences do sometimes occur repeatedly, developing into a periodic pattern that becomes a planned part of the person's devotional and spiritual practice. I came across an example of this development while interviewing a man of the Kāyasth caste from Chandigarh who was on a group pilgrimage to the major Devī temples. In a discussion of his long-standing devotion to the Goddess and the miracles she had performed for him, he volunteered the information that he had recently started to "play," describing his experience as follows:

> I do *pūjā* twice a day. When I go to a *jagrātā*, I get the experience of possession. I see Devī seated on a lion, and my head starts whirling around. This has been happening for five or six months now. . . . I get a feeling of wind (*pavan*) overwhelming me like a whirlwind and see the image of Devī. I am not afraid of this experience. I sit in front of a flame every day and concentrate. The wind comes when I am listening to a beautiful song. At first my wife worried that I would renounce the world, but now she and the children realize what it is.[9]

This informant's description of a vision (*darśan*) of the Goddess accompanied by the sensation of wind is typical of possession experience. The vision of the Goddess and the statements she makes while inhabiting her vehicle are the major signs that distinguish possession by Devī from possession by other deities or spirits.

In a performance situation such as a *jagrātā*, possession is often found to be planned, even orchestrated, plus which there seems to be a progression from an initial spontaneous incident to more controlled and periodic possessions. A woman may start to become possessed on a specific day of the week, such as Tuesday or Friday, or on the eighth day of the bright fortnight of the lunar month—days traditionally associated with Goddess worship. When news of this spreads outside her family, people may come on these days to sing devotional songs, offer her gifts, and ask for her help as an oracle or healer. The woman may start to hold ritual functions in her home on a regular basis; she may be invited to participate in these events at others' homes. She may build a small shrine or temple and/or start making pilgrimages with her devotees to Devī temples. In this way, a small cult begins to form.

During the spring and fall Navarātras and the ten-day festival during the month of Sāvan (July–August), pilgrimage places such as Jvala Mukhi, Chintpurni, and Naina Devi are besieged by these women (called Mātās, "mothers") and their entourages. They come from villages and towns all over the greater Punjab, bearing red flags and other offerings. They bring drums, cymbals, and musical instruments—nowadays even a cassette tape player—and set up "stage" in the temple courtyard. After lighting incense and a lamp, they start drumming and singing, and the Mātā begins to "play." People in her entourage and other pilgrims at the temple approach the Mātā to worship, make a small cash offering, and then ask for a prophecy or favor. At any given time during the festival season, and occasionally at other times, one can see several of these performances going on at once amidst the other temple activities: *pūjā* (ritual offerings), *āratī* (waving of the flame), ecstatic dancing and singing, the ritual shaving of childrens' heads, and the worship of virgin girls. Pilgrims eat and distribute *prasād* (consecrated food), priests recite the *Devī Māhātmya,* and people shout the ubiquitous cry of joy, *Jay mātā dī* ("Victory to the Mother").

The goddess Śerāṅvālī is like the great gods Viṣṇu and Śiva in her power, purity, and universality. At the same time, she shares characteristics such as accessibility, immanence, and intimacy with the lesser deities and saints. While the great male gods of the Hindu pantheon do not generally possess their devotees, the more minor divinities do. When I asked informants why the Goddess possesses people, whereas Viṣṇu and Śiva do not, they were usually unable to provide a reason. One informant, however, the secretary of the newly built Bābā Bālak Nāth temple in Chandigarh, gave this explanation:

> Bābā Bālak Nāth and Devī can both enter a man or a woman. Just as there are different branches of the government, so do different gods have different functions. Full avatars (incarnations of the Divine) do not enter people. Viṣṇu and so forth do not. But Mā is *śakti*; she is everywhere. Therefore, she does not fall into the category of avatar.[10]

The monistic identification of spirit and matter found in Śākta theology may help explain why possession by the Goddess occurs far more frequently than possession by such supreme male deities as Viṣṇu and Śiva. As we have noted, male deities do possess human devotees, but these tend to be lower-level functionaries such as Bābā Bālak Nāth or Guggā Pīr, with the occasional exception. The cults of Narasiṃha in Himachal Pradesh and Venkaṭeśvara in Andhra Pradesh—both incarnations of Viṣṇu—involve divine possession, but these are atypical.

The general understanding of possession is that the Goddess plays in people and speaks through them as a means of helping her devotees and revealing her *śakti*. She may also wish to castigate those who have committed some evil or issue a demand that she expects her devotees to fulfill. It is not unusual for new temples to be built or old images to be "rediscovered" as the result of a command from the Goddess speaking through a possessed medium. A small temple in a village that is now part of the city of Chandigarh, for example, was built in the late nineteenth century after a young girl became possessed by the Goddess and told the villagers that only by building a temple could they eradicate a severe epidemic. Similarly, Nainā Devī temple was built on a hillside outside Kalka in 1950 on the orders of the Goddess, who entered a small girl and commanded those listening to dig up an ancient image of Nainā Devī that lay buried and forgotten there.

There are various explanations as to why some people get possessed and not others. Some say that it is solely due to the divine play of the Goddess. Others say that it is the fruit of karma or because of a *saṃskāra* (mental impression or predisposition) from a past life. Others say that it is the reward for faith and devotion to Devī. Sometimes it runs in a family; the *śakti* is passed from generation to generation. Or it can be the result of a spiritual discipline (*sādhanā*) in which one attempts to bring on possession as a means of identifying with the Goddess.[11] Purity is also cited as a requirement for a suitable vehicle; she should not eat meat, drink liquor, or be unchaste. That is why young girls below the age of puberty and unmarried women are thought to be especially suitable vehicles for the Goddess.[12]

Charges of chicanery, commercialism, and exploitation are not uncommon in connection with possession, even among those who consider themselves devotees of Śerāṅvālī. An informant who grew up in a village near Jullunder told me that, in his childhood, during the yearly pilgrimage to Chintpurni fights would break out between rival parties over whether or not a possession was legitimate. He summed it up as follows.

> When one camp undertakes a pilgrimage out of reverence, and the other for commercial purposes, there is a clash. When a group holds a *jagrātā* with commercial intent and a girl becomes possessed (*devī khelnā*), it is often a fake. Some groups have several women who regularly stage these possessions. My father had a friend with a red turban who used tests for distinguishing real possession from fake. He would take an iron rod and prod the woman with it. An even more foolproof method is to put a lighted incense stick under the person's nose. If the possession is real, she will not flinch. There was a group who used to come to Cintpurni every year from about 1950 to 1955 who would

> stage possession. They would do this every night. We did not mind it if they did it on their own, but they used to do it in public when other *jagrātā*s were going on. Then fights would break out. Our group would not let them have a session inside the temple, because they were using it as a regular business. They would also have *jagrātā*s at their home and made quite a bit of money out of this.[13]

People will also ask the possessed person questions in order to test her clairvoyance—a mental rather than physical test. They might, for example, ask how much money is in someone's pocket. A certain amount of skepticism thus exists as to the validity of possession, at least in individual cases.

The same informant, however, recalled a case of what he considered to be a valid, spontaneous possession. During a *jagrātā* to which four different singing parties had been invited, a young woman started to "play." She had always been a devotee of Devī but had recently been married into a family that ate meat and drank liquor. During her possession, she was tested by a leader from one of the singing groups, who put lighted incense under her nose and struck her with a metal bar. She did not flinch. She spoke as Devī and ordered all people who were drunk to leave the *jagrātā*. After this, the young woman was so drained that she had to remain in bed for two months. As for her in-laws, they were so shaken by the experience that they became vegetarians and teetotalers.[14]

Hinduism does not draw a clear dividing line between divine and human; gods can become humans and humans can become gods. There are numerous forms of worship of deified humans such as ancestors, heroes, gurus, *satī*s, yogis, *siddh*s, and *nāth*s. Similarly, certain women who are regularly possessed are worshiped as Mātās or living goddesses, as manifestations of Śerāṅvālī. Such a woman is said to embody the *śakti* of the Goddess during her possession—that is, to become a human icon. But the sanctity of the possession experience also carries over into her normal life, and she gradually becomes a religious specialist and the object of worship. This process occurs with varying degrees of elaboration, and individual cases are extremely idiosyncratic, as there is no formal or centralized institution for this phenomenon. Let us look, then, at a specific case involving two family members, which, while not "representative," will illustrate the nature of the human-divine exchanges that may occur during Goddess possession.

THE HUMANITY OF POSSESSION: THE MOTHERS OF GUMTI VILLAGE

My first encounter with Mātājī and her niece the Little Mother occurred quite by accident in October 1982 (see figure 18). Accompanied by my friend Manjit, a research scholar in social anthropology at Punjab University, I paid a visit to Jayantī Devī, a small hilltop temple in the Shiwalik hills of Punjab, about an hour's bus ride from Chandigarh. When we arrived at the temple, we found a group of about fifteen people seated inside singing devotional songs. Among them were three women who seemed to be particularly significant: an elderly woman in a plain cotton sari and two others, one middle-aged and one very young but identically dressed in the bright red *salvār-kamīz* outfits typical of Punjabi brides. The elderly and middle-aged women took turns leading the singing in Hindi and Punjabi, and from time to time the elderly woman would recite verses in Sanskrit from the *Devī Māhātmya.* The young woman sat quietly throughout the session with head bowed, her eyes glazed and her body swaying from side to side; she seemed to be crying.

Manjit was intrigued by the "red ladies" and could hardly wait to ask about them. One of their devotees, whom I will call Mr. S., explained that the two women lived in the village of Gumti, near Shahabad Markanda (in the Ambala district of Haryana), where they have their own temple. When the older of them was five years old, he said, she received a boon and Mātā entered her; as a result she has remained unmarried. The younger woman is her niece, who has been entered by Kālī Mātā owing to a blessing from her aunt. The elderly woman who accompanied them, Mr. S. went on to say, is Devkī Mātā, a saintly and respected lady from Chandigarh who is active in organizing religious functions but who does not become possessed. As the result of later conversations with Mr. S., other devotees, and the Gumti Mātās themselves, and by observing these women in ritual and nonritual contexts at their home and on their subsequent visits to Chandigarh, I was able to piece together a general picture of their lives and cult.

The two Mātās belong to a well-to-do Brahmin peasant family that originally lived and owned land near Lahore, then in West Punjab. The elder Mātā's mother had first started receiving the *śakti* after her marriage, and she passed it on to her daughter, who started "playing" at about age five. After the partition of the Punjab in 1947, the whole family moved to the Haryana village where they now live. The mother died on the way in Amritsar after drinking some polluted water, but her daughter, who at the time of our meeting was about forty-five, had passed the *śakti* on to her brother's daughter nine years earlier, when the girl was about seven years of age. The child used to fight with her brothers and sisters. One day her aunt said to her, "Kālkā, don't fight." From that time on, the little girl began to get the "wind" of the goddess Kālkā, another name for Kālī—whereas her aunt gets the "wind" of Vaiṣṇo Devī. Kālī and Vaiṣṇo Devī are generally considered to be the fierce and gentle manifestations of Śerāṅvālī, respectively, so the two balance each other. The niece is referred to as "Little Mother" (Choṭī Mātā) or "Devatā" (meaning a minor god), while the aunt is called by the honorific Mātājī. Mātājī has some control over her possession, whereas the younger is still very inexperienced. Neither of the two women is married; both say that celibacy makes it easier for them to maintain the purity necessary for a ve-

Figure 18. Mātājī and the Little Mother after a *jagrātā* in Chandigarh. Photograph by Kathleen M. Erndl.

hicle of the Goddess. They have the same guru, Rāmānand Svāmī, an ascetic who lives near Kurukshetra.

Many of Mātājī's followers are refugees from West Punjab like herself—some of whom knew her mother—who have settled in Chandigarh, Ludhiana, Ambala, Delhi, and other places in East Punjab and Haryana. Gradually, the local people have started to visit her too, as they hear about her powers and miracles. The people of Haryana tend to identify her with Bālā Sundarī, a goddess enshrined in nearby Nahan (in Himachal Pradesh), who is the tutelary goddess of many families in the area, whereas West Punjabis tend to identify her with Vaiṣṇo Devī. But both groups say that each goddess is an aspect of Mahādevī, the Great Goddess.

Apart from the general desire for *darśan*, the reasons people visit Mātājī fall into three categories: prophecy, healing, and material gain. During possession performances Mātājī "tells things," such as when would be a good day to begin an enterprise, whether or not one will succeed in a given endeavor, whether or not one should trust a certain person. Sometimes she makes such predictions in response to a question; other times she volunteers the information. The devotees tell a story about a man whom Mātājī had warned not to go on a certain trip. He went anyway, and his train collided with another one near Ambala. And once she volunteered the information to Mr. S. that in his past life he had been an M.A. student in a particular village who had committed suicide because he failed an exam. Upon inquiry, Mr. S. found out that there had indeed been such a person in that village. The Goddess will also castigate someone if something does not please her. For example, if there is a menstruating woman in the crowd witnessing the possession, she will tell her to leave.

Healing and granting material welfare are both called boons. People come to Mātājī for these while she is in her normal state of consciousness as well as when she is possessed. Her devotees make offerings of sweets, flowers, money, and the like to her, taking some back as *prasād*—which is supposed to have healing power. I have seen many people bringing small packets of cloves or cardamom seeds to be blessed, or bottles of water that Mātājī holds in her hands for a few moments, toying with the lid, and then hands back. These are then consumed at home to cure whatever disease the devotee is suffering from.

Numerous stories have grown up around Mātājī's healing and wish-granting powers. A woman from Ambala said that she used to come to Gumti once a month for a *jagrātā*. Then, for about seven years after her husband's death, she did not make her monthly visit, although she would come from time to time when her child had an exam. After a while, she developed an ulcer and her face became swollen. Around this time, she went to another village to visit some relatives. There she met a fortune-teller who told her that she had forgotten to worship Mā ("Mother")—that she used to go somewhere and should go back. After this, she came to Gumti to meet Mātājī, and her problems went away. Others attribute their marriages, or their jobs, or their success in examinations to Mātājī's grace.

At first, Mātājī had only one small room in which to receive devotees. There is also some talk to the effect that, in those days, her elders did not approve of her becoming a cult figure and tried to put obstacles in her way. Because of pressure from devotees and out of fear of the Goddess's wrath, however, they allowed her to continue, rather than forcing her to marry. Of course, the fact that both Mātājī and the Little Mother remained unmarried and childless made it much easier for them to pursue their spiritual lifestyle: in some ways they are more like ascetics than householders. In contrast, a married woman like Tārā Devī, about whom I have written elsewhere, has had to enlist her husband's cooperation and juggle child care and domestic responsibilities with the demands the Goddess has placed upon her as a medium and healer.[15]

The biggest watershed in the institutionalization of Mātājī's cult came in 1969 when her temple was built and an image of her late mother consecrated. The temple is dedicated to the Nine Durgās. Mr. S. informed us that the temple was built according to a blueprint specified by Kālī, who entered Mātājī and, speaking in Bengali, said that she had come from Calcutta with instructions.[16]

Mātājī and her niece are now installed in a large temple complex at one end of the village, its entrance marked by a large gateway atop which "Śrī

Prabhāveśvarī Navadurgā Mandir" ("Blessed Prabhāveśvarī's Nine-Durgā Temple") is inscribed. Prabhāveśvarī is Mātājī's given name. The gateway leads into a compound containing living quarters, cattle sheds, and guest rooms. These face a large courtyard, on the south side of which is the temple, consisting of one large, square room. The central image is of Durgā/Śerāṅvālī flanked by Hanumān and Bhairava. On the walls surrounding the Durgā image are carved images of the nine Durgās, with the addition of Sarasvatī at one end and Kālī at the other. West of the temple is a pit where fire sacrifices are performed by a Brahmin during the festival of Navarātra. Directly opposite the temple, on the north side of the courtyard, is an elevated platform on which an image of Śiva sits.

On the west side of the courtyard is a large audience hall equipped with a wooden platform, where the two Mātās sit during their possession performances. At the back of this hall is a doorway leading to their private rooms; adjoining their sitting room is a small shrine housing the image of Mātājī's mother. Behind these rooms is a large open area edged by several rooms and sheltered verandas that is used as an outdoor kitchen and eating area during special functions. The people who currently live in this compound are Mātājī, the Little Mother, the Little Mother's parents, a servant who takes care of the animals, and a priest who tends the temple. The priest, a wandering ascetic with long matted hair, is a native of Bengal who took up residence with Mātājī at the command of the Goddess.

Mātājī's establishment is obviously expensive to keep up. Most of the funds come from devotees, although some come from her family's farm income. She owns a car, and her devotees have bought her a refrigerator and a telephone, on top of which they sponsor her trips and pilgrimages. It is still, however, an informal association. Devotees may come and do service at the temple, but no formal hierarchy exists among them. Mātājī maintains control over all the affairs of the temple. When, for example, one of her close devotees tried to form a temple committee, Mātājī refused, saying only that there was no need for it. Mātājī also makes a point of not discriminating among devotees: she welcomes people of all castes. Once, when she found out that her relatives were giving out more *prasād* to family than to others, she ordered them to distribute it equally. It is said that they broke out in a rash that refused to heal until they did so.

While welcoming members of all castes, Mātājī at the same time places a strong emphasis on certain Brahminical or "Sanskritic" practices. All food prepared on the premises or brought and offered to Mātājī must be strictly vegetarian. As her devotees explain, vegetarianism is required because Mātājī is the Goddess in Vaiṣṇava form. Thus, even though the Little Mother is possessed by Kālī—who is generally carnivorous—she is still under Vaiṣṇava influence. When Mātājī went to Calcutta, she refused to go inside the famous Kālī temple there because goats were being sacrificed. Although

Mātājī has had little formal schooling, she has great respect for the Sanskrit language, regularly sponsoring readings from Sanskrit texts and Sanskritic rituals. (Her own languages are Hindi and Punjabi, both of which she speaks fluently.) Mātājī also arranges for a *jagrātā* once a month and nightly possession performances when she is in residence.

The annual festival at Gumti is Image Consecration Day, which celebrates the installation of the Nine-Durgā temple and Mātājī's mother's image on May 29, 1969. The festival consists of a nine-day recitation of the *Devī Bhāgavata Purāṇa* in Sanskrit, culminating on May 29 with a fire sacrifice. Several devotees (not necessarily Brahmin priests) perform the recitation each morning and evening; between recitations the text is wrapped in a red cloth and kept in the Nine-Durgā temple next to a pot around which barley sprouts are planted. The celebration of this annual festival clearly has been patterned after that of the traditional Navarātra, although it is not identical in every detail. The *Devī Bhāgavata Purāṇa* has been substituted for the *Devī Māhātmya,* and the festival exhibits a higher degree of informality, occasioned perhaps by the presence of lay recitants rather than a Brahmin priest.

When I attended the celebration in 1983, the fire sacrifice was not held on May 29 but instead took place a day or two later because the *Devī Bhāgavata Purāṇa* recitation had started a day late that year. A carnival-like atmosphere pervaded. Visitors had set up stalls outside the compound, where they sold ice cream, tea, and various snacks, while devotees provided free ice water inside. Several hundred people came and went, visiting the temple, going for an audience with Mātājī in her back room, and chatting with friends. A lavish communal meal consisting of thick chapattis, lentils, cooked squash, sweet rice, and salty rice was available all afternoon. In the afternoon, a band of the sort one might find at a wedding played in the courtyard, while some of the women, mostly the very young and the elderly, danced. Some important devotees from Chandigarh had brought new clothes for the main Durgā image in the temple. First they dressed the Little Mother in a new red gown and scarf; then they dressed the image in identical clothing.

On that day I also met another Mātā who stays with Mātājī from time to time, as well as coming to visit on special occasions. A seventeen-year-old Baniyā (merchant-caste) woman from a village near Kurukshetra, she goes by the name of Bhadrakālī, after the goddess who enters her. She had been getting the "wind" since she was about eight years old: during a *Satyanārāyaṇ Kathā* in a friend's house, she fell down and started shaking.[17] Her family took her first to the hospital and then to the Kālī temple in Patiala. There she received a "direct vision" (*sākṣāt darśan*) of Devī, after which she started coming to Gumti to meet Mātājī. The girl told me that Mātājī, having identified her possessing goddess as Bhadrakālī, had refused to accept her as her disciple, saying that to do so would be inappropriate since Bhadrakālī is the seniormost manifestation of the Goddess. "Bhadrakālī" has continued an informal association with Mātājī, however, and performs possession from time to time at Gumti. She has also become a disciple of Mātājī's guru, Rāmānand Svāmī, whom she met through Mātājī when he came to Gumti for a feast. Bhadrakālī considers her role as the Goddess's vehicle to be her life's work and does not plan to marry. She would like to pass the power on to someone else when she gets older. Although she does not have much of a following today, her validation by the Gumti Mātā and her participation in functions at Gumti may lead to the future development of a cult.

Besides presiding over functions that take place at Gumti, Mātājī and her niece are often on tour. They go on pilgrimage to Goddess temples with groups of devotees several times a year, and they are frequently invited to perform at *jagrātās* or other functions in their devotees' homes in various towns and cities—and nowadays they receive more invitations than they can handle. A small group of devotees coordinates their travel arrangements and accommodations. I attended several *jagrātās* in and around Chandigarh at which the Mātās of Gumti were the featured attraction; it was at one of these that the incident described at the beginning of this chapter occurred.

THE DIVINITY OF POSSESSION: THE STORY OF NANDĀ AND NANDLĀL

From a devotee's point of view, there are various ways in which the Goddess manifests herself in the world, making herself available to her followers. Among these, possession is notable because it is visible and accessible, as well as allowing verbal communication between the devotee and the Goddess as well as allowing the human vehicle to participate in her power. In telling the story of the Mātās of Gumti, I have focused on how possession by the Goddess can transform a woman's identity and purpose in life. I have also suggested ways in which such possession serves to heal individuals and communities, inasmuch as it provides an indirect language for the expression of tensions and problems and a means to resolve them. In other words, I have concentrated on the "human" aspects of possession. Yet from an insider's perspective it is the "divine" aspects of possession that remain most important. So, by way of conclusion, let us return to the Goddess herself by looking at a story told at many *jagrātās* just before the dramatic moment when coconuts are offered to the Goddess. This oral narrative illustrates the Goddess's various modes of manifestation and the place of possession among them.[18]

> There once was a potter named Icchū Bābā who had a daughter named Nandā and a son named Nandlāl. He had an image of the Goddess that had been discovered and dug up from the earth. Every day Nandā and Nandlāl would worship the image by lighting a flame, singing devotional songs, and distributing *prasād*. The contractor who had sold the potter his land found out about the valuable image and tried to claim it as his own, but Icchū Bābā would

not give it up. The case came before the village council, which decided that the image should be put back on the spot where it had been unearthed; then the image would return by itself to its rightful owner. Icchū Bābā put the image on his head and took it to that spot, lamenting, "How can I take your name when you are no longer in my house?" On the way back, he met his children, Nandā and Nandlāl. They said, "Why are you crying? The image has flown back and is in a niche in our house."

People heard about the miraculous image and started coming from near and far, saying that it would grant any wish. The contractor became jealous and went to complain to Emperor Faruq Shāh in Delhi: "A certain Icchū Bābā, a potter of village Narela, has lit a flame in front of an image of Mātā and has collected more money than is in your treasury." The emperor then ordered his soldiers to bring the potter to court. When the soldiers arrived at Icchū Bābā's house, they found him very ill. Not wanting to be responsible for his death, they arrested the two children instead and took them to Delhi. Nandā lit the evening flame before she left, vowing that she would return by morning to light the morning flame.

The emperor had the two children put in jail, saying that he would decide what to do with them the next day. Nandā and Nandlāl prayed to the Mother: "Who will light your flame? If we your devotees die here, who will believe in you?" Then, with the Great Mother's power, the emperor's lion-throne began to shake. In her wind form (*pavan rūp*), Mother had come to the aid of her children. She put a trident on the emperor's chest, telling him that he would have to release the children if he wanted to keep his kingdom intact. The emperor apologized to the Mother and became devoted to her. He told his soldiers to take the children back to Narela village before morning.

At this point in the story, the Goddess has appeared in "wind form," shaking the emperor's lion-throne in order to protect the two children. Besides being a symbol of royal authority, the lion is, by virtue of its status as the Goddess's own vehicle, a symbol of her superior power and authority. The story continues:

When Nandā and Nandlāl reached the village, they found that their father had already died. They continued the same practices that their father had established—lighting the flame, singing devotional songs, and distributing *prasād*—but added a new one: making a pilgrimage on foot every year to Jvālā Mukhī, the temple where the Goddess resides in the form of a flame. Years passed this way. Finally, Nandā died, becoming the Mother's beloved forever. Nandlāl continued his duty year after year, until finally he became too decrepit.

He made one last trek to Jvālā Mukhī, hobbling all the way. He cried so much that the Mother's feet were bathed in his tears. Mother appeared directly before him and asked why he was crying. He said, "Don't you know? Because I will be unable to come to your court (*darbār*) any more." She replied, "Whenever you want my *darśan*, light a flame at home and have a *jagrātā*. You will get my *darśan*."

One year later, Nandlāl called all the devotees and announced that Śerāṅvālī would manifest herself at his *jagrātā*. Everyone assembled and waited expectantly, but by three in the morning she still had not come. They started to taunt Nandlāl, saying that he was lying in his old age and trying to get money. Nandlāl beseeched the Mother over and over again to remember her promise and save his honor.

The Great Mother was aroused from sleep by these supplications. She mounted her lion and emerged from the cave. Her servant, Laṅgur Vīr, asked where she was going in the middle of the night.[19] She replied that a devotee had called her to his *jagrātā*. Laṅgur Vīr said, "What a great devotee he must be if the ruler of the three worlds is leaving her place to go to him. If he is a greater devotee than I who serve you night and day, I would like to get his *darśan*." So she took him along.

The Mother took the form of wind (*pavan rūp*). When she reached Narela village, she said to Laṅgur Vīr, "Laṅgur Vīr, it is not right for us to go inside in our own forms. Why? Among the congregation seated there are those who are not devoted to me. But there is one child, Nandlāl, who has lit my flame. He is attentive to me. Let us go and give him *darśan*." Then the Mother took the form of a five-year-old girl seated in the congregation. The girl's hair flew about wildly. When the girl started "playing," devotees started running away. Why? Because at that time, no one knew anything about "playing." The Mother said, "Fear not, my children. I am here to take care of you, Nandlāl, to deliver you."

Here, then, the Goddess—having assumed "wind form" and not wanting to grant a direct (*sākṣāt*) *darśan* to unbelievers—enters into a young girl and starts to "play." The story further states that this is the origin of possession as a means by which the Goddess reveals herself to devotees. The story concludes:

The Mother gave her *darśan* to Nandlāl and asked, "What offering have you brought in honor of my coming?" Nandlāl had forgotten to bring anything, so he cut off his head and offered that. The Mother was pleased and joined it back to his body, offering him a boon. He asked that in the future, devotees should be allowed to offer something else, instead of a head. So she gave him the boon that in the future she would accept a coconut and consider it a head. That is why in the present world age (the Kali Yuga) we offer coconuts to the Mother. Therefore, the coconuts we offer here—tonight at this *jagrātā*—are considered by the Mother to be heads.

In the course of explaining why devotees offer coconuts, this story also functions as a charter myth for the phenomenon of Goddess possession. It illustrates the Goddess's epiphanies, the various forms in which she manifests herself and in which devotees experience her: the miraculous carved image found in the ground; the flame lit daily in household worship; the wind that enters the emperor's lion-throne and makes it shake; the eternal flame at Jvala Mukhi; the direct vision (*sākṣāt darśan*) she presents to Nandlāl; the "wind form" by which she travels from her cave dwelling to his house; and again the wind through which she possesses the five-year-old girl. Of these, the direct vision in which she manifests herself to Nandlāl ranks highest. It is the full epiphany reserved for those who have demonstrated the highest faith by worshiping the Goddess in her other forms. All other forms are "disguised" epiphanies: devotees must make a leap of faith to accept them as being the Goddess herself. In the story, the Goddess does not appear before the entire *jagrātā* congregation in her direct form. Instead, she chooses to enter and speak through a five-year-old girl, knowing that true devotees will recognize her. The Mother thus possesses in order to reveal—and sometimes, simultaneously, to conceal—herself. In so doing, she transforms not only herself but her vehicle and her devotees as well.

Still, the story does not make the relationship between the Goddess and the five-year-old girl absolutely clear. Did the Goddess appear in the form of a girl who had not previously been there, or did she enter the body of a girl who was already present in the congregation? The matter is open to interpretation. However, the ambiguity in the story recalls the ambiguity of the issue with which we began this essay: Is it the Mother who possesses, or is it the Mother who is possessed? To answer exclusively one way or another would presuppose a dualistic mind-set that is foreign to Hindu ways of thinking about the Goddess and *śakti*. *Śakti* is not an object or an entity; it is an all-pervasive force. It can be present in greater or lesser degrees; it can move around and become manifest in various forms. Indeed, it is this very fluidity of identity among the myriad forms of the Goddess and between divine and human beings that is so essential to understanding the phenomenon of Goddess possession.

NOTES

1. Material for this chapter is taken from my book *Victory to the Mother: The Hindu Goddess of Northwest India in Myth, Ritual, and Symbol* (New York: Oxford University Press, 1993) and from more recent research I have conducted on village women healers in the Punjab and Himachal Pradesh, India. Fieldwork was funded by Fulbright-Hays research fellowships in 1982–83 and 1991.

2. Manuel Moreno, "God's Forceful Call: Possession as a Divine Strategy," in *Gods of Flesh, Gods of Stone: The Embodiment of Divinity in India*, ed. Norman Cutler, Joanne Waghorne, and Vasudha Narayanan (Chambersburg, Pa.: Anima Books, 1985). For a recent study that makes excellent use of this approach in a context outside India, see Karen McCarthy Brown, *Mama Lola: A Vodou Priestess in Brooklyn* (Berkeley: University of California Press, 1991).

3. See also, for example, Margaret Trawick Egnor, "The Changed Mother, or What the Smallpox Goddess Did When There Was No More Smallpox," in *Contributions to Asian Studies*, vol. 18, *South Asian Systems of Healing*, ed. E. Valentine Daniel

and Judy F. Pugh (Leiden: E. J. Brill, 1984), pp. 24–45, in which I describe the possession of a woman in Madras by the goddess Mariamman. See also the essay in this volume by Sarah Caldwell, on the goddess Bhagavati in Kerala.

4. See Susan Wadley, "The Spirit 'Rides' or the Spirit 'Comes': Possession in a North Indian Village," in *The Realm of the Extra-Human: Agents and Audiences,* ed. Agehananda Bharati (The Hague: Mouton, 1976), pp. 233–52; John M. Stanley, "Gods, Ghosts, and Possession," in *The Experience of Hinduism,* ed. Eleanor Zelliot and Maxine Berntsen (Albany: State University of New York Press, 1968), pp. 26–59, esp. p. 26; and Gananath Obeyesekere, "Psychocultural Exegesis of a Case of Spirit Possession in Sri Lanka," in *Case Studies in Spirit Possession,* ed. Vincent Crapanzano and Vivian Garrison (New York: Wiley, 1977), pp. 235–94, esp. p. 290.

5. Ann Grodzins Gold, "Spirit Possession Perceived and Performed in Rural Rajasthan," *Contributions to Indian Sociology* (n.s.) 22, no. 1 (1988): 35n. Peter J. Claus distinguishes between spirit possession and spirit mediumship, defining the former as "an unexpected intrusion of the supernatural into the lives of humans" and the latter as "the legitimate, expected possession of a specialist by a spirit or deity, usually for the purpose of soliciting the aid of the supernatural for human problems" ("Spirit Possession and Spirit Mediumship from the Perspective of Tulu Oral Traditions," *Culture, Medicine, and Psychiatry* 3, no. 1 [1979]: 29). Although his point is well taken, I prefer not to make such a hard-and-fast distinction, as there is often considerable overlap, as well as transition, from one to the other.

6. Paul Hershman, "Hair, Sex and Dirt," *Man* (n.s.) 9, no. 2 (1974): 277.

7. An example of this kind of song is "Dātī de darbār kanjakāṅ kheḍdiyā," written by Camanlāl Jos̀ and sung by Narendra Cancal (Polydor Records no. 2392894). The words are printed in the pamphlet *Mātā dīyāṅ bheṭāṅ, ghar ghar vic mahimā terī* (Delhi: Aśokā Prakāśan, n.d.), pp. 7–10.

8. For a full-length study of the concept of play in Hinduism, see David Kinsley, *The Divine Player: A Study of Kṛṣṇa Līlā* (Delhi: Motilal Banarsidass, 1979).

9. Interview, Cāmuṇḍā Devī temple, 9 June 1983.

10. Interview, Bābā Bālak Nāth temple, 13 May 1983.

11. This seems to be the case in the ceremony described by Ruth S. Freed and Stanley A. Freed, "Two Mother-Goddess Ceremonies of Delhi State in the Great and Little Traditions," *Southwestern Journal of Anthropology* 18, no. 3 (1962): 246–77. I am also personally familiar with the case of a male astrologer in a Kangra village who, as a result of performing an arduous religious regimen, acquired the magical power (*siddhi*) of being able to act as a medium and transmit the words of the goddess Dakṣiṇakālī. He was in such demand for this skill that his activities as a medium eventually displaced his astrology business.

12. The same idea is operative in the Kumārī cults of Nepal, in which specially chosen young girls occupy a ritual position as a goddess until their first menstruation. See Michael Allen, *The Cult of Kumari: Virgin Worship in Nepal* (Kathmandu: Tribhuvan University, 1975).

13. Interview, New Delhi, 14 February 1983. Similar cases of conflict have been recorded from the late nineteenth century, during the heyday of the Ārya Samāj reform movement. See Kenneth W. Jones, *Arya Dharm: Hindu Consciousness in Nineteenth-Century Punjab* (Berkeley: University of California Press, 1976), p. 190.

14. Interview, New Delhi, 12 January 1983.

15. For more on Tārā Devī and on the relationship between the Goddess and women's lives, see my essay, "The Goddess and Women's Empowerment: A Hindu Case Study," in *Women and Goddess Traditions,* ed. Karen King (Minneapolis: Fortress Press, forthcoming).

16. This tale is interesting in light of the fact that Mātājī is usually possessed by Vaiṣṇo Devī, not Kālī. I have the impression, though, from what devotees have told me, that before her niece started becoming possessed by Kālī, Mātājī herself was alternately possessed by both forms of the Goddess. The fact that the order to build the temple came from her fierce form—Kālī—of course made it even more compelling.

17. *Satyanārāyaṇ Kathā* is a Vaiṣṇava story and vow that is performed in the various vernacular languages in many parts of India.

18. The story to follow is taken from an oral Punjabi version related by a group named Śrī Śām Rangīlā and Party of Ambala that I taped at a Viśāl Bhagavatī Jāgraṇ (a public *jagrātā* on a grand scale) in Chandigarh on 7 and 8 November 1982. The story of Nandā and Nandlāl is told during the *jagrātā* as an alternative to the story of Dhyānū Bhagat, just before the offering of coconuts, to explain why they are offered. I have heard several oral versions of this story but have encountered no written versions so far.

19. Laṅgur Vīr, whose name means "Monkey Hero," is a local form of Hanumān, the divine monkey who, in other contexts, is associated with the god Rāma. Here, though, he is the companion and bodyguard of the Goddess. For more on Laṅgur Vīr and the connection between the Goddess and Rāma, see Erndl, *Victory to the Mother,* pp. 4, 41–42, 126, and 160–61.

BHAGAVATI
Ball of Fire

Sarah Caldwell

DEVĪKOPAM: THE WRATH OF THE GODDESS

As we walk through the village lanes and over a stone bridge, we admire the beautiful landscape: paddy fields nestled under the dark green hills, cows calmly munching cool green grass, coconut palms waving at the edges of the fields, just where the hills begin to rise. The sun is setting and a slight breeze is beginning to relieve the oppressively humid heat of the day. It is the month of Kumbham in southern Kerala, harvest time, the start of the intensely hot summer months before the monsoon rains, and the fifth month of my fieldwork on the temple rituals dedicated to the fierce goddess Bhagavati.[1]

Welcoming visitors at the entrance to the temple ground are two large plantain stalks heavy with fruit, ripe golden coconuts, and flowers. Inside, the energy is intense and colorful; many things are happening at once. Crowds of people are milling about as musicians play in front of a low, tile-roofed shrine. The heavy drums, covered in gold and red brocade and suspended horizontally around the slim waists of the heavily perspiring young male drummers, resound with deep and complex rhythms. Oboelike instruments pierce the evening air as four instrumentalists serenade the representation of the goddess stationed in their midst: the curved sword of Kāḷi, painted as if covered in blood, a white cloth folded in an accordion fan below, sits atop a red and gold palanquin, which is paraded around the temple. While the musicians play before the display of Kāḷi's weapons, at the entrance to the shrine women are making offerings to a clay pot covered in a red cloth, which also represents the goddess.

Hundreds of people are already here in the large temple compound. The men are mostly involved in the carrying and displaying of bullock carts to entertain the goddess. The smell of liquor strong on their breath, they are particularly exuberant as they shout and dance and pull the effigies through the yard of the temple compound. The women and girls cluster around the shrines or the tea shops lining the yard, keeping a safe distance from the activities of the men.

The main event of the temple festival is a drama of battle, which takes place after the midnight hour. The fierce Bhadrakāḷi, represented by a special actor wearing a heavy wooden headdress and elaborate costume, celebrates her violent victory over the demon-king Dārika. Bhagavati, the predominant deity of Kerala, is a form of the pan-Indian goddess Kālī. As Bhagavati she is a benevolent protectress, but in her more common angry and violent form, she is referred to as Bhadrakāḷi.[2] She holds various weapons in her right hands, which may number from two to thirty-two, and, in her left, symbols of the "left-handed" way—the head of the demon she has decapitated, a bowl to catch the blood dripping from his severed neck, bells used by the oracles she empowers, snakes. She is hot, full of rage, sexually dangerous, but she is also a loving mother whose blessing ensures prosperity and fertility. She is a mother, a virgin, and a warrior. She resides in a special tree, she loves the color red, she loves blood, colored powders, music and dance, and humor. She is covered with smallpox, but she is lovely. She is evoked and feared by her devotees, who hope to control her through the performances they carry out. She is beautiful and fierce. She is the coconut tree, the paddy field, and the forest.

On the floor inside the temple building we find the *kaḷam*—a large multicolored rice-flour picture of Bhadrakāḷi into which the goddess is to be installed temporarily.[3] Her feet are shown with toes pointed downward, straddling the prone and bloodied corpse of Dārika. His head is severed, and his entrails spill out where her long curved sword has pierced his abdomen. Bhadrakāḷi's three bulging eyes, red and white, stare out at us, the only three-dimensional protrusions other than the two small red breasts built up of raw paddy rice; her four arms hold a fistful of weapons, the head of Dārika, a snake, and a bowl to catch the demon's blood. Three folds at her middle enclose the prominent navel, necklaces hang from her neck, and stars and flowers dot her long loose black hair. A square red cloth is suspended like a tent over the *kaḷam*. It is fringed with tender coconut leaves into which are tied areca nuts, small bananas, and bunches of mango leaves. On the floor surrounding the *kaḷam* are brass lamps lit with oil wicks, plantain leaves heaped with piles of rice, ripe coconuts with coconut flowers on top; by the goddess's feet are puffed rice and bananas (see figure 19). Four ladies sit opposite the shrine area, hands folded in prayer to the goddess before them. Only men, however, are allowed to mount the platform where the *kaḷam* is installed, to perform the ritual worship of the goddess.

Pounding drums shake the small building as the *kaḷam* artist draws large black circles around Bhadrakāḷi's staring eyes, rousing the goddess and call-

Figure 19. Rice-flour drawing of Bhagavati, fully enlivened with her fierce energy, by the artist Varanattu Narayana Kurup. Photograph by Balachandran.

ing her into the drawing. The musicians sing a mournful song (*kaḷampāṭṭu*) describing her attributes and worshiping her, as the soul-splitting drums get louder and louder, faster and faster. The attendant priest lights the oil-wick lamps outside the doors of the shrine and opens the doors to reveal the main image of the goddess, a crude granite stone with three eyes and a mouth, completely smeared with red powder. A weird wailing sound emerges from the inner sanctum, like someone being pierced, and a man runs out holding the goddess's sword in his right hand, jumping and moaning, a red cloth at his waist, long hair and beard flowing, brass bells at his arms, ankles, and hips. This is the oracular representative of the goddess, the *velicchappadu (veḷiccappāṭu)*, who is possessed by her spirit and carries it forth into the outer compound to empower the performance to come.[4] The oracle runs around the inner shrine erratically, shaking his anklets with a wild look in his eyes. As the image of the goddess is brought from the shrine, the women are hooting loudly—*ullullullullu!*—and loud firecrackers and sparklers are set off behind the temple. Quietly, as more firecrackers go off, the *kaḷam* is erased by the artist, who waves a green plantain leaf that encloses a burning wick in his left hand. With his right he pulls down some coconut leaves from the hanging decorations with which to sweep away the colored-powder drawing of Bhagavati, leaving only the protruding face and breasts. Then, dropping the leaves, he uses the fingers of his right hand to erase the face and breasts and places the powder on a fresh plantain leaf, to be given as a blessing (*prasādam*) to the sponsor of tonight's rituals—in this case a young man—and others present. The ladies apply the powder to their foreheads. Through this sequence of acts, the spirit of the goddess has been released from the drawing and is being taken to the outer compound for the further rituals.

The action now shifts to a large pavilion outside the shrine where an elaborate *guruti*, a blood offering to the evil spirits of the forest, is about to take place. As heavy "demonic drums" pound their mesmerizing beat, the priests are preparing huge bamboo grids, plantain stalks, coconuts, and bowls of red *guruti* liquid.[5]

Now it is time to take Bhagavati in procession to collect the evil spirits (*bhūtam*) who will assist her in the war against Dārika. These evil spirits reside in a group of trees about half a kilometer from the temple. Everyone begins to stir, forming two lines behind the bearers of six small pyramids made of banana plant stalks and topped by small fire torches. These are a form of portable shrine. The whole retinue proceeds up the hill and then down the road to the shrine of the evil spirits. The young men lead, bearing on their heads the banana-stalk structures; each of them is sponsored by a family group that walks along attending to the oil torches. Following them are the *tālappoli*—two lines of women with plates holding wicks, coconut-shell lamps, areca flowers, and colored flowers. I hustle in amongst the women and hurry along behind them. Behind us walk the drummers, torch bearers, the oracle, and the glittering image of Bhagavati carried palanquin-style by two bearers.

We walk down the dark country road like this, torches flaming, drums beating, ladies hooting (even I try it). Our eerie feminine hooting seems to pierce the night. As I move within this slow, sedate group of women, flanked by the lines of excited men, the bright torches, and the gleaming golden image of the enlivened, fierce goddess illumined only by fire and moon, I begin to feel I really am walking in a bunch of forest spirits. We are calling ghosts in the dead of night, far from home and the ordered routines of daylight and village. It feels dangerous and thrilling. As we walk along, people come out of their houses to salute Bhadrakāḷi. They have put oil lamps out on the stoops, and they stand with folded hands as we pass. We arrive at the small group of trees and circle them, collecting the ghosts and spirits that will accompany Bhadrakāḷi to the war.

Back at the temple pavilion we all crush around the stage area, when suddenly the two actors playing Kāḷi and Dārika run wildly into the shrine: Kāḷi is being held by the *velicchappadu*. They look as if they are possessed: wide vacant stares, erratic, violent movements, full of unrestrained energy. The two men—handsome, slim, and muscular—are dressed only in short skirts. Dārika has a red skirt over a white cloth twisted around his waist; his face is painted green with a white line around the jaw and red lips; a simple white cloth is tied on his head. Kāḷi wears a gold-colored blouse, raised to expose the nipples and full lower part of the amazing blue breasts—very large, round, and prominent. (The whole breast and blouse ensemble is a prop made of highly lacquered wood.) Around her waist she wears lacquered wooden belt-ornaments. Like Dārika's, her face is green, with black around the eyes and red lips, and some white and red "pox" pustules of lime have been pasted on the cheeks. Although her expression is fierce, she is a young, very beautiful, sexy-looking Kāḷi—a Dravidian warrior goddess. A small headgear is attached to the top of the actor's head, its coconut-frond hair is let loose and then cut into small strips with an iron knife by the oracle, in order to release its power.

The ladies around me seem oblivious to the performance: they are more interested in eating peanuts and talking, or mildly scolding their children. Some are sleeping. Meanwhile, Kāḷi is looking furious—her eyes wide and her mouth open. Staring intently, she brandishes an iron sword while she dances to the heavy beat. Now the drumming stops. The priest fixes her anklets, lifts Kāḷi's breastplate for ventilation, and fans the perspiration from the chest of the actor, who is drinking a soda. We are surprised to see grey hair on his chest. How bizarre this small grey-haired man looks standing half-naked with white frills attached to his behind and huge breasts at his front.

Thin, hardened tamarind twigs beat out the rhythmic refrain on the taut skin of the drumheads—**1** 2 3 4 / **1** 2/ **1**. This is very powerful. The drums are so hypnotic.[6] The arms and chests of the five strong young drummers shine as they bend forward and backward in perfect unison. I'm starting to get drawn inside myself—I feel different. It's hard to write notes or be objective. Laji, my field assistant, also has stopped writing. Dārika continues to dance in squares around the flickering oil lamp. Listening to the pulsating drumbeat, I become entranced. There is something so sensual and masculine about the drumming—powerful, passionate, incessant. One tall, handsome drummer watches me swaying slightly to the rhythm; he seems to play to me. I lose my self-consciousness and enter the energy of the drumming with them. Somewhere the actors are flashing knives at each other. I'm lost in the drums and barely notice Dārika. The eyes of the drummers are so wild, like wolves. They seem to look through me.

Then the oracle comes running out with the headgear (*mudi*)—enormous and very heavy—and holds it before the image of Bhadrakāḷi in the main shrine, while the ladies once again hoot loudly—*ullullullullu*! The *mudi (muṭi)* is about four feet high and wide and is shaped like a leaf. The oracle places the enormous *mudi* atop the head of the actor, who now becomes the goddess Kāḷi herself. Two men hold torches in front of Kāḷi as she stalks around slowly, then faster. The actor can barely sustain the weight of the *mudi*; he almost drops it. They put ash on his hands. He steps onto the stool—quite a sight—and turns about, stamping his feet, his ankle bracelets jingling. The oracle removes the *mudi* and seats Kāḷi on a stool, with the *mudi* resting on the ground in front of her. As they fan her, they again lift the breasts to cool the actor down. The breasts are the source of great heat.

Now it is the dead of night. The drama of Bhadrakāḷi and Dārika has been unfolding to the deep voices of the drums for several hours. As each scene begins, the actors dance and spin, carefully making offerings of prayers and flowers to the deity of the oil lamp at the center of the performance area, the *kaḷiviḷakku*, which has been enlivened with the spirit of the goddess. The actors' movements are accentuated by the occasional brilliant green flare of the torches, made of oil-soaked rags tied to branches, onto which are thrown handfuls of *telli* powder, an indigenous medicine extracted from tree resins. It has a beautiful smell, fresh and pungent, as well as an antiseptic effect, which once served to eradicate smallpox germs in the area. Bhadrakāḷi is a fever goddess, and the offering of this ritual performance is said to cure any pox diseases afflicting villagers by satiating her blood thirst and cooling her down from her raging, overheated state.

It is the deepest part of the night of the most dangerous day of the week, the time when ugly and bloodthirsty demons move abroad in search of their victims. It is a time when people should be safe and asleep in their beds, doors and windows shut, protected from the evils of the dark. But they are not in their beds. They are here, women, men, and children, in full view of the night sky, the unhealthful mists of evening, the frightening spirits of a Friday night, watching the battle of Bhadrakāḷi and Dārika on the dry, barren paddy fields of the village temple grounds.[7] All night the actors and priests have been flirting with the dark powers at large. Indeed, everything has been calculated to call forth those powers and to invite them into the performance arena, into the person of the actor himself, into the body of Bhadrakāḷi dancing *mudiyettu*.[8]

And now it is time. Kāḷi begins to veer madly into the audience, wildly waving her sickle-shaped iron sword in blood lust for Dārika's head. People jump up from their seats and run for the safety of the shrine as she chases Dārika erratically around the temple ground. Suddenly her heavy headdress begins to slip, her steps falter, she swoons and begins to tremble violently, her eyes rolling up into her head, her arms flailing. She is helped to her seat near the flame, her headdress removed, the energy temporarily contained and controlled, her body cooled.

An enormous crowd is watching now—there are easily a thousand people present, and all eyes are riveted on the action in the pavilion. A conch shell is blown as Kāḷi puts the *mudi* on again and stamps out the small rice-powder drawing that was under the stool. Everyone hoots. Kāḷi's dancing is more rhythmic now; the actor's concentration seems to have improved. Her naked stamping to the beat of the drums is very sexual, contrasting sharply with the staid, controlled movements of Kerala women in public. The legs swathed in white paste and laden with brass anklets thrust heavily downward into the dirt like elephants trampling a forest floor, the movements reminiscent not of the graceful, controlled classical art forms of Kerala but rather of the aboriginal dances of the hill tribes. Now Dārika is smearing the "blood" offering of the *guruti* all over his body, thereby feasting the spirits and sending them away to their forest dwellings. The torches flare up with fragrant green light.

After about five hours, as the dawn breaks, Kāḷi symbolically beheads Dārika, removing the colorful wooden headdress and hair, which she waves before the oil lamp, chanting in Sanskrit. Parents then bring their infants forward for Kāḷi to bless, which she does by waving them before the lamp and applying a spot of lampblack to their foreheads. Some say that the sight of the gruesome Kāḷi so startles the sleeping infant who is awakened in this manner that he becomes brave and strong for life. Others merely wish to obtain the blessings of the now benevolent goddess, at this moment of her victory, at the height of her *śakti*, her power.

Mothers in the audience scoop up their sleeping children, collect their belongings, and follow disheveled husbands through the dew-damp brown paddy fields to their homes nearby. Birds flit about in the thin morning light, their songs brightening the misty air. Back inside the temple, the performers are removing their makeup and drinking hot tea. I, too, lift my heavily sleeping little one, take blessings from the *mudi*, and, shouldering my bag of notebooks and my tape recorder, head for home.

AGNIGOLAM: BALL OF FIRE

The performance of *mudiyettu* and related art forms is a divine offering, not an entertainment. Its primary purpose is to please and to appease Bhagavati; the reaction of the spectators is, in theory, irrelevant. Yet the special circumstances under which the drama is performed lead actors and audience together to a heightened devotional state that transforms the actors' consciousness. One veteran, who has played the part of Kāḷi twenty to thirty times annually for more than forty-five years, described his inner experience of this transformation:

> After the entrance of Kāḷi, during that war [with Dārika], we find it difficult to control ourselves. We cannot control ourselves. We feel lots of special energy in our mind and also in the body. At that time we are in the war. At first we will feel some weakness. I'm telling you my experience. After this, a sudden change comes. Without our knowing, some power comes into us. At this time, all the audience will be concentrating on us, with great faith in their hearts. So when all these people are looking at us with such divine power, that same divine power gets into us. We as well as they get totally immersed in the divine power. . . . When there is this divine power everywhere, everyone including us gets totally mixed up in the divine power of God.[9]

As the performance intensifies, Kāḷi will enter the actor's body and consciousness as a great inner heat:

> [When possessed by Kāḷi, I feel] that I've lost my self-consciousness. It is a great feeling. I feel my head to be heavy. There is no other thought. When others see that abnormal running, jumping and all, they take the headgear from my head. Then we lose our self-consciousness. After losing the self-consciousness, we will be very hot. We experience a lot of heat in the body. That feels [just like] sweating in the hot sun. Along with the sweat and heat our emotions also change. We feel so angry toward the other actors. Our eyes also will appear red. Then the headgear and the weapon will be taken away and that spirit will go off on its own. When the weapon and the headgear are removed, she [Kāḷi] gets cooled and comes down to normal. The actor will drink some black coffee or some flavored boiled water, while people fan him. After fanning, when the sweat is all gone, then they tie the *mudi* on the head again.[10]

Heat is everywhere in the performance: in the oppressive summer night air, in the large oil-wick lamp holding the sacred presence at the center of the drama's action, in the fire torches that accompany the actors wherever they move, and within the body of the actor, as sweat and anger. This is no accident, for the goddess herself is of the form of fire. The male actor must deeply identify with this female, heated form:

> After putting on the dress and makeup, we feel that we are Kāḷi. That feeling is there in our mind always as a special excitation. We fix the picture of Bhagavati in our mind, and her supernatural power (*caitanyam*) enters our body. The picture of Bhagavati is of a woman. Bhagavati was born from the third eye of Śiva. Śiva sends her out with all his anger fixed in her. He puts his anger into

> her. She goes out with the aim of killing Dārika. It can only be called a fire ball (*agnigolam*). To represent that fire ball, we light a fire torch (*pantam*) on both sides. When you light that torch and throw the incandescent powder (*telli*) onto it, it blazes up with a loud noise: boo! boo! In the stories and all, when we talk about Kāḷi's power . . . she is the power born from Śiva's anger.[11]

The stories to which Balakrishnan Marar refers are collectively called the *Dārikavadham*, "The Killing of Dārika," a tale that appears in both oral and written versions throughout Kerala and forms the basis of the performance rituals dedicated to Bhagavati.[12] Weaving together elements of various Purāṇic versions of the stories of the fierce goddess but adding elements found in none of these, the *Dārikavadham* appears to be unique to Kerala. A brief version of the story is as follows: The demon Dārika, after intense ascetic practice, secured a boon from the god Brahmā that he would be invincible and could not be killed by any man. He began to harass the world and commit numerous depradations. When the great ascetic deity Śiva came to know of the misdeeds of Dārika, he became infuriated and created the goddess Bhadrakāḷi to kill the demon. Full of wrath, he opened his fiery third eye, and the enormous flaming form of Bhadrakāḷi emerged. She was huge, wore a ferocious look, and had innumerable heads, hands, and legs. When Śiva requested Bhadrakāḷi to destroy Dārika, she went through the forest and sought the help of the bloodthirsty ghosts and spirits who lived there. When Dārika saw Bhadrakāḷi and her largely female army coming, he only laughed and dismissed her, forgetting that his boon of invincibility did not prevent his being killed by a woman. After a fierce battle, Bhadrakāḷi and her assistants finally finished him off, and the goddess began to return home to Kailāsa, full of wrath and excitement and holding the head of Dārika in her left hand. When she reached Kailāsa, her father Śiva attempted to calm her wrath by dancing naked before her and offering her worship. She was satisfied and henceforth began to receive offerings from devotees as a boon from Śiva.[13]

Whereas male performers experience profound devotion and inner identification with the fierce goddess, other, rather different reactions are often evoked in the audience. Especially typical was this sentiment expressed by an elderly lady of a royal family whose temple sponsors *mudiyettu* annually: "We actually worship Bhagavati out of fear. It's simply fear. See, if we do anything wrong, if we commit any mistake, we fear she will punish us. It's for that reason we have devotion (*bhakti*) for her. [Actually] it's not devotion, it's a kind of fear. It's something inside . . . an anxiety inside the mind."

As my time in Kerala stretched from weeks to months, and as I adjusted to the horrendous tensions that accompany every attempt to enter another society deeply, that "anxiety inside the mind" came more and more into focus in my work. What struck me most about the scores of performances dedicated as offerings to Bhadrakāḷi that I witnessed in my first six months of fieldwork was their anxious aura of intense emotions ordinarily forbidden open expression. Whereas villagers and city folk alike seemed to value self-control, consideration, humility, and lack of conflict with others as the primary virtues of social life, it was violence, closely followed by sexuality and heavily interlaced with satiric humor, that seemed to predominate in the village festivals. I often saw inebriated men break into quarrels at such events. On one occasion a serious fistfight broke out in the wee hours of the morning during the enactment of the battle between Kāḷi and Dārika. The fight erupted numerous times during the performance and had to be subdued forcibly by friends of the combatants. At several temples we were told legends of the accidental murder of the actor playing Dārika by the actor playing Kāḷi, who lost control and became too strongly identified with his bloodthirsty heroine. In all such cases the victim was murdered by his father or maternal uncle, in a pattern that suggested oedipal conflict.

The fact that these stories seemed ultimately to revolve around male power relations (even when one of the males appeared in the guise of a female) reinforced my suspicion that the Kāḷi we were seeing in these performances represented the inner fears and feelings of men more than of women. After all, only men may participate in the rituals and dramatic enactments of *mudiyettu* and its related art forms. Women, though present, perform only perfunctory and peripheral ritual roles—namely, the processional *tālappoli* welcoming the goddess as a housewife greets a distinguished guest, and the ululation performed as the enlivened headgear is donned by the actor playing Kāḷi. During the performance, however, the women tended to remain in protected groups huddled close to the temple walls, avoiding the boisterous and often frightening activities of the men. While men could drink, misbehave, scream, run, and laugh during performances, women never broke their cool, controlled demeanor, never returned the smiles or teasing of the wolf-eyed men, never shouted or ran. Nor did they give way to the strong tides of desire and anger that washed through the temple courtyard in the wake of the cruel, powerful Bhagavati, as she ran naked, shouting and brandishing her sword to chase and conquer her impudent masculine foe. Young men and boys trailed the goddess, laughing, shouting, and waving branches of leaves to invoke and heighten her furious divine energy. But the women remained silent and still.

Living as a woman in a society that imposed the most stringent standards of feminine self-discipline and self-denial gave me some insight into the level of mental anxiety that both men and women may experience in such an environment, especially in matters relating to social intercourse, and, in particular, the control of female sexuality.[14] A fifty-five-year-old widowed mother of five related a tale to me that indicated the prominence of this theme in her own consciousness:

> Once when Śiva and Pārvatī were traveling, they saw a place lit up with all sorts of lights, and Pārvatī asked her husband, "What is that place?" Śiva told her "Please don't look at that—thousands of prostitutes are there." Pārvatī did not know what he meant, and she asked Śiva what that was. When he explained that to her, she cursed the prostitutes, saying they should have three breasts so no man would look at them. Śiva told her any woman has desires and is capable of the same behavior, even herself, and asked her to remove the curse. Pārvatī just laughed scornfully and refused. Then one day when Pārvatī was alone, Śiva came to the house in the form of a cloth merchant selling saris. Pārvatī liked one of the saris very much, but the man was not willing to sell it for money. He wanted something else from her. She had to surrender to him, and though she got the sari she also got the same curse she had given the prostitutes: a third breast appeared on her chest. Śiva then revealed himself and reminded her of her words at the brothel. She repented and he removed the curse.[15]

Despite Kerala's high literacy rate and generally excellent living conditions, as well as a tradition in some castes of matrilineal inheritance, attitudes toward women remain highly restrictive. Women should not speak with, look at, walk with, or befriend men, nor may they laugh in the presence of men other than family members, except in rare circumstances. Modesty, reticence, and self-control before men or elders are the ideal of feminine behavior. Even working women told me of the humiliating gossip that arises should they behave familiarly with a male colleague or even shake his hand in the office. Except in the most liberal urban settings of Trivandrum and Ernakulam, a woman cannot ordinarily walk alone in the street or arrive home after dark without being the object of vicious gossip attacking her moral character.[16] Sexual mores are, as in most of India, conservative, with no dating or cross-sex socializing permitted (although mixed groups of young people may talk together in a college setting), and nearly all marriages are arranged by parents or guardians within the caste. Owing to higher education and the frequent travel of young men to the Gulf states for work, marriages often are delayed—until men are in their late twenties or early thirties, and women somewhere between twenty-two and thirty. Large dowries are also expected from the bride's family, further delaying and limiting marital opportunities for many young women from less wealthy families. During the entire period from puberty to marriage—a minimum of seven years and as many as eighteen or more—a girl is expected to remain a virgin, pure in mind as well as body, and males also are denied sexual outlets with women of their own status and age group.[17]

By most standards this situation would be judged highly restrictive and hard to endure, both physically and psychologically. The extremely hot and humid climate, the very minimal attire of young men in villages (often just a thin, short cloth tied around the waist), and extended family groups living in close quarters make this enforced abstinence an even greater austerity.[18] This is particularly true for women, who in many cases spend their leisure hours watching suggestive romantic movies, serials, and dances on the television but are strongly discouraged from showing any interest in sex.[19] Girls are encouraged to keep busy; they are told that too much sleep is "unhealthy" and are carefully guarded by both family and prying neighbors, who watch out for any signs of romantic or sexual involvement, real or imputed, that could destroy a girl's chances of a suitable marital alliance. Although complaints about this situation or even any open acknowledgment of female feelings and frustrations are generally taboo, and a tense silence on such topics is nearly always maintained, several young women did express their dissatisfaction and suffering to me when a sympathetic ear was offered, in some cases for the first time in their lives. Two young women in their mid-twenties, one an English teacher in a cosmopolitan town, and the other the eldest daughter of a performer of traditional Kerala folk arts living in a remote village, voiced similar discontent, longing, desire, and even anger at their respective situations, which they felt quite powerless to change. In both cases, lack of family finances was the bottom line preventing them from achieving fulfillment either in marriage or in pursuing further studies. A woman who is one of many sisters, and whose family cannot afford her dowry, may well have to accept a life of celibacy, living at home and caring for her parents until their deaths. Unlike most married women I interviewed, these two mature, unmarried women were both fervent devotees of the fierce goddess Bhagavati, enthusiastically relating her legends and stories to me and frequently visiting her temples "for mental peace."[20]

The mental suffering of young women, particularly their frustration and anger over repressed sexual needs, is a vital theme in Kerala folklore and popular culture. Malayali films and novels present updated versions of the pervasive and ancient folktales about *yakṣi*s (Sanskrit: *yakṣī*)—unhappy, seductive, and bloodthirsty female tree spirits out to entice and destroy upstanding, virtuous men. The legend generally follows the same pattern: A Brahmin man is walking home from the temple on a moonlit night, when he encounters a beautiful, voluptuous maiden standing alone on the road before him. Her bewitching smile and the fragrance of jasmine enveloping her utterly dazzle him. Shyly she requests his protection to accompany her home. On the way the man's amorous desire grows even more intense, and the lady seems willing. In the morning the bloody entrails of his body are discovered hanging from the trees and the *yakṣi* is nowhere to be seen. In a version of this legend published in *Temples and Legends of Kerala*, the Brahmin escapes by ducking into the home of his guru, who instructs his disciple to touch his body while looking at the enticing female: "Lo! It was an apparition, a fiendish woman with fierce eyes and protruding teeth. Little did Guptan Nambudiri realise that he was in the clutches of a terrible yakshi out to entice men and devour them."[21] In this version of the story, the Brahmin seeks the help of Bhagavati, who destroys the *yakṣi* and throws her into a pond, the water of which turns red as blood.

HEAT AND LUST: THE BLOODTHIRSTY VIRGIN

This published account is associated with one of the temples most renowned for curing the mental disturbances of young unmarried or recently married women, as well as madness in general: the Chottanikkara Bhagavati Temple in the Ernakulam district of Kerala. In fact, it was the favorite temple of one of the young ladies I interviewed, who stated that she "got no mental peace" if she did not visit Chottanikkara Bhagavati at least once a month. When showing me how she worshiped the goddess and describing her to me, she emphasized enthusiastically that "she is a virgin, you know." She clearly identified with the goddess and believed in her power to relieve the special tensions of young women. On numerous visits to Chottanikkara, I witnessed the daily *tuḷḷal* dance performed by the mentally afflicted in front of the shrines of Śiva and Bhadrakāḷi. *Tuḷḷal* is a jumping, hopping dance undertaken in a fit of possession, fever, or madness. One extreme form of treatment for mental illness prescribed by astrologers is the offering of *guruti* (the same blood substitute I earlier described) to Bhadrakāḷi at Chottanikkara, the mad person also banging a large iron nail into a special tree in which evil spirits reside, using nothing but the forehead and fists to drive it in. This treatment, while drawing blood from the victim's head, also releases the evil spirit believed to be possessing the person and fixes it to the tree. The Bhadrakāḷi shrine in the lower part of the Chottanikkara Bhagavati temple complex is the site where the *yakṣi* of our legend was destroyed. The infamous red pool is still there, as is the *pālā* tree (a favorite residence of *yakṣi*s and evil spirits), its bark studded with thousands of heavy iron nails.

The *tuḷḷal* danced by the mad women at Chottanikkara was overpowering to me in its expression of extreme anguish. All rules of female propriety were controverted by the wild screaming and shameless jumping of the women, their matted hair flying about loose, dirt clinging to their faces, obscenities pouring from their angry tongues. Anxious family members hovered about the young women and girls, watching their movements sadly, in hopes of a cure, only interfering when they seemed to be in danger of injuring themselves in their violence. As I watched the group of hopping, screaming dancers before the shrine, one girl suddenly broke from the pack and tore madly into the temple compound, running and screaming until an older male relative gently restrained her. While I wondered what suffering could drive a woman to such extreme antisocial behavior, the obvious parallel to the dancing of Bhadrakāḷi in *mudiyettu*, which I had witnessed at so many temple festivals, came painfully to mind.[22]

Yet despite the obvious resemblance of the possessed Kāḷi dancer's behavior to real female possession and madness, it is striking that women are prohibited from participating in the public rituals of Kāḷi, except in the *tālappoli* (the welcoming of the goddess with a procession of lights) and as spectators. Even in their homes, I found that women tend to shy away from the worship of Kāḷi, often directing their faith toward more benevolent deities such as Krishna, Śiva, Pārvatī, or family ancestors. In the temple performances, women are never permitted to enact the role of Kāḷi or perform as oracles (*velicchappadu*).[23] I asked the wife of one prominent performer who specializes in the role of Kāḷi about this, and she explained:

> Women can't perform *mudiyettu* because of menses. I have much bleeding and sickness at each period. I can't touch any food. People think menses is bad. We can't enter the temple. If a woman goes in the temple when she is menstruating, she will fall to shivering, have epileptic fits, or be possessed. My mother told me so. The old women say that if a woman goes in at that time, she will lose her eyes and go mad. Women don't have much power. If we ask small things from Devī, we will get them—not big things. Men have more power. For work and such, men have more. Only at the time of birth do women have power. At other times, men dominate.[24]

Omana's statement echoed the response I invariably received when questioning both men and women about the prohibition on female performers in the ritual arts of Kāḷi: menstruation was the key—indeed the only—factor preventing their participation. At first this response seemed to conform neatly to the sterotyped Hindu attitudes about the "impurity of women" often noted by feminist scholars. But the remainder of Omana's remarks illumines a possible deeper meaning of the menstrual taboo, revealing something more complex than the simple oppression of women by men: that is, a concern with the proper management of the potent forces of female reproductivity. The symptoms that will be suffered by a woman who breaks the well-known Hindu taboo on a menstruating woman entering the temple are the *very same symptoms* that must be manifested by the male representatives of Bhagavati in the temple rituals. Shivering, fits, and possession are the very signs that the fierce goddess is entering the performer and enlivening the ritual. They are the form of Bhagavati's revelation of herself, and, as Omana's comments suggest, these symptoms reflect the ambivalent and essential powers of female sexuality. The performer enacting the role of Bhadrakāḷi in the ritual dramas of Kerala dons an entirely female costume (with an emphasis on prominent breasts) and a stylized female demeanor, including voice modulation, posture, and movements. The goddess's oracular representative, the *velicchappadu,* is also clearly if more subtly feminine in his dress and behavior. He grows his hair long like a woman, ideally does not have a moustache, uses turmeric all over his body as women do, and dons the archaic ritual dress of a high-caste female.[25] One troupe leader put it clearly: "He should be like a lady."[26] This is a remarkable prescription: the ritual representative of the goddess must be *like* a lady, but must not actually *be* a lady.

One clue to this conundrum may be found in glosses of the Malayalam word *tuḷḷal*, commonly used to refer to possession dances in Kerala. *Tuḷḷal* describes a wide variety of things, including those artless displays of pure misery at Chottanikkara and the possession dances of professional oracles, as well as the highly sophisticated temple arts taught in government-supported institutions. The dictionary provides a revealing set of related meanings that may illumine the underlying symbolism of possession dance. Consider the following series of etymologically related words:

> *tuḷḷal*, n., jumping, leaping, hopping, skipping; prance, prancing; fretting and fuming with anger; tremor; involuntary motion as of demoniac possession; dance; a kind of stage-play with the accompaniment of rhythmic dance and music, usually performed in temples.
>
> *tuḷḷalppani*, n., a burning fever, a fever with hot and cold fits.
>
> *tuḷḷuka*, v.i., to jump, to hop, to frisk, to dance, to palpitate; to shiver or tremble with anger; to shiver and dance uncontrollably and vehemently as in demoniac possession.
>
> *tuḷḷicchi*, n., an unruly or ungovernable sort of woman; a flirt; an arrogant woman [slang usage].[27]

This series of glosses suggests an underlying cognitive relation between certain emotions, their physiological manifestations, and spirit possession. It appears that uncontrollable anger can lead to shivering and trembling, fits and possession, and can manifest itself physically in fever, uncontrolled dancing, and jumping. The ritual *tuḷḷal*s of temple arts would appear not only to mimic but actually to invoke these states of uncontrollable emotion, in order thus to control and remove them. In the performance of *mudiyettu* this is demonstrated by the repeated exciting and cooling of the goddess, which culminates in possession.

Yet it is the last entry in the glossary that captures our attention the most. A *tuḷḷicchi (-icchi* is merely a feminine ending, here added to the stem *tuḷḷu-*) is a woman who is "unruly," "ungovernable," "arrogant," and worst of all, "a flirt"—that is to say, the opposite of all that a Malayali lady should be. These adjectives might also well describe the behavior of Bhadrakāḷi in the performance, as well as that of the mad women at Chottanikkara. The lack of control displayed by all these undesirable female models centers around the double taboos against anger and sexuality. A woman who displays vehement anger, particularly a scolding wife or mother, is referred to in folk speech as "a real Bhadrakāḷi." The physical symptoms marking a *tuḷḷicchi* are identical to those punishing the errant female who enters a temple while menstruating, according to Omana: shivering, fits, possession. It is her sexuality that is the source of the difficulty, and that is what must be controlled.

But why is menstruation the pivotal point around which this complex of anger, female sexuality, power, and control appears to revolve? One point of view that has frequently been presented in both scholarly literature and Hindu doctrine turns on the notion of pollution, which regards menstrual blood as defiling and dirty, and hence as negating the purity of sacred power in high-caste Hinduism.[28] Yet this view does not fully explain the role of anger, sexuality, and power that is so central to the Bhagavati cult of Kerala. Menstruation is clearly the sign of reproductive potential, the ability to bear children, which, according to Omana, is the only form of power allowed to women in her world: "Only at the time of birth do women have power. At other times, men dominate." In fact, the celebration of first menses is one of the central life-cycle rituals among Kerala women, although its popularity is beginning to wane.[29] The symbolism of the rite celebrates the fertility of the young girl, likening her to the budding coconut and ripening paddy, the mainstays of Kerala diet. The tender young buds of the coconut tree, lovely and promising as the breasts of a young virgin girl, are placed before her in a large measure of raw paddy rice, and she is presented with the auspicious items given to a bride. But menstruation, while signaling the potential for fertility and birth, also implies a danger: the intense emotions of sexual desire believed to accompany physical maturity may lead the girl to disaster if they are not restrained and controlled until her marriage.[30] Menstruation also may have another negative meaning, which is the failure to conceive. In a married woman, menstruation signals the loss of a potential fetus, a death of sorts.[31] In menstruation, then, death, desire, and heat are intimately interwoven; it is the symbolism of menstruation that lies at the root of the complex belief system expressed in the Bhagavati temple rituals.

A menstruating woman is considered to be "hot," both physically and emotionally, within the Indian system of indigenous medicine known as the Āyurveda.[32] This heat, like that described by the Kāḷi performers, manifests itself physically in perspiration and emotionally in unruly emotions like anger and lust. It may also be manifest in pustulant fevers such as smallpox or chicken pox, which, as in much of India, are seen as visible signs (*darśanam*) of the presence of the fierce goddess.[33] An item of folk medicine further links female sexuality and heat, for acne eruptions on a woman's face are interpreted as a sign of a "hot" nature (in other words, excessive sexual desire). Certain liquids and foods are taken daily, both internally and externally, to cool the body and emotions, which are intimately linked. Kerala women apply coconut oil to the head, hair, and entire body—an "oil bath"—and use fresh turmeric on their faces and bodies as a coolant and cosmetic. These treatments are more important for women in a "hot" state, as they are just after menstruation (a woman traditionally remained in seclusion and did not bathe during the first four days of her menses) and during pregnancy. Although men also take oil baths and eat cooling foods, they are generally considered to be naturally "cooler" in the indigenous medical system. And of course men do not ordinarily undergo the periodic transformations in their physiological and emotional state that women do (though the Kāḷi enactment during temple rituals provides such an opportunity).

Virgin girls and women are associated with *yakṣis* in the male imagination. Most men that I interviewed believed that unmarried women, as well as married women whose husbands are away (30 to 40 percent of the adult male population leave Kerala to work for long periods in the Persian Gulf, returning home only briefly each year or two), are voraciously sexual, and that they secretly desire the attentions and teasing of men.[34] George, a married man in his thirties, explained to me (through a male translator) that "in the olden days people believed that when they slept . . . these kinds of people [virgins] would come in dreams and have [sex] with us . . . [producing] nocturnal emissions. . . . These kinds of people enter our body, and cause us to ooze [fluid]. They drain us and drink it. That's the belief."[35]

The deity Bhadrakāḷi is conceived of in Kerala as an unmarried, virgin girl—beautiful, hot, and dangerous—and is also clearly associated with *yakṣis*. Like "hot" women, she, too, receives cooling offerings of bananas, coconut, and rice. These please and placate her. Her heat is directly associated with her virgin state, and, like the *yakṣis* and virgins of dreams, her desire and anger make her thirsty for male life fluids. In folktales and legends, the *yakṣi* is a vampire, drinking the blood of her victims while seducing them; but George's statement makes the symbolism more explicit: it is *semen* that the virgin demoness wants from her victim. This essential fluid fertilizes and cools the hot female womb but weakens and drains the man who gives it—in the *yakṣi* stories, even to the point of death. The motif of drinking blood is clearly a symbolic displacement of the intaking of semen by the vagina, and in some stories and medical pronouncements the two fluids are interchangeable.[36] In some versions of the *Dārikavadham* story, for example, the demon Dārika has been given the boon of reproducing himself ad infinitum: each drop of his blood that falls upon the earth immediately springs up into a thousand more of him.[37] Because of this ability, he is known as *raktabījāsura*: blood-seed-demon.

In Malayalam (the language of Kerala) *bījam* means reproductive seed or semen. Both males and females possess it, and it is closely related to blood. In folk conceptions of reproductive physiology, it is by heating the body and arousing sexual desire that both males and females produce (or "ooze," in George's words) their sexual fluids—that of the woman in the form of blood and that of the man as semen. The mixing of these two emotionally generated fluids leads to fertilization and life. Thus, the heat of the female's desire is requisite to conception, but this process inevitably requires a "sacrifice" of the male to the female, an offering of his life fluids that is tantamount to blood sacrifice and leaves him somehow less vital, closer to death.

This sacrifice of essential male fluids is enacted in the remainder of the story: Dārika is conquered by Kāḷi, who enlists the help of the insatiably bloodthirsty Vētāḷam, a horrible female forest ghost. Her enormous tongue spreads over the entire battlefield and, as Kāḷi kills Dārika, Vētāḷam laps up the endless river of blood so that no more Dārikas can be born from the contact of his blood with the earth. Dārika is thus destroyed by the direct controversion of his infinite autofertility: his *yakṣi*/demon/vampire/virgin opponents "drain and drink" his precious life fluids (in George's phrase), thereby destroying his vitality and killing him.[38]

The rituals and folklore of another important Bhagavati temple in Kerala reinforce the association of the fierce goddess with the image of the sexually aggressive and insatiable virgin woman. The Kodungallur Bhagavati temple in central Kerala is renowned for its unusual annual festival at the asterism of *Meenam Bharaṇi* (in the month of March–April). On this day, the temple, closed until this century to any but the highest castes, was thrown open for ritual pollution by low-caste people. This pollution was accomplished in various ways: through the mere presence of low-caste men and women but also through drunken dancing, highly obscene songs and gestures directed toward the goddess, the presence of hordes of *velicchappadu* (oracles—including female oracles from the hilly tribal areas), who danced possessed and cut their heads with swords to produce blood, swift running around the temple, and the blood sacrifice of vast numbers of cocks.[39] This blood sacrifice having been outlawed for several decades, today thousands of chickens are thrown over the temple walls and *guruti* is offered instead; but the other polluting practices continue largely unabated, despite objections from various reform-oriented Hindus.[40]

George discussed the Kodungallur *Bharaṇi* with my field assistant, Laji:

L: So are there any obscene songs there at *Bharaṇi*?

G: Yes, there are. She is an unmarried lady, right? [Very secretively:] So she is pleased or made happy at least by singing these obscene songs.

L: This Kāḷi, right?

G: Yes, this Bhagavati. There is a belief that Bhagavati remains unmarried. . . . So . . . [by our] singing these obscene songs, . . . she can be made happy. These songs are sung with *tuḷḷal* dancing. People go there and please her and come back once a year. It is for this reason that they dress up this oracle and go once a year.

L: Those who have not married—unmarried virgins—do they have more interest in sex (*kāmam*)?

G: That's right. If she had been born as a human being she would have all those interests.

L: So it is to fulfill her lust that these enactments are done, these oracles' performances, obscene songs, and so on?

G: Yes, to make her happy. Once a year everyone takes all these pains and comes, to do all the sacrifices and enactments.

L: Well, that's true, but is it somehow related to her lust, her desire?

G: Yes, they sing to extinguish her desire. These songs and other activities, like *tuḷḷal,* calm her lust.

L: And unmarried ladies have more of it?

G: Yes, but she [the anthropologist] shouldn't feel bad because I am saying that. You should be careful in explaining it.[41]

Although most people denied any direct relation between the sexual desires of virgins (or any other female emotions) and the nature of Bhagavati, George's statements imply that the public worship of the virgin Kāḷi in Kerala reveals in part an attempt to resolve concerns about female sexuality. Bhadrakāḷi is modeled on a virgin female, whose sign is menses, who is perceived as suffering from an unfulfilled desire for sex and procreation, whose lack of fulfillment is one source of her anger, and who requires the blood sacrifice of a male to cool and satisfy her "thirst." Her emotional and physical needs are intimately interdependent, regulated by heat and coolness, dryness and wetness, and subject to penetration by outside agencies of consciousness. Extreme imbalances in this delicate system are reflected in extraordinary behavior like spirit possession, and the crucial balance may be restored physical, emotional, and spiritual remedies.

This conflation of psychology, physiology, and the supernatural in the larger-than-life persona of Bhagavati relates not only to personal well-being but to the health of society as a whole. Bhagavati is, first and foremost, a deity of the soil, the matron goddess of Kerala. It is to Bhagavati that the first fruits of the paddy harvest are offered at the Onam festival in late August. She is propitiated in songs at the harvest as well as at the time when paddy seedlings are transplanted. Bhagavati is also the soul of the ubiquitous coconut tree, for which some say Kerala is named. One of her common epithets is *kurumba,* which means "tender coconut." Tender coconut leaves hang from the *mudi* of the possessed actor as the strands of her hair; her breasts are made of brightly painted coconut shells; and toddy, the fermented sap of the coconut tree and a favorite intoxicant, is first drawn on Tuesday and Friday, days sacred to Bhadrakāḷi (and on which both *tuḷḷal* and the offering of *guruti* often take place). One could say that Bhagavati is the earth itself. This association is demonstrated by the following legend, which explains the origin of the Chottanikkara Bhagavati temple:

> The place where the temple stands today was once a dense forest inhabited by tribals. Among them was a notorious dacoit by name Kannappan. . . . One day he had a dream in which Mother Sakti appeared before him and told

him . . . [his] cowshed would be sanctified by the presence of her idol and that of Vishnu. The next day Kannappan repaired the shed and found the idols. He built a temple and spent the rest of his life in the worship of the Devi.

After the death of Kannappan the temple fell in ruins as the place became uninhabited. One day a Pulaya (outcaste) woman who had come to cut grass sharpened her scythe against a stone which started to ooze blood. The horror-stricken woman shrieked aloud and the Pulayas in the neighborhood came running to the spot. They, in turn, informed the learned Edathu Nambudiri, who, visiting the spot, realised that there was divine *Chaitanya* of Parasakti at the place. . . . It was Edathu Nambudiri who built a shrine, performed pooja and administered the temple for several years.[42]

In this story the sign of the divine energy of the goddess, whose idol had been lost, is the oozing of blood from a stone when it is sharpened by the scythe of a low-caste female agricultural worker.[43] The scythe used for the cutting of rice paddy in Kerala is a curved iron tool, which strongly resembles the ritual sword of the goddess Bhadrakāḷi.[44] In the temple festival described at the outset of this essay, it was the curved sword stained with blood that represented the goddess and to which the drummers played so feverishly. In addition to its martial significance, the sword also evokes the sacrifice of the paddy plants to the hunger of humans, the scythe cutting down the dry, ripe golden stalks, heavy with plump seed, with its sharp, curved iron blade. Once again, hunger and heat impel death and sacrifice; through the satiation of biological need, balance and coolness are restored, and the cycle begins anew. The bleeding rock is analogous to the menstruating goddess, the virgin girl, and the potentially fertile earth, which awaits only the offering of cooling, fertilizing rain to remove her overheated anguish so that she can proffer her life-giving fruits.

Does the earth suffer? In the blistering dry heat of late April and May, everything suffers. Before irrigation, the crop lands of Kerala would have lain fallow from February to May, getting drier and drier as the harvest was gathered before the monsoon rains. These hot months after the harvest mark the temple festival season, when *mudiyettu* and other rituals emphasizing violence and blood sacrifice are performed as offerings to Bhagavati. It is also the time when, until forty years ago or so, the people of Kerala celebrated the menses of the earth goddess in an agricultural ritual called *uccāral*:

At the end of Makaram (January–February), when the second crop has been harvested, the year's agricultural operations are supposed to be over, and Mother Earth, *Bhumi Devi*, is considered to rest during the hot weather until the first shower begins. At the beginning of this period the Malayali observes a festival in honour of the Goddess's menstruation, which . . . is supposed to take place at this time.[45]

For three days no agricultural work may be undertaken, granaries are closed, and paddy is not sold. This period represents the seclusion of the menstruating earth goddess (human women are also secluded for three days). On the fourth day the granaries reopen, and landlords go to repossess their fields. In some *uccāral* festivals, "straw models of cattle are taken in procession to the temples of Bhagavati," much as described in the opening section of this essay.[46]

This overt connection between Bhagavati temple rituals, agriculture, and puberty and menstrual rites has been lost over time and is not now recognized by most people. However, the leader of a well-known temple performance troupe from northern Kerala, E. Kalidasan, clearly related the *guruti* offering to both harvest cultivation and female fertility. As he explained it, this offering of *guruti* by the sprinkling of red water on the ground "represents the menstruation of Bhagavati. The earth gives birth to plants in the same way a mother gives birth to a child after the menstrual period. So the earth must also be mature."[47] According to Kalidasan, all the temple arts devoted to Bhagavati are closely related to farming culture.

Whereas the legend of the bleeding rock at Chottanikkara intertwines the life of the goddess's image with that of the living earth through the indirect symbolism of menstruation, a legend from Chengannur makes this association explicit. According to temple legend:

> It is a wonder of wonders that even today the deity which is cast in *panchaloha* [an alloy of five metals] gets her periods, a phenomenon which is not heard of in any other temple.
>
> 'In olden days it used to occur regularly every month. Now only three or four times a year,' said . . . the head priest of the temple speaking to this writer.
>
> He or his assistant . . . on opening the [inner sanctum] early morning removes the *nirmalyam* (previous day's decoration of the deity) and hands it over to the Varrier attendant along with the white *udayada* (petticoat) without looking at it. The Varrier examines the dress closely and if there are signs of bleeding sends it to . . . the temple Tantri. There the lady of the house scrutinises the cloth again and confirms the menses.
>
> The *udayada*, after the occurrence, is available for sale to the public. Though the rate fixed by the Devaswom is only Rs. 10/–due to its being a rarity it is grabbed by devotees by paying hundreds of rupees, booking it well in advance. Among the dignitaries who bought this, we are told, are the late Sir C. P. Ramaswami Aiyar and ex-President Shri V. V. Giri.
>
> The sanctum is kept closed for three days when the Goddess gets menses. . . . On the fourth day, the bathing ceremony . . . is conducted by taking the image in procession on a female elephant to the nearby Pampa river. Innumerable devotees, especially women with *thalapoli* (holding lamps), accompany this.[48]

The reason for the image's miraculous menstruation, according to this temple text, is that when Satī's body was cut into pieces by Mahāviṣṇu after her humiliation at the sacrifice of Dakṣa, it was "at Chengannur the yoni mandala or the female reproductive organ [fell], which explains why the

Devi gets her monthly periods here."[49] Vaidyanathan goes on to relate that a British colonial officer who scoffed at this belief found his wife suddenly stricken with incessant menstrual bleeding, which only desisted when he worshiped the goddess at the temple. The details of the rituals surrounding the menses of Chengannur Bhagavati explicitly reenact the traditional puberty ceremony of high-caste girls of Kerala, now falling into disuse. Kamala Das, in her autobiographical work *Ente Bālyakaḷasmaraṇa* (My childhood memories), describes the procession of the young high-caste girl, who is carried on the back of an elephant to bathe in the river after her first menstrual seclusion.[50] The examination of the first menstrual bloodstains on the white petticoat was once a form of divination, from which the future of the young woman could be read.[51] This evidence suggests that, just as Bhagavati is modeled on the virgin female, the female puberty rite is the prototype of all Bhagavati rituals performed in the Kerala temple today.

Agnigolam, the "ball of fire" described by Balakrishnan Marar as the essential being of Bhagavati, is a multifaceted entity.[52] The fire that is generated by the oil-soaked rag torches held before the steaming, sweating, possessed performer who has been inspired by the angry goddess is only the external sign of a deep inner experience of a heat that penetrates not only the body but the soul. The ritual reenactment of the anguish and anger of the goddess pleases and satisfies her. She is cooled through the offering of flowers and fruits, of *guruti*, and of the head of Dārika, but also by the very real suffering of the male actor who bears her weight with his whole being. At the end of the ritual drama, as the dawn breaks, the exhausted actor falls to the ground and the goddess is tamed, transformed from a bloodthirsty virgin to a benign and loving mother who will offer fertility and protection to her devotees for another year.

EMPATHY OR ENVY?

The dramatic rituals that celebrate the goddess Bhagavati in Kerala temples clearly are modeled around images of female sexuality, with both its promises and its perceived dangers. Whether emulating the joyous rites of a girl's first menstruation or the terrifying consequences of desire gone out of control in possession and madness, these ritual arts are dominated by men: men acting as and in the place of women.

This fact forces us to confront the difficult question of how these art forms differentially serve men and women. We have reviewed some causes of the frustration, anxiety, and anger that arise in the lives of young women in Kerala but seem to find little outlet. Perhaps even less so today than in the past, there are few ritual arts, performances, or diversions that women alone control and direct and through which some of this pressure could be relieved.[53] Certainly the Bhagavati cult has no female component, and, as we have seen, women are prohibited from direct participation in its temple rituals. For the most part, women appear self-controlled and contented, seldom acknowledging or expressing these frustrations. Only in extreme cases, when the pressure becomes too much, does inner suffering erupt in the symptoms of "hysteria" and madness. Does the suffering of the male performers in *mudiyettu* reflect an attempt at empathy for the women's plight, providing vicarious relief to them? Does the honoring of the goddess honor women? Or is it a demonstration of deep envy and fear of a perceived female power that men feel they can never really own?

Observing the stiff, controlled bodies and faces of the women in the performances I attended, I did not feel that these rituals were designed to help, relieve, or honor their pain and struggles. The women were peripheral, both as ritual participants and as spectators. When I interviewed them, they were unable or unwilling to draw any parallel between Bhagavati and themselves. If they secretly identified with the furious Kāḷi, they never showed or admitted it. Their devotion, such as it was, was motivated by fear, not love. They constantly deferred to their menfolk both in knowledge and in personal interest where the Bhagavati rituals were concerned.

Yet there are hints. The burning eyes of a young girl silently listening to her father discussing her imminent marriage to a stranger, the tense choking back of tears by a wife whose husband prohibits her from visiting a neighbor's house, the hysterical weeping at the loss of a beloved mother—all point to the river of emotions running deep under the still surfaces of composure and modesty. Women's jokes, songs, and stories: these are other places to look.[54] For example, a ninety-year-old Brahmin widow, Savitri, related the following legend to me about the origin of her own family temple, at which *mudiyettu* is performed every year in early April. This story illustrates a more homey, sympathetic view of the goddess than the vampirelike *yakṣis* or bloodthirsty warriors of the men's imaginations. Savitri refers to "the place of delivery," a small room in the house where menstrual seclusion as well as childbirth take place. In her story the goddess is strongly attracted to this exclusively female and highly "polluted" space and must be forcibly relegated to the pure, male-controlled temple where she is eventually installed in the form of her sword:

> An ancestor from here worshipped Bhagavati. He brought her here from Kodungallur and installed her. . . . Bhagavati told him, "I shall come walking towards the [temple door] here and face toward the north." The temple door in Kodungallur is toward the north. She is the savior of all the people in this area. She is very powerful. [It happened like this.] An old Nambudiri [Brahmin priest] worshiped her image at Kodungallur and brought it from there. . . . She went to the [Brahmin's house]. Remember I told you about the place of delivery and all? It is said that she immediately ran in there. So one

> woman of the family said, "Look, delivery and menstrual blood are here. You cannot stay here." "Okay, place my sword somewhere, and build an abode for me wherever you find the sword," the goddess replied. Then when the Nambudiri returned after his bath, he saw the sword on the red stone there. At that he remembered that Bhagavati had said the temple door should face north, so he built a temple to her in that way.[55]

Savitri's story makes Bhagavati a covert ally of women, who nonetheless must help the goddess assume her proper place in the male ritual world. The goddess may not remain in the "place of delivery" but must take her place with the men. When she does so, however, it is not as a living, breathing female but in the symbolic form of her sword that she agrees to be installed. The distance implied by this transformation provides a possible answer to our question about empathy and envy. Something is lost as the female experience enters the male imaginative realm. The male coopting of female suffering in ritual does not seem to help women much. Male performers and spectators identify with female energy to gain more power, not to empower women. The performances and stories of Bhagavati, rather than providing role models of female defiance and independence, serve rather to reinforce cultural ideas about the inherent danger a woman holds for men, which it is her responsibility to contain and control.

Yet in my dealings with Kerala women, I was not convinced that they had fully internalized these negative roles, although they outwardly acquiesced to them. They seemed rather to be merely tolerating a system they accepted as unjust but unchangeable. For the most part, women were more involved in the difficult business of everyday living than in the imaginative world of Bhagavati. Men, however, really seem worried about and deeply interested in dangerous feminine sexuality and its symbolic manipulation.[56] Fear and envy feed each other in a complex psychological process that invites deeper analysis and reflection.

These conclusions show us that the view one gets of the powerful ritual dramas of Bhagavati differs depending on where one sits. The opening of this chapter revealed my own perspective. But through the eyes of the male performer of Kāḷi, it looks something like this:

> When all these people are looking at us with such divine power, that same divine power gets into us. We as well as they get totally immersed in the divine power. . . . When there is this divine power everywhere, everyone including us gets totally mixed up in the divine power of God.[57]

Yet amongst the many viewpoints, there is also that of the performer's wife, watching silently from the sidelines:

> Before my marriage, I had never seen *mudiyettu*, even though my family is of that performing caste. When I first saw my husband dressed as Kāḷi, I felt fear

> on seeing his face. I said, "I won't look at him," and I ran away. It makes me feel strange to hear the men calling my husband, "Kāḷi, Kāḷi." But it is a religious offering, so I don't feel too bad.[58]

We cannot know how Bhagavati sees the drama, but it is our duty to embrace as many other views as fully as we can. By reflecting on this rich performative tradition from a myriad points of view, we can glimpse some of the personal meaning of this "ball of fire" for the men and women whose world the goddess inhabits. Through all her transformations in time and space, Bhagavati continues to dance at the edges of our scholarly and social consciousness, pointing to a world we can perhaps only partly understand, but we must feel deeply whenever it is near.

NOTES

1. The field research on which this account is based was supported by generous grants from the American Institute of Indian Studies and the United States Educational Foundation in India, for which I am extremely grateful. The descriptions in the first section are a composite of my field notes, taken during several different performances, and written narratives. By blending these two with the extensive comments offered by my informants, I have attempted to capture the real-life experience of ritual performances devoted to the goddess Bhagavati in central and southern Kerala. Although a number of important structural features of such performances are mentioned here, this description should not be taken as a complete ethnographic account. My present purpose is only to suggest the emotional and phenomenological tenor of such events.

2. Although the name Bhagavati (Sanskrit: Bhagavatī) means simply "goddess," in Kerala this term usually refers more specifically to a fierce, independent female deity, known throughout the Hindu world as Durgā or Kālī. The relationship between the pan-Indian Kālī/Durgā and local village goddesses has been the subject of a great deal of scholarship. For excellent summary discussions, see David R. Kinsley, *The Sword and the Flute—Kālī and Kṛṣṇa: Dark Visions of the Terrible and the Sublime in Hindu Mythology* (Berkeley: University of California Press, 1975), pp. 81–126, and *Hindu Goddesses: Visions of the Divine Feminine in the Hindu Religious Tradition* (Berkeley: University of California Press, 1986), pp. 95–211; and Kathleen M. Erndl, *Victory to the Mother: The Hindu Goddess of Northwest India in Myth, Ritual, and Symbol* (New York: Oxford University Press, 1993), pp. 18–36.

My informants routinely interchanged the names Bhagavati, Bhadrakāḷi, and Kāḷi, often in the same sentence. Clearly, they did not seem to see much difference between them. In general, the name Bhagavati is synonymous with the generic Devī, and, as such, it can indicate a benevolent form of the goddess, in particular. The name Bhadrakāḷi, however, refers unequivocally to the goddess in her violent form. For the purposes of this essay, I will follow the Kerala usage, interchanging the three terms as I feel most appropriate, according to the context.

3. In this essay, all Malayalam words are transliterated using standard Library of Congress system, with the exception of *mudi (muṭi), mudiyettu (muṭiyēṟṟu)*, and

velicchappadu (veḷiccappāṭu). For ease of reading, these three words have been given spellings that more closely approximate their pronunciation in English. Many terms derived from Sanskrit, including proper names such as Kāḷī (Kālī), undergo phonetic and orthographic changes in Malayalam. Spellings in this essay conform to standard Malayalam usage.

4. The role of the *velicchappadu*—a figure unique to Kerala—is described in detail by H. H. Kerala Varma Thampuran in "Kali Cult in Kerala," *Rama Varma Research Bulletin* 4 (1936): 77–97. The presence of an oracular representative of the goddess appears to be a holdover from pre-Brahmanical religion, when shamans functioned as priests. The fact that the Nambudiri Brahmins retained this ritual figure when they took over temple worship, assigning the role to a non-Brahmin ritual specialist (usually a Nāyar male), indicates the strength and importance of this indigenous tradition. The *velicchappadu* performs a part separate from that of the possessed actor who plays Bhadrakāḷi during the performance. For one thing, he is permanently attached to the temple, whereas the actors are hired for particular events (although they may have hereditary rights to perform at a given temple). But the *velicchappadu* also exists in a special relationship to the goddess, sharing her substance when possessed by her and functioning as her vehicle and oracle. He can both understand and control her. Thus, the *velicchappadu* guides and controls the possessed Kāḷi-actor, as if he actually were the goddess. This intricate pattern of relationship and representation merits further ethnographic study.

5. *Guruti* (known in some parts of Kerala as *gurusi*) comes from the Tamil *kuruti*, "blood." Since the outlawing of blood offerings, *guruti* has been made from a mixture of turmeric and calcified lime, which turns a brilliant red when mixed with water. Originally used by Nambudiri Brahmins as a blood substitute in certain sacrifices to the ancestors, turmeric-lime *guruti* is now integral to nearly all temple rituals in central and southern Kerala.

"Demonic drums" refers to a particular category of drums, known as *cenda*, which is subdivided into two types: *deva* and *asura*. As might be expected, *deva* drums may be used only in pure (*sāttvik*) offerings to benevolent deities, whereas the drum used during the blood sacrifice is the *asura cenda*, or demonic drum. Since the drum actually functions to summon the deity, it is crucial to use the proper instrument.

6. The *tālam*, or cycle of beats, is the rhythmic basis of the musical accompaniment, and specific *tālams* must be played at different times during the performance. The heavy, plodding beat of this particular *tālam* is associated with the onset of spirit possession.

7. Tuesday and Friday are days said to be sacred to Bhadrakāḷi, and many possession rituals to honor the fierce goddess occur on these days. Performances are scheduled, however, around the annual temple festival (*utsavam*), which is held on a date considered to be the birthdate of the goddess of that particular temple and may not always fall on a Tuesday or Friday.

8. *Mudiyettu (muṭiyēṟṟu*, literally, "the carrying of the headgear") is the general name given to this type of possession performance in central Kerala, which consists of a full dramatic performance in seven set scenes. Accompanied by singers and a small percussion orchestra, seven fully costumed characters enact the story of Bhadrakāḷi's birth and the killing of Dārika through a mixture of dance and speech.

In southern Kerala, the performance is less structured, and it may go by other names such as *muṭiyēṭuppu, paṟaṇēṟṟu,* or *kāḷiyuṭṭu.*

9. Balakrishnan Marar, interview, Muvattupuzha, Kerala, May 1992.

10. Siva Raman Marar, interview, Muvattupuzha, Kerala, May 1992.

11. Balakrishnan Marar, interview, Muvattupuzha, Kerala, May 1992.

12. The name Dārika is interchangeable with Dāruka, an alternate spelling. In speech and Malayalam writing, the former is preferred; in Sanskrit texts, the latter.

13. Major elements of this story resemble portions of the *Devī Māhātmya* and the *Devī Bhāgavata Purāṇa,* but it is the *Liṅga Purāṇa* (1.106) that comes closest to the Kerala account and actually mentions the demon Dāruka. According to a reference in David Dean Shulman, *Tamil Temple Myths: Sacrifice and Divine Marriage in the South Indian Śaiva Tradition* (Princeton: Princeton University Press, 1980), a Tamil text known as the *Tirukkuvam* contains a version of this legend (see p. 103, n. 64). To my knowledge, no scholar has clearly pinpointed a textual origin for the story as it appears in Kerala. It has been published in Sanskrit and Malayalam many times under titles such as *Bhadrakālī Māhātmyam, Bhadrolpathi,* and *Dārukavadham,* but these texts appear to some analysts to be Sanskritized versions of an oral tale. Whatever its textual antecedents, however, the story is alive and well in oral transmission: some version of it was known to nearly everyone I met in Kerala. The full story is more complex than the version I have just presented, incorporating more episodes and more characters. In the interest of brevity and simplicity, only the most essential elements have been included here. The full version of the story appears in my dissertation, "Oh Terrifying Mother: The *Mudiyettu* Ritual Theater of Kerala, South India" (University of California, Berkeley, 1995).

14. Of course, as a privileged Euro-American research scholar with the freedom to leave the society at will, I could never hope entirely to replicate the experience of women in Kerala. Still, as the result of completely adopting the Kerala style of dress, food, and etiquette, getting closely involved with a number of Malayali families on whom my behavior—good or bad—reflected powerfully, and having almost no contact with other Westerners, I experienced significant changes in my own feelings and attitudes over the eighteen months of my fieldwork. This immersion, I feel, allowed me to share in significant ways the experience of Kerala women.

15. Paraphrased from my notes on the story as narrated in January 1992 by Madhavi, a widow of Ezhava caste who resided in Trichur District.

16. This prohibition varies according to age and status. Thus, a younger, higher-status female is more subject to these taboos than is an older or lower-status one, who apparently has less to protect.

17. Nur Yalman, in his well-known article, "On the Purity of Women in the Castes of Ceylon and Malabar" (*Journal of the Royal Anthropological Institute* 93, no. 1 [1963]: 25–58), reviews the "sadistic" control of the sexuality of Brahmin women in premodern Kerala. Given the rule by which only the eldest son of a Nambudiri Brahmin family could marry a Brahmin woman (the others were relegated to unofficial unions with lower-caste Nāyar women), a majority of Brahmin women were forced to remain virgins, living in total seclusion within their parental homes until their deaths. Although further ethnographic and historical research is necessary, it seems likely that the current seclusion and prohibitions on the behavior of even Nāyar and

Ezhava unmarried women (many of whom previously enjoyed more freedom of action) is a form of Sanskritization—the hope being that emulating this earlier Brahmanical custom will confer a gain in status. This phenomenon may also be observed in upper-class Muslim and Christian homes in Kerala.

18. Women, by contrast, are expected to cover the body from neck to toes at all times. This modesty in dress is the more remarkable in that Kerala women did not cover their breasts at home (and many did not do so even in public) until about fifty years ago. Before that time, a single white cloth tied at the waist was the normal attire for both sexes, except on formal occasions. It may be that delayed sexual relations, the seclusion of women who previously enjoyed more freedom, and increased prudery in dress may be attempts to raise social status through imitations of the customs of both North Indian high castes and the Victorian English. Certainly, enormous social and cultural changes have swept Kerala since Indian independence in 1947, and such drastic shifts in domestic life reflect these changes.

19. Obviously men also would be subject to the same psychological pressures, but the modest dress and demeanor of females, along with the freer social atmosphere for young men, perhaps make these pressures somewhat less onerous than they are for women.

20. I interviewed some twenty-five women in depth, of various castes and ranging in age from thirteen to ninety-one. Despite some differences in their responses, all expressed certain common themes alluded to here, particularly in regard to their early womanhood and married life. I have highlighted the aspects of women's experience that pertain to the symbolism of feminine power in the male Bhagavati cult; these remarks should not be taken as a final sociological assessment of the condition of women's life in Kerala.

21. K. R Vaidyanathan, *Temples and Legends of Kerala* (Bombay: Bharatiya Vidya Bhavan, 1988), p. 103.

22. As in other areas of India, mental imbalance is traditionally believed to be a sign of possession by an evil spirit, either male or female—but, significantly, *not* by Kāḷi or any other *deva* (divine being). Exorcism is the remedy, as described earlier. Few individuals in Kerala avail themselves of modern clinical psychiatry, as it still carries a heavy social stigma. Even so, a common medical disorder treated at psychiatric clinics is the old-fashioned Victorian malady "hysteria," the symptoms of which might otherwise be regarded as spirit possession. Hysteria is considered to be a disease almost exclusive to women. Dr. Jagadambika of Alwaye, a practicing psychiatrist, noted the intimate relationship between the symptoms of hysteria and sexual dysfunction (personal communication, November 1992). Interestingly, her patients described the same feelings of inner heat, trembling, and rage that typify the inner experience of possession reported by actors performing *mudiyettu.*

23. The *velicchappadus* associated with temples are exclusively male. Female *velicchappadus* do exist, but only in the hilly tribal areas of Palghat region. These female oracles come to the Kodungallur Bhagavati temple at Bharaṇi and participate in the rituals of pollution, cutting their heads along with the male oracles. To my knowledge, no fieldwork has been done among these female oracles, who are reluctant to speak with outsiders. I was told by several local scholars that they are the last of the female shamanic priests who perform important ritual roles in these tribal societies.

It also seems quite likely that the male *velicchappadus* in fact modeled their behavior on these female shamans, whose role was superseded in the Aryanized lowlands.

24. Omana, wife of Varanattu Narayana Kurup, interview, Trichur, Kerala, February 1992.

25. Thampuran, "Kali Cult in Kerala," p. 82.

26. E. Kalidasan, personal communication, December 1991.

27. C. Madhavan Pillai, *NBS Malayalam English Dictionary* (Kottayam, Kerala: National Book Stall, 1989), p. 493.

28. This point of view is so well known that individual references are too numerous to mention. The traditional viewpoint is summarized in Johann Jakob Meyer, *Sexual Life in Ancient India* (1930; repr. Delhi: Motilal Banarsidass, 1971), pp. 225–28. For a discussion of the relative values of impurity and auspiciousness in menstrual blood, see Frédérique Apffel Marglin, *Wives of the God-King: The Rituals of the Devadasis of Puri* (Oxford: Oxford University Press, 1985), esp. pp. 57–59. Wendy Doniger O'Flaherty reviews the psychological and symbolic meanings of menstrual pollution in *Women, Androgynes, and Other Mythical Beasts* (Chicago: University of Chicago Press, 1980), chap. 2 ("Sexual Fluids"). An excellent overview of theories of menstrual pollution is presented in *Blood Magic: The Anthropology of Menstruation*, ed. Thomas Buckley and Alma Gottlieb (Berkeley: University of California Press, 1988), pp. 25–34.

29. For brief ethnographic accounts of these rites in Kerala, see Kathleen Gough's "Female Initiation Rites on the Malabar Coast," *Journal of the Royal Anthropological Institute* 85, pt. 1 (1955): 45–80; and Yalman, "On the Purity of Women." Extensive data on individual castes are presented in L. K. Anantha Krishna Iyer, *The Tribes and Castes of Cochin*, 3 vols. (1909; repr. New Delhi: Cosmo Publications, 1981).

30. This concern led to scriptural injunctions to marry a girl before puberty; it may also be the origin of the *tāli*-tying rite in traditional Kerala, performed on young girls in anticipation of marriage; see Yalman, "On the Purity of Women."

31. The notion that menstruation implies death was expressed as far back as the Upaniṣads; see A. S. Altekar, *The Position of Women in Hindu Civilisation from Pre-Historic Times to the Present Day* (Benares: Benaras Hindu University, 1938), p. 67.

32. See E. Valentine Daniel, *Fluid Signs: Being a Person the Tamil Way* (Berkeley: University of California Press, 1984), p. 189; Susan S. Wadley, "The Paradoxical Powers of Tamil Women," in *The Powers of Tamil Women*, ed. Susan S. Wadley (Syracuse: Syracuse University, Maxwell School of Citizenship and Public Affairs, South Asia Series no. 6, 1980), p. 164.

33. One young woman who had suffered a severe case of chicken pox when she was eighteen told me that white-colored pox is considered a blessing from the goddess, whereas black pox pustules represent a curse and the goddess's anger. Her pustules, luckily, had been white.

34. I interviewed approximately fifty men in depth on matters relating to temple arts, family life, and religious beliefs. Many of these were performing artists with whom I established trusting relationships over the course of eighteen months. Sensitive matters such as sexual practices or obscene folklore were only probed after sufficient trust had been established, and I relayed my questions through male translators (one an elderly gentleman, one a young bachelor).

35. George is a pseudonym. Although George is a Christian, he has an intense interest in Hindu religion and folklore. He also has an outstanding collection of folk masks and is somewhat of a local authority on folk religion. I have chosen to quote George's response to my questions regarding sexuality as it was the most forthright and direct, overtly confirming the views expressed in folklore and popular culture. The responses of other men whom I interviewed are discussed in detail in chapter 6 of Caldwell, "Oh Terrifying Mother."

36. See O'Flaherty, *Women, Androgynes*, pp. 33–35; Shulman, *Tamil Temple Myths*, p. 103.

37. This motif obviously replicates the story of Raktabīja found in the second episode of the *Devī Māhātmya.*

38. Many scholars have studied the pervasive theme of male sacrifice in the mythology of the Hindu fierce goddess; see especially Shulman, *Tamil Temple Myths*, pp. 176–316; and Kinsley, *Hindu Goddesses*, pp. 95–122, 200–208. Often this theme is given a psychoanalytic interpretation, as castration anxiety or as a reverse projection of an infantile male desire to devour the mother; see G. Morris Carstairs, *The Twice-Born: A Study of a Community of High-Caste Hindus* (Bloomington: Indiana University Press, 1958), pp. 156–69; Gough, "Female Initiation Rites"; Sudhir Kakar, *The Inner World: A Psycho-analytic Study of Childhood and Society in India*, 2d ed. (New York: Oxford University Press, 1981), pp. 52–112; Gananath Obeyesekere, *Medusa's Hair: An Essay on Personal Symbols and Religious Experience* (Chicago: University of Chicago Press, 1981), pp. 1–51 passim and pp. 150–59; and O'Flaherty, *Women, Androgynes*, pp. 81–129. While these explanations are very compelling, a fair evaluation of them requires in-depth exploration of individual case histories and personality studies that are beyond the scope of this article (but see Caldwell, "Oh Terrifying Mother," for an in-depth discussion). Here I wish only to present an explanation that makes sense in relation to indigenous concepts of fertility that are more or less conscious.

39. For an extensive historical study of the Kodungallur temple and the Bharaṇi festival, see V. T. Induchoodan, *The Secret Chamber: A Historical, Anthropological and Philosophical Study of the Kodungallur Temple* (Trichur, Kerala: Cochin Devaswom Board, 1969). Induchoodan's authoritative study includes quotations from eyewitnesses of the festival in earlier centuries that provide evidence of orgiastic behavior, the baring of female oracles' breasts before the image of the goddess in the shrine, and extensive blood sacrifice.

40. In April 1993 the obscene songs were successfully banned from the festival, owing in large part to the influence of the Bharatiya Janata Party (BJP), India's major fundamentalist Hindu political party. Similar attempts were made in the nineteenth century.

41. Interview by author, Trichur, Kerala, February 1992.

42. Vaidyanathan, *Temples and Legends of Kerala*, pp. 108–9. I also collected this legend (or close variants of it) orally at several other Bhagavati temples.

43. This motif cogently telescopes several layers of social stratification and historical periods of religious change peculiar to Kerala. It seems likely that Bhagavati as she appears in Kerala temples today was originally an autochthonous, tribal deity, whose nature was modified and adapted to the ethos of various distinct groups. The Bhagavati of *mudiyettu* represents a kind of middle ground; she is an Aryanized, San-

skritized refinement of the tribal deity, who yet maintains many autochthonous characteristics, including possession, dancing to spirit drums, the use of fire, and blood sacrifice. It is significant that the temple origin myth quoted here acknowledges the power of the originating indigenous religion by giving an essential role in the discovery of the divine image to a tribal or low-caste agricultural worker (here a member of the Pulaya caste, one of the most "polluting" groups in the traditional caste hierarchy). Although it is the low-caste worker who inadvertently brings forth the "divine *Chaitanya* of Parasakti" through causing the stone to bleed, only the high-caste Nambudiri priest can properly diagnose and manage the spiritual situation, converting the spot into the site of a temple. The added element of a *female* low-caste worker underscores the antistructural position of the autochthonous spirituality, which exists in tension with high-caste, Aryan religion. Similar issues of power relations and historical realities expressed in Kerala temple legends are explored by J. Richardson Freeman, Jr., in "Purity and Violence: Sacred Power in the Teyyam Worship of Malabar" (Ph.D. diss., University of Pennsylvania, 1991), pp. 416–756, passim.

44. The technical term for the scythe is *arivāl*, the sword used to cut rice (*ari*). The word denoting the ritual weapon of the goddess may be spelled either *a̱ruvāl* or *a̱ravāl*. In all three cases the term refers to a sword used for cutting, and the associated verb implies cutting, sawing, reaping, severing, and killing. This ambiguity built into the linguistic term for the ritual sword expresses the conflation of harvesting and death (more specifically decapitation and the spilling of blood-seed), which is at the base of my argument here.

45. Iyer, *Tribes and Castes of Cochin*, 2:78.

46. Ibid., 2:79. See Marglin, *Wives of the God-King*, pp. 234–35, for an account of a similar but more elaborate festival in Orissa.

47. E. Kalidasan, interview, Calicut, Kerala, December 1991.

48. Vaidyanathan, *Temples and Legends of Kerala*, p. 46.

49. Ibid., pp. 48–49. Śākta tradition typically associates this event with Kamarupa, Assam.

50. This reference was given to me orally by Payipra Radhakrishnan, secretary of the Kerala Sahitya Academy. I have not been able to locate this work, which may have been published as a series of articles in the weekly publication *Matrubhumi*. The same ritual was described to me by various informants in other interviews.

51. Iyer, *Tribes and Castes of Cochin*, 1:203–8.

52. The English expression "ball of fire" connotes much that the Malayalam word *agnigolam* implies in this context: a female who is both angry and sexual, dangerous and exciting.

53. A possible exception is the ritual of *sarpam tuḷḷal*, performed by the lower-caste Pulluvan community, in which virgins are possessed by serpent deities. Even so, the men of this caste still control nearly all the elements of the ritual except the actual possession, which must be carried out by virgin girls (who are said to be "of one mind" with the snakes); the singing of the ritual songs is also performed by women professionals of that caste. Other female expressive arts and rituals include songs sung by Brahmin women in temples (*brāhmiṉi pāṭṭu*), the folk dances performed at the Onam holidays, the Tiruvātira bathing festival of the Nāyar women, marriage songs, and puberty songs. None of these has been adequately studied in Kerala. Moreover, many of these exclusively feminine expressive arts are rapidly declining

in popularity, as they are considered "old-fashioned" by the current generation of young women. It is notable that the higher the status of the ritual art form, the less likely it is that women will be allowed to participate; conversely, women assume more extensive ritual roles as one moves down the status hierarchy or into the private domestic sphere.

54. Scholars are increasingly looking to women's folklore for illuminating insights into the alternate worldviews of the disempowered gender. Outstanding recent examples of such studies include Ann Grodzins Gold and Gloria Goodwin Raheja, *Listen to the Heron's Words: Reimagining Gender and Kinship in North India* (Berkeley: University of California Press, 1994); Kirin Narayan, "Birds on a Branch: Girlfriends and Wedding Songs in Kangra," *Ethos* 14 no. 1 (1986): 47–75; Velcheru Narayana Rao, "A Rāmāyaṇa of Their Own: Women's Oral Tradition in Telugu," in *Many Rāmāyaṇas: The Diversity of a Narrative Tradition in South Asia*, ed. Paula Richman (Berkeley: University of California Press, 1991), pp. 114–36; and A. K. Ramanujan, "Two Realms of Kannada Folklore," in *Another Harmony: New Essays on the Folklore of India*, ed. Stuart H. Blackburn and A. K. Ramanujan (Berkeley: University of California Press, 1986), pp. 41–75. Unfortunately, as my research in Kerala focused primarily on the exclusively male art form of *mudiyettu*, I was not able to explore women's folk traditions as fully as I would have liked, although I plan eventually to undertake further research in this area.

55. Savitri, interview, Alwaye, Kerala, February 1992. The northern orientation of the deity is unusual in a Kerala temple: benign deities normally face east; demonic ones face west. Kodugallur Bhagavati is well known for her idiosyncratic position facing north. Although the exact reasons for this orientation remain a matter of speculation, it may reflect a historical connection between Kodungallur Bhagavati and fierce goddesses propitiated in Tulunad (southern Karnataka) or other regions to the north of Kerala. These goddesses, it is said, have such a strong desire to go toward the north that they must be restrained in certain performances or they may be lost forever.

56. See Lynn Bennett, *Dangerous Wives and Sacred Sisters: Social and Symbolic Roles of High-Caste Women in Nepal* (New York: Columbia University Press, 1983), for similar conclusions drawn from a very different social and cultural milieu.

57. Balakrishnan Marar, interview, Muvattupuzha, Kerala, May 1992.

58. Omana, wife of Varanattu Narayana Kurup, interview, Trichur, Kerala, February 1992.

SATĪ
The Story of Godāvarī

Lindsey Harlan

As I was sifting though audiocassettes of Rajasthani folk music a few years ago in a small shop in a Jodhpur bazaar, my eyes fell upon a tape entitled *Satī Godāvarī*.[1] The striking cover featured a brilliant blue sky into which leapt red-orange flames engulfing the body of a turbaned, mustached man. This man was lying on the lap of a smiling *satī* who was performing devotions with prayer beads while holding up a book, possibly a copy of the *Bhagavad Gītā*, an iconographic detail that sometimes appears on *satī* stones.

I was particularly interested in the fact that the singers of *Satī Godāvarī* were male. The *satī* songs with which I was familiar are the "night vigil" (*rātijagā*) songs that Rajput women sing on auspicious occasions, particularly weddings.[2] Unlike these songs, which tend to be brief and repetitious accounts of the preparations made by a *satī* before she goes to the pyre and/or enumerations of the jewelry and types of makeup that the *satī* wears, and unlike the *satī* narratives that women tell informally, which contain the barest of plots, this *satī* account was extremely long and detailed. Like many folk epic performances, *Satī Godāvarī* was composed of alternating stretches of spoken and sung narrative. While one man told the story, the other punctuated the narrative with fervid exclamations, such as "Victory to Satīmātā!" and "Bravo!"

When I was invited to contribute to this volume an essay on the *satī*—a wife who joins her deceased husband on his pyre or follows him to death shortly thereafter—my mind returned to this performance, a hasty translation of which I had made in the field and which was now gathering dust in my attic.[3] It occurred to me that an exploration of this performance could allow access to some of the more important and widely shared assumptions that attend the concept of the *satī* ("good woman"). It also reveals interesting peculiarities of this narrative, which departs in significant ways from the accounts found in women's night vigil songs and in the *satī* stories with which I am familiar. The detail that the story of Godāvarī provides, combined with the emotive performance style in which the tale is related, gives it an unusual vividness.

My investigation will be broken into three parts. I begin with a terse summary of the story, which comprises synopses of the episodes and provides details that strike me as particularly useful in demonstrating general assumptions underlying the notion of the *satī* and for illustrating the distinctiveness of this *satī* story. Dividing the story into three sections, I will next analyze the episodes each contains. The last, rather speculative part of the essay then scrutinizes the story in terms of some of the perspectives and tensions that the narrative seems to exhibit.

THE STORY OF SATĪ GODĀVARĪ

In Somal village near Byawar there was a woman who died as a *satī*.

Invocation:
O God, your world is so strange:
Fools become rich while devotees wander poor;
Good women (*satīs*) are without clothing while prostitutes wear
  polyester;[4]
Seven times I have become a *satī* and now in this
Kali Yuga, I have come again, Krishna!

Refrain:
The flower dies, but the scent remains.
The name of Godāvarī, daughter of Jagad Dās, is immortal!

There was a man named Madhu Dās and Godāvarī was his wife. They were from the Sādh caste. They worshiped God and served him in his temple. Madhu Dās became gravely ill. His wife, realizing he was going to die, decided that she would become a *satī*.

Madhu Dās went for a final viewing (*darśan*) of God. Godāvarī followed him to the temple and said to Krishna, "I will be a *satī*." When her husband heard this, he scolded her, saying she shouldn't speak so casually, as if she were in some *dharmśālā* or watering place.[5] Then he staggered home.

Godāvarī wept and "trembled like a peacock." She said that without her husband, she had no one. So she went to the temple and petitioned Krishna for permission to become a *satī*. She asked him to protect her modesty, and Krishna responded, "Don't worry; I'm with you," and he promised her that her name would be famous.

When the villagers began to suspect Godāvarī's intentions, they became worried. Some thought she'd lose her nerve and while burning, run through the village and set it on fire. They also were afraid that the police would come and beat them for allowing a *satī* to die in the village. They decided to cremate Madhu Dās's body quickly and without his wife's knowledge, but she returned from the temple before they could do so. Godāvarī went to him and grabbed his wrist and as she did, his spirit returned "like an electric current."

Some girls managed to pry Godāvarī's hand from her husband's wrist, and Madhu Dās's spirit again departed. Godāvarī went home weeping, but when she arrived and found everyone else weeping, she told them that they should be happy. This enraged her mother-in-law, but Godāvarī told her that she would "make everyone illustrious" and that she would save her father's family, her husband's family, and her mother's brother's family (in which her mother was raised). She promised to make the whole village of Somal illustrious and wash away the sins of the people who lived there. But then she warned everyone not to stop her, as God was with her.

Godāvarī asked her mother-in-law for the key to the inner apartments so that she could bathe herself and put on her ornaments and makeup (*śṛṅgār*), but her mother-in-law told her that if God were on her side, he would open the lock. So Godāvarī asked Sūraj, the sun, to break the lock with his rays: the lock was soon ashes.

Still the villagers scoffed. One remembered that just recently Godāvarī had burned her finger and had made a big fuss about it. So the villagers plotted to stop her. They sent for Godāvarī's good friend, a potter-caste girl name Dhāpū. The messengers tried to persuade her to come by telling her that since she was Godāvarī's close friend, the police would arrest her and beat her. Dhāpū did not think this would happen, so they had to offer her a bribe, some fine land with good wells on it. Then she agreed. Before going to see Godāvarī, however, she stopped to see the *ṭhākur,* the lord of the village, to try to convince him that he should stop Godāvarī for her. Since he is the *ṭhākur,* she said, the police would hold him responsible. But the *ṭhākur* said he wouldn't interfere because Godāvarī was a devoted wife and such women save their lineages (*kul*s).

Dhāpū went to Godāvarī and warned her that being a *satī* was just too difficult and that Godāvarī would probably fail. Realizing that Dhāpū had some ulterior motive, Godāvarī cursed her to be a leper. Immediately, Dhāpū's fingers and toes fell off, and the remaining stubs "shriveled up like peanuts." Dhāpū begged her to take back her curse, but Godāvarī would not change her mind.

The villagers then decided to persuade a printmaker to pour bluing (which is considered extremely inauspicious) on her, which would remove her *sat* (goodness, moral substance; that which makes her a *satī*). Godāvarī, however, caused him to spill the bluing on himself and cursed him to be childless.[6] She ignored his pleas for mercy.

The villagers then sent for Godāvarī's adoptive father, whom they hoped would stop her. His wife, however, persuaded him not to interfere but to worship the *satī* and give her appropriate offerings.[7] He went with wife to see Godāvarī, who asked him to get her a band for her procession to the pyre. He brought her a superb band, one that could play English disco music.

Meanwhile, the *ṭhākur* had a change of heart. He came to Godāvarī and told her that he had not given his permission for Godāvarī to become a *satī,* as was required. So Godāvarī cursed him to be a babbling idiot. Immediately his tongue grew thick and he started stuttering. He begged her to take back the curse, but she would not do so.[8] When the *ṭhākur* got back to his fort, he asked his two queens to ask the *satī* for blessings. Being in purdah, they couldn't approach her directly, but they sent her offerings. Godāvarī said that each of them would be blessed with a son, but that one would be stupid and the other deaf.

The villagers then sent for a businessman to whom Godāvarī's husband owed money. When this man demanded money from Godāvarī, she said she was pleased that he had come because failing to repay the debt would have had negative consequences in her next life. She tried to repay him with a handful of sand—presumably this would have turned into riches—but the man said he wanted something valuable and snatched her necklace. The *satī* cursed him to be blind and made his eyes fall out. In agony, he pleaded with her, but to no avail.

The villagers sent for another man to whom Godāvarī's husband was indebted, but Godāvarī made this man fall off his camel and made the camel run away. This put him in terrible trouble, as the camel belonged to the *ṭhākur* of his village. Godāvarī felt sorry for him and said that the camel would soon return.

Godāvarī ascended the pyre and called on Sūraj to help her. The sun's rays then fell on the pyre and ignited it. While she burned, she said that she would grant a boon to anyone who would sleep at the pyre for seven nights. A man from the Megwal caste did this, and after seven nights the *satī*'s voice spoke to him, asking what he desired. He responded that he wanted her to unlock his heart. He promised to tell her story and to remain near her always.

THE NARRATIVE: DEVOTION, INTENTION, AND TRIUMPH

Devotion

While the narrative flows in one continuous performance, I find it useful to divide it into three sections in order to get at some of its dominant features. The first section establishes the narrative squarely within the framework of *bhakti*—devotional religion. The invocation of Krishna introduces a common theme in *bhakti:* the rewards of devotion are not tangible, earthly ones. Material comforts are not payments one can expect for dedicating one's life to God. At the same time, the invocation hints at another *bhakti* theme, the idea that the rich (and often the rich are the powerful, high-ranking members of society) are not privileged in terms of access to God. Good people, devoted people, are the ones whom Krishna loves, even if they lack status, wealth, and power.[9] As members of the Sādh community, Godāvarī and her husband do not belong to a high caste.[10] Their Krishna *bhakti* brings to *satī* immolation an orientation expressed clearly in the *Bhagavad Gītā* (9.26): God's grace is available to everyone. *Bhakti*'s elevation of the lowly in God's eyes would seem, by inference, to legitimize the practice of *satī* immolation in a lower caste; *satī* immolation has been most common among higher castes, particularly the martial castes.[11] This story has Krishna himself giving Godāvarī permission to become a *satī*.

That Godāvarī and her husband are Vaiṣṇavas is in itself interesting. Among Rajputs, *satī* immolations generally occur within Śaiva-Śākta contexts, if there is any sectarian association at all. *Satī* songs and stories do not usually mention *satī*s' associations with deities, but the stone pavilions in which Rajput *satī* stones are found often contain Śaiva-Śākta imagery. In Rajasthan it is common for stones to face images of *liṅga*s and *yoni*s, the male and female symbols appropriate to Śiva and Śakti, respectively. Moreover, while *satī* stories and songs do not invoke the Purāṇic tale of Śiva and his wife Satī, the story is well known, as it is elsewhere in India.

Because Vaiṣṇavas are generally vegetarian and abhor animal sacrifice, the idea of a Vaiṣṇava *satī*'s sacrifice of herself seems odd.[12] In Rajasthan, *satī* immolation is commonly referred to as a *bali*, a sacrifice of a living victim.[13] Might not Godāvarī's Vaiṣṇavism account at least in part for the community's persistent resistance to allowing her to die as a *satī*? As we shall see, there are other factors that bear on the extreme apprehension felt in the community—the fear of police retribution being prominent among them—but the sectarian aspect ought not to be discarded as we attempt to discern the various elements and nuances of the tale's context.

Prominent and important as the invocation to Krishna and Krishna's subsequent sanctioning of Godāvarī's death are in providing a devotional context for this *satī* sacrifice, they are not the only devotional elements that appear in this rich narrative. Sūraj, the sun (Sanskrit: Sūrya), also plays a major part in the story. He serves as an enabler: he unlocks the door that prevents Godāvarī from doing her *śṛṅgār*, that which identifies her as an auspicious wife, and he ignites the pyre, which allows her to realize her goal of dying a *satī*. He also serves as a compelling divine witness: he reveals Godāvarī's overflowing of *sat*, goodness, thereby enabling her to become a *satī*. In this capacity he is not unlike Agni, who proves to skeptics the purity of the heroine Sītā in the *Rāmāyaṇa* when she enters his flames and remains unscorched. He makes visible what is invisible: the pristine character of the wholly devoted wife.

The participation of Krishna and Sūraj in the narrative provides two sources of authority for Godāvarī's death on the pyre. Krishna's blessing reflects *bhakti,* pure and simple. Sūraj's help implies *bhakti* but also shows that Godāvarī is fated to die as she does. His promotion of fate is indirectly approved by Krishna, who says at one point that Godāvarī's death is in fact the result of fate, *kismat.* Thus, Godāvarī's *bhakti* is joined by fate as a source of authority for the course of action she has adopted. Alongside these two sources stands another, karma. At the end of the invocation Godāvarī proclaims that seven times previously she has been a *satī* and now she has returned to become a *satī* once again. (She repeats this claim later in the story.) Godāvarī's ability to be a *satī* is supported by her previous action, karma, which enables her to develop *sat* and become a *satī* more easily than would otherwise be possible. It serves notice that Godāvarī is entitled to *satī* status because of her previous meritorious actions as a *satī.*

Godāvarī's claim that she can be a *satī* because she has been one before is a peculiarity of the narrative. In the narratives with which I am familiar there are no parallel instances of *satī* immolation earning a woman the right to die as a *satī* yet again.[14] Moreover, the fact that Godāvarī says she has been a *satī* seven times previously is intriguing, as generally the seventh time at anything is charmed: it works a transformation in one's status and fortune or in the efficacy of one's actions. For example, *satī*s' curses tend to last seven generations, then expire. Thus, one might expect that the seventh death would have led Godāvarī to an automatic, ultimate rest and release from reincarnation, but this is not the case. Alternatively, the mention of seven previous deaths might tempt one to infer that the seven deaths were prerequisites, after which the eighth will surely put an end to the cycle of rebirth, but the story offers no such certainty.[15] On the contrary, toward the end of the story, Godāvarī thanks the businessman for reminding her of her husband's debt so that in her next life she can avoid the negative fruits of not repaying a loan.[16]

In any case, the idea of seven deaths as a *satī* connotes extreme auspiciousness (as the number seven always does) and conveys added authority. Moreover, the implication that the prior *satī* deaths were in past world ages (*yugas*), while the current one is in the present, degenerate Kali Yuga, lends the narrative a broadly mythic framework that endows it with additional authority. As a narrative motif, the appearance of divine beings in past ages and then again in the present explains the particular significance of the present manifestation and demonstrates that divine beings are indeed involved in the currently miserable human condition. The gods Śiva and Indra appeared in previous ages before being freed of their sins and founding pilgrimage places (Banaras, Madurai) in the present. Ekliṅg Jī, an incarnation of Śiva, is believed to have come to Mewar (southwest Rajasthan) in each of the previous ages before manifesting himself to the first member of the dynasty of Mewar kings in this Kali Yuga and then establishing himself at Kailashpuri, a thriving pilgrimage spot near Udaipur. In short, the idea of progressive appearances throughout the *yugas* culminating in the present makes the story of Godāvarī resonate with divinity. It also suggests to any audience the wisdom of appreciating the opportunity that this veteran *satī* presents for those undertaking her service and giving her their devotion.

Although the matter of seven previous *satī* deaths may be unusual, the ambiguity of the afterlife destiny of the *satī* is not. Women who die this way are transformed into supernatural beings who protect their families after their deaths. They are also said to attain liberation (*mokṣa*) because of their self-sacrifice, although they are often held to share the destiny of their husbands, which some interpret to mean that the *satīs* are reborn as the wives of their reincarnated husbands. Some, however, believe that *satīs* transfer a portion of their merit to their husbands and thus enable them to achieve high rebirths or even residence in heaven. And people frequently hold several of these ideas at once. *Satīs* are thought to be blissful liberated souls, yet they are also understood as watchful divine guardians of their families; they are thought to be divine, yet also to share their husbands' fates. With *satīs*, as with many types of departed spirits, notions about destiny are often unclear, fluctuating, or contradictory. Hence, it is not terribly surprising that Godāvarī is born a human wife of a human husband again and again yet is also seen as an utterly pure supernatural being, a status that is particularly clear by the end of the story. In much the same way, competing ideas of *bhakti* (and divine intervention), fate, and karma all serve as sources of authority for Godāvarī's immolation.[17]

Karma as a source of authority places the credit for Godāvarī's ability squarely on her own shoulders: she has earned the death she now seeks. But there is another source of authority, one already hinted at, that credits Godāvarī with mastery over her destiny: her own divinity. Quite late in the story Godāvarī is actually referred to as a goddess. When she curses the fickle *ṭhākur* who interferes with her plans, he addresses her as the goddess Bhavānī. While one may be tempted to dismiss his use of this title as flattery, such a dismissal could well deny an important aspect of Godāvarī's identity. Although people do not generally refer to *satīs* as goddesses (*devīs*), they do understand *satīs* as possessing the supernatural abilities of goddesses. In fact, the difference between a goddess and a *satī* is one of classification, rather than power. Moreover, the iconography at some *satī* memorials appears to suggest a homology between the *satī* who sacrifices herself for her husband and the goddess (represented in the form of a *yoni*) who sacrifices herself for Śiva (represented in the form of a *liṅga*).

That Godāvarī is called Bhavānī toward the end of the story may reflect an understanding of Godāvarī as a goddess or goddesslike being right from the beginning of the story. If Godāvarī has been divine since her first instance of becoming a *satī*, then her subsequent appearances may be regarded as avatars—incarnations or "crossings-down," on the divine model—as well as the result of previous meritorious actions. As Stuart Blackburn has shown, a continuity exists between the notion of the divine status acquired by humans who die special (usually violent) deaths and the idea of an avatar: in sum, those who go up, may come down.[18] The issue of which comes first, divinity or human incarnation, becomes a chicken-egg question, as deities often take on human incarnations, then die violent deaths.[19] It is possible to read the story in either direction: woman to goddess (through karma, fate, *bhakti*) or goddess to woman (for her own reasons or *līlā,* divine play). The multidimensionality that inheres in the identity and status of Godāvarī reflects not only the richness of the text but the spectrum of ideas about divinity and the afterlife that can be found in Rajasthan as well as elsewhere in India.

While these sources of authority tell us much about the context of Godāvarī's death and reveal possible facets of her identity, they also hint at the need for legitimation and proof expressed throughout the text. What follows the introductory segment of the text can be read as a chronicle of doubt and anxiety gradually leading toward a resolution in the form of the *satī*'s ritual self-sacrifice.

Intention

The second section begins with the illness and death of Godāvarī's husband, which are in effect framed and punctuated by Godāvarī's three statements of her intention (*saṃkalp, vrat*) to become a *satī*. As we have seen, the first, which appears at the end of the invocation, sets the story within the broader context of Godāvarī's history as a devoted wife through the ages. It thus establishes the story's trajectory even before the plot proper begins. The second comes when the ailing Madhu Dās visits the temple and overhears his wife's vow to be a *satī,* which he dismisses as loose talk. The third, which follows Madhu Dās's death, proves the sincerity of Godāvarī's resolve, despite her husband's skepticism and reprimand.

This threefold declaration of intention seems necessary in the text as a prelude to the episodes that follow, which repeatedly challenge the idea that Godāvarī has the resolution or the constitution to die a *satī*. The vows express her determination to sacrifice herself, which is considered in Rajasthan an aspect of the *satī*'s *sat,* the goodness she has gained by previous sacrifices of will and desire. Like the ascetic renouncer (*sannyāsī*), the good wife ideally deprives herself of any wishes that do not serve the end she seeks: to preserve her husband's longevity, welfare, and happiness. She does this by obeying the commands of her husband, his parents, and his older brothers and their wives, and by observing religious fasts; such acts train her to endure privation and enable her to summon divine assistance when her husband or children are in peril. The consequence of self-deprivation is power, whether it be the power to enlist the gods in protecting her husband or the power to die as a *satī* if, despite her efforts at protecting her husband, her husband dies before her.[20]

Although this power is the consequence of self-deprivation, it is manufactured through the medium of the *sat* that the *satī* builds through self-denial. *Sat* is not just an abstract quality of character; it is a physical substance that changes the constitution of the women in whom it resides and grows. It is something of a moral fuel, which both results from self-sacrifice and conduces toward self-sacrifice, including the ultimate self-sacrifice of life should the husband of this "good woman" die. Actually, it would be more precise to say that this fuel results from the intention to perform acts of self-sacrifice, for it is intention that generates both pure, good (*sāttvik*) action and pure, good character (*sat*). This is demonstrated most clearly in the celebrated instances in which a fiancée becomes a *satī,* although she has not even had an opportunity to perform self-sacrificing actions for her future husband. There are many stories of young fiancées who empty themselves of personal desire and gain *sat* simply by intending to be loving and selfless wives. These women are often held up as superb examples of *satī*s, because they sacrifice themselves for men whose mere names or portraits have inspired them to abandon selfishness and ultimately life itself. Their intention to perform future acts of self-sacrifice enables them to generate *sat* and become *satī*s.

The importance of intentionality is also seen in the fact that the *satī*'s *sat* generally becomes manifest after she voices her intention to die as a *satī* in the form of a vow. This vow is an observable index of inward goodness (though not a definitive one, as the continued skepticism in this narrative makes clear), but it is also a representation of the woman's change in status. Generally speaking, a wife cannot harbor the ambition of becoming a *satī* before her husband dies because to do so would be, in effect, to will that her husband's death precede hers; such a wish would belie her possession of *sat.* Even though the Godāvarī narrative deviates from this rule by allowing Godāvarī to utter her vow while her husband is still alive, it is clear from the very beginning that the husband is going to die (he is extremely ill), as the very title of the performance, *Satī Godāvarī,* announces. Thus, the exception does little to undermine the usual pattern.

Once the *satī* makes a vow, her *sat* begins to manifest itself as heat. *Satī*s are often said to be too hot to touch and hence to restrain from mounting a pyre.[21] The moral fuel that begins to burn generates the powers to perform miracles, pronounce curses, and confer blessings—much as the renouncer's sublimated sexual heat (*tapas*) generates these powers—and is thought ultimately to spark a conflagration that consumes the bodies of the *satī* and her husband. Even when a pyre is lit by another person or, as here, by the rays of the sun, the fire that consumes the *satī* and spouse is assumed to have been ignited internally, by her *sat.* Here Godāvarī's *sat* either causes a fire that burns independently of the sun's fire or serves as the catalyst causing Sūraj to emit rays and light the fire.

The woman whose *sat* becomes manifest (either by her vow or, if skepticism remains, by the miracles, curses, and blessings she performs, as well as by her eventual death on the pyre) is considered to have always intended to preserve her husband, despite his death prior to hers. Because of this imputed good will, the *satī* is never understood as a widow; rather, she is termed a *sahagāminī,* "one who goes with" (her husband). And because the *satī* is not viewed as a widow, she is supposed to dress as an auspicious, married woman. (Hence the importance of the *satī*'s *śṛṅgār* in songs and stories.) Whereas the widow is expected to abandon decoration of all types, lament openly, and begin penances for her failure to predecease her husband, the *satī* is expected to wear all her ornaments and make-up (as she did when she first entered the household as a bride), comport herself with composure or even joy, and process with self-assured dignity to the pyre.[22]

Although Godāvarī conforms loosely to this stipulated mode of comportment, she deviates from the standard, at least temporarily, in some notable ways. Instead of being wholly self-controlled and intent on her reunion with her husband, she trembles. Twice the story says that she is so overcome by grief that she "shakes like a peacock." Moreover, instead of maintaining a serene or joyful countenance as *satīs* should, she breaks into tears. Only later, and quite suddenly, does she realize that crying is inappropriate and begin to urge family members to share her joy. These lapses in self-restraint, which she eventually overcomes, make Godāvarī more human and accessible as a protagonist, even as they provide ammunition for the skeptics who contest her resolve and thus her *sat.*

Skepticism about a woman's possession of sufficient *sat* to be a *satī* is a pervasive motif in *satī* narratives. The prevalence of the motif is not surprising: in India, as elsewhere, the authencity of many venerated religious figures is doubted by their contemporaries, and particularly by those closest to them, people who know their weaknesses and shortcomings. With *satīs*, as with saints, familiarity often breeds contempt. Thus, in Godāvarī's case, the chain of doubt begins with her husband, then spreads to her husband's family members and the villagers. Apart from this universal problem of skepticism vis-à-vis religious personages, there is the particular problem that, in the case of housewives, the actions that formulate *sat* are simply the repetitious, everyday actions expected of women who love their husbands. While heroes gain *sat* by performing acts of bravery on the battlefield, women gain *sat* by quietly setting aside their preferences when these run counter to their husbands' or in-laws' interests and by routinely giving up certain foods on fast days. Their sacrifices tend to be unimpressive, even invisible, as good wives ought not to protest if an order interferes with their personal wishes. Furthermore, even women who attempt to sacrifice their desires sometimes draw condemnation for the decisions they make. For example, women who disobey their husband are criticized, but so are women who allow their husbands to do things that are destructive to their well-being, such as drinking, gambling, and fighting. Arguing with a husband is wrong, but so is letting him stray from his duty, his dharma. Thus, even women with the best intentions must sort through options, set priorities, and risk criticism. The development of *sat*—unseen and tied to intention, not action—is a business that guarantees neither popularity nor favorable reputation during one's life. The *satī* 's death thus affords retroactive confirmation of a motivation toward self-denial that might otherwise have gone unnoticed and unappreciated.

Given that the characters in *satī* narratives are often skeptical, at least to some extent, of the protagonist's possession of *sat,* the fact that the first thing a *satī* must do is to apply her *śṛṅgār,* to beautify herself, is particularly striking. In dressing as a nonwidow, the *satī* appears in the eyes of the doubtful as a strumpet seeking the attention of other men. Godāvarī's mother-in-law accordingly expresses shock and dismay when Godāvarī asks for the key to the inner apartments so that she can adorn herself. She also makes things difficult for Godāvarī by asking her to prove that God is behind her as she readies herself for the pyre.[23] Sūraj's incineration of the lock then offers the family the proof it requires, while also foreshadowing the ultimate conflagration that will offer all other skeptics final proof: immolation on the pyre.

Triumph

We have seen that *sat* may be generated by intention but requires proof in action. The remainder of the story consists of a series of such proofs, which, though dramatic, only gradually and incrementally dispel the seemingly overwhelming doubt surrounding Godāvarī. That these proofs are necessary demonstrates not only the villagers' assumption that Godāvarī lacks credibility but also their foolish faithlessness: they express the view that Godāvarī will not die a *satī*—that she might even lose her nerve at the very end, while she is burning, and then run through the village, setting it on fire.[24] On the one hand, the villagers employ several agents to dissuade Godāvarī from dying a *satī;* their success would have proved that there was a deficit in her *sat.* On the other, they make an attempt to remove the *satī*'s *sat* (they persuade a printmaker to pour bluing on her), which at the very least indicates an acknowledgment of the possibility that she could possess the requisite *sat* to be a *satī.* But it also demonstrates a subtler kind of faithlessness—fear. The villagers are portrayed as worrying that they will be subject to beatings because of the *satī*'s virtue. Moreover, they are unwilling to sacrifice their welfare to aid the woman whose death, if she is what she says she is, will make their village illustrious and pardon them of all their sins.

With each instance of resistance, the *satī* demonstrates her *sat* by destroying the lives of those who are designated to execute the villagers' plots of interference. Each of her destructive demonstrations of power presumably earns her credibility, but each requires a sacrifice of the sort an insulted or neglected goddess might demand. She is like Śītalā, the goddess of pustular diseases, who exacts punishment that is both curse and blessing: the punishment harms while at the same time converting the faithless to faithfulness, whether they be those stricken with disease or those who watch an epidemic in horror and fear.[25] And wrathful or not, she is, like Śītalā, understood as a mother, a *mātā,* who nurtures.[26]

One interesting feature of the Godāvarī narrative is the fact that the *satī* does not curse family members who exhibit faithlessness. She ignores the skepticism of her husband (as one would expect, because at this point she is not yet empowered as a *satī*—her husband is still alive), and she gently corrects her mother-in-law's opinion of her by performing a miracle. In other narratives, however, *satī*s frequently curse in-laws. Rajput women often explain such curses as instructive acts that inspire faith within the family. But if Godāvarī exercises restraint where others unleash fury, she amply makes up for this leniency by an unparalleled exhibition of wrath toward nonfamily members.

Counterbalancing this apparent hostility toward the villagers is Godāvarī's statement that she has come to help them. Here again the narrative differs from Rajput narratives, which characteristically extend a *satī*'s protection only to her family members and occasionally close friends. Rajputs generally construe as malevolent curses afflicting people who do not belong to these categories. As the unfortunate *ṭhākur,* in all probability a Rajput himself, explicitly says in the narrative, *satī*s save their lineages (*kul*s).[27] The martial context in which most Rajasthani *satī* narratives occur (*satī*s' husbands are usually killed in combat) demonstrates time and time again that protecting the good of the family often requires the destruction of its enemies, both aggressors who would harm its members or take its property and detractors who would insult it and so rob it of fame and illustriousness. Hence, the *satī* can be extremely hostile to and destructive of nonrelatives; she harms them without offering any instruction or ultimate solace and protection.

Godāvarī, however, far from limiting her protection so strictly, in fact extends her blessing to all the villagers. She even includes some outsiders who have business in the village: her last acts are to spare one outsider (her only case of amending a curse) and to grant a boon to another outsider who sleeps on her pyre. Thus, unlike the vast majority of Rajput *satī*s, Godāvarī appears as a potential protector of all faithful petitioners. Her general accessibility both distinguishes her from the familiar Rajput family protectresses and renders the many severe curses she pronounces paradoxical. Godāvarī is cruel to be kind.

PERSPECTIVES AND TENSIONS: SOME SPECULATIONS

A crucial question remains: why is the utter devastation of so many victims required to dispel the villagers' doubt? To put this another way, why are so many people in the narrative so deeply skeptical and slow to learn their lesson? We can begin to understand why people are portrayed as so suspicious if we focus in a little more closely on two things: who is telling the story and what the story reveals about the understanding of women as potential possessors of *sat.*

With regard to the first matter, as in the case of epics the people singing this story are professionals, and the plot of the story they are performing is like that of epics—full of detailed episodes, which yield both length and drama. Without the series of incidents recounting Godāvarī's manifold curses, there would be little of this story to tell. Moreover, again as in the epics, one good story deserves another: the recurring curses serve as vivid variations on a theme. Each repetition carries the performance toward its climax, at which point the *satī* ascends the pyre and puts an end to all resistance. Further increasing dramatic tension are the frequent and rhythmic repetitions of the refrain, which constantly proclaim the *satī*'s immortality (the main point of the story) and so impatiently anticipate the finale on the pyre, despite the villagers' persistent attempts to prevent it. In addition, the narrative—true to its performance format—is full of entertaining characterization and metaphor, which enhance the vividness of the cursing incidents and so render them particularly devastating and cruel. Thus, for example, the *satī* does not curse Dhāpū merely to develop leprosy in due course but to develop the advanced disfiguring symptoms of the disease right then and there: Dhāpū's toes and fingers immediately shrivel up like little peanuts. Her erstwhile "sister" begs for mercy, but Godāvarī tells her to be still or be ready to endure more punishment. The striking detail, as well as the memorable simile, renders the *satī*'s wrath and the human wreckage all the more evident.

The combination of these features makes this performance extremely different from the informal *satī* stories that Rajput women tell in their households, stories that tend to contain the barest, most essential facts and only one curse (or at most two or three), if they contain any at all. The streamlined nature of these narratives supports the broad generalization that women's stories are often less elaborate than men's, as I have found to be true in my work in Rajasthan and A. K. Ramanujan has observed in South India.[28] Of course, this may be so simply because most professional storytellers are men.[29] Furthermore, especially in North India, where women have often been subject to purdah and other travel restrictions, men will have had greater opportunities to attend professional performances, which could in turn influence their storytelling styles.[30]

To whatever extent the gender of the performers may be reckoned as a discrete factor separable from their professionalism in accounting for the length, detail, repetitiousness, and cruelty of the Godāvarī story, the narrative contains fluctuating and discontinuous perspectives that stimulate insights about the patriarchal culture within which the performance occurs. Faith in "*satī* mothers" (*satīmātās*) is widespread in Rajasthan, yet the *satīmātā* narratives from the area reveal overwhelming and obdurate skepticism about the capacity of individual women to qualify as *satīs*. As we have seen, doubt both pervades and structures the Godāvarī narrative: it serves as catalyst for the series of curses that moves the story toward its vindicating conclusion.

It is not hard to understand why there would be such skepticism about the ability of individual women to die such self-obliterating sacrificial deaths. First, consummation by fire is an unimaginably grisly and painful form of death: it is difficult to imagine anyone choosing to perish in flames.[31] Moreover, as already noted, holy persons or saints (whatever their gender) are often ignored, or even ridiculed, in their own day. And yet one must ponder why folklore interrogates women who intend to sacrifice themselves on the pyre but does not challenge the ability of heroes to don saffron and sacrifice themselves in what Rajasthanis term a *saka*—an unwinnable, bloody battle. Such heroes are worshiped much as *satīs* are worshiped—as family protectors who increase familial fame and fortune. Unlike *satīs*, they are simply assumed to possess the requisite *sat* to die as they have determined to die.[32] While in both women's and men's hero narratives (including folk songs) women often try to stop men from leaving for battles in which the odds against them are unbeatable, these attempts are portrayed as stemming from love (for brothers, fathers, husbands, and sons), not from doubts about the character and ability of the men.

There are many other reasons for the skepticism and general negativity shown *satīs* in folklore. One factor is surely a diffuse but still powerful psychological ambivalence about according power to females, particularly to women near and dear. Much has been written on the phallocentric ambivalence implicit in the characterization of goddesses, who are "mothers" (like *satīs*, they are often called *mātās*) protecting their children, yet controlling them, threatening their (male) sexuality, and demanding self-sacrifice.[33] Moreover, this assumed danger to the male pysche has become generalized: the characterization of goddesses as benign yet threatening is not limited to some distinct genre of men's stories. Rather, the ambivalence toward the mother has shaped the understanding of female power that finds its way into the stories both women and men tell.

This ambivalence would account at least partly for a problem that makes conceptualizing the *satī* a slippery task. This is a basic problem of theodicy: if the *satī* is purely good, purely *sattvik,* how can she also be powerfully destructive?[34] Discomfort over the contradiction of having good but powerful mothers has doubtless contributed to the tendency of many well-known Indian myths to bifurcate the goddess into two personae: one demure and nurturing, the other aggressive and rampaging. This split image keeps some "mothers" pleasing to behold and safely approachable yet sees others as terrifying in appearance and demanding of bloody sacrifice (of a surrogate beast, if not oneself). Women's narratives, as well as various other types of folklore, often challenge this bifurcated vision, which tries to separate female goodness from female power but then has to reassociate goodness with at least some degree of power, since without power females cannot protect, be they goddesses or simply women. *Satī* stories, in particular, must preserve the *utter* goodness of the woman (after all, the *satī* is by definition the embodiment of goodness) yet accord her some power: the power to do good and to force others, even cruelly, to obey her commands, which are for their own good. The *satī* story resists attempts to keep goodness and real power—namely, uncontrolled and unchanneled power—separate.

To be considered alongside the psychological dynamics that figure in the paradoxical attitude exhibited toward *satīs* in *satī* narratives (dynamics I have only been able to touch upon here) is the Hindu understanding of the social order, which is shaped by the principle of hierarchy. This principle subjugates lower castes to higher castes and women to men. Whereas Hindu culture recognizes the power of individual goddesses, which often exceeds the power of gods, it proves reticent when it comes to asserting that any particular woman can outdo her husband. In cases where a *satī* dies with a husband who is himself a hero, the *satī* achieves a soteriological equality with her spouse—but, in heroic narratives, the preeminence of the hero is maintained by the fact that he dies first, his example explicitly or implicitly inspiring his wife's (or wives') actions. In the iconography of memorial stelae his image is central and predominant (even though such stelae are often referred to as "*satī* stones"). In cases where the husband is an ordinary sort of fellow, however, like Madhu Dās in *Satī Godāvarī,* there can be no question but that the woman is the one who has preeminence and superior power. Her death, not her husband's, will both assure him of a place in heaven or a better rebirth and be highly beneficial to his family and community. While this is good news for all, it also undermines the gender hierarchy, according to which a woman should play a subordinate and supportive role.

In sum, there are various reasons for the pervasive ambivalence that accompanies the veneration of individual *satīs*. The persistence of this attitude, however, is rather striking when one considers the benefits to be derived from having a *satī* in the community, some of which are clearly stated in *Satī Godāvarī*. Becoming illustrious, the *satī* makes everyone illustrious. The *satī* not only epitomizes female virtue but serves as an emblem of the entire community's virtue. More than this, she removes whatever moral failings individual community members may have: she renders them sinless. She makes tangible the community's claim to purity and the status that purity conveys. *Satī*s are, in short, status symbols and, as such, are especially valuable to communities that seek to raise their social status by emulating the traditions of higher-status groups.

There are other reasons why a community would want to celebrate the decision of one of its women to become a *satī,* although here I can mention just a few.[35] It is often said that by becoming a *satī* a woman escapes the devastating condition of widowhood. Widows are often seen as pitiable creatures who have outlived their usefulness, whereas *satī*s are seen as having perfected their duty as women. Death as a *satī* also rescues a woman from a life of loneliness (hence Godāvarī mourns her husband's death and cries out, "Who is there here for me?") and from the shame of failing to protect her husband (hence Godāvarī asks Krishna to protect her reputation for modesty by giving her permission to die a *satī*).[36] And if she is unfortunate enough to have married into an inhospitable or cruel family, it spares her a life of abuse.

*Satī*s also become immortal protectors. Devotees believe that *satī*s who are properly propitiated bring wealth and success. They cure the sick, make the barren fertile, and prevent or ease family tensions and discord. Moreover, the *satī* 's death relieves the family of having to provide for her. Anti-*satī* activists often hold that this is a major reason society perpetuates the practice of *satī* immolation. Pro-*satī* forces, however, do not tend to mention this as a benefit, and they dismiss the claim that it serves as a motivation for *satī* veneration. Regardless of the perspective taken, it cannot be denied that many widows in Rajasthan, like many widows elsewhere in India (and like many old people in cultures around the world), do not wish to be a burden to their families and feel guilty about the expenditure of resources (not only money, but time) that their upkeep requires. Immolation is a solution, although a drastic one: it relieves them of this burden, but at the cost of their lives.

Another economic aspect of *satī* veneration to which anti-*satī* activists call attention—and *satī* devotees do not—is the growing tendency of *satī*s to draw large crowds of worshipers, thereby turning their towns or villages into prosperous pilgrimage sites.[37] Many are concerned that, lured by the prospect of substantial profit, people may allow greed to motivate their veneration of *satī*s—and perhaps even to tempt them to coerce a woman into becoming a *satī,* so that they can make money housing and feeding pilgrims and selling devotional offerings and *satī* souvenirs.

Given the many benefits that having a *satī* in the community confers and given the ultimate outcome of the *Satī Godāvarī* narrative, is it not surprising that the story represents the community as strongly averse to Godāvarī's death and ready to throw up barricades? Another reading of the text might lead one to conclude that the villagers protest too much. In providing episode after episode of resistance, the narrative shows us that the villagers have done everything they possibly could do to prevent the *satī*'s immolation. The result: the villagers are rendered guiltless. While the *satī* portrays them as beneficiaries of her death, they proclaim themselves victims. She'll burn their town down; perhaps they will be the ones to perish in flames. Moreover, she'll cause them to suffer beatings at the hands of the police. In sum, the repeated protest can be read as a litany of self-protection and self-justification. Not only has the *satī* prevailed in her implicitly voluntary decision to die on the pyre, but she has actually forced her fellow villagers to accept her decision. Their professed doubt, despite repeated manifestations of Godāvarī's *sat* and power, serves to substantiate their innocence: her blood is not on *their* hands.

The skepticism, then, cuts both ways. Providing grounds for Godāvarī's display of *sat* and the power that it generates, skepticism allows her to prove that, though a woman, she is virtuous and strong. But it also provides justification for the villagers' evidently grudging but inevitable acceptance of a woman's self-sacrifice.[38]

While it is tempting to read the motif of doubt as leading, teleologically, to the validation of Godāvarī's death on the pyre, to do so without looking at the development of the plot and the variety of episodes that the plot comprises would be to miss some salient commentaries on gender and caste. The plot is too detailed to allow comprehensive exegesis, but in closing I would like to focus on two features of the story line that vividly illuminate the nature of skepticism and of justification.

The first feature I would mention is the progression of doubt from the husband to his family and then outward to the community and beyond. The structure of the story serves to reinforce a notion implicit in the early episode in which the husband dismisses his wife's vow to be a *satī*: the husband is the paradigmatic male whose doubt of female *sat* reverberates through society and echoes throughout the rest of the story. While the husband's skepticism foreshadows the general reaction, Godāvarī's compliant response (quite obligatory because she is a *satī*) does not indicate that this *satī* accepts all the social norms that her marriage to her husband would impose. By convention, the wife is to obey her in-laws as she does her husband and to be loyal to them as she is to him. Yet Godāvarī subtly but powerfully challenges the norm of exclusive obedience and loyalty. When she opposes her in-laws' denial of her status and assures the family of the future benefits to be had from her death, she contextualizes her promises of reward to her conjugal family by naming it as but one in a series of three primary beneficiaries of her death: her in-laws' home appears second in a list that begins with her father's home and ends with her mother's brother's home. The *satī* thus subverts the premise so prominent in the dominant discourse about women's dharma to the effect that a wife owes her exclusive loyalty to her husband's family. Her blood relatives literally surround her conjugal kin in a way that might even suggest encompassment. The list indicates a marked, if temporary, resistance to her in-laws' expectations, as do many passages in various genres of women's songs and many features of women's ritual practices. In short, when the *satī* assigns joint custody in her legacy—some benefits flowing to her in-laws, some to her natal family—she would seem to be uttering a fleeting but striking call of protest against male authority. She will protect whom she pleases.

It should be noted that while the *satī*'s designation of joint beneficiaries indicates resistance to the normative paradigm, it does not radically challenge the foundation of patriarchal assumptions that underlie the practice of *satī* immolation. Godāvarī does not question the practice of *satī* immolation, nor does she ponder whether dying a *satī*'s death is really beneficial for women such as herself. Such questions simply do not arise. Godāvarī challenges the presumption that she *herself* cannot be a *satī* and the notion that she must be loyal to only her in-laws and their community. But she would hardly serve as an exemplar for those who do not accept the premise that *satī* immolation is a moment of empowerment for women.

The second aspect that merits special attention is the recurring insertion of the *ṭhākur* into the narrative. The *ṭhākur* stands as the traditional pinnacle of authority in the village. *Ṭhākur*s were responsible for governing men, just as husbands are responsible for governing wives. In addition, *ṭhākur*s were responsible for the welfare of widows, since their husbands were no longer there to take care of them. In demanding that Godāvarī seek permission from her lord (that is, himself) before dying on the pyre, the *ṭhākur* is requiring that she recognize his authority and comply with whatever decision he might make.

But Godāvarī refutes his authority, dismissing his claim to have the right to decide her fate for her. Her decision to curse him to be an idiot would seem to indicate that she already thinks him an idiot for even daring to suggest that he could interfere with her plans. In disregarding his orders, she challenges his right as a man and a member of the ruling caste to tell her what to do. Both gender and caste hierarchies are thus threatened by her independent determination of the path she will follow.

Godāvarī's protest against the *ṭhākur* and his authority is not meek or fleeting. She ruins him and then later his progeny as well: he is the only character subjected to two curses. What makes the double damnation especially interesting is that the second curse takes the shape of a blessing. The *satī* offers a boon to the queens who worship her (she blesses them with children), but this boon is disaster in disguise (the children will have severe defects). As far as the *ṭhākur* is concerned, Godāvarī is merciless and relentless.

Set against these two episodes of *ṭhākur*-cursing is the final attempt at obstruction, because of which Godāvarī curses a moneylender to lose his camel but then decides to have him recover the camel in a few days when she learns that her curse will get the moneylender in trouble with the *ṭhākur* of his village. In this episode—the only episode in which Godāvarī modifies a curse to the victim's benefit—Godāvarī demonstrates her solidarity with a person dominated by a ruler. The juxtaposition of this incident with the *ṭhākur* episodes and its placement as the prelude to her death reinforce the message that Godāvarī has no special respect for the traditional heads of local hierarchies. She will do what she will do; no one can get in her way.

The *ṭhākur* incidents remind us that this narrative, though sharing a basic premise upheld by higher castes that *satī* immolation brings fame to a community, departs from the dominant discourse in that it challenges the authority of the dominant caste over the community. But again, the narrative does not question the institution of *satī* immolation: it does not reflect on whether *satī* immolation is a worthy vehicle for resisting caste dominance. Rather, it assumes that this high-caste practice is laudable and that Godāvarī's community has a right to benefit from it, just as high caste communities do.

The conjoining of protest against male domination and protest against caste domination is a common theme in *bhakti* devotionalism, which maintains the inevitable equality of souls in God's eyes. The Vaiṣṇava context of Godāvarī's story might allow us to predict that these themes would arise.[39] And as in much *bhakti* literature, while the protest indicts hierarchy on soteriological, not sociological, grounds, the conviction of soteriological equality tends to corrode established patterns of social dominance. Hence, the protest Godāvarī makes against the *ṭhākur*'s authority cannot but demote him in the eyes of others. Godāvarī will not be alone in envisioning the *ṭhākur* as an idiot.

In short, Godāvarī's protests serve to undermine basic assumptions about gender and caste. In undermining these assumptions, however, they do not challenge the sacrality of *satī* transformation or *satī* veneration. Godāvarī's actions serve to combat any skepticism about a woman's ability to earn *sat* and thereby accrue power of a transcendent nature. They also demonstrate that no one, whether husband or ruler, can control the woman who has perfected her traditional dharma. But in asserting the autonomy of women in this respect, the narrative repeatedly illustrates a conviction that when a woman dies on her husband's pyre, no one else is responsible for her action. The *satī* has agency. It is she who makes the decision as to whether she will or will not perish in flames, a decision that the community cannot revoke or repeal.[40] If the *satī* is ultimately shown as powerful, then the community can appear to others, and to itself, as both victimized by and benefiting from a woman's self-sacrifice. In *Satī Godāvarī,* the practice of immolation is never challenged in a woman's voice. In fact, it is championed most vehemently by the woman who achieves immolation after overcoming skepticism and interference.

NOTES

1. The performance, sung by Nainaram-Jaitaram, was recorded by Yuki Cassettes, Delhi (1990). Paul Courtright sent me a copy of a similar recording by Nainaram on Senior Systems, Delhi, n.d.

2. See Lindsey Harlan, *Religion and Rajput Women: the Ethic of Protection in Contemporary Narratives* (Berkeley: University of California Press, 1992), and "Women's Songs for Auspicious Occasions," in *Religions of India in Practice,* ed. Donald S. Lopez (Princeton: Princeton University Press, 1995), pp. 269–80.

3. I am grateful to R. S. Ashiya for transcribing this performance and for helping me formulate a rough field translation.

4. This reference to polyester and the later reference to disco music are intriguing. Because, as I have said, I picked up this tape in a bazaar and did not have the opportunity to do much investigating, I lack historical and ethnographic information that would help me locate and contextualize the narrative. The references to polyester and disco may well be modern additions: anachronisms of this sort are not uncommon in heroic narratives. Another possible such instance is the narrative's reference to police beatings. *Satī* immolation is now illegal in India, and accomplices may be apprehended, tried, and imprisoned. The fear of police beatings expressed in the narrative may well reflect a present-day concern about breaking the law against *satī* immolation. Although all three of these possible anachronisms could truly be indices of a relatively recent *satī* immolation, the fact also remains that Satī Godāvarī is not a well-known *satī* even in the region in which she is said to have lived. I have spoken about the narrative with various residents and with scholars who have worked in the area, and they could tell me little about her. If there had been a *satī* immolation during the disco era or afterward, one would expect it to have aroused a good deal more publicity.

5. A *dharmśālā* is a place where pilgrims can stay when visiting holy places. Such a stay also allows for the exchange of information about places to eat and things to see, as well as other chitchat. Madhu Dās's admonition that the temple is not a watering place refers to the fact that, when village women go to fetch water from a temple tank or well, they often dally to chat, joke, and gossip.

6. Specifically, she said he would have no children each time he was reincarnated in the present world age (the Kali Yuga).

7. These are a coconut, money, and cloth, the traditional offerings made to a *satī* at a shrine.

8. Or at least not entirely, perhaps: she declared that as long as her memorial stone was hot, he would remain in the same predicament. R. S. Ashiya takes this to mean that the *ṭhākur* would be an idiot during the day, when her stone would be heated by the sun, but not at night. An alternative interpretation is that because her memorial would always be hot (with *sat*), he would always be an idiot.

9. On subaltern groups in Vaiṣṇava discourse, see Kumkum Sangari, "Mirabai and the Spiritual Economy of Bhakti," *Economic and Political Weekly* 25 (7 and 14 July 1990), special articles, pp. 1470–71.

10. Sādh, also referred to as Sād and Sādhu, is a sectarian caste with relatively low status, although it is by no means ranked among the very lowest castes. Its members worship Krishna and other forms of Viṣṇu.

11. In Rajasthan people tend to associate *satī* immolation with the Rajputs, although there are notable exceptions. Romila Thapar has noted that *satī* immolation is most common among the martial castes, which have relatively high status. See her essay "In History," in the special issue of *Seminar* entitled "*Satī: A Symposium on Widow Immolation and Its Social Implications*" (*Seminar* no. 342 [February 1988]: 14–19. There are *satīs* in other communities, but higher castes are often suspicious of lower-caste *satīs*; see Harlan, *Religion and Rajput Women,* pp. 120–21. This century has witnessed the rise of large intercaste cults devoted to *satīs* from various communities. On this development, see Paul B. Courtright, *The Goddess and the Dreadful Practice* (New York: Oxford University Press, forthcoming).

12. The word *Vaiṣṇava* itself is often used to mean vegetarian. See Kathleen M. Erndl, *Victory to the Goddess: The Hindu Goddess of Northwest India in Myth, Ritual, and Symbol* (New York: Oxford University Press, 1993), p. 5.

13. While meat offerings are sometimes worked into Vaiṣṇava worship, they are made not to Viṣṇu but to a guardian deity. For more on the recipient of the *satī bali,* see Harlan, *Religion and Rajput Women,* pp. 130–31. On Vaiṣṇava *satī* sacrifices, see Lata Mani, "Cultural Theory, Colonial Texts: Reading Eyewitness Accounts of Widow Burning," in *Cultural Studies,* ed. Lawrence Grosberg, Cary Nelson, and Paula Freichler (New York: Routledge, 1992), p. 401.

14. While carrying out research for *The Goddess and the Dreadful Practice,* however, Paul Courtright encountered a few similar claims.

15. I have come across narratives in which the effects of a *satī*'s curse lasted until the seventh generation; in two cases, such curses were held responsible for the barrenness of kings for six generations.

16. The text allows for two readings: either Godāvarī will be reborn in any case, or else she would have been reborn if the money lender had not appeared and allowed her to repay her husband's debt.

17. Ambiguity in conceptualizing the locus or destiny of the dead is not, of course, peculiar to Hindu India. For example, Christians frequently visit the dead at graves and yet hold that the dead reside in heaven.

18. See Stuart H. Blackburn, "Death and Deification: Folk Cults in Hinduism," *History of Religions* 24, no. 3 (1985): 255–74.

19. For an interesting example, see David Dean Shulman, "Outcaste Guardian and Trickster: Notes on the Myth of Kāttavarāyan," in *Criminal Gods and Demon Devotees: Essays on the Guardians of Popular Hinduism,* ed. Alf Hiltebeitel (Albany: State University of New York Press, 1989), pp. 35–67. Since time is itself cyclical, the question of determining which status—human or divine—is original often becomes meaningless.

20. The word generally used to denote the power wielded by women is *śakti,* but Rajput women tended to use the word *sat* to mean both the source of power (goodness) and the power itself. On self-deprivation and power, see Holly Baker Reynolds,

"The Auspicious Married Woman," in *The Powers of Tamil Women,* ed. Susan S. Wadley (Syracuse: Syracuse University, Maxwell School of Citizenship and Public Affairs, South Asia Series no. 6, 1980), pp. 50–60.

21. This claim appears in many *satī* narratives, including those pertaining to the famous case of Rup Kanwar, who died on her husband's pyre in 1987 under much-debated circumstances. See note 37, below.

22. On composure, see Lata Mani, "Production of an Official Discourse on Sati in Nineteenth-Century Bengal," *Economic and Political Weekly* 21, no. 17 (26 April 1986): WS32–40; and Rajeswari Sundar Rajan, "The Subject of Sati: Pain and Death in the Contemporary Discourse on Sati," *Yale Journal of Criticism* 3, no. 2 (1990): 1–23.

23. The mother-in-law says that even though Godāvarī was raised in a good family, she behaves badly, a contradiction that reveals the mother-in-law's inability to accept the idea that Godāvarī could be exceptional enough as a daughter-in-law to die a *satī.*

24. This concern is not unfounded, for women did sometimes change their minds. See Mani, "Cultural Theory, Colonial Texts," pp. 397–400. Here, the concern that Godāvarī might set the whole town on fire is, of course, exaggerated. It evokes an image reminiscent of the scene in the *Rāmāyaṇa* in which Hanumān ignites Laṅkā with his burning tail. In general, the major fears surrounding a potential change of heart are that a woman will be permanently disfigured and/or incapacitated by her burns and that her change of heart will reveal her previous hypocrisy and her current cowardice, both of which will bring shame to her family and community.

25. See Edward C. Dimock, "A Theology of the Repulsive: The Myth of the Goddess Śītalā," in *The Divine Consort,* ed. Hawley and Wulff, pp. 184–203.

26. See ibid., and see also Ralph W. Nicholas and Aditi Nath Sarkar, "The Fever Demon and the Census Commissioner: Śītalā Mythology in Eighteenth- and Nineteenth-Century Bengal," in *Bengal: Studies in Literature, Society and History,* ed. Marvin Davis, (East Lansing, Mich.: Michigan State University, Asian Studies Center, 1976), pp. 3–68.

27. Exceptions to this are a few *satī*s who have become famous enough to gather large followings. See p. 242 and n. 37, below.

28. See A. K. Ramanujan, "Two Realms of Kannada Folklore," in *Another Harmony: New Essays on the Folklore of India,* ed. Stuart H. Blackburn and A. K. Ramanujan (Berkeley: University of California Press, 1986), pp. 41–75.

29. I am grateful to Ann Gold and Gloria Raheja for discussions on this point.

30. It is also possible that the narrative was in some sense created or crafted by a man. The final miracle described in the story—in which the *satī* grants the boon of keeping her forever in his heart to the Megwal who shows devotion by sleeping at her pyre—may be something of a signature line. He might be the man who composed the story, way back when, or the legendary first raconteur in a line of people who transmitted the narrative until it was finally passed on to professional singers.

31. Rajasthanis I encountered often remarked that it is impossible to understand how *satī*s can die as they do. While there is a widespread belief that *satī*s do not feel pain—so deep are they in their meditation on their husbands—the people I knew often described a *satī*'s death by fire as excruciating.

32. I discuss the concepts of *sat* and heroic death in "Hero Veneration," a book manuscript in progress.

33. One of the better-known expositions of this appears in Sudhir Kakar, *The Inner World: A Psycho-analytic Study of Childhood and Society in India,* 2d ed. (New York: Oxford University Press, 1981). See also Karen McCarthy Brown, "Good Mothers and Bad Mothers in the Rituals of Sati," in *Sati, the Blessing and the Curse,* ed. John Stratton Hawley (New York: Oxford University Press, 1994), pp. 91–99.

34. On theodicy in Indian thought generally, see Wendy Doniger O'Flaherty, *The Origins of Evil in Hindu Mythology* (Berkeley: University of California Press, 1976).

35. See the articles in *Manushi* 42–43 (September–December 1987) and in *Seminar* no. 342 (February 1988). See also Mani, "Cultural Theory, Colonial Texts"; Gayatri C. Spivak, "Can the Subaltern Speak? Speculations on Widow-Sacrifice," *Wedge* nos. 7–8 (Winter/Spring 1985): 120–30; John Stratton Hawley, introduction and afterword in *Sati, the Blessing and the Curse,* ed. Hawley (pp. 3–26 and 175–86), as well as several other essays in that volume, including "The Roop Kanwar Case: Feminist Responses" (pp. 101–30) and "The Continuing Invention of the Sati Tradition" (pp. 159–73), both by Veena Talwar Oldenburg, and Ashis Nandy, "Sati as Profit versus Sati as a Spectacle" (pp. 131–49).

36. Widows are, moreover, seen as lacking a socially approved outlet for their sexual desires, which leaves them sexually unsatisfied. Consequently, they are thought to be easily seduced (or even libidinous seducers) and are thus potential threats to family honor (*izzat*). In contrast, *satīs* are understood as having had all their sexual needs satisfied by their husbands and therefore having retained their modesty (*laj*), much to their families' credit.

37. The most famous example of this is Rup Kanwar: in the first two weeks after her immolation, some two hundred thousand people flooded into her village. See Hawley, introduction and afterword, in *Sati, the Blessing and the Curse,* ed. Hawley. See also the reflections on Rānī Satī in Sudesh Vaid, "Politics of Widow Immolation," *Seminar* no. 342 (February 1988): 20–23, esp. p. 21; and Sangari "Perpetuating the Myth," ibid., pp. 24–30, esp. p. 25. On the spread of such profitable cults in Rajasthan, see Paul Courtright, "The Iconographies of Sati," as well as Oldenburg, "The Roop Kanwar Case," and Nandy, "Sati as Profit versus Sati as a Spectacle," all in *Sati, the Blessing and the Curse,* ed. Hawley, pp. 27–49, 101–30, and 131–49, respectively.

38. The skeptical reaction of the villagers also demonstrates how sacrificers often render themselves victims. On this subject, see René Girard, *The Scapegoat* (Baltimore: Johns Hopkins University Press, 1986).

39. On protests against gender and caste hierarchies in another Rajasthani context, see Sangari, "Mirabai and the Spiritual Economy of Bhakti," pp. 1470–71.

40. On agency and *satī* immolation, see Mani, "Cultural Theory, Colonial Texts," and "Production of an Official Discourse on Sati." See also Oldenburg, "The Roop Kanwar Case," pp. 124–25, and "The Continuing Invention of the Sati Tradition," p. 170, in *Sati, The Blessing and the Curse,* ed. Hawley.

BHĀRAT MĀTĀ
Mother India and Her Militant Matriots

Lise McKean

The identity of the patriarchal Indian nation-state and its citizenry has been, and continues to be, expressed in terms of devotion to the goddess Bhārat Mātā, Mother India. This essay presents two examples of how a Hindu nationalist organization, the Vishva Hindu Parishad (World Hindu Council) has propagated this devotional complex: its 1983 All-India Sacrifice for Unity (*Ekātmatā Yajña*) and the temple it has built to Bhārat Mātā. The Sacrifice for Unity involved a six-week nationwide tour of an image of Bhārat Mātā, during which crowds worshiped her and listened to speeches delivered by religious leaders and other public figures. Six months before this event, the VHP had consecrated its eight-story Bhārat Mātā temple in the pilgrimage town of Hardwar (see figure 20). As is well-known, issues of national culture, religious identity, gender, and class are embedded in both past and contemporary formulations of devotion to Bhārat Mātā. And although the destruction of the Babri Mosque in Ayodhya, the campaign to build a Rāma temple there, and the cult of Bhārat Mātā are distinct phenomena, all pertain to the politics of nationalism and to the Hindu nationalist movement of the 1980s and 1990s.

A young woman ascetic, Sadhvi Rithambra, who is a member of the VHP's committee of religious leaders, often invokes Bhārat Mātā when she speaks at rallies.[1] Her speeches explode with rage and hatred, directed primarily against Muslims: they are so inflammatory that the government has banned the sale of cassette recordings of them. She tells her audience that Muslim atrocities against Hindus—which began when they invaded India, desecrated Hindu temples, and raped Hindu women—have neither ceased nor been avenged. Muslim separatists in Kashmir, she claims, are using "red hot irons to burn the slogan 'Long Live Pakistan' on the thighs of our Hindu daughters."[2] She exhorts the crowd to remember the blood of Hindu martyrs who

Figure 20. Billboard at the Hardwar railway station.

died in 1990 during their attempt to build a Rāma temple in Ayodhya. She insists that the fight to build this temple is tantamount to the fight to preserve their civilization, national consciousness, honor, and self-esteem. References to the need for Hindus to protect themselves from brutal enemies intensify the emotive power of her speeches—a strategy widely used by nationalists and other groups to forge and consolidate a collective identity. The audience simultaneously experiences and affirms this collective identity and imagined community when Sadhvi Rithambra leads a chant that begins and ends with invocations of Bhārat Mātā. The chant links the audience with gods of the past and Hindu martyrs of the present: all are children of Bhārat Mātā.

The historian Partha Chatterjee emphasizes the complementarities between nationalist discourse and the cultural identity of the middle class under British rule.[3] Analysts of contemporary Hindu nationalism highlight the interrelations among support for the nationalist movement, global and domestic economic transformations, and changes in middle-class identity and practices.[4] Work by feminists demonstrates how nationalist discourse, first during British rule and later in the postcolonial nation-state, articulated the "woman question" in terms of the requirements of changing cultural and economic practices of the upper and middle classes.[5] Under colonial rule, the emergent Hindu patriarchy's differentiation of social space into public and private spheres required a new vision of the ideal woman. This ideal woman should be a wife and a mother. She should be as frugal and fastidious in her housekeeping as she is devout and knowledgeable about religious traditions. She should be sweetly subordinate to her husband yet sufficiently educated and informed to provide satisfying companionship. The welfare of her family and particularly her husband depended upon her spiritual powers, which were earned through the performance of rituals, scrupulous chastity, and incessant self-sacrifice. This ideal image attributed to virtuous wives and mothers the capacity to inspire their husbands and sons to become heroic nationalists. Sangari and Vaid argue that this particular ideal woman is ideological because from a diverse array of possibilities, specific gender roles have been selected and universalized. Given this process of gender construction, "the formation of desired notions of spirituality and womanhood is thus part of the formation of the middle class itself, wherein hierarchies and patriarchies are sought to be maintained on both material and spiritual grounds." Reminding readers of the importance of caste and class inequalities to the study of gender in India, Sangari and Vaid argue that the current politicization of religious identities "has given a new lease of life to patriarchal practices under 'religious' sanction."[6] In short, patriarchal projects are embedded in the Hindu nationalist movement.

The discourse and practices of Hindu nationalism create specific subjectivities, while contesting others. The promoted subjectivities are commonly articulated in terms of the duties of Bhārat Mātā's children and are differentiated according to age, gender, and socioeconomic and caste status. "Matriots"—the term is mine—are Bhārat Mātā's devoted and dutiful children who constitute an ideal, loyal citizenry, and militant matriots are those who, ever eager to assert their devotion, readily construe events as offenses against Bhārat Mātā. The narrative of militant "matriotism" might be read as an oedipal drama of the patriarchal nation-state. The nation is figured as a loving Mother surrounded by her devoted children; the secular state and Muslims (as heirs of Muslim invaders) figure as the tyrannical Father. Whether celibate or supported by their devoted wives, Bhārat Mātā's sons are valiant protagonists whose struggle is a righteous patricide, a conquest that simultaneously liberates the nation—the Mother and her children—and enables her sons to enjoy the power and riches they have successfully wrested from the malevolent Father.

This theme of patricide is the subtext of a history of Bengal written by Sarala Devi, a member of the privileged and sophisticated Tagore family.[7] The history's hero, Pratapaditya, is singular among Bengali landlords for challenging the authority of a Muslim king. When criticized by her uncle, Rabindranath Tagore, for making a known patricide the hero of Bengali history, Sarala Devi defended her choice by saying that she presents Pratapaditya not as an ideal moral being but as a brave and manly Bengali—a defense that conveniently valorizes a code of conduct for militant matriots. In fact, Sarala

Devi organized a group of young Bengali men who pledged to her in front of a map of India that they would sacrifice their lives fighting for independence from British rule. In 1903 Sarala Devi's group instituted an annual festival of heroes, held on the second day of Durgā Pūjā, the great festival in honor of the warrior-goddess Durgā. Included in the third of these celebrations was a dramatic performance of Bankim Chandra Chatterjee's anti-British novel *Ānandamaṭh,* "Monastery of Bliss." When the performance ended, the crowd began to chant the song "Bande Mātaram": its lyrics and imagery, which praise the goddess Bhārat Mātā, recur throughout *Ānandamaṭh.* "Bande Mātaram" subsequently became the nationalists' rallying cry.

Bhārat Mātā's apotheosis in her present form dates back clearly to this Bengali novel, in which she inspires her children, under the leadership of the male Hindu ascetic Mahatma Satya, to vanquish the British and restore peace and prosperity. Bankim's novel marks the invention of a tradition—a tradition of "matriotism" that combines European political concepts of the nation-state, progress, order, and patriotism with a complex heritage of the mythological elaboration and ritual worship of Hindu goddesses (*devī, śakti*) that is particularly strong in Bengal. However, as the burgeoning literature on nationalist ideologies and national cultures demonstrates, invented traditions are not static. They are continually reinvented in specific contexts to produce and challenge dominant constructions of class, religious and gender identities. In India diverse groups—bourgeois social reformers, Hindu and secular nationalists, peasant leaders, feminists—and even Nehru himself have fashioned for their own purposes this invented tradition of imagining India as a Hindu goddess.

The 1992 English edition of *Ānandamaṭh* includes the dedication made by the translator, B. K. Roy, to Benjamin Franklin and Aurobindo in 1941, together with his seven-page preface. Roy declares that Bankim's "great achievement for India was that he made patriotism a religion and his writings have become the gospel of India's struggle for political independence."[8] He discusses the song "Bande Mātaram" and explains how it became the nationalists' call to duty. It inspired both Gandhian pacifists, who suffered atrocities in British jails, and Aurobindo-like revolutionaries who were sent to the gallows for "loving their own country" and died with the "sacred mantra of Bande Mataram on their lips."[9] In Roy's opinion, *Ānandamaṭh* "set forth the principle of unselfish militancy as taught by Krishna in the *Bhagavat Gita,* the Bible of the Hindus."[10] The translator celebrates Bankim for founding a lineage of revolutionaries, a lineage that militant Hindu nationalists have not only kept alive down to the present but also claim as their own.

The literary style of *Ānandamaṭh* more closely approximates the Hindu epic than the British novel. Characters, their relationships, and their actions serve to evoke a range of emotions in the audience: sorrow and anger, fear, disgust, and the desire for revenge. Bankim's expressive powers reach their greatest intensity in his elaboration of the religious devotion of Bhārat Mātā's children, a devotion so powerful that it purifies and liberates both the mother and her children. The rapacious British have enslaved Bengal; they have brought famine and despair. Under the leadership of the ascetic Mahatma Satya, the Order of the Children protects the good and punishes the wicked British and their collaborators. The audience visualizes Bhārat Mātā when the Mahatma leads Mahendra, a potential disciple, to three rooms, each containing a different form of Bhārat Mātā. In the first room is Bhārat Mātā before the British conquest: "a gigantic, imposing, resplendent, yes, almost a living map of India." In the second room stands a tearful Bhārat Mātā wearing rags, with a sword hanging over her head. The Mahatma explains, "She is in the gloom of famine, disease, death, humiliation and destruction." But if the sword signifies how the British keep India in subjection, it also suggests how Bhārat Mātā will be freed. In the third room a heavenly light radiates from "the map of a golden India—bright, beautiful, full of glory and dignity!" The Mahatma says, "This is our mother as she is destined to be." Excitedly, Mahendra asks when Bhārat Mātā will be so radiant and cheerful again. The Mahatma replies, "Only when all the children of the Motherland shall call her Mother in all sincerity."[11]

After testing his devotion, the Mahatma initiates Mahendra, whose property and riches are used to build an iron storehouse for the Order's treasury and a factory in which to make weapons. The Mahatma explains that two types of Children join the Order. Those like Mahendra are few; he chooses them himself. They receive a secret, higher initiation that makes them leaders of the Order. They vow to give up wealth, pleasure, and personal attachments until they achieve their goal of purifying Bhārat Mātā from the pollution of alien domination. Death is the penalty for breaking this vow. The second type consists of the householders and beggars who present themselves when summoned for warfare and receive a share of the spoils. The speeches of their leaders quicken their devotion to Bhārat Mātā, which in turn inspires ferocity in battle: "the fire of anger was in their eyes, and the passion of stern determination on their lips, and one could hear brave words of revenge from their mouths."[12] In addition to the main plot, which culminates in the victory of the Order of the Children over the British, there are two important subplots involving two women whose husbands are leaders of the Order. They combine their duties as virtuous wives with active devotion to Bhārat Mātā, inspiring and reinforcing their husbands' heroism. One waits patiently for her husband to return; the other, in the guise of a male ascetic, joins her husband in the Order. The story eventually reveals that only self-sacrificing devotion to Bhārat Mātā can bring the questing heart what it desires: a liberation that is at once political and spiritual.

The Bhārat Mātā cult propagated by contemporary Hindu nationalists combines the devotional and heroic imagery of *Ānandamaṭh* with a set of elements defining Hindu-ness (*hindutva*) formulated in 1922 by the archetypal militant Hindu, V. D. Savarkar. He defined as Hindu those who consider India not only their holy land—a land sanctified by the presence of Hindu gods and the blood of its heroic martyrs—but also the land of their ancestors. Hindus are a race and a nation with a common origin and blood, a shared culture and civilization. Savarkar stressed the importance of the struggle against Muslim and British enemies to the formation of the Hindu national identity. The Indian subcontinent may be the holy homeland of *hindutva,* but as Savarkar envisioned it, *hindutva* "is compatible with any conceivable expansion of our Hindu people. . . . The only geographical limit of Hindutva is the limit of our earth."[13]

The VHP brought Savarkar's vision to life in 1983, with its All-India Sacrifice for Unity (*Ekātmatā Yajña*). The six-week event required careful planning. Shrines mounted on the backs of trucks took Bhārat Mātā, Gaṅgā Mā (Mother Ganges), and Śiva to the people for mass rituals of public worship. Included as well was a mobile Bhārat Mātā temple. Mounted on a truck, it traveled as part of a cortege modeled on the journeys (*yātrās*) of great temple deities, during which they can be seen and worshiped outside the precincts of sacred enclaves. For such *yātrās*, deities are enshrined on huge wooden carts known as *rath*s. The VHP's Sacrifice for Unity sent an updated version of the *rath yātrā* through cities, towns, and villages from Hardwar in the north to the southern tip of India at Kanyakumari.

Bearing a statue of Bhārat Mātā and an enormous ritual vessel containing Ganges water, the procession of vehicles made accessible the promise of power and auspicious abundance associated with Goddess worship. The procession traversed three principal routes, starting and finishing in major Hindu pilgrimage centers and stopping en route in other pilgrimage places as well as various villages, towns, and cities. In the commemorative volume, *Ekātmatā Yajña* (see figure 21), VHP officials repeatedly assert that the purpose of the sacrifice is to promote national unity and that the event has no relation to politics. They attribute its success to the "grace of God, blessings of Saints and cooperation of the public" and to the "full cooperation" of the government and bureaucracy.[14] A color photo shows VHP officials meeting with the president of India to discuss the upcoming event. The volume reports that many district magistrates and high-ranking police officials presided over ceremonies. It also recounts the extensive media coverage of the sacrifice: there were more than 150 press conferences before and during the event, as well as radio and television reports.

Describing the Sacrifice for Unity as a ritual sacrifice "in the Vedic sense," the volume declares that "through its medium, young and old, male and female, all of them forgetting their own identities and differences" gathered

Figure 21. Cover of the Vishva Hindu Parishad's "Sacrifice for Unity" souvenir volume.

to worship Bhārat Mātā and Gaṅgā Mā (p. 13). Yet forgetting is not all that is involved. VHP rituals actively fashion social identities and differences, as well as instructing people in the appropriate expression of a specific type of Hindu identity. As the VHP's aristocratic president Maharana Singh Mewar explained to an audience, the Sacrifice of Unity had as its purpose to instill feelings of devotion in the nation. If the sacrifices of freedom fighters liberated Bhārat Mātā from British rule, then this sacrifice would restore the unity of India and earn for its participants the honor of being called "Children of Bhārat Mātā" (p. 4). Reportedly sixty million people, whom the VHP volume calls Hindu brethren, participated in the sacrifice. Though they belong to different sects and practice different customs, all share the same "pure attitude." "We are one. Our happiness and sufferings are one. There is no inequality, no untouchability, no reservations, no high and low" (p. 4). Christian and Muslim participants "proved that irrespective of their mode of worship all of them are Hindus culturally and nationally" (p. 13). Here, as elsewhere, the VHP attacks "class conflict" as detrimental to national unity. It attributes the success of the *Ekātmatā Yajña* to the support not only of diverse religious groups but also of a broad spectrum of economic groups: "The weak and downtrodden depressed classes and the industrialists all had shown their keenness to make their bit of contribution" (p. 14). A discussion of poverty and the efforts of the VHP to ameliorate it closes with a plea for money: "In our society sacrifice is very important, but after the sacrifice one must make a donation" (p. 8). The VHP also raised money by selling small pots of Ganges water.

By conducting ritual ceremonies on the mall at India Gate in New Delhi, the VHP occupied the epicenter of the national capital for one day. Here, hundreds of local processions met up with the main one. A huge crowd filled the expanse adjacent to India Gate, where shrines were set up for worship. After the rituals had been completed, VHP officials and religious leaders delivered speeches from a high stage adorned by a huge backdrop of Bhārat Mātā and Mother Ganges. They repeated the claims that the Sacrifice for Unity had no political purpose and that the VHP no connection with politics. Religious leaders then praised the "holy work" of the sacrifice, from which would come the "organization and unity of Hindu society" (p. 85). Thanking Delhi's religious leaders for publicizing the event and encouraging people to attend, the VHP officials called the finale of the sacrifice a new beginning. They also pledged to undertake further projects: the celebration of an annual Unity Month throughout India, the establishment of Centers of Awakening, and the construction of a World Hindu Brotherhood Center in Delhi. Through these and other projects the VHP successfully capitalized on the monetary, institutional, and symbolic profits it earned as organizer and patron of the sacrifice. These profits then enabled the VHP to mount more aggressively and effectively its campaign to destroy the Babri Mosque and build a temple on the supposed site of Rāma's birth in Ayodhya.

SWAMI SATYAMITRANAND GIRI: VHP LEADER AND FOUNDER OF HARDWAR'S BHĀRAT MĀTĀ TEMPLE

The VHP's Bhārat Mātā temple in Hardwar, like the Sacrifice for Unity, provides a means both to popularize Hindu nationalist ideology and to raise money for the movement. The temple guidebooks, available in Hindi and English, celebrate the extraordinary devotion of its founder, Swami Satyamitranand Giri, to Bhārat Mātā.[15] The swami's hagiography details his frequent tours in India and overseas, during which he solicited money for the VHP, ostensibly for the temple's construction.[16] The temple's eight stories house pantheons of deities, saints, nationalist heroes, and virtuous women—figures important to the VHP's ideology. The temple is also a site of socioreligious activities, a place where local residents, pilgrims, tourists, religious leaders, and politicians participate in rituals and celebrations sponsored by Satyamitranand and the VHP.

Religious leaders who run establishments in Hardwar and in nearby Rishikesh hold important positions within the VHP. Of the thirty-nine members of the VHP's council of religious leaders, of whom Satyamitranand is one, four have their headquarters in Hardwar and Rishikesh, and many other VHP members have ashrams and temples in these pilgrimage centers as well. Swami Satyamitranand Giri, whose name and photograph can be found on numerous pages of VHP literature, has his headquarters in Hardwar at the Bhārat Mātā temple. Along with the Dalai Lama and the head Ladakhi lama, three Shankaracharyas, and two former vice chancellors of Banaras Hindu University, the VHP names Satyamitranand among those who supported the formation of the VHP.[17] Satyamitranand's name appears on the first page of another VHP booklet, together with the names of ten other VHP founders, and later he is listed as a VHP trustee and member of the Commission on Religion, which is noted as having convened in Hardwar.[18] Like thirteen other religious leaders and two industrialists, Satyamitranand has "adopted" a district—Ajmer, Rajasthan. Adoption involves distributing patronage and establishing institutions, the purpose of which is to "uplift" backward sections of society, promote Sanskrit, prohibit cow slaughter, renovate temples, and build schools. Foremost among the duties of those who adopt districts, however, is to stop the conversion of Hindus to "alien faiths" and "to integrate those returning to their ancestral faith."[19]

When I met Satyamitranand at his Hardwar headquarters, he told me of his trips around the world to visit his devotees. He also spoke of having resigned his post as Shankaracharya of Bhanpura Math in Madhya Pradesh because it restricted his activities, particularly his travel abroad. I was not given the opportunity to ask the numerous questions I had about his organization, the Bhārat Mātā temple, and his involvement with the VHP. Instead, after a few minutes Satyamitranand dismissed me, saying that he was busy preparing for another trip abroad. Most of my attempts to engage personnel at his ashram and the Bhārat Mātā temple in conversation were also rebuffed. One lay disciple who was sitting in the temple early one morning, however, was more talkative. He had come for a long visit to Hardwar from Ahmedabad. He said that he had retired, that his children were grown and settled, and that he only wanted to serve his guru, Satyamitranand. His service entails sitting in the temple for four hours each day, chanting mantras and keeping an eye on visitors. In return he receives food and accommodation at Satyamitranand's ashram, adjacent to the temple. This devotee lamented that even now that he had come to Hardwar, he rarely had a chance to meet with his guru because Satyamitranand was usually away. Rubbing his fingers together, he said that Satyamitranand often travels to the United States and Canada to raise money for the temple, going on to explain that Satyamitranand has a particularly strong following among Gujarati Patels in India and overseas. He also pointed out that Satyamitranand had to give up his post as Shankaracharya in order to "do more *sevā*" (religious service).

Before I learned about Satyamitranand's involvement in the VHP through reading its literature, I had inquired at the local newspaper about the location of the offices of the Hardwar branches of the Rashtriya Swayamsevak Sangh (RSS), the most important and long-standing Hindu nationalist organization of the twentieth century, and of the VHP. The editor directed me to Satyamitranand's Bhārat Mātā temple. Later, when visiting the VHP's headquarters in New Delhi, I asked Ashok Singhal, the general secretary, about Satyamitranand and his relation to the VHP. He replied vaguely, saying merely that Satyamitranand had ties with the organization; only later, after studying the VHP literature, did I learn just how extensive these ties are. Singhal's office was adorned with icons of Hindu nationalism: a picture of Durgā inside an outline of India; a picture of the Rani of Jhansi; a statue of Krishna and Arjuna in their war chariot; a photograph of Jayendra Saraswati, the Shankaracharya of Kanchi; and several images of the sacred syllable *om.* The manager of a small ashram near the Bhārat Mātā temple told me that when Satyamitranand's links with the RSS earned him the disfavor of Indira Gandhi's government, he sponsored a big sacrifice (*yajña*) in Hardwar, during which prominent swamis and politicians spoke approvingly of Indira Gandhi. Their relations had become even more cordial by 1983, when Indira Gandhi attended the ceremonies marking the consecration of the Bhārat Mātā temple. And it was Satyramitranand who, also in 1983, conducted the rituals preceding the departure of the Sacrifice for Unity procession from Hardwar.

Rajkumar Sharma, Hardwar's leading publicist for its Brahmin priests and a former Janata party member of the Uttar Pradesh legislative assembly, estimated that the VHP holds assets worth at least fifty million rupees. He also mentioned that he is a member and knows Ashok Singhal, and that in July 1988 he had attended the VHP's Sādhu Sammelan (Ascetics' Convention) in Hardwar. Satyamitranand's ashram helped organize the convention and housed many of its participants. According to Sharma, the principal issues discussed at this VHP gathering included cow protection, the liberation of Rāma's birthplace in Ayodhya, and the conversion of Hindus to

Christianity and Islam. He said that in order to counter foreign influences that threaten the culture of Bhārat (India), the convention decreed that if Indians regard Rāma and Krishna as "national heroes" and touch India's sacred ground three times with their head while saying "Bhārat Mātā kī Jai" (Hail, Mother India), then they may belong to "any religion." In short, the participants in the convention urged all Indians to worship the deities sacred to Hindu nationalists.

WE ARE ALL CHILDREN OF BHĀRAT MĀTĀ

Satyamitranand's hagiography, *Divyalok,* discusses at length his devotion to Bhārat Mātā and how it compelled him to build a temple where Hindus could worship Bhārat Mātā and learn about Bhārat's religious culture. Like Savarkar and other Hindu nationalists, Satyamitranand teaches that Bhārat has the oldest culture in the world and is the land where God has repeatedly chosen to be incarnated. Sages and saints are born in Bhārat to teach the path of devotion. Although there was already a Bhārat Mātā temple in Banaras, Satyamitranand wanted to build one in Hardwar to acquaint visitors with Bhārat Mātā's "cultural, spiritual and divine glory."[20] Temples to many other gods filled Hardwar, but there was no temple for Bhārat Mātā. Satyamitranand therefore decided to build a temple where visitors could worship not only Bhārat Mātā but also Bhārat's other gods, great saints, heroes, and *satī*s. Having resolved to build such a temple, Satyamitranand and his worldwide organization, the Samanvaya Parivār (Family of Harmony), began to work to raise money for its construction. According to *Divyalok,* Satyamitranand was disheartened when funds were not immediately forthcoming. He prayed for help, and soon his devotees in India and abroad as well as the VHP were organizing rallies and *yajña*s to raise money. The book's account of the fund-raising campaign records the various places where Satyamitranand spoke and how much money he collected. On a previous visit to the Rajasthani city of Bardoli, Satyamitranand had been installed in a pantheon of nationalist heroes, along with Subas Chandra Bose and Mahatma Gandhi. When he came again during his Bhārat Mātā Temple fund-raising tour, he was presented with nearly four million rupees.[21] In 1978 he presided over the ground-breaking ceremonies for the monumental eight-story temple in Hardwar, built at an estimated cost of ten million rupees.

Satyamitranand chose May 15, 1983, the anniversary of the birth of the first Shankaracharya, as the date for the consecration of the Bhārat Mātā temple. Announcements were published in newspapers throughout India inviting "all citizens" to attend. Invitations were also sent to heads of religious sects and to politicians. People began arriving several days in advance so as not to miss the many events leading up to the consecration. On May 14 Satyamitranand led a kilometer-long procession through Hardwar to the temple. One Hardwar resident who witnessed it reportedly commented that he had not seen such a huge and grand procession in fifty years, likening it to Hinduism's largest gathering, the Kumbh Mela.[22] Satyamitranand also brought in five hundred Brahmins trained in Vedic ritual to perform a Viṣṇu *yajña.* The festivities included recitations of sacred texts, a performance by a *Rām Līlā* troupe from Mathura, lectures by religious leaders, banquets for ascetics, and numerous other ritual activities. Prime Minister Indira Gandhi arrived punctually at the time appointed for the consecration. The principal consecration rituals were conducted by the Shankaracharya of Dvaraka; Indira Gandhi participated by performing *āratī* before the statue of Bhārat Mātā. After worshiping Bhārat Mātā, she sat on stage with religious leaders and addressed the audience. Over a hundred thousand people are said to have attended the event.

The following year Satyamitranand's devotees from India and abroad were invited to Hardwar to attend a five-day spiritual camp. Five hundred people gathered to receive his blessings and be honored for their assistance in building the Bhārat Mātā temple. The camp was inaugurated by Swami Chidananda, a VHP member and the head of Divine Life Society, and several other religious leaders also addressed this select gathering of Bhārat Mātā's devotees and Satyamitranand's followers. One week after the conclusion of this camp, the procession in connection with the VHP's All-India Sacrifice for Unity arrived in Hardwar. *Divyalok* is silent about Satyamitranand's involvement, but VHP sources say he figured prominently in ceremonies held in Hardwar and elsewhere in northern India. Materials for the following discussion of the temple and its relation to the Hindu nationalism of Satyamitranand and the VHP are drawn from my own visits to the temple and from the English and Hindi guidebooks published by Satyamitranand's organization and sold at the temple.

While the devotional tone is more pronounced in the Hindi guidebook, the English book is printed on better-quality paper and has glossy color photographs of the temple and the statue of Bhārat Mātā on its front and back covers, respectively. The front cover of the Hindi version has a drawing of the temple with the orange Hindu flag flying above it and an *om* above that—insignia of the VHP (see figure 22). On its back cover is a photo of Satyamitranand, with text below. The first paragraph reads like a précis of Savarkar's "Essentials of Hindutva": "We are all children of Bhārat Mātā. Our country is one, our society is one, our civilization is one, our culture is one, our relations are blood relations."

The English guidebook, *Bharat Mata Mandir: A Candid Appraisal,* opens with a discussion of the reasons why Satyamitranand decided to build a temple in honor of Bhārat Mātā. His decision is depicted as arising from a "vision," an "almost divine inspiration" that "dawned on Pujya Swami Satyamitranand Giri Maharaj in an auspicious tranquil moment."[23] After sharing his

Figure 22. Cover of the Hindi guidebook to the Bhārat Mātā temple in Hardwar.

vision with a few close disciples, he began to speak publicly about the need to build a Bhārat Mātā temple in Hardwar. The text draws readers into an intimate, inclusive relation with its arguments by using first-person-plural pronouns: "We may wonder about the basis for the iconic representation of Bharat Mata." It assures readers that worship of the Divine Mother is universal and normative; it is "as old as civilization" and exists in India as it did in "all ancient cultures." In India, the Divine Mother as the "Cause off [*sic*] Creation, as the symbol of Primal Energy and the source of Power—Shakti—is well within our comprehension." As the text points out, Tantric practitioners worship the mother as goddess at "shakti-peeths" (*śakti-pīṭha*s, places of the Goddess's special power) throughout India. There are "iconic manifestations" of the Divine Mother as the rivers Ganga and Yamuna, and as the *Gītā*—so "why not then Bharat Mata????" (p. i).

Indeed, such a manifestation of Bhārat Mātā is necessary because "to us all Mother-Land is sacred" (p. i). A temple would not only propagate the worship of Bhārat Mātā but would also be a medium through which to enlighten visitors about the power and glory of the holy motherland:

> May this beautiful, yet powerful symbol of Mother India entice the hitherto uncommitted passerby, who happens to be a chance visitor, to the glory of Bharat Mata in her manifold facets, to the vastness of her resources and power, to get a glimpse of her history, culture, traditions, and hopefully, be rejuvenated. . . . It is hoped that a visit to the shrine will be a satisfying and lasting spiritual experience that will inspire devotion and dedication to Mother-Land. (pp. i–ii)

The iconic representation of Bhārat Mātā in sculpture is described as both an artistic expression and a devotional act, and the temple serves to promote this devotional attitude toward Bhārat Mātā, something that "historians and mythological story tellers may have missed" (p. 1). Satyamitranand selected Hardwar as the site for the Bhārat Mātā temple because the town is famous for the austerities that ancient sages performed there; it is "the holiest of holy pilgrim centers." Every year "millions of Indians and others" retreat from "the din and bustle that engulfs our modern world" and come to Hardwar for an atmosphere "sublime, captivating, full of divine vibrations" that can "uplift the human heart." Thus, the temple gives visitors both aesthetic and spiritual satisfaction by presenting "a unique majestic appearance soothing to the eye and the mind" (p. ii).

In addition, the temple is said to synthesize the best of ancient and modern architecture. This notion of a synthesis of the traditional and the modern also informs ideas concerning Hinduism and Hindu society promoted by the VHP and its affiliated religious leaders, who claim to interpret ancient traditions so as to adapt them to the conditions of modern life. Not everyone, however, concurs with this opinion of the temple's architecture. Many

Indians told me that the temple is imposing but as ugly as an office or apartment block; it lacks the beauty and grandeur befitting a temple. An Indian architect working in Delhi, who visits Hardwar several times a year, asserted that the Bhārat Mātā temple "is not architecture but it is an important vision of India's unity." When I asked him what he thought the political implications of worshiping India as a Hindu deity might be, he replied, "Villagers like the temple, especially the views of Hardwar which can be seen from the top." The English guidebook, however, does not restrict to villagers the pleasure of this view from the top: "The view of the Himalayas: of the Sapta Dhara [seven streams, said to have been formed so that, during its descent, the Ganges would bypass the ashrams of the seven ancient sages]; of the scenic view of entire campus of the Sapta Sarowar area from the balconies of this floor, is breath-taking and transquilizing [*sic*] to the eye" (p. 18).

The temple's embodiment of the vision of India's unity, of the nation's history and heritage, is a recurrent theme in the guidebook. Even though India "is saturated with temples" and its entire landscape is "an Abode of God," the Bhārat Mātā temple meets the urgent need to "keep our history and heritage alive." This knowledge "about our ancestry, about the founders of our faith, culture and tradition . . . is often sadly lacking." Muslim and Christian youths are said to be more knowledgeable about their heritage than Hindu youths: "Can we afford such gross nescience about our ancestry, about our heritage?" (p. iii). In addition to its purpose of fostering devotion to Bhārat Mātā, the temple is said to commemorate "the persons who have generated the alpha and gamma [*sic*] of our culture" and to offer visitors "a glimpse of our nation's illustrious sons and daughters: saints and seers, philosophers and theologians, the originators of our unique thought; gallant men and women who have sacrificed their lives for the nation." By thus presenting the nation's lineage of illustrious forebears, the Bhārat Mātā temple is said to inspire in visitors "pride, faith and confidence in Bharat, and a resolve for dedication to the cause of our Motherland" (p. iii). Through its presentation of the motherland as an object of devotion and sacrifice, the temple, like the VHP, defines national identity in terms of Hindu piety and activism. Such an identity contributes to the VHP's ability to mobilize large numbers of people for specific Hindu nationalist causes—notably, the All-India Sacrifice for Unity, the demolition of the Babri Mosque at Ayodhya, and the construction of a Rāma temple on the site of the mosque.

The temple guidebook sets forth how the Bhārat Mātā temple explicitly aims to provide for its visitors an emotional experience of religious and national unity. By unifying sectarian diversity "under one umbrella," the temple strives to promote an appreciation for the diversity of religious teachers as "different interpreters of the Same Manifest." This presentation of diversity as encompassed by unity is alleged to be the basis for instilling "the feeling that 'We are one,' 'Bharat Mata is our mother'" (p. iii). The ideology of

Hindu nationalism as expounded by Savarkar and the VHP creates a composite religious and national identity. It figures loyalty to the nation in terms of devotion to and sacrifice for one's sacred motherland. The temple guidebook asserts that "religion and nationhood should be complementary to each other. Religion motivates culture while nationhood evokes sacrifice for one's religious identity. Nothing of lasting value can be achieved without this sense of self-sacrifice and dedication. The welfare of our nation demands sublimation of our individualistic drives and the creation of a true spirit of humanism and brotherhood" (p. iv).

The Bhārat Mātā temple also furnishes a means for teaching a particular conception of Indian history, even though so numerous have been the contributors to the "many millennia of our history" that it is impossible to include all of them in a single temple. Regarding the principles informing the selection of personages who have "created our unique, intransient civilization," the text offers an ambiguous explanation: "to apply a criteria [*sic*] of selection would defeat the aim. Bharat Mata Mandir is just a humble effort at highlighting some important epochs in our social history that may encourage further research" (p. iv). Despite the guidebook's claim, my subsequent research suggests that the figures included in the Bhārat Mātā temple were carefully selected according to specific principles, primarily relating to the themes that structure the Hindu nationalism of the VHP, as prefigured in Savarkar's militant teachings. These principles do not, however, pertain exclusively to Hindu nationalism; there is some overlap with other forms of Indian nationalism.

The deities represented in the temple are the VIPs of the Hindu pantheon. Some are worshiped throughout India; others are the leading deities of particular regions, who are worshiped at major pilgrimage centers. The Hindu nationalist tenet asserting that Sanātanīs, Jains, Buddhists, Ārya Samājīs, and Sikhs are all Hindus is enshrined in the level of the temple that is specifically dedicated to saints and religious teachers. But before examining in detail the contents of the temple, let us look at the next section of the guidebook, where Satyamitranand further explains the temple's purpose. This explanation is framed by a narrative that charts Satyamitranand's entire achievement—from the temple's conception through to its construction and consecration. The narrative also provides an occasion for Satyamitranand to set forth and apply principles of Hindu nationalism.

BHĀRAT MĀHĀTMYA: THE LAND OF DIVINE REVELATIONS AND SPIRITUAL GLORY

Satyamitranand praises the glory of Bhārat Mātā and the holy soil of the motherland. The incarnations in Bhārat of Śiva, Krishna, Rāma, and all the gods of heaven, as well as the presence of saints and religious teachers, have consecrated the soil of Bhārat. The ideals and values they embodied and taught have created the culture and nation of Bhārat; their presence has "divinised this land." Satyamitranand celebrates the preeminence of spirituality in the holy land of Bhārat, holding the most important feature of Bhārat's "matchless and prodigious" soil to be its capacity to nurture the spiritual. "The unique, singular feature of this holy land of India is that it fosters and sustains spiritual life: it is the land leading in the world for yoga and ecstasy. The august tree of spiritualism grows and thrives on this land, through its branches and subbranches and spreads far and wide and bestows gentle peace and sweet transcendence to us all who absorb it." Like Vivekananda, Aurobindo, Tagore, Mahatma Gandhi, and others, Satyamitranand contrasts Bhārat's spirituality with the rampant materialism of Europe and America. Bhārat's reputation is such that "for the quest of the saffron of spiritualism the entire universe is drawn to the sacred soil of Bharat. There is no equal to it" (p. 3).

Bhārat Mātā may be the divine embodiment of Bhārat's holy soil, but like a Hindu woman, her identity is defined in reference to a male: "As I ponder over the format and facet of Bharat Mata I fancy that total aspect of her is symbolized in Lord Shankara." Satyamitranand envisions Śaṅkara (Śiva) as the "Supreme Lord—the Lord of Lords" and as the "characterization of our nationhood" (p. 1). Satyamitranand equates "our nationhood" with Śiva's status as the supreme overlord, an equation that embeds within the concept of nation the ideals of Hindu militancy and ascetic discipline. The menacing trident and the sacred syllable *oṃ*, more recently deployed by the VHP, have long been emblems of Śiva, the "Supreme Lord," whose asceticism augments his already awesome powers. Furthermore, the concept of Śiva as "Lord of Lords" also suggests the political ambitions of militant Hindu nationalists: to gain control of the Indian state. Hindu nationalists use symbol, ritual, and discourse to forge innumerable links among culture, politics, religion, and nation. In his discussion of nation and culture Satyamitranand does not use the term *Hindu*; he uses either *Bhārat* or *India*. However, he not only equates the nation with a Hindu god and goddess but also pronounces that "the culture flowing through her is portrayed in the life of Lord Rama. It is difficult to conceive of a culture in the absence of nationhood while the absence of culture cannot give entity to nationhood. Thus we need both: Lord Shankara as the manifestation of our nationhood and the modesty and adeptness as personified by Lord Rama" (p. 1).

Rāma is widely revered by Hindus as the divine embodiment of dhamra—he is duty incarnate. For Satyamitranand, however, Rāma is culture incarnate; he provides the model for proper social and religious conduct. Just as both the VHP and Satyamitranand represent themselves as being concerned with social problems, so is Rāma portrayed. Had he not been exiled from Ayodhya, "he would have forgone personal experience of the problems of the multitude in India" (p. 8). Even "without rolling in the Indian soil" Rāma could have achieved "his goal of social uplift" (pp. 3–4). However, Rāma chose to "flounder" in Bhārat's soil as a child and to traverse it during his exile in order "to inspire the future generations in the piety of the soil of Mother India" and to "set standards and norms of socio-moral intelligence" (p. 9). The text implies that by emulating Rāma's self-sacrificing adherence to dharma, that is, his deference to all figures of patriarchal authority—his father the king, his Brahmin gurus and priests—Indian society will be able to achieve "social uplift" and solve its problems. Through his exemplary actions and his blessings, Rāma "gives contentment to one and all." While Śiva symbolizes nationhood and Rāma is the manifestation of ideal culture, Satyamitranand further names Krishna as the "'persona-grata' of such idealised personality" and proclaims that these three male Hindu deities represent the totality of Indian culture: "Thus, the total panorama of Indian culture would appear to be a synthesis of the personalities of Lord Rama, Lord Krishna, and Lord Shankara" (p. 9).

According to Satyamitranand, Indian culture owes its idealism to Hindu gods and its continuity to saints and ascetics. Through their divinely inspired knowledge and their travels throughout Bhārat and the world, Hindu saints interpret scriptures and propagate the principles of Indian culture. Satyamitranand extols sainthood, which he defines as "piety coupled with strict self-discipline," as constituting the eternal roots of both culture and nation. It has "penetrated the heart-centre of our nation and planted the imperishable Banyan tree (like the one on the River Ganges at Prayag) of our culture" (p. 2). Shankaracharya and Vivekananda receive special attention in Satyamitranand's discussion of saints. They are revered for their teachings on, and achievement of, self-realization and for founding monastic institutions. Satyamitranand belongs to the ascetic order founded by Shankaracharya, and his depiction of him suggests a venerable progenitor for the VHP's mission to unify Hindu society and codify Hindu rituals and beliefs. Shankaracharya's mission was to "synthesize and unite the strands of ethos and logos of our worship"; he traveled throughout India conducting religious discussions and disputations, which enabled him to "scrutinize, collate and authenticate our theology" (p. 9). In order to propagate his teachings, he established four ascetic orders, one each in the north, south, east, and west of India.

Satyamitranand introduces several other religious teachers, devotees, and saints—all of whom are declared to be ubiquitous in the holy land of Bhārat. Whenever dharma grew weak, saints stepped in to strengthen tradition and "thus rejuvenated and rescued our culture in times of peril." When despair brought desolation to human hearts, the Krishna devotionalism taught by Caitanya brought hope to the masses. On other occasions, when "Indian life was dissipated" on account of "foreign invasions, laxity, indifference and internal quibbles," Gyaneshwara, Namdev, and Shahjobai "rescued our society and re-established its splendour and tradition" (p. 10). Like Savarkar, Satyamitranand reserves a special place for Rāmdās, guru of the Maratha warrior Shivaji. His passage concerning Rāmdās echoes Savarkar's paean to the guru, who, like Krishna in the *Bhagavad Gītā,* inspired his disciple to do battle. It also encodes within it Savarkar's claim that the Hindu nation owes its continued existence to Maratha warriors and that Hindus should emulate Maratha militarism and heroism: "At another time in our history when physical exertion and inaction had demoralised our nationhood, our able Guru Ramdas preached chivalry, competence and confidence to his great disciple Shivaji Maharaj, who rose to the occasion, obtained the blessings of Mother Bhavani and became the saviour of our culture and inspired gallantry among his compatriots" (p. 10).

From among the many saints who have contributed to the continuity of Indian society and culture, however, Satyamitranand singles out Swami Vivekananda as representative of all saints. He highlights the same qualities and achievements of Vivekananda that his own disciples attribute to him, particularly his popularity both in India and abroad for dynamic and persuasive speeches that express a modern approach and pride in his Indian heritage. Satyamitranand praises Vivekananda's message of fearlessness and strength: "India needed 'muscles of iron,' 'nerves of steel' and a 'gigantic will'" (p. 11). This imagery connotes the political goals of Hindu nationalism: militarization, industrialization, and a centralized, authoritarian state.

Having detailed the reasons for building the Bhārat Mātā temple, Satyamitranand summarizes them in the final section, "A Moment of Volition." Readers once again hear Satyamitranand thinking aloud, as he wonders if all these marvelous aspects of Bhārat Mātā would remain buried in history books. Next, he asks how they could be "meaningfully projected in some monumental form that can inspire the odinnary [*sic*] man of India and enrich and uplift his life," before concluding on a practical note: "If the total aspect of the excellence of Bharat Mata can be capitalised in one place to enable recapitulation of its glorious past, it could serve as an impartial motivation conducive to the future prosperity of the nation. Is this not obligatory?" (p. 11). Satyamitranand recalls having speculated that Lord Brahmā may have erred in giving him, a poor ascetic, the mission of building the Bhārat Mātā temple. He accepted the responsibility, however, and attributes its fulfillment to divine will. Indeed, he proved himself skillful in raising money for building this monumental structure that provides a means to enshrine and popularize Hindu nationalism. But the Bhārat Mātā temple is also a means to solicit monetary donations that fund other organizations and campaigns led by Satyamitranand and his allies in the VHP and elsewhere.

A COVETED STATUS OF NATIONAL SIGNIFICANCE

The guidebook describes the Bhārat Mātā temple as unique, "a pioneer in its field," a "marvel of engineering skill" that has "acquired a coveted status of national significance" because it is a shrine designed to "spread a message of universal harmony and brotherhood" in a country with a variety of religions and languages (p. 13). From its 180-foot summit visitors gaze down on Hardwar and the temple's lofty golden dome can be seen from afar.

Entering the temple, visitors are greeted by a statue of Bhārat Mātā (see figure 23). Thus can "the sons and daughters of Bharat Mata get a glimpse—Darshan—of the Mother whose love flows to her subjects in abundance" (p. 14). The inspiration for the Bhārat Mātā statue is attributed to Bankim Chandra Chatterjee's poem "Bande Mātaram." The guidebook links Bhārat Mātā to the freedom struggle by explaining that Bankim visualized her during the movement for independence from British rule. Although the statue could not include all the nuances and details expressed in "Bande Mātaram," it manifests them in an abbreviated form. Bhārat Mātā holds a milk urn in one hand and sheaves of grain in her other hand and is accordingly described as "signifying the white and green revolution that India needs for progress and prosperity" (p. 13). But the milk urn suggests other chains of significations that the text does not discuss—cows, the cow protection movement, gifts to Brahmins—as well as recalling ritual vessels like the ones filled with Ganga water that were worshiped and sold during the VHP's Sacrifice for Unity. A sign in Hindi and English identifies the statue as Bhārat Mātā. Below that is another sign evocative of the Indian flag: black letters on a white background, with a green and orange border. The Hindi script reads, "Vande Bhārat Mātaram" ("Praise to Mother India"). At the front point of the triangular pedestal is the symbol *oṃ*, in orange. Large brass oil lamps burn on either side of the statue. The shrine also incorporates Tantric elements of goddess worship by including a *yantra*, an abstract geometric icon of the goddess. On the wall behind the statue "the mighty Bharat Mata Yantra is installed to give her power and glory" (p. 13).

Like another *yantra*, a large map of India is mounted on a raised platform located in the center of this ground-floor shrine. On it are marked mountains and rivers, major centers of Hindu pilgrimage, and "all important centres of culture" (p. 13). The map thus represents the political boundaries of the Indian state while inscribing its topographic features in terms of Hindu cosmography. Besides the statue of Bhārat Mātā and the map of India, upon entering the temple visitors also see large color photographs of Satyamitranand, Indira Gandhi, the Shankaracharya of Dvaraka, and others who

Figure 23. Postcard of the Bhārat Mātā statue located on the entry level of the Bhārat Mātā temple.

participated in the temple's consecration ceremonies. The next three floors above the entry level contain shrines dedicated to the nation's heroes, *satīs*, and religious teachers:

> The stalwarts in any nation can be categorised as: the heroes on the battle front; the noble women of character at home; and the philosophers who have given ideas and set ideals. By the grace of the LORD, our culture is endowed with in-

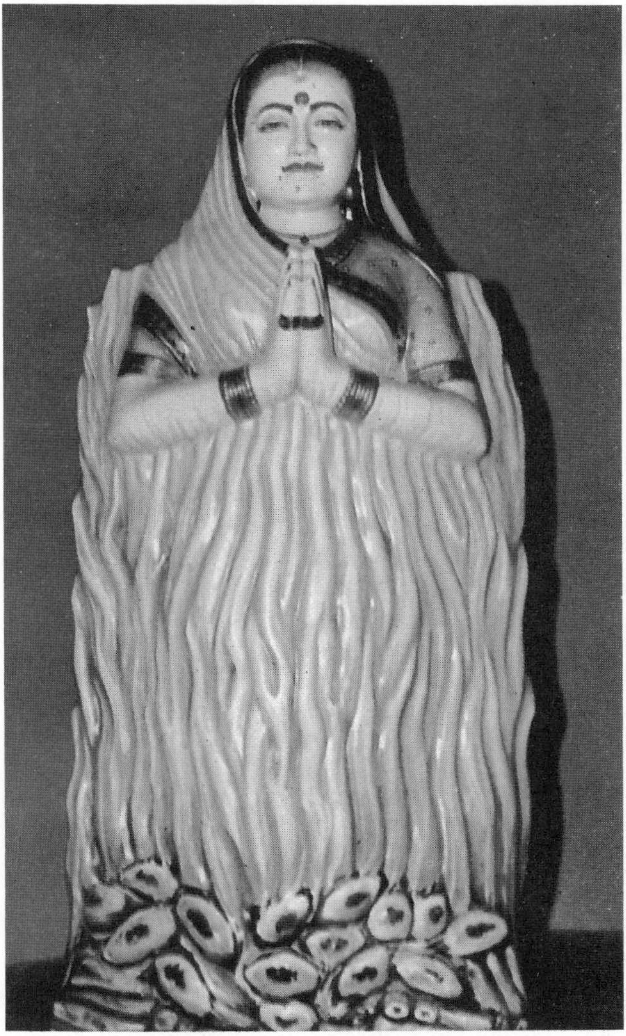

Figure 24. Postcard of Satī Padminī, one of the two statues of women in flames located in the Satī shrine at the Bhārat Mātā temple.

numberable [*sic*] brave gallantry (SHOOR), chaste womanhood (SATEE) and pious Acharyas and pious Saints (SANT). This is true not only for our past history but also for the present generation. It is hoped that the visitors to the Shrine will be able to pay their respects to them under one roof, and get inspiration from them for their own life. (p. 14)

As the guidebook further explains, although it may seem as if the temple includes too many manifestations of deities and heroes, holy men and women, each floor of the temple was consecrated by the Shankaracharya of Dvaraka and constitutes an autonomous shrine.

The Shrine of Heroes occupies the second level. Like the shrines on four other floors, it consists of a large room with statues in display cases lining three walls. The fourth side opens onto a veranda and views of the Ganges. Signs in Hindi and English identifying the figures are propped against the bases of the statues. Bhārat's forebears are worshiped in this shrine for the sacrifices they made to defend the sacred motherland and the Hindu religion: "The first floor is dedicated to the sacred memory of our valiant ancestors, bold and gallant sons and daughters of Bharat Mata, who sacrificed their lives for the patriotic cause of protecting the Sanatan Dharma and the glory of the Motherland" (p. 14). Satyamitranand and his associates selected a dozen personages to include in this shrine: Madan Mohan Malaviya, Veer Savarkar, Subhas Chandra Bose, Mahatma Gandhi, Maharana Pratap, Chatrapati Shivaji, Guru Govind Singh, the Rani of Jhansi, Shaheed Bhagat Singh, Chandra Shekhar Azad, Hemu Kalani, and Asphak Ulla.

The selection of these figures is consistent with the lineage of Hindu nationalists that Satyamitranand and the VHP have constructed for themselves. This lineage draws upon those whom Savarkar celebrated as defenders of the Hindu nation—Maharana Pratap, Shivaji, Guru Govind Singh, and the Rani of Jhansi. Mounted upon her horse with baby swaddled on her back, the Rani of Jhansi raises her sword with one hand, holding the reins and her shield in the other. Both her clothing and her horse's caparison are green and orange, the colors of the Indian flag. During Satyamitranand's visit to Bardoli, in Rajasthan, local notables described him as combining the qualities of two great men who had previously visited the city: Subhas Chandra Bose and Mahatma Gandhi. These two heroes of the independence movement are installed in the Bhārat Mātā temple as representatives of militarism and nonviolent noncooperation, respectively. Pandit Malaviya—the founder of Banaras Hindu University, a Hindu political leader, and an organizer of Brahmin priests in Hindu pilgrimage centers—is enshrined among these protectors of *sanātan* (eternal) dharma. Savarkar also stands with these national stalwarts, these "heroes on the battle front," whereas Nehru is conspicuously absent in this configuration of India's lineage of freedom fighters.

The floor above the Shrine of Heroes houses the Satī Shrine, which the guidebook describes as "dedicated to the glory of Indian Womenhood from Vedic times to the present era, symbolizing the chastity, loyalty and dedication of Indian wedlock" (p. 15). A Sanskrit verse extoling the virtues of women is presented as evidence of the "sense of respect and reverence shown to our women," the guidebook arguing that such evidence refutes the opinion of those who think women are oppressed in Indian society. This assertion belongs to the discourse upholding the high status of women in traditional Hindu society. Still pervasive today, this discourse perpetuates the apologetics of conservative, upper-caste Hindu men who were responding to critiques made by the British and by Hindu social reformers, critiques often directed against the practice of *satī*.[24] The critiques, like the practice and worship of *satī*, continue to this day. Hardwar is believed to be the site where the goddess Satī avenged her father's insult to her husband, Śiva, by jumping into the sacrificial fire, and two of the twelve "beautiful manifestations" in the Satī Shrine show a woman engulfed in flames. Satī Padminī, a Rajput queen, is celebrated for leading the women of Chitor to kill themselves after their husbands were defeated in battle by a Mughal army (see figure 24). With flames rising out of the wood and up to her shoulders, Satī Padminī's half-open eyes and beatific smile make her look as if she is in a blissful trance. Her hands are pressed together in a gesture that suggests she is respectfully fulfilling her duty and politely greeting those who come for her *darśan*. Flames are etched upon her fair forearms, making her glass bangles glow.

Besides its two graphic symbols of the "chastity, loyalty and dedication of Indian wedlock," the Satī Shrine includes wives of sages and other women who are exemplars of wifely virtue. Continuing the clockwise circuit of the statues, the visitor reaches the last *satī*, a figure who looks incongruous amidst the finery and glory of Indian womanhood. In a plain white dress, suggestive of a widow rather than an auspicious Hindu wife, stands Annie Besant. She stares severely and clutches a book in one arm; on her feet are heavy, sensible shoes. Her inclusion in the Satī Shrine can be interpreted in various ways. Annie Besant was a leading figure during the early days of the Congress Party and the independence movement; she supported the campaign for a Hindu University and praised the spiritual riches of Hindu civilization. For visitors less familiar with the specifics of Annie Besant's career in India, however, her presence might signify that even Western women aspire to the status of Hindu *satī*.

Above the Shrines of Heroes and Satīs is the Shrine of Saints, which consecrates a national lineage of religious teachers. Discussing this shrine, the guidebook reiterates the belief that sainthood is central to Indian culture:

> In a world of luxury, lust and power, Indian culture has upheld the ideals of Sainthood. This floor is dedicated to our great philosophers and Saints, who have infused unity in us, who have rejuvenated us; through love, devotion and knowledge they gave us inspiration, through captivating speeches they enriched our culture, through pious, austere life they set norms for our way of life. (p. 15)

Twenty-four statues crowd the shrine, so as to include the founders and teachers associated with all major Hindu sects and ascetic orders. Figures associated with other religious groups—Sikh, Jain, Buddhist—that are embraced by the VHP's conception of "Hindu" are also displayed here. The

Figure 25. Postcard of Bhagwan Shankar (Śiva) as he appears in the Mount Kailāsa shrine on the top floor of the Bhārat Mātā temple.

saints worshiped in this shrine are: Valmiki and Tulsidas, Rāma's inspired devotees; the Buddha; the Jain saint Mahavir; Nanak, the first guru of the Sikhs; Chaitanya, the Bengali devotee of Krishna; and Ramdas, the guru of Shivaji. Also housed in the Shrine of Saints are the great religious philosophers of the south—the "miniature incarnations" of Indian culture: the original Shankaracharya, along with Ramanujacharya, Nimbarkacharya, Vallabhacharya, and Madhvacharya. Other saintly religious teachers depicted are Udasin Acharya Chandraji, Rang Avdoot, Garibdas, Raskhan, Hirjibapa, Narasingh Mehta, Gyaneshvara, and Shirdi Sai Baba (who perhaps doubles as a reference to the currently popular Sathya Sai Baba). Notably, all three members of the triad associated with the Ramakrishna Mission are also present: its founder Vivekananda and his guru Ramakrishna, together with Ramakrishna's wife and disciple, Sharada Ma—who is the only woman included in this assembly of spiritual teachers. Nearby stands the statue of Aurobindo, the anti-British revolutionary who later retired from active participation in politics to devote himself to spiritual pursuits at his ashram in Pondicherry. Finally, the alliance between the Arya Samaj and the VHP earns a place in the Shrine of Saints for Swami Dayananda Saraswati, the man who founded the Arya Samaj and propounded the supremacy of Vedic knowledge.

Although not formally a shrine, the Assembly Hall on the next floor gives visual expression to tenets of Indian and Hindu nationalism that celebrate the unity of all religions and the unified diversity of the peoples and cultures of Bhārat. Painted on the walls are "important Dharma Sutras from all the religions of India: Hindu, Muslim, Christian, Parsee, Sikh, Jain, Buddha." Just as the VHP presents the cooperation of Hindus, Christians, and Muslims in the Sacrifice for Unity as evidence of the unity underlying all religions, so the guidebook describes the quotations inscribed in the Assembly Hall as "illustrating the brotherhood of man in a world of many beliefs and '-isms'" (p. 16). In addition to the passages from scriptures, the Hall is also decorated with a series of paintings, each labeled with the name of an Indian state and depicting landscapes, temples, facial types, and clothing associated with that state. Modern technology is also recruited to the cause of national unity: the guidebook promises the imminent installation of an electronic computer that will answer question of cultural interest—although two years after the guidebook's publication, the computer had not yet arrived.

Above the Assembly Hall is the Śakti Shrine, dedicated to various forms of the goddess. Its thirteen statues of the "divine mother" are described as "the embodiment of spiritual and moral strength, the triumph of Truth over evil" (p. 16). The guidebook refers to the *Markandeya Purāṇa*'s enumeration of Durgā's nine "invincible" manifestations, and each is represented in the Śakti Shrine as a form taken by Durgā in order to slay a particular beastly foe. As noted earlier, the VHP is also partial to Durgā: the cover of *Ekātmatā Yajña* (the commemorative book celebrating the Sacrifice for Unity) shows Durgā leaning on her lion, the orange Hindu flag in her hand. Bhārat Mātā embodies the power of the divine mother to bestow prosperity, whereas the iconography of Durgā emphasizes her power to vanquish enemies. In addition to the nine forms of Durgā, the Śakti Shrine also presents Sarasvatī, the goddess of knowledge and music, and Ved Mātā Gayatrī, the divine form of the sacred mantra. Two further forms of *śakti* are figured in the shrine, which the guidebook associates with specific regions of India: Jagadambā of Gujarat and Meenakshi (Mīnākṣī) of South India. Of the many popular regional forms of the goddess, Jagadambā may have been selected because Satyamitranand's Gujarati followers, both in India and abroad, contributed money for the temple's construction, while Meenakshi, the fish-eyed goddess worshiped at the prosperous Madurai temple in Tamil Nadu, may have been included in the shrine as a tribute to Hindus of South India.

Enshrined in the seventh and penultimate level of the Bhārat Mātā temple are nine forms of Viṣṇu. The guidebook describes these incarnations of Viṣṇu as symbolizing "Devotion (Bhakti) with Domination," as well as providing a Sanskrit quote that emphasizes Viṣṇu in his form as "Destruction to Wrongdoers" (p. 17). By highlighting Viṣṇu's punitive powers, the guidebook affirms the duty and moral authority of righteous rulers to subjugate those whom it names as enemies of Hindu dharma. The shrine displays incarnations of Viṣṇu that are popular throughout India: Sītā-Rāma, Lakṣmī-Nārāyaṇa, Rādhā-Krishna. It also displays incarnations that have important but more regional followings: Dattatreya, Śrī Nāthjī, Ranchod Rāijī, Veṅkateśvara, Akṣara Puruṣottama, and Viṭṭhala-Rukmiṇī.

Visitors must climb stairs to reach the summit of the Bhārat Mātā temple, where Mount Kailāsa, the abode of Śiva, is depicted. Describing this topmost level, the guidebook states: "The massive Sanctum Sanctorum of this floor presents a wonderful view of Mount Kailas. In the center, under the huge dome, Lord Shiva is seated deep in meditation, a Maha Yogi." With its glittering white plaster crags, the sanctum's mountainous scene resembles a stage set. Several statues of Śiva, representing his different aspects, populate the pinnacle. The central, dominant statue (see figure 25) shows Śiva in solitary meditation, the form in which "he glorifies renunciation and asceticism: the qualities adored and adopted by seekers after Truth in India" (p. 17). He wears, and is seated upon, animal skins. Cobras are entwined around his silver body, while another cobra rises out of the matted locks coiled on top of his head. The glistening cascade of the descending Ganges flows through his hair. Stuck in the ground next to Śiva is his trident, from which hangs the drum on which he beats his terrifying rhythms.

Behind the solitary meditating Śiva, viewers see him in a family portrait, in which he sits with Pāvatī and his elephant-headed son, Gaṇeśa. In the wings of the shrine stand two other forms of Śiva, one of which shows him as an androgyne, "an idealization of Purusha and Prakriti or Shiva and Shakti in one moorti [image]" (p. 18). Satyamitranand had earlier asserted his vision of Śiva, the Supreme Lord, as symbolizing the whole of Bhārat Mātā. Here, Śiva's representation as half woman provides an iconic referent for his capacity to symbolize this totality. The fourth statue of Śiva shows him in his well-known form as Naṭarājā, the Lord of Dance, in which, surrounded by a circle of fire, he dances destruction upon the body of Māyā (illusion). The guidebook extols the statue maker's genius in making a "unique piece of art" that "concurs beautifully with the notion of perpetual motion as investigated by modern science" (p. 18).

The guidebook repeatedly assures readers that the statues in the Bhārat Mātā temple have been consecrated and are worshiped with the proper rituals. However, unlike visitors to other temples, who bring food, cloth, and other goods as ritual presentations to the deity, visitors to the Bhārat Mātā temple arrive empty-handed. There is no bell to ring to announce one's presence; no priest awaits devotees to accept their offerings and give them *prasād*. With its statues in glass display cases, all dutifully labeled, the temple seems more like a museum of Hindu nationalism than a living Hindu temple. However, as is common in temples and ashrams, here, too, visitors are encouraged to donate money. A temple attendant ritualizes the act of donating money by marking donors' foreheads with red powder—a practice not only common in many temples but appropriate in other ritual settings—and by issuing receipts.

The guidebook's discussion of how donations to the temple are used echoes the pronouncements of both Satyamitranand and the VHP regarding their support for charitable projects that further national unity:

> It is our resolve to utilise all gifts and endowments received at the shrine towards the further service of our Vanavasi Brethren—the forest and hill dwellers, and the Harijans [Untouchables]. Along with this, a portion of this endowment will be utilised for the education of Brahmin youth in proper Vedic rites, rituals and research. We earnestly hope that in this way Bharat Mata Mandir can contribute to the socio-economic needs of our nation. (p. iv)

The training of Brahmins as Vedic ritualists and scholars, like "service" to tribals and untouchables, are heralded as ways in which the Bhārat Mātā temple uses its income to further the cause of strengthening the nation. Such activities are similarly undertaken, and similarly portrayed, by the VHP and by Satyamitranand.

ŚAKTI EX MACHINA

The Bhārat Mātā temple, which houses multiple elements of Hindu nationalism, purveys to its visitors a particular configuration of national identity in accordance with its vision of India's unified culture and religion. The temple encourages visitors to imagine their identities as devoted sons and daughters of Bhārat Mātā, to be edified and inspired by the ideals and the deeds of their heroic and saintly forebears, and to prove their devotion by dedicating themselves as "matriots" to the defense of the holy motherland. Visitors to the Bhārat Mātā temple are enjoined to "depart with the noble concept that we all belong to One Family" (p. iv). The Bhārat Mātā temple, like the All-India Sacrifice for Unity and the campaign to destroy the Babri Mosque and build the Rāma temple in its place in Ayodhya, are both ends and means. They function as sites for the production and dissemination of national identity and cultural forms. They furnish a means for raising money, as well as for attracting official and popular support for the Hindu nationalist movement. Although movements to establish a Hindu state in India have waxed and waned for nearly a century, events surrounding the destruction of the Babri Mosque suggest that the Hindu nationalist movement's political power, financial backing, and respectability among upper- and middle-class Hindus has never been greater. Its successes relate to complex dynamics associated with domestic and transnational political economy and the religocultural politics of nationalism.

Following the demolition of the Babri Mosque in December, 1992, Muslims in Pakistan and Bangladesh retaliated by attacking Indian consulates, businesses, and Hindu temples. Governments of Arab countries condemned the mosque's destruction, while in Britain news about Ayodhya prompted firebombings of Hindu temples and cultural centers, in addition to a mosque and a Sikh *gurdwārā*. South Asian leaders feared that white racists would use this violent incident as an opportunity for further attacks on people of color. In New York, Black Muslims protested outside the United Nations. In Dakha, twenty thousand people gathered to march to Ayodhya and rebuild the mosque, although the Bangladeshi government announced that it would stop the march at the border. The various international responses to the destruction of the mosque indicate that the politics of Hindu nationalism is not bounded by India's borders. The Bangladeshi government may be able to prohibit protesters from crossing into India, but no single government can halt transnational flows of money and support to Hindu nationalist groups, or to their opponents.

The strategies behind struggles for power involve the use of cultural media to inculcate specific subjectivities and sensibilities; they also involve organizational secrecy and dissimulation. In the case of India, strategic deception makes it difficult for researchers and the public—and perhaps even the government—to obtain information about the Hindu nationalist movement's covert activities and sources of support. The movement's ability to organize networks of leaders and followers at local, national, and international levels is, however, apparent. Related to this ability is the movement's use of diverse media—television and radio, tapes and videocassettes, mass rallies and festivals, pilgrimage, and rituals—to promulgate its ideology, as well as to raise money and attract supporters.[25]

The most militant members of the Hindu nationalist movement consider their ultimate goal to be the transformation of India into a Hindu state, whereas less militant Hindu nationalists emphasize the "protection" of the interests of a dominant Hindu majority within the framework of a secular state. It is difficult to know how many Hindu nationalists fit the former description and how many the latter, since to maintain its international respectability the movement's publicists often mask, or even deny, the desire to create a Hindu state. Rather, they define Hindu nationalism in cultural terms and distance it from politics. Yet the range of identities and emotions that the Hindu nationalist movement both constructs and imparts remains inextricable from the ideology propounded by the militants who destroyed the Babri Mosque and who have targeted two thousand other mosques for destruction. The cult of Bhārat Mātā, in combination with militant matriotism, assists the Hindu nationalist movement by positing a dire dilemma. It proposes that Hindus must either fight for the cause of Hindu unity, a fight that should culminate in the establishment of a Hindu nation-state, or else suffer the demise, defeat, and extinction of the Hindu people.

NOTES

1. See Sudhir Kakar, "When Saffron Speaks," *Sunday Times of India,* 19 July 1992.

2. Quoted in *ibid.*

3. See Partha Chatterjee, *Nationalist Thought and the Colonial World* (Delhi: Oxford University Press, 1986), and "The Nationalist Resolution of the Women's Question," in *Recasting Women: Essays in Indian Colonial History,* ed. Kumkum Sangari and Sudesh Vaid (New Brunswick, N.J.: Rutgers University Press, 1990), pp. 233–53.

4. See Achin Vanaik, *The Painful Transition: Bourgeois Democracy in India* (London: Verso, 1990). For further discussion, see Richard G. Fox, introduction and "Hindu Nationalism in the Making, or the Rise of the Hindian," both in *Nationalist Ideologies and the Production of National Cultures,* ed. Richard G. Fox (Washington, D.C.: American Ethnological Society, 1990), pp. 1–14 and 63–80. See also Lise McKean, *Divine Enterprise: Gurus and the Hindu Nationalist Movement* (Chicago: University of Chicago Press, 1996).

5. See especially the essays collected in *Recasting Women,* ed. Sangari and Vaid.

6. Kumkum Sangari and Sudesh Vaid, "Recasting Women: An Introduction," in ibid., pp. 10, 2.

7. See Uma Chakravarti, "Whatever Happened to the Vedic *Dasi*?" in ibid., pp. 27–87, esp. pp. 62–64.

8. Basanta Koomar Roy, translator's introduction, in Bankim Chandra Chatterjee, *Ānandamaṭh* (1941; repr. New Delhi: Vision Books, 1992), pp. 13–20, at p. 18.

9. Ibid., p. 13.

10. Ibid.

11. Chatterjee, *Ānandamaṭh,* trans. Roy, p. 43.

12. Ibid., p. 63.

13. V. D. Savarkar, *Hindu Rashtra Darshan,* vol. 6 of *Samagra Savarkar Wangmaya* (*Writings of Swatantrya Veer V. D. Savarkar*) (Poona: Maharashtra Prantik Hindusabha, 1964), p. 74.

14. Vishva Hindu Parishad, *Ekātmatā Yajña*, ed. Ramashankar Agnihotri and Dattatreya Tiwari (New Delhi: Vishva Hindu Parishad, n.d.), pp. 13–14. Page references to this volume will hereafter be given in the text.

15. The English guidebook is Samanvaya Sewa Trust, *Bharat Mata Mandir: A Candid Appraisal* (Hardwar: Samanvaya Publications, 1986); the Hindi is Swami Satyamitranand Giri, *Bhārat Mātā Mandir* (Hardwar: Samanvaya Publications, 1990).

16. See Krishnakant Chaturvedi and Brahmajeet Sharma, *Divyalok: Parivrājak kī Divya Yātrā* (Hardwar: Samanvaya Prakashan, 1986).

17. Vishva Hindu Parishad, *The Hindu Awakening: Retrospect and Promise* (New Delhi: Vishva Hindu Parishad, n.d.), pp. 7–8.

18. Vishva Hindu Parishad, *Vishva Hindu Parishad: Messages and Activities* (New Delhi: Vishva Hindu Parishad, n.d.).

19. Vishva Hindu Parishad, *Hindu Awakening,* p. 37.

20. Chaturvedi and Sharma, *Divyalok,* p. 22.

21. Ibid., p. 24.

22. Ibid., p. 26.

23. Samanvaya Sewa Trust, *Bharat Mata Mandir,* p. i. Page references to this volume will hereafter be given in the text.

24. See Chakravarti, "Whatever Happened to the Vedic *Dasi*?" and Lata Mani, "Contentious Traditions: The Debate on *Sati* in Colonial India," both in *Recasting Women,* ed. Sangari and Vaid, pp. 27–28 and 88–126.

25. See Tapan Basu et al., *Khaki Shorts and Saffron Flags* (New Delhi: Orient Longman, 1993). For a discussion of the use of audiocassettes by Hindu nationalists, see Peter Manuel, *Cassette Culture: Popular Music and Technology in North India* (Chicago: University of Chicago Press, 1993), pp. 236–56.

EPILOGUE
The Western Kālī

Rachel Fell McDermott

This . . . is . . . an invitation to all women to join in the search to find out who we really are, by beginning to know our past heritage as more than a broken and buried fragment of male culture.[1]

I believe that Hinduism does indeed contain a model and image that could be used to fit the needs of today's women, and that this model lies at the very heart of Hinduism itself. This image centers on the goddess Kali and her many manifestations. I also believe this image must be extricated from patriarchal interpretations and understandings that have clouded its essential meaning.[2]

The Hindu goddess Kālī is of great interest among a variety of modern thinkers and writers, who approach her from several perspectives. Ever since the mid-1970s, with the publication of David Kinsley's wonderfully accessible account of her history and interpretation, Kālī has increasingly become a subject of scholarly research among those who study Hindu religion and culture.[3] In addition, other writers and scholars have found Kālī an exciting figure for reflection and exploration, notably feminists and participants in New Age spirituality who are attracted to goddess worship. Although these two groups are by no means identical, a significant area of overlap occurs in literature written primarily for and about women's spirituality. Even a cursory investigation of the women's and New Age sections in bookstores reveals an astonishing recent upsurge of interest in goddesses of all types. One can buy books on the history of goddess spirituality, on goddesses from specific geographic regions, and on the empowerment and healing available, especially for women, through the active worship of a female deity. There are also reference works such as *The Concise Lexicon of the Occult* and *The New Age Dictionary* (both of which include entries on Kālī).[4] Books are not the only items for sale, however; one can also choose from a variety of calendars, almanacs, diaries, posters, greeting cards, bookmarks, Tarot card decks, and cassettes—all of which have the goddess as their main theme. As a spate of recent book reviews and newspaper articles indicates, such new materials and ideas are gradually capturing the attention of the media as well.[5]

Kālī does not play a very big part in this interest in goddess figures, as the majority of the goddesses discussed are of Greek and Roman origin. Nor do all the authors who write on Kālī hold identical viewpoints. But she is the most frequently cited Hindu goddess in books that go beyond the Greek and Roman materials, and for a few writers she is very important. The Kālī of many of these writers is, however, quite a different deity from the Kālī of Hindu India, and it is the purpose of this essay to attempt to ascertain exactly where the dissimilarities lie.

THE CONTEXT OF GODDESS WORSHIP

Women's spirituality is by no means coterminous with goddess spirituality, as a wide variety of approaches have been adopted by Western women who are sensitive to issues of gender within the context of religion. Some, for instance, choose to remain within their existing religious traditions, usually Jewish or Christian, and work to reform oppressive attitudes and linguistic usage. Among such women are those who want to neuterize or androgynize the language in which we speak of God, while others find it more appealing to introduce feminine terminology alongside the standard masculine forms. But in neither case is an anthropomorphic goddess attractive. Even among women who leave Western religious traditions behind entirely, the worship of goddess figures is not the only alternative; many women do not like anthropomorphism at all, whether the deity be male or female, preferring instead to think of the divine in terms of creative and destructive energy, or the affirmation of female beauty and power. As Carol P. Christ notes in her article "Why Women Need the Goddess," some women feel that the positing of a goddess "out there" is part of the patriarchal worldview that they are trying to expunge.[6]

There is also considerable diversity among women who do choose to find meaning and renewal from a goddess or goddesses. Some of the most controversial books of recent years, for instance, approach the topic of goddess spirituality from a historical or archaeological standpoint, searching for evidence of goddess worship in ancient cultures. Riane Eisler, Marija Gimbutas, Monica Sjöö and Barbara Mor, Charlene Spretnak, Starhawk, and Merlin Stone are a few of the more well-known authors in this arena, but many others are following suit.[7] The majority of such studies treat of European and Near Eastern history, although comparisons with non-Western cultures are also frequently made. Sometimes the argument for the existence of goddess-worshiping societies is linked with claims about their social structure: where women held power, goddesses reigned. In general, these studies are characterized by a search for a new historical understanding of

Western civilization and its origins; almost uniformly, the writers of these volumes use their findings to criticize and lament the destruction of goddess-centered cultures by patriarchal groups.

Aside from the historical and archaeological quest for goddess spirituality, there is also the psychological exploration of the meaning of the goddess in today's world. Authors who write from this vantage point seek less to prove historical facts than to establish the existence and usefulness of goddess archetypes in the process of psychological healing. Especially influential in this regard have been the works of Carl Jung, Robert Graves's *The White Goddess: A Historical Grammar of Poetic Myth* (1948), and Erich Neumann's *The Great Mother: An Analysis of the Archetype* (1955). Many feminists are critical of Carl Jung, citing a patriarchal bias in his discussion of feminine symbols.[8] Nonetheless, his insights into the mother archetype have made him a potent source of inspiration; many authors draw upon his ideas in one form or another in an attempt to integrate Jungian and feminist thinking.[9]

Still a third type of book on goddess spirituality, while it may draw upon the findings and theories of the historical and psychological works mentioned above, emphasizes instead the practical aspects of goddess worship. Here one finds an effort to formulate positive religious traditions for women through the use of rituals, meditations, affirmations, pictures, and exhortations to self-discovery. Whether the goddesses in question derive from the Greco-Roman tradition, from a living non-Western culture, or from an inner experience, they are seen as symbols of and models for women's empowerment.[10]

As one would expect, even from this very quick glance at the various perspectives on goddess spirituality, tremendous diversity exists in the literature. In general, the interest in goddesses is a popular phenomenon and has no leader or geographic center. Writers range from university scholars to religious practitioners, artists, novelists, and therapists, and they approach their material from the disciplines of history, anthropology, religion, art, psychology, and women's studies. Some are men; more are women. Most of the authors whose work informs this essay are American, Canadian, or European, although Indian views, where available, have also been incorporated. Just as varied as the personalities of the authors are the genres they employ: although the majority of sources are books and articles, equally if not more fascinating methods for conveying the meaning of goddess worship to women today can be found in an array of poems, interviews, artworks, songs, and rituals.

Given the wide spectrum of attitudes involved, attempts at generalization are bound to be inadequate and misleading. Moreover, the intellectual effort to categorize and classify has in recent years come under fire for its insensitivity to individual experience and for its reification of "the other."

Hence, an essay that self-consciously chooses to summarize a growing, creative body of literature on women's spirituality may, in its very conception, be a contradiction in terms.[11] In spite of, or in awareness of, these methodological snares, the question of Kālī still deserves exploration. How is she being depicted in such literature? And how might we understand the adoption of this Hindu goddess into a non-Indian setting?

KĀLĪ IN FEMINIST AND NEW AGE LITERATURE

Her Characteristics

The inclusion of Kālī in the expanding genre of works on goddess spirituality must be seen in the overall context of burgeoning interest in comparative religion among writers of all kinds. While it is true that several influential authors of the late nineteenth to early twentieth centuries, such as Tylor, Briffault, Bachofen, Jung, and Neumann, drew upon a vast array of data from around the world, only since the 1980s have the insights gleaned from this material been popularly applied in works on and for women.[12] Numerous books are now being published that act as compendia or encyclopedias of goddess and heroine lore, spanning either thousands of years within a single geographic area or encompassing numerous figures from many parts of the world.[13]

One result of this increased interest in a wide variety of goddesses is the tendency to compare and contrast, and particularly to see in similar figures the indication of common symbolic meaning. For example, Kālī is repeatedly compared with goddesses who are said to preside over love and war, or who are paradoxical, or who have a dangerous character. The two most frequently cited goddesses in this vein are the Sumerian Inanna and the Babylonian Ishtar. Others include the Egyptian Isis, the Anatolian Cybele, the pre-Hellenic Gorgon, Greek goddesses such as Hecate, Demeter, Artemis, Rhea, Aphrodite, Athene, and Astarte, Minerva of Rome, Anath of Syria, the Aztec Coatlicue, Morrigan and Cailleach from Ireland, the Hebrew Lilith and Shekinah, the Black Virgin, the American Indian Spider Woman, and a host of hags, harpies, furies, and wicked stepmothers.[14] Typically such comparisons are made on a psychological or symbolic level, but a few authors go further, positing historical connections and influences. The most striking instances of this interpretive approach come from Barbara G. Walker's many books; she claims that Indo-European linguistic roots account for many similar names and figures spread over large geographical areas. In her estimation, Finland's Kalma and Ireland's Cailleach derive from the same Sanskrit root as Kālī, and "the Greek Psyche, Roman Anima, Gnostic Sophia, and Cabalistic Shekina [are] all based on the Shakti" of Indian philosophy.[15] We will return to a consideration of this type of statement in the concluding section of this essay.

Several authors devote whole sections of their books, or whole poems, to Kālī. If one takes an overview of such material, there seems to be one characteristic of the goddess, as she is understood and portrayed in this literature, to which the writers give most importance. This is Kālī's nature as a union of opposites, as a paradoxical deity who combines within herself the poles of creation and destruction, birth and death, love and fear. This dual aspect of her character is implied by her epithet "Terrible Mother."

This emphasis on Kālī as a coincidence of opposites is understandable, given the feminist critique of attitudes that deny the earthier, more bodily and sexual side of existence. In 1983 there appeared an important article on this very point, by Rita M. Gross. In her often-quoted "Hindu Female Deities as a Resource for the Contemporary Rediscovery of the Goddess," she argues that there are six principal ways in which modern Western women's thinking and meditating on the goddess can be enriched by an understanding of Hindu beliefs and claims about their goddesses. These six characteristics are the bisexuality of deities in general, and the goddess's own strength and capability, her embodiment of polarities and opposites, her role as a mother, her universal range of activity, and her explicit sexuality. In her discussion of the third of these images, the coincidence of opposites, of which Kālī is her prime example, Gross writes that this type of symbolism is "exceedingly important in theistic imagery but . . . also seems to be very weak in current Western religious imagery." Moreover, "this is perhaps the area in which we most need help in re-imaging the goddess, since it seems unlikely that any of our present resources prompts us to develop this symbolism."[16] The fact that most of the feminist and New Age authors under review find Kālī's complexity and multiple polarities to be so significant points to the far-sightedness of Gross's remarks.

Kālī's typical iconography, in which the fearsomeness of her ornaments and her dance on the cremation ground are mitigated by her smiling face and signs of reassurance, offers a graphic illustration of the opposites she embodies, as most authors note—either verbally or by including drawings. Some take as representative, however, a rather unusual depiction of Kālī found in the India Museum, London, and reproduced by both Heinrich Zimmer and Erich Neumann.[17] This North Indian statue shows Kālī squatting on the inert body of a corpse, whose entrails she is devouring. Not surprisingly, relying upon such a singular portrayal of the goddess has led to overstatements concerning her destructive side (see figure 26). In an even more marked example of the same tendency, one author, although commenting on Kālī's usual depiction, interprets her two fearlessness- and boon-conferring hands to be malicious in intent: one hand is raised in a gesture of peace "to trick the unwary," while the other "forms a claw, ready to pinion its next victim."[18] Thus, even though what appeals to most writers is Kālī's ability to symbolize both the loving and the terrifying

Figure 26. "Kali: Queen of Swords," an illustration from the Barbara Walker tarot deck. Reproduced by permission of U.S. Games Systems, Inc., Stamford, Connecticut. Copyright 1986.

sides of life, the latter half of her character is often stressed at the expense of the former.

Kālī's multifaceted nature is also described through an allusion to the three phases of the moon, waxing, full, and waning, which are compared to the stages of a woman's life. These are said to be represented by the Virgin, the Mother, and the Crone—associated with white, red, and black colors, and with purity, maternity, and wisdom, respectively. Most of the feminists who use this imagery to describe Kālī state that, in her complexity, she incorporates all three phases. But occasionally she is said to epitomize just one—the Crone, or dark aspect.[19]

In choosing to depict Kālī as a deity of polarities and opposites, many authors are stating what they feel to be her true nature. In the opinions of most, this essential and intriguing attribute of Kālī has been forgotten or suppressed, in favor of a one-sided, usually fearsome portrayal. A pressing challenge to modern women is therefore to recover and reclaim this wholeness in Kālī, and hence in themselves. A brief glance at some feminist and New Age views of history and patriarchy will help to clarify this point.

Kālī in History

The description of Kālī as a paradoxical union of opposites frequently forms the basis for an alternative view of history and/or a critique of patriarchy. Many thinkers follow the lead of Bachofen and others in postulating several stages in the development of human history. According to this schema, at least by the early Neolithic period (eighth millennium B.C.E.) matriarchal societies, characterized by the worship of goddesses and the social elevation of women, were widespread. These were eventually subjugated, however, by patriarchal peoples, the progenitors of our present male-dominated cultures, who wrested power from women and tamed, or marginalized, their goddesses.[20] The link between goddess worship and women's status is often explicitly affirmed in this literature; as Paulette Boudreaux says, "it is important to remember that in ancient pre-historic times when people worshipped the Mother as Absolute, women were respected and revered as agents of the Great Mother on earth."[21]

Significant for the discussion of Kālī is the consequences that patriarchal attitudes had for the goddesses of early matriarchal societies. Like Kālī, such goddesses are typically stated to have been powerful agents of creation and destruction, who contained within themselves a balance of opposites. But patriarchal groups, fearing the female deities of the peoples they had conquered as embodiments and symbols of female energy, split apart what once was whole and demonized them. "Paradox is split into dualism, an act characteristic of patriarchal consciousness."[22] All demonic manifestations of these goddesses, including Kālī, therefore "developed from the religious and political domination of Goddess-worshipping cultures by the patriarchal invaders."[23]

Particular historical statements made in connection with Kālī generally begin with the pre-Aryan Dravidians and Harappans in India, who are said to have been goddess-worshiping matriarchal societies. They revered Kālī and other ancient female deities, who are said to date from Neolithic or prehistoric times, and their religiosity was Tantric in orientation. As soon as the Aryans arrived and conquered these peaceful peoples, however, the process of demonization was unleashed on the indigenous goddesses. The Aryans' male priesthood felt threatened by the feminine element, so powerfully portrayed in deities such as Kālī, and hence emphasized her dark, sexual aspects in an attempt to discourage people from her worship.[24] This development can also be regarded as a fragmentation of the goddess. Again, patriarchal thinking is directly responsible:

> She also has her benevolent aspect, but the functions became increasingly severed. . . . No doubt as men engaged more and more in wanton slaughter of their own kind for plunder and power, the more they needed to project this split in their own psyches onto the Goddess. The benevolent Kali becomes virtually a separate pale goddess, a passive mother, a sex partner without power. . . . The Bronze Age Kali is split into the Death Goddess, or the Sex Goddess, or the Mother Goddess—but no longer is she the one cosmic process containing all aspects and polarities.[25]

The Aryans demonized Kālī, it has been claimed, by naming the fourth and worst *yuga*, or era, after her (the Kali Yuga), by borrowing her supreme attributes to award to their own male gods, and by making their disparaging associations of her black color with low status.[26]

Although the majority of authors who treat of Kālī's origins and subsequent demonization do so from the historical perspective outlined above, some interesting twists to this argument can be found in the literature. For instance, a few writers prefer to discuss Kālī in terms of psychology, rather than history, arguing that the demonization occurred at the level of archetypes. "Although Kali has been distorted into a Terrible Mother archetype who devours or represents physical killing, she actually represents death of the ego and the regenerative power of the sexual mysteries."[27] Even more fascinating are two other variations on this theme. One author reverses the patriarchal process, saying that Kālī's *loving* side has been made to overshadow her deeper, more complex nature, while another claims that although the East has been able to maintain insight into the paradoxical union of opposites in its goddesses, it is the West that has split and demonized Kālī.[28]

Despite a minority view that champions the insights of Indians regarding the spiritual essence of their goddesses, most books and articles on women's spirituality present Hinduism as a religion of patriarchs and patriarchal attitudes. Kālī's fragmentation by such a religious ethos has not only misrepresented her; in addition, it has robbed women—Indian and non-Indian—of access to their own inherent wisdom and power.

Reclaiming Kālī's Wholeness

As a general phenomenon, goddess spirituality is attractive for women because it makes possible an affirmation of the female body, of women's anger and aggression, and of the changing cycles of life which menstruation and birth so readily illustrate.[29] The same is true of Kālī: the very characteristics that patriarchy repressed and demonized—her potent, sexual, dark side—can be claimed as liberating for women, within a context of wholeness and balance. Taking the cue from India, where Kālī's dual nature is still available to some degree, some feminists find the goddess and her coincidence of opposites to be a source of empowerment:

> The image of Kālī has become important in contemporary feminist consciousness in an attempt to recover imagery more compatible with the reality of female power, anger, and assertion. . . . Kālī's reminder of the dark, avenging side of life, and the power of rage, readied for action, poised against the contemporary backdrop of a plundered and wounded earth, is a vision of spiritually energizing female power far removed from the benevolent mercy and accepting patience of Lakṣmī or Mary.[30]

> This book, like all my work, is dedicated to the Dark Goddess, who has been rejected and demonized by patriarchal culture and lies dormant in all women. Her awakening is the source of energy and healing power, for us as individuals and for the planet.[31]

Kālī's relevance for modern women is not only part of an ongoing intellectual discussion, however. In two intriguing, albeit disparate, cases, therapists recount instances of personality transformations in patients to whom the Kālī archetype had become meaningful. Edward C. Whitmont tells the story of a mother who ended up in therapy with him because she wanted to kill her child. The goddess appeared to her in her dreams and helped her both to channel her aggression and to learn to nurture. In another case, recorded by Manuela Dunn Mascetti, a South Indian woman was jailed for killing her husband and three children with a kitchen knife, while thinking she was possessed by Kālī. The moral drawn for therapy is that while it is essential for adequate ego-functioning that aggression not be repressed, its release, or its activation as the Kālī archetype, can be dangerous—if eventually healing.[32]

Feminist poetry offers another indication that a recognition and reclamation of the dark side of Kālī can be beneficial for women on a personal level. Two striking examples are the poems of Suzanne Ironbiter and May Sarton, each of whom internalizes the symbolism of Kālī for the purpose of self-examination and healing. In *Devi,* the first half of which is Ironbiter's English version of the Sanskrit *Devī Māhātmya,* the poet herself takes the part of Durgā. In the third episode of the Sanskrit text, Kālī issues forth from Durgā's angry forehead in order to help her slay demons. Here is Ironbiter's rendering:

> I contract my brows in a frown. In the flat of my forehead
> a gaping grows with my scowl.
> Kali, my Blackness,
> steps from my head, from the cranial pit,
> great hole of my anger—Kali Karalavadana,
> my Blackness whose mouth is a hole, raw as a wound,

whose tongue is a cleaving sword,
and the world at her feet is a world drained of light,
gashed open and bleeding.[33]

A similar depiction of Kālī, though less anchored in the Hindu texts, is that by May Sarton. In "The Invocation to Kali," Sarton uses the goddess to represent that which she dreads yet must face and integrate:

The kingdom of Kali is within us deep.
The built-in destroyer, the savage goddess,
Wakes in the dark and takes away our sleep.
She moves through the blood to poison gentleness.

She keeps us from being what we long to be;
Tenderness withers under her iron laws.
We may hold her like a lunatic, but it is she
Held down, who bloodies with her claws.

How then to set her free or come to terms
With the volcano itself, the fierce power
Erupting injuries, shrieking alarms?
Kali among her skulls must have her hour.

It is time for the invocation, to atone
For what we fear most and have not dared to face:
Kali, the destroyer, cannot be overthrown;
We must stay, open-eyed, in the terrible place.

. . .

It is time for the invocation:

Kali, be with us.
Violence, destruction, receive our homage.
Help us bring darkness into the light,
To lift out the pain, the anger,
Where it can be seen for what it is—
The balance-wheel for our vulnerable, aching love.
Put the wild hunger where it belongs,
Within the act of creation,
Crude power that forges a balance
Between hate and love.

Help us to be the always hopeful
Gardeners of the spirit
Who know that without darkness
Nothing comes to birth
As without light
Nothing flowers.

Bear the roots in mind,
You, the dark one, Kali,
Awesome power.[34]

These poems and others like them provide vivid illustrations of the role that Kālī plays in the lives of some women: by accepting the part of themselves that had been repressed and feared, they allow themselves a new psychological and spiritual integration. As such, Kālī is a goddess of transformation.

If the suppression of the dark side of Kālī, and of women, has occurred because of patriarchy, the healing of that fragmented consciousness helps undo the unhealthy effects of patriarchal thinking. This is true not merely in the sense of popular education through the intellectual activity of reading books; claiming the demonic powers of the dark goddess in a personal, emotive manner brings strength, wisdom, and relief.

> Kali and Durga were like mirrors, reflecting back everything I had been afraid of in myself. . . . The darkness of these female gods comforted me. It felt like a balm on the wound of the unending white maleness that we had deified in the West. They were the dark side of everything I had ever known about God.[35]

> I seemed to feel a special perverse kinship with my vision of Kali. She frightened me not at all. I sensed something liberating about the very concept of ugliness and horror simultaneously expressed as feminine essence as opposed to Western civilization's unrealistic view that ugliness automatically negated femininity.[36]

At base, this is the significance of the search for Kālī among women in the West today; her symbolism offers healing in a male-dominated world. For many, this statement could be made much stronger: not only her symbolism but the goddess herself "struggles to bring the feminine principle into the forefront in this world again."[37]

Experiencing Kālī

There are many ways of approaching the goddess and learning from her how to integrate opposites within oneself. Most authors, in fact, even if they are writing historical or discursive accounts, add an exhortatory and inspirational flavor to their texts, and in many books the attempt to include an experiential dimension goes even deeper. For instance, some writers draw upon Kālī's iconography, either in its traditional Indian depiction or in a Western form, to teach and invite (see figure 27). Karen LaPuma, in *Awakening Female Power: The Way of the Goddess Warrior,* asks the reader, after calling attention to the severed head in Kālī's lower left hand: what do you need to let go of in your life? She urges that one sever and release all that encumbers—a sort of "let go and let the Goddess" approach.[38] Paulette Boudreaux places this method of self-examination in a more general context: "to work at understanding the symbolism of Kali is to move towards acceptance of oneself."[39]

Figure 27. "Kali," by Katinka June van Lamsweerde, 1985, pen and ink. Reproduced by permission from Paulette Boudreaux, "Kali Ma," *Woman of Power: A Magazine of Feminism, Spirituality, and Politics* no. 3 (Winter/Spring 1986): 61.

Other, more physical or practical approaches to the understanding and worship of Kālī involve singing, prayer, ritual, Tarot readings, and astrology. One can buy numerous cassette tapes dedicated to goddesses—although the majority of these are produced by Indian gurus or their disciples. One Western exception is *From the Goddess,* a tape of music sung by

Robert Gass and the musical group On Wings of Song; the cassette consists of the interweaving of three goddess chants, one of which is Deena Metzger and Caitlin Mullin's "Isis, Astarte, Diana, Hecate, Demeter, Kali, Inanna."[40] Various authors also encourage making Kālī a subject of guided meditations, prayers, litanies, and mantras. Here, for instance, is the suggestion of Barbara Ardinger: "If you don't want a traditional mantra, select a goddess name and do a few minutes of research to find out what her attributes and associations are. Then, keeping what you have learned in mind, sound her name . . . Kaaaaallllliiiii. Sound it often."[41] She also proposes substituting names of goddesses, such as Isis and Kālī, in the Christian hymn "Jesus loves me, this I know."[42] Additional examples abound.[43]

Certainly the most striking arena, however, in which Kālī has been incorporated into the sphere of contemporary women's spirituality is that of ritual. Even though there seem to be relatively few instances of Kālī's inclusion in ritual settings, the ones that do exist are fascinating. For instance, Janet Ferrar and Stuart Ferrar's *The Witches' Goddess* devotes an entire chapter to "Goddess Recipes," one of which is for the blending of "Kali incense." Sandalwood chips, jasmine chips, rose petals, and two drops of one's own menstrual blood are combined and burned during private meditation at the onset of one's period.[44] Zsuzsanna E. Budapest, in *Grandmother Moon,* offers two rituals that center on Kālī. One, which emphasizes her destructive side, is performed for the purpose of revenge. On the night of the dark moon one builds an altar to Kālī, places on it various chicken and fish bones, and writes the name of the person to be harmed on a piece of paper backwards five times. The paper is then to be smeared with one's own menstrual blood and placed under a black candle.[45] The second ritual stresses Kālī in her creative, potent aspect, as the giver of sexual pleasure. Again, one builds an altar, although this time it is to be beautiful, with a tablecloth, flowers, and red candles. Wine, tinkling bells, and incense are offered. Before masturbating, one says "Kali Ma" four times, followed by, "I surrender to your flow . . . , You are dancing within me. As I touch myself you are loving me." At the conclusion of the ritual prescriptions, Budapest remarks, "Kali Ma has brought me good luck and lovers. She gives results fast, so be careful what you ask for."[46]

Kālī also takes her place within the experience of New Age goddess spirituality through Tarot cards and astrology. Both Vicki Noble and Barbara G. Walker have created their own Tarot decks, and each has used the image of Kālī to indicate transformation through the dark powers within.[47] And, in an effort to take back the astrological calendar from the male gods of the Greeks, Merlin Stone has proposed a configuration of female deities; in this schema, Gemini is assigned to Pārvatī and Kālī.[48]

In sum, Kālī is a symbol of wholeness and healing, associated especially with repressed female power and sexuality. Some writers approach her historically, others psychologically, and still others ritually. All, however, view her as a positive—if potentially dangerous—aid to internal transformation. Though she is not nearly as popular in contemporary books on goddess spirituality as are her Greek and Roman counterparts, she has definitely entered the discourse, for she is the most oft-cited of the Hindu goddesses. Interest in her among those committed to women's spirituality seems certain to continue.

KĀLĪ IN THE WEST: ISSUES AND QUESTIONS

The preceding pages have been almost entirely descriptive, little attempt having been made to evaluate or comment upon any of the materials presented. In what follows, we will take a closer look at some of the points already raised, bringing in for comparison data and interpretations originating in Hindu India, particularly in Bengal, one of the regions in which Kālī is most popular.

Common Perspectives from India

In a number of respects, the Western portrayal of Kālī, as summarized above, is corroborated by indigenous Indian interpretations. First, Kālī is indeed a paradoxical deity, especially since the advent, in eighteenth-century Bengal, of devotional movements focused on Kālī. Over the course of her history she has grown in complexity and functional scope, such that she is not only the demon-slayer of the *Devī Māhātmya,* or the embodiment of the highest reality, as in the Tantras, but also the universal mother of compassion.[49] Second, one can find examples in Indian history of the attempted suppression of Kālī imagery and worship. Her Tantric rites have always outraged many people, Hindus and non-Hindus, in addition to which evidence exists of mutual hostility between Vaiṣṇavas and Śāktas, particularly since the time of Caitanya in early-sixteenth-century Bengal. Moreover, in his description of the late-eighteenth-century context of Rammohan Roy's struggle against idolatry, the practice of *satī,* and ritual worship, Ashis Nandy writes that Kālī became "the new symbol of a treacherous punitive mother, eager to betray and prone to aggression. She also came to be associated with almost all the other major rituals generally cited as instances of the cultural decadence of the age, and against which Rammohan Roy and almost every other reformer of the region fought."[50] Work on a slightly later development in Bengali history, the nationalist movement at the end of the nineteenth century, has shown that such attitudes persisted: male elites fostered an ideal for women's spirituality that conflicted with a Kālī-like model of independent female action. Women were to be the guardians of purity and morality, and therefore an unrestrained reverence for women as manifestations of the divine mother was deemphasized.[51] This antagonism toward

Kālī and her rituals is mirrored in Rabindranath Tagore's play *Sacrifice*, written in the early twentieth century.[52]

A third area in which the Indian materials provide justification for Western claims pertains to the status of women. Hindu women have certainly suffered greatly at the hands of societal mores and attitudes, and there is a large and growing literature, both in India and abroad, on the history and current practices of such social ills as *satī*, child marriage, child labor, the plight of widows, and bride burning. A number of recent books and articles on the general subject of the role of women in world religions discuss the religious underpinnings of social customs.[53] Many of these trace the oppression of Hindu women to a societal ambivalence, or even fear, in the face of their dual powers of benevolent fertility and malevolent aggression.

Fourth, Indian literature offers a few examples of Hindu women who use the image of Kālī in a manner reminiscent of that suggested by Western feminists: for strength, self-determination, and wholeness. For example, Sanjukta Gupta writes about three Śaiva women saints of the medieval period who achieved social and spiritual autonomy by identifying themselves with Kālī's example.[54] Sumanta Banerjee has, moreover, uncovered evidence that eighteenth-century Bengali women of the lower orders sang about Kālī standing on top of her husband, Śiva, as a means of social protest. Here is Banerjee's English translation of a *jhumur*, a type of dance song:

> The hussy has thrown the bloke flat on his back,
> With her foot on his chest.
> Wordless she stands, glaring in anger.[55]

Even though songs based on the theme of Kālī were, for women and men alike, much less popular than those about Rādhā and Krishna, and even though women of the upper echelons of society joined with men in being scandalized by the type of song quoted above, the existence of a few such specimens shows that some women, at least, were making use of the potency of Kālī's symbolism. Another example from this region and time period is provided by Lou Ratté's research into the differences between men's and women's use of Kālī during the early nationalist movement. Whereas men claimed her as the destructive goddess calling them to self-sacrifice on behalf of their country, women saw in Kālī the benevolent mother, grieving over her children's suffering.[56]

Evidence for the use of Kālī imagery among modern feminists in India today is very hard to find in the published literature. The vast majority of books and articles written by Indians who are in the women's movement prefer to address the economic, political, and social variables affecting women; discussion of religious issues of a specific nature, such as how a particular goddess can help to empower women, is almost nonexistent. Clues that such religious perspectives do in fact exist, however, are not lacking. A modern Hindu woman, for example, in an interview with a Western feminist magazine, speaks of Kālī as a powerful symbol for women in the grip of poverty.[57] And the premier feminist publishing house in India goes by the name of Kali for Women.[58]

An initial foray into the published material from India thus indicates that several of the currently dominant Western views of Kālī are consonant with available data from Kālī's land of origin. As far as her paradoxical nature, the occasional attempt to suppress her worship, the unequal status of women, and her potential as a female role model are concerned, there seems to be at least partial overlap between East and West. Yet there are difficulties, as well.

Problems with Western Interpretations of Indian Materials

The biggest stumbling block facing a student of the Hindu religious tradition who tries to accept Western feminists' accounts of Kālī, as outlined above, is the use these writers make of history. From a scholarly standpoint, it seems irresponsible to write about the ancient matriarchal societies of India, the Dravidian and Harappan, without acknowledging that the existence of matriarchies, both as a general fact of human history and as a specific claim regarding India, is a fiercely contested issue. The theory of an evolution in human development from matriarchy to patriarchy, as postulated by Bachofen, Tylor, and others, has now been completely discredited, and most anthropologists agree that truly matriarchal societies, in the sense of absolute rule by women as a class, never have existed, at least not in any culture known to us. In the case of the Indus Valley civilization, of which Harappa was a leading city, there is no conclusive evidence to prove that this culture had a matriarchal social structure, or even that the Harappans exclusively worshiped a female deity or deities.

Many feminist thinkers, working in a variety of disciplines, have raised these and other critiques of the literature that is the subject of this essay. In general, such criticisms focus on what constitutes the legitimate interpretation of scanty data: when is one overinterpreting, or treating as assumptions what ought to be taken as hypotheses? In addition, they argue that no necessary relation can be demonstrated either between the existence of powerful goddess imagery and an elevated status of women, or between the existence of ritual fertility objects and a goddess-centered society.[59] And the postulation of primordial matriarchies may have a certain suspect quality in another regard: if women were once responsible for the conceiving of goddess figures, then one is relieved of the delicate problem of attempting to reclaim female deities who must originally have been primarily the product of male thinking.

Another problem with the discussion of goddess spirituality is the widespread tendency to write and speak of the "Goddess" as a divine power or concept that unifies all separate female deities everywhere. Even with respect to the Indian subcontinent one cannot really talk about such an idea, from the historical and textual viewpoint, until the sixth century, when the *Devī Māhātmya* was composed; there is no proof that prior to that time people conceived of an overarching female power behind all individual goddess figures.[60] This issue becomes even more complicated when one's frame of reference expands to include goddesses from Europe, the Near East, and other parts of the world. To claim that goddesses who are similarly depicted must be forms of the same Great Goddess is to dehistoricize and decontextualize one's material. After all, just because two goddesses look alike superficially does not imply that they have the same meaning in their respective cultures or that they are equivalent in any more than a personal sense—that is, to the person who perceives the similarity.

With respect to Kālī herself, it is simply not true that *as a historical figure* she can be dated to an ancient, Neolithic period. Her name first occurs in the *Muṇḍaka Upaniṣad* (1.2.4), written sometime around 500 B.C.E; there Kālī is one of the eight tongues of Agni, the god of fire. The earliest stories in which Kālī appears as a deity in her own right date from the epic period, the centuries immediately preceding and following the Common Era, but it is not until the sixth century *Devī Māhātmya* that she rises to prominence and is equated with other goddesses. Her iconography is also of fairly recent origin: the typical Bengali depiction of Kālī, in which she stands astride Śiva, is not attested prior to seventeenth-century Tantric literature. Certainly, it is not "primordial" in any historical sense.

Other statements made about Kālī in Western literature are also questionable from the standpoint of history and context. Several authors take as universal truth claims or stories found in Sanskrit texts without acknowledging that these texts themselves have a history. One such declaration—a rather startling one—is that Kālī invented the Sanskrit alphabet. The most interesting example of this assertion comes from Barbara G. Walker's *Woman's Encyclopedia*:

> The *Encyclopaedia Britannica* devoted five columns to Christian interpretations of the Logos without ever mentioning its origin in Kali's *Om* or Creative Word. . . . Indo-European languages branched from the root of Sanskrit, said to be Kali's invention. She created the magic letters of the Sanskrit alphabet and inscribed them on the rosary of skulls around her neck. . . . In short, Kali's worshippers originated the doctrine of the Logos or creative Word, which Christians later adopted and pretended it was their own idea.[61]

This interpretation of the garland of skulls is an esoteric and symbolic understanding of Kālī's iconography, derived from the Tantric tradition. But the carriers of such an interpretation, the Sanskrit Tantras, date to no earlier than the eighth-century C.E.—about two thousand years after the Vedic form of Sanskrit had begun to develop! Another instance of the misuse of textual material concerns the *Skanda Purāṇa:* together with the arrival of the Aryans, this text is blamed for the origin of duality and racism in Hindu religion. The fact that the earliest sections of this Purāṇa were apparently not written down until the eleventh century—when Hinduism was hardly in its infancy—is not taken into account.

If texts are not properly contextualized, neither are ideas and words that exhibit surface resemblances. The most extreme examples, again, come from the work of Barbara G. Walker. Not only is Kālī's triple nature as Virgin, Mother, and Crone said to have influenced the triune concepts of the Celts, the Norsemen, the Egyptians, and the Arabs, but "even Christians modeled their three-fold God on her archetypal trinity."[62] Moreover, corresponding to the goddess's three aspects were three types of priestesses who attended her shrines: *yoginīs*, or virgins; *mātṛs*, or mothers; and *ḍākinīs*, or crones.[63] Finally, Eve's name is dependent on Kālī, and Jesus's conception of a law of moral consequences derives from Kālī's law of karma.[64] These statements are odd in the extreme.

Naturally, much of this confusion and misrepresentation stems from a lack among these authors of knowledge of Hindu history. A glance at their bibliographies helps explain why: only a handful of the books surveyed for this essay draw upon materials written by scholars of the Hindu religious tradition.[65] The majority instead rely chiefly on other popular feminist sources, almost none of which base their interpretations on a close reading of Kālī's Indian background. Moreover, being unfamiliar with the original languages in which texts were written can lead to other errors of interpretation. With respect to Sanskrit, the most typical mistake in this literature occurs with regard to the name Kālī itself. Spelled without its diacritics, Kālī is easily mistaken for Kali. But the term *Kali* originally referred to the worst possible throw of the dice and was later personified as Kali, the *male* demigod who presides over the fourth and most decadent of the four Hindu ages, the Kali Yuga. To state that the Kali Yuga illustrates the demonization of Kālī is to base an argument on a straightforward case of inadequate transliteration.

But perhaps the most fundamental problem with the presentation of Kālī in the literature discussed above lies with the concept of demonization. It is certainly true that demonization as a phenomenon occurs repeatedly throughout Indian history, and indeed throughout the histories of all world cultures: objectifying one's antagonists as the "other" and perceiving them as evil or inhuman is part of a natural human tendency to reify. It is also a fact that Indians who are hostile to the ritual worship of Kālī have demonized her; of this we have already seen a few examples. Problematic, however, are claims about specific instances of demonization, such as the Aryan invasion, destruction, and appropriation of Indus Valley culture in the second millennium B.C.E. Recent scholarship has raised doubts as to whether this "invasion" occurred at all or (if it did) in such a uniform manner as was previously believed.[66] Furthermore, it is hard to accept, from the historical point of view, that Kālī's development as a *whole,* from her beginnings to the modern era, has been characterized by demonization. David R. Kinsley and others have carefully charted the growth of Hindu beliefs and conceptions about Kālī over the course of the last two thousand years, and if there is any progression to be discerned, it is the opposite of demonization. The feminist view is that Kālī was degraded from a paradoxical, all-encompassing deity, whose votaries understood her as the cosmic embodiment of polarities, to a fragmented, dark, and dangerous goddess, through the willful intervention of patriarchy; hence the need for a contemporary revaluing of her darkness and a reclamation of her wholeness. But the historical record indicates that portrayals of Kālī's character have generally progressed in the opposite direction—from a minor, bloodthirsty goddess toward a universally compassionate mother. If one travels to Bengal, one will see the results of this slow transformation: the images of Kālī are beautified as much as possible (see figure 28), many of them disguising her nakedness with the dress and ornaments of a domesticated married woman (see figure 29). In short, while individual groups in various regions may indeed have demonized the goddess, and while a few depictions of her still convey a sense of her more horrific side (see figure 30), Kālī's history overall is one of growing benevolence and increased complexity (see figure 31), rather than purposeful disfigurement and contraction.[67]

An intriguing aside concerns the different perceptions of patriarchy's relation to Kālī, depending on one's cultural point of view. For the most part, Western women writing on Kālī have been struck with her fearsome demeanor, which they have then blamed on patriarchal attitudes. In contrast, women growing up in India, who are daily exposed to a Kālī of beautified aspect, a Kālī who is the loving mother of all, do not emphasize her dread character. In their opinion, if there is to be any critique of patriarchy, it is the excessive "sweetening" of the goddess that must come under attack, as it has downplayed her more powerful, sexual, independent side.[68]

The issue of the use of history is a point of some contention among feminist writers, as we saw above with respect to the controversy over matriarchies. Some, who are critical of the type of argumentation that blames patriarchy for most modern evils, charge that history is being manipulated to suit present needs. A good example of such a critic is Joan B. Townsend; she feels that what is helpful as an idea or a psychological concept is dangerous when claimed to be actual fact. "My argument is not with the myth and the use of the myth in giving women a new sense of self and of the divine, but with the tendency of some to treat the myth as historical fact." She presents the view

Figure 28. A *pūjā* image of Kālī, central Calcutta, 1989.

of history outlined by many feminists as a revitalization movement, with its typical view of time as beginning with a golden age, followed by a calamity, leading to a utopian hope. To her, such a false and oversimplified construction of history is not ultimately beneficial to the women's movement:

> If we build unity on an alleged Goddess of an alleged old religion and matriarchy, it is built on sand. If the sand of basic assumptions is eroded, as it easily can be with careful scholarship, the myth will collapse, and with it may go the unity and strength of the movement associated with the assumptions. There are many such examples in the history of revitalization movements. For example, the Ghost Dance of the North American Plains Indians of the 1890's collapsed when the buffalo and the dead did not return as promised, and the ghost shirts did not protect the people. They lost faith in the entire movement.[69]

Behind the problem of historical interpretation is the issue of authority. Who interprets correctly? What status do texts and indigenous traditions have in the reading of history? When the available texts represent such a scanty and unrepresentative a picture of Hindu life over the centuries, especially in regard to the experience of women, who is to say that one imaginative reconstruction is further from the truth than another?[70] In the end,

Figure 29. The central image at the Lake Kālī temple in southern Calcutta, 1990.

the historical critique may not matter in the slightest to the feminist and New Age projects of many authors, as Kālī, or any other goddess, transcends the sphere of historical investigation (which may itself be initiated and poisoned by patriarchy). For "Kali eludes any attempt to place her in any historical, ethnic, or cultural perspective. As a numen of the untamed feminine, the Dark Devi is the embodiment of the powers of women which have been so long suppressed, denigrated, or denied by patriarchy."[71] But in refusing scholarly accounts of history a legitimate place in the discussion of

Figure 30. Postcard of Kālī, purchased in Calcutta, 1992. Courtesy of David R. Kinsley.

goddess figures, it would seem that the potential for intimacy and depth is also lost. Is it sufficient, in developing a love relationship with a divine being, just to "take a few minutes of research" to acquaint oneself with her characteristics?[72] From the standpoint of devotionalism, a thorough investigation into the many backgrounds of the beloved in her land of origin would be a true sign of love and reverence.

Figure 31. Postcard of Mahākālī, purchased in Calcutta, 1991.

A second difficulty encountered in many Western writings about the goddess Kālī pertains to their treatment of Indian women. Although Hindu women are not typically the main subject of feminist narratives on goddess spirituality, insofar as they have suffered from the same patriarchal process that demonized their female deities, they are of substantial interest. As stated above, many Western assumptions about the experience and oppression of women in India are true. But as Frédérique Apffel Marglin argues in her article "Female Sexuality in the Hindu World," "Westerners' understanding of female sexuality in the Hindu world has been strongly colored by cultural meanings from Western traditions. All too often, familiar meanings have been projected onto less familiar cultural facts. The Hindu world is complex."[73] Marglin goes on to provide a complement to the perception that Hindus (especially Hindu men) see their women as dangerous and impure, owing to their association with blood and sexuality, by bringing forward the equally important Hindu concept of auspiciousness. As opposed to the polarity of purity and impurity, which can serve to justify male domination over polluting womanhood, the scale of auspiciousness and inauspiciousness ranks women more positively. Auspiciousness is the power of life and is nonhierarchical; not only do women embody this quality but so also do menstruation and intercourse. Hence, there are attitudes native to Hindu India that strongly affirm women.

Others writing in this vein point to the independence and respect accorded to women in the various devotional traditions of India, the fact that men are often seen as deliverers and rescuers within the context of a Hindu woman's life, and the fundamental difference between East and West regarding the value of equality.[74] Finally, we have the assumption on the part of many Western feminists that the discovery of Kālī as a liberating model for women is of universal relevance. Some Indian feminists do not find this an attractive point of view, fearing that a close identification between women and goddesses may lead to a dehumanization that denies the real needs of real women—especially Indian women.[75]

CROSS-CULTURAL BORROWING

The most fundamental issue arising from this discussion—one even more important than the question of "correct" interpretation—concerns the adoption of other people's religious symbols. Can one borrow out of context, but do so meaningfully? Drawing on the work of Clifford Geertz, Carol Christ and other feminists argue that because symbols act as vehicles for and reflections of social thought, old ones must be changed and new ones created in order to foster more positive ideas about women.[76] Seen in this light, the whole point of the emphasis on goddess spirituality is to introduce new ways of thinking about and approaching the divine, so as to change social attitudes. This, for example, was the intention of Rita Gross's article on the role of Hindu female deities as a resource for contemporary feminists, cited above. A significant obstacle to the realization of this goal, however, is the problem of achieving sufficient ritual or community participation to effect the transfer of the goddess from a merely conceptual image to a concrete symbol functioning within a realistic framework.[77] Indeed, four years after the appearance of her article on Hindu deities, Gross published another on the Buddhist Vajrayogini tradition, into which she had been initiated. Preferring a living, authentic tradition of oral transmission to a spirituality bolstered by books and solitary imaginations, she wrote: "Because this was transmitted to me by a genuine spiritual master, I do not have to struggle to reinvent the wheel, discovering Kālī or whatever, and then to spit out some private personal interpretation. And I do not have to be alone or in an artificially separated community to express all this richness."[78] As Gross discovers, it is hard to import the worship of a goddess from another culture: religious associations and connotations have to be learned, imagined, or intuited when the deep symbolic meanings embedded in the native culture are not available. Even if one knows a lot about India, as Rita Gross indeed does in relation to Kālī, the lack of public reinforcement of one's chosen religious symbolism makes the path difficult. Despite the enthusiasm for Kālī among many in the women's spirituality movement, she has not yet become a part of mainstream Western religiosity; there is no community able to transport her on a continuing and subtle basis into Euro-American culture.

And yet there are compensations. As this foray into the many goddess histories, psychological explorations, poems, and rituals illustrates, there is every indication that popular interest in goddess spirituality is on the rise in the West—and, in other ways, in India. The chances of new symbols and attitudes becoming mainstream, therefore, increases proportionately. Moreover, most Westerners who worship Kālī do not do so to the exclusion of other goddess figures; she is part of a wider group of deities, all united under the umbrella term, the Goddess, who, taken together, provide ample scope for reflection. At the present time, in fact, the success of Kālī as an emerging deity in Western consciousness depends heavily on this continuing fascination with goddess figures in general. Then, too, as is shown in the histories of all cross-cultural religious transplants, Kālī devotionalism in the West must take on its own indigenous forms if it is to adapt to its new environment. This is already occurring, both in the larger context of women's spirituality, much of which would be foreign to Hindus, and also in the specific way that Kālī is currently being depicted. As much as, from a historical perspective, one might deplore many of the statements about Kālī one encounters in this literature, one must also recognize the proliferation of such lore as natural in the process of cultural adaptation. Symbols have their own lives. So do goddesses. One should not expect Kālī in the West necessarily to look like Kālī in the East. Just as she has had a complicated and dynamic history of interpretation in India, so will she in the West. And as long as her inclusion in historical studies, psychological and therapeutic contexts, and ritual manuals helps to heal divisions in women's lives, the Western Kālī of feminist and New Age spirituality will deserve to be seen as a genuine goddess of transformation.

NOTES

1. Merlin Stone, *When God Was a Woman* (New York: Harcourt Brace Jovanovich, 1978), p. xxv.

2. Lina Gupta, "Kali, the Savior," in *After Patriarchy: Feminist Transformations of the World Religions,* ed. Paula M. Cooey, William R. Eakin, and Jay B. McDaniel (Maryknoll, N.Y.: Orbis Books, 1991), p. 16.

3. David R. Kinsley, *The Sword and the Flute—Kālī and Kṛṣṇa: Dark Visions of the Terrible and the Sublime in Hindu Mythology* (Berkeley: University of California Press, 1975). Kinsley also discusses Kālī in his contribution to the present volume and in *Hindu Goddesses: Visions of the Divine Feminine in the Hindu Religious Tradition* (Berkeley: University of California Press, 1986), chap. 8.

4. On Kālī, see Gerina Dunwich, *The Concise Lexicon of the Occult* (New York: Citadel Press, 1990), p. 92; and Alex Jack, ed., *The New Age Dictionary: A Guide to Planetary Family Consciousness* (Tokyo and New York: Japan Publications, 1990), p. 99.

5. See, for example, "The Ultimate Mother (Goddess Worship Makes a Comeback)," editorial, *New York Times,* 12 May 1991, p. E16; Richard N. Ostling, "When God Was a Woman: Worshippers of Mother Earth Are Part of a Goddess Resurgence," *Time,* 6 May 1991, p. 73; Judith Weinraub, "The New Theology—Sheology: Mystical Women's Spiritual Movements Gaining Momentum . . . and Adherents," *Washington Post,* 28 April 1991, p. F1; Jay Matthews, "Did Goddess Worship Mark Ancient Age of Peace?" *Washington Post,* 7 January 1990, p. A8; Sonia L. Nazario, "Is Goddess Worship Finally Going to Put Men in Their Place? Spiritual Movement Reveres Mother Earth and Power of Female Energies," *Wall Street Journal,* 7 June 1990, p. A1; and Peter Steinfels, "Idyllic Theory of Goddesses Creates Storm: Was a Peaceful Matriarchal World Shattered by Patriarchal Invaders?" *New York Times,* 13 February 1990, p. B5.

6. Carol P. Christ, "Why Women Need the Goddess: Phenomenological, Psychological, and Political Reflections," in *Womanspirit Rising: A Feminist Reader in Religion,* ed. Carol P. Christ and Judith Plaskow (San Francisco: Harper and Row, 1979), p. 278.

7. See, among others, Riane Eisler, *The Chalice and the Blade: Our History, Our Future* (San Francisco: Harper and Row, 1988); Marija Gimbutas, *The Goddesses and Gods of Old Europe, 6500–3500 B.C.: Myths, Legends, and Cult Images,* new ed. (Berkeley: University of California Press, 1982), and *The Language of the Goddess: Unearthing the Hidden Symbols of Western Civilization* (San Francisco: Harper and Row, 1989); Monica Sjöö and Barbara Mor, *The Great Cosmic Mother: Rediscovering the Religion of the Earth* (San Francisco: Harper and Row, 1987); Charlene Spretnak, *Lost Goddesses of Early Greece: A Collection of Pre-Hellenic Myths* (1978; Boston: Beacon Press, 1992); Starhawk, *The Spiral Dance: A Rebirth of the Ancient Religion of the Great Goddess* (San Francisco: Harper and Row, 1979); and Stone, *When God Was a Woman.*

8. The principal critique of Jung centers on the monolithic nature of his anima/animus polarity. Feminists argue that the characteristics of each pole are taken as eternal and hence as prescriptive for human behavior. See Carol P. Christ, "Symbols of Goddess and God in Feminist Theology," in *The Book of the Goddess Past and Present: An Introduction to Her Religion,* ed. Carl Olson (New York: Crossroad, 1983), pp. 231–35; Naomi Goldenberg, *The End of God: Important Directions for a*

Feminist Critique of Religion in the Works of Sigmund Freud and Carl Jung (Ottawa: Ottawa University Press, 1982); and Merlin Stone, introduction to *The Goddess Re-Awakening: The Feminine Principle Today,* comp. Shirley Nicholson (Wheaton, Ill.: Theosophical Publishing House, 1989), pp. 15–16.

9. Jung first articulated his ideas on the mother archetype in *Symbols of Transformation: An Analysis of the Prelude to a Case of Schizophrenia* (1912). See *The Collected Works of C. G. Jung,* trans. R. F. C. Hull, 2d ed., 20 vols. (Princeton: Princeton University Press, 1966–79), vol. 5 (1967). See also his *Archetypes and the Collective Unconscious,* in ibid., vol. 9, pt. 1 (1968). A "revisioned" Jung has been proposed in several books, two of the most influential being James Hillman's *Archetypal Psychology: A Brief Account, Together with a Complete Checklist of Works* (Dallas: Spring Publications, 1982); and *Feminist Archetypal Theory: Interdisciplinary Re-Visions of Jungian Thought,* ed. Estella Lauter and Carol Schreier Rupprecht (Knoxville: University of Tennessee Press, 1985). Many modern feminist and New Age authors write from a psychological viewpoint, often explicitly drawing upon Jungian thought. See, for example, Jean Shinoda Bolen, *Goddesses in Everywoman: A New Psychology of Women* (San Francisco: Harper and Row, 1984); Kathie Carlson, *In Her Image: The Unhealed Daughter's Search for Her Mother* (Boston: Shambala, 1989); Christine Downing, *The Goddess: Mythological Images of the Feminine* (New York: Crossroad, 1981); Joan Chamberlain Englesman, *The Feminine Dimension of the Divine* (Philadelphia: Westminster Press, 1979); Gareth S. Hill, *Masculine and Feminine: The Natural Flow of Opposites in the Psyche* (Boston: Shambala, 1992); Manuela Dunn Mascetti, *The Song of Eve: An Enchanted Journey into the Myths and Symbols of the Feminine* (New York: Simon and Schuster, 1990); Sylvia Brinton Perera, *Descent to the Goddess: A Way of Initiation for Women* (Toronto: Inner City Books, 1981); Edward C. Whitmont, *Return of the Goddess* (New York: Crossroad, 1982); and Jennifer Barker Woolger and Roger J. Woolger, *The Goddess Within: A Guide to Eternal Myths That Shape Women's Lives* (London: Rider, 1990).

10. Examples include Barbara Ardinger, *A Woman's Book of Rituals and Celebrations* (San Rafael, Calif.: New World Library, 1992); Hallie Iglehart Austen, *The Heart of the Goddess: Art, Myth, and Meditations of the World's Sacred Feminine* (Oakland: Wingbow Press, 1990); Zsuzsanna E. Budapest, *The Grandmother of Time: A Woman's Book of Celebrations, Spells, and Sacred Objects for Every Month of the Year* (San Francisco: Harper and Row, 1989), and *Grandmother Moon: Lunar Magic in Our Lives—Spells, Rituals, Goddesses, Legends, and Emotions under the Moon* (San Francisco: Harper and Row, 1991); Judith Laura, *She Lives! The Return of Our Great Mother: Myths, Rituals, Meditations, and Music* (Freedom, Calif.: Crossing Press, 1989); Vicki Noble, *Motherpeace: A Way to the Goddess through Myth, Art, and Tarot* (San Francisco: Harper and Row, 1982); Gloria Orenstein, *The Reflowering of the Goddess: Contemporary Journeys and Cycles of Empowerment* (Pittsburgh: Pittsburgh Peace Institute, 1990); Diane Stein, ed., *The Goddess Celebrates: An Anthology of Women's Rituals* (Freedom, Calif.: Crossing Press, 1991); Barbara G. Walker, *Women's Rituals: A Sourcebook* (San Francisco: Harper and Row, 1990); and *The Womanspirit Sourcebook,* ed. Patricia Wynne (New York: HarperCollins, 1988).

11. This point is argued by Emily Erwin Culpepper, "Contemporary Goddess Theology: A Sympathetic Critique," in *Shaping New Vision: Gender and Values in American Culture,* ed. Clarissa W. Atkinson, Constance H. Buchanan, and Margaret R.

Miles (Ann Arbor: UMI Research Press, Harvard Women's Studies in Religion Series, 1987), pp. 51–71.

12. Each of the authors mentioned attempted to incorporate world history into his developmental scheme. See Robert Briffault, *The Mothers: The Matriarchal Theory of Social Origins,* 3 vols. (1927; New York: Macmillan, 1931); Johann Jakob Bachofen, *Das Mutterrecht* (1861), abr. and trans. Ralph Manheim, in *Myth, Religion, and Mother Right: Selected Writings of J. J. Bachofen* (Princeton: Princeton University Press, 1967); Erich Neumann, *The Great Mother: An Analysis of the Archetype* (1955), trans. Ralph Manheim, 2d ed. (New York: Pantheon, 1963); and Sir Edward Burnett Tylor, *Primitive Culture: Research into the Development of Mythology, Philosophy, Religion, Language, Art, and Custom* (London: John Murray, 1871). For Jung, see note 9, above.

13. One can watch this growth of attention to unconventional goddess traditions even by comparing the two books edited by Carol P. Christ and Judith Plaskow. *Womanspirit Rising* (1979) contained three introductory articles on goddess worship, whereas *Weaving the Visions: New Patterns in Feminist Spirituality* (San Francisco: Harper and Row, 1989) includes studies of Native American, African American, and Haitian deities. That interest in goddess traditions has broadened in scope is strikingly illustrated by the titles of a number of recently published books: Patricia Monaghan, *The Books of Goddesses and Heroines* (New York: E. P. Dutton, 1981); Barbara G. Walker, *The Woman's Encyclopedia of Myths and Secrets* (San Francisco: Harper and Row, 1983), and *The Woman's Dictionary of Symbols and Sacred Objects* (San Francisco: Harper and Row, 1988); Austen, *The Heart of the Goddess: Art, Myth, and Meditations of the World's Sacred Feminine;* Mascetti, *The Song of Eve: An Enchanted Journey into the Myths and Symbols of the Feminine; After Patriarchy: Feminist Transformations of the World Religions,* ed. Cooey, Eakin, and McDaniel; Pamela Allardice, *Myths, Gods and Fantasy: A Sourcebook* (Bridport, Eng.: Prism Press, 1991); Anne Baring and Jules Cashford, *The Myth of the Goddess: Evolution of an Image* (London: Viking Arkana, 1991); Carolyn McVickar Edwards, *The Storyteller's Goddess: Tales of the Goddess and Her Wisdom from around the World* (San Francisco: Harper and Row, 1991); and Merlin Stone, *Ancient Mirrors of Womanhood: A Treasury of Goddess and Heroine Lore from around the World* (Boston: Beacon Press, 1991).

14. For additional names, plus a discussion of the feminist exploration of such goddesses as part of the creation of a woman-centered culture, see Emily Culpepper, "The Spiritual Movement of Radical Feminist Consciousness," in *Understanding the New Religions,* ed. Jacob Needleman and George Baker (New York: Crossroad, 1978), pp. 224–25.

15. Walker, *Woman's Encyclopedia of Myths and Secrets,* p. 929. For her comments on Kālī, see Barbara G. Walker, *The Skeptical Feminist: Discovering the Virgin, Mother, and Crone* (San Francisco: Harper and Row, 1987), p. 192.

16. Rita M. Gross, "Hindu Female Deities as a Resource for the Contemporary Rediscovery of the Goddess," in *The Book of the Goddess Past and Present,* ed. Olson, pp. 217–230, at pp. 222, 223.

17. See Heinrich Zimmer, *Myths and Symbols in Indian Art and Civilization,* ed. Joseph Campbell (1946; repr. Princeton: Princeton University Press, 1971), pl. 68; and Neumann, *The Great Mother,* pl. 66.

18. Allardice, *Myths, Gods, and Fantasy,* p. 127.

19. For examples of how authors use this tripartite nomenclature, see Paulette Boudreaux, "Kali Ma," in *Woman of Power: A Magazine of Feminism, Spirituality, and Politics* no. 3 (Winter/Spring 1986): 62; Charlene Spretnak, introduction to *The Politics of Women's Spirituality: Essays on the Rise of Spiritual Power within the Feminist Movement,* ed. Charlene Spretnak (New York: Anchor Press, 1982), p. xvii; and Walker, *Woman's Encyclopedia of Myths and Secrets,* p. 258. In another publication, Walker identifies Kālī with the third phase in a woman's development: see "The Terrible Crone," chap. 4 in *The Crone: Women of Age, Wisdom, and Power* (San Francisco: Harper and Row, 1985), p. 71. Demetra George does the same, aligning all dark goddesses with the dark, or Crone, aspect of life: see her *Mysteries of the Dark Moon: The Healing Power of the Dark Goddess* (San Francisco: Harper and Row, 1992), pp. 31–33.

20. For three modern examples of this line of argument, see Elinor W. Gadon, *The Once and Future Goddess: A Symbol for Our Time* (San Francisco: Harper and Row, 1989); Stone, *When God Was a Woman;* and Whitmont, *Return of the Goddess.*

21. Boudreaux, "Kali Ma," p. 61.

22. Sjöö and Mor, *Great Cosmic Mother,* p. 182.

23. Patricia Reis, *Through the Goddess: A Woman's Way of Healing* (New York: Continuum, 1991), p. 63.

24. Authors who in general share this view of Indian history include Kathleen Alexander-Berghorn, "The Dark Devi: An Interview with Shuma Chakravarty," *Woman of Power: A Magazine of Feminism, Spirituality, and Politics* no. 8 (Winter 1988): 17; Austen, *Heart of the Goddess,* pp. 78–79 (entry for "Kali Ma"); Boudreaux, "Kali Ma," p. 60; Edwards, *Storyteller's Goddess,* pp. 141–42; Gadon, *Once and Future Goddess,* p. 83; Buffie Johnson, *Lady of the Beasts: Ancient Images of the Goddess and Her Sacred Animals* (San Francisco: Harper and Row, 1988), p. 172; Sjöö and Mor, *Great Cosmic Mother,* p. 219; and Barbara G. Walker, *The Crone,* pp. 76–78.

25. Sjöö and Mor, *Great Cosmic Mother,* pp. 182–83.

26. Barbara G. Walker, in her *Woman's Encyclopedia,* argues that Kālī's three functions as creator, maintainer, and destroyer were taken from her and given to the male gods, Brahmā, Viṣṇu, and Śiva (p. 489). The *Skanda Purāṇa* is occasionally cited as evidence of racism and sexism in the depiction of Kālī. See, for instance, Stone, introduction to *The Goddess Re-Awakening,* comp. Nicholson, pp. 9–10. As we will shortly see, however, no etymological link in fact exists between Kālī and Kali.

27. Noble, *Motherpeace,* p. 82.

28. For the former position, see Gupta, "Kali, the Savior," p. 33; for the latter, see Caitlin Matthews, *Sophia, Goddess of Wisdom: The Divine Wisdom from Black Goddess to World Soul* (London: Mandala, 1991), pp. 56–57.

29. For more detailed discussions of these points, see Christ, "Why Women Need the Goddess," pp. 273–87; and Starhawk, "Witchcraft as Goddess Religion," in *Politics of Women's Spirituality,* ed. Spretnak, pp. 49–56.

30. Linda E. Olds, "The Neglected Feminine: Promises and Perils," *Soundings: An Interdisciplinary Journal* 69, no. 3 (1986): 226–40, at p. 234. Recovery of Kālī's original symbolism is possible only because, in spite of the harm done to her by patriarchal attitudes, glimpses of her deeper meaning still persist. Some authors speak of "survivals" from Neolithic belief and ritual, while others, who are somewhat less pessimistic, state that Indian women, in particular, have never lost sight of the goddess's true nature.

31. Vicki Noble, dedication to *Shakti Woman: Feeling Our Fire, Healing Our World—The New Female Shamanism* (San Francisco: Harper and Row, 1991).

32. The former case is described in Whitmont, *Return of the Goddess,* chap. 1 ("A Modern Theopany"); the latter in Mascetti, *Song of Eve,* pp. 90–91.

33. Suzanne Ironbiter, *Devi* (Stamford, Conn.: Yuganta Press, 1987), p. 22.

34. In *She Rises Like The Sun: Invocations of the Goddess by Contemporary American Women Poets,* ed. Janine Canan (Freedom, Calif.: Crossing Press, 1989), pp. 149–53. For further examples, see Merlin Stone's poem "Kali," in *Ancient Mirrors of Womanhood,* pp. 222–23; and Lucille Clifton's poem "Kali," in *Cries of the Spirit: A Celebration of Women's Spirituality,* ed. Marilyn Sewell (Boston: Beacon Press, 1991), pp. 249–50.

35. China Galland, *Longing for Darkness: Tara and the Black Madonna, A Ten-Year Journey* (New York: Viking, 1990), pp. 28, 31.

36. Walker, *Skeptical Feminist,* p. 194.

37. Boudreaux, "Kali Ma," p. 60.

38. Karen LaPuma, with Walt Runkis, *Awakening Female Power: The Way of the Goddess Warrior* (Fairfax, Calif.: SoulSource Publishing, 1989), pp. 123–27.

39. Boudreaux, "Kali Ma," p. 61.

40. *From the Goddess* was produced in 1989 by Spring Hill Music, Boulder, Colorado.

41. Ardinger, *Woman's Book of Rituals and Celebrations,* p. 40.

42. Ibid., pp. 41–42.

43. For instance, see the "Women's Freedom Litany," printed in *Womanspirit* 1, no. 3 (1975): 6. The last lines read, "In the names of Kali, Ishtar, Isis, Mary, and all lost goddesses whom we come now to realize, for all women everywhere—freedom forevermore!" Hallie Iglehart Austen offers a slightly different means of identifying with and worshiping goddesses: for each goddess listed in her book *The Heart of the Goddess,* she provides a short descriptive sketch, a picture, a meditation, and a prayer.

44. Janet Ferrar and Stuart Ferrar, *The Witches' Goddess: The Feminine Principle of Divinity* (London: Robert Hale, 1987), p. 71.

45. Budapest, *Grandmother Moon,* pp. 112–14.

46. Ibid., pp. 204–6.

47. Vicki Noble's "Tower" card is a "symbol of Kali's cutting off the head—ego death, the end of mental control"; she devotes five pages (pp. 118–22) of *Motherpeace* to an explanation of this particular card. Barbara G. Walker's "Queen of Swords" card portrays Kālī in Walker's favorite pose: eating the innards of her corpse-vehicle. *Woman of Power: A Magazine of Feminism, Spirituality, and Politics,* no. 5 (Winter 1987) has a black-and-white photo of this card (p. 66). For Walker's explanation of its meaning, see her *Secrets of the Tarot: Origins, History, and Symbolism* (San Francisco: Harper and Row, 1992), pp. 222–24.

48. Stone, *Ancient Mirrors of Womanhood,* p. 417.

49. For a succinct overview of this development of Kālī's persona, see Kinsley, *Sword and the Flute,* pp. 81–126.

50. Ashis Nandy, "Sati: A Nineteenth-Century Tale of Women, Violence, and Protest," in his *At the Edge of Psychology: Essays in Politics and Culture* (Delhi: Oxford University Press, 1980), p. 9.

51. Malavika Karlekar, *Voices from Within: Early Personal Narratives of Bengali Women* (Delhi: Oxford University Press, 1991), pp. 71–72. Karlekar is reporting on research conducted by Partha Chatterjee.

52. See the *Collected Poems and Plays of Rabindranath Tagore* (New York: Macmillan, 1967), pp. 407–27. Originally written in Bengali (its Bengali title is *Bisarjan*), the play was first staged in 1900.

53. Sumanta Banerjee, "Marginalization of Women's Popular Culture in Nineteenth-Century Bengal," in *Recasting Women: Essays in Indian Colonial History*, ed. Kumkum Sangari and Sudesh Vaid (New Brunswick, N.J.: Rutgers University Press, 1990), pp. 126–79; Denise Lardner Carmody, "Hindu Women," chap. 3 in her *Women and World Religions*, 2d ed. (Englewood Cliffs, N.J.: Prentice-Hall, 1989); Sudhir Kakar, "Feminine Identity in India," in *Women in Indian Society: A Reader*, ed. Rehana Ghadially (New Delhi: Sage Publications, 1988), pp. 44–68; Klaus Klostermaier, "*Śakti*: Hindu Images and Concepts of the Goddess," in *Goddesses in Religion and Modern Debate*, ed. Larry Hurtado, University of Manitoba Studies in Religion no. 1 (Atlanta: Scholars Press, 1990), pp. 143–61; Frédérique Apffel Marglin, "Female Sexuality in the Hindu World," in *Immaculate and Powerful: The Female in Sacred Image and Social Reality*, ed. Clarissa W. Atkinson, Constance H. Buchanan, and Margaret R. Miles (Boston: Beacon Press, 1985), pp. 39–59; Kana Mitra, "Women and the Hindu Tradition, in *Women's and Men's Liberation: Testimonies of Spirit*, ed. Leonard Grob, Riffat Hassan, and Haim Gordon (New York: Greenwood Press, 1991), pp. 83–103; Sara S. Mitter, *Dharma's Daughters: Contemporary Indian Women and Hindu Culture* (New Brunswick, N.J.: Rutgers University Press, 1991); Vasudha Narayanan, "Hindu Perceptions of Auspiciousness and Sexuality," in *Women, Religion, and Sexuality: Studies on the Impact of Religious Teaching on Women*, ed. Jeanne Becher (Philadelphia: Trinity Press International, 1990), pp. 64–92; Sandra P. Robinson, "Hindu Paradigms of Women: Images and Values," in *Women, Religion and Social Change*, ed. Yvonne Y. Haddad and Ellision B. Findly (Albany: State University of New York Press, 1985), pp. 181–215; Manisha Roy, "The Concepts of 'Femininity' and 'Liberation' in the Context of Changing Sex Roles: Women in Modern India and America," in *Women in Indian Society*, ed. Ghadially, pp. 136–47; Susan S. Wadley, "Women and the Hindu Tradition," in ibid., pp. 23–43; and Katherine K. Young, "Hinduism," in *Women and World Religions*, ed. Arvind Sharma (Albany: State University of New York Press, 1987), pp. 59–103.

54. See Sanjukta Gupta, "Women in the Śaiva/Śākta Ethos," in *Roles and Rituals for Hindu Women*, ed. Julia Leslie (London: Pinter Publishers, 1991), p. 198. The three saints that Gupta discusses are Kāraikkāl Ammaiyār of the Tamils, Akkā Mahādevī of Karnataka, and Lallā Dēd of Kashmir. Of the three, the most intriguing is Kāraikkāl, who in two of her four extant poems describes how, as a ghoul attending on Kālī, she watched Kālī's dance competition with Śiva in the forest. Gupta asks in regard to the second saint, the naked wandering Akkā Mahādevī: "Did she want to emulate Kālī, the fierce goddess, a benign mother to her devotees but the killer of her enemies?"

55. Banerjee, "Marginalization of Women's Popular Culture," p. 157.

56. Lou Ratté, "Goddesses, Mothers, and Heroines: Hindu Women and the Feminine in the Early Nationalist Movement," in *Women, Religion, and Social Change*, ed. Haddad and Findly, pp. 351–76.

57. Chakravarty, "The Dark Devi," p. 59.

58. Kali for Woman was founded in 1984 by Ritu Menon as India's first feminist publishing house. For a brief overview of the types of women's movements in India

today, see Elisabeth Bumiller, *May You Be the Mother of a Hundred Sons: A Journey among the Women of India* (New York: Random House, 1990), p. 129. Longer treatments are Vibhuti Patel's "Emergence and Proliferation of Autonomous Women's Groups in India, 1974–1984," in *Women in Indian Society*, ed. Ghadially, pp. 249–56; and Leslie J. Calman, *Toward Empowerment: Women and Movement Politics in India* (Boulder, Colo.: Westview Press, 1992).

59. For writers critical of the matriarchy theory, see Carolyn Fluer-Lobban, "A Marxist Reappraisal of the Matriarchate," *Current Anthropology* 20, no. 2 (1987): 341–59; Olds, "The Neglected Feminine"; James J. Preston, "Goddess Worship: Theoretical Perspectives," in *The Encyclopedia of Religion*, ed. Mircea Eliade, 20 vols. (New York: Macmillan and Free Press, 1987), 6:53–58; and Joan B. Townsend, "The Goddess: Fact, Fallacy, and Revitalization Movement," in *Goddesses in Religion and Modern Debate*, ed. Hurtado, pp. 180–203. A particularly lively debate on this same subject, with responses, a counterresponse, and a counter-counterresponse, is contained in the appendix to *The Politics of Women's Spirituality*, ed. Spretnak, where Sally R. Binford's critique of the matriarchy theory, entitled "Myths and Matriarchies" (pp. 541–49), is critiqued in turn by Merlin Stone and Charlene Spretnak, to whom Binford then responds.

60. See Thomas B. Coburn's *Devī-Māhātmya: The Crystallization of the Goddess Tradition* (Delhi and Columbia, Mo.: Motilal Banarsidass and South Asia Books, 1985).

61. Walker, "Kali Ma," in *Woman's Encyclopedia of Myths and Secrets*, pp. 489 and 491.

62. Ibid., p. 492. Her reference for this claim is Merlin Stone's *When God Was a Woman*, p. 17.

63. Ibid. The three types of "priestesses" mentioned are Kālī's attendants, to be sure. But there is no evidence to support Walker's claim that they were functionaries on a human plane as well.

64. Walker, *Women's Rituals*, p. 181. As Walker remarks, "The name of Eve may have originated with Kali's Ieva or Jiva, the primordial female principle of manifestation; she gave birth to her 'first manifested form' and called him Idam (Adam)" ("Kali Ma," in *Women's Encyclopedia of Myths and Secrets*, p. 491).

65. The bibliographies of China Galland, Elinor W. Gadon, Suzanne Ironbiter, Buffie Johnson, Caitlin Matthews, Linda E. Olds, and Sylvia Brinton Perera include various scholarly sources on Hindu religion, including the works of David R. Kinsley; *The Book of the Goddess Past and Present*, ed. Olson; *Mother Worship: Theme and Variations*, ed. James J. Preston (Chapel Hill: University of North Carolina Press, 1982).

66. Representative examples include Romila Thapar, "Ideology and the Interpretation of Early Indian History," in her *Interpreting Early India* (Delhi: Oxford University Press, 1993), pp. 1–22; and Edmund Leach, "Aryan Invasions over Four Millennia," in *Culture through Time: Anthropological Approaches*, ed. Emiko Ohnuki-Tierney (Stanford: Stanford University Press, 1990), pp. 227–45.

67. See my "Evidence for the Transformation of the Goddess Kālī: Kamalākānta Bhaṭṭācārya and the Bengali Śākta *Padāvalī* Tradition" (Ph.D. diss., Harvard University, 1993).

68. Lina Gupta's article, "Kali, the Savior," is a good example of this perspective. She argues that although patriarchy has understood Kālī solely as a loving mother and spouse, a deeper reading of the textual material provides evidence for a more ambivalent, potent, and sexually independent deity.

69. Townsend, "The Goddess: Fact, Fallacy, and Revitalization Movement," pp. 182, 198.

70. For a longer discussion of some of these questions, see Dawne McCance, "Understandings of 'The Goddess' in Contemporary Feminist Scholarship," in *Goddesses in Religion and Modern Debate,* ed. Hurtado, pp. 165–78, esp. pp. 173–74; and Mary Jo Weaver, "Who Is the Goddess and Where Does She Get Us?" *Journal of Feminist Studies in Religion* 5, no. 1 (1989): 49–64.

71. Kathleen Alexander-Berghorn, introductory remarks to her interview with Shuma Chakravarty, "Dark Devi," p. 17.

72. Ardinger, *A Woman's Book of Rituals and Celebrations,* p. 40.

73. Marglin, "Female Sexuality in the Hindu World," p. 39.

74. For a discussion of some of these points, see Suma Chitnis, "Feminism: Indian Ethos and Indian Conviction," in *Women in Indian Society,* Ghadially, pp. 81–95.

75. See Indu Prakash Singh, *Indian Women: The Captured Beings* (New Delhi: Intellectual Publishing House, 1990), p. 6.

76. Christ, "Why Women Need the Goddess," pp. 273–87.

77. Larry D. Shinn develops this point further in "The Goddess: Theological Sign or Religious Symbol?" *Numen* 31, no. 2 (1984): 175–98.

78. Rita M. Gross, "I Will Never Forget to Visualize That Vajrayogini Is My Body and Mind," *Journal of Feminist Studies in Religion* 3, no. 1 (1987), p. 80.

GLOSSARY

NOTE: Many names and terms found within individual entries below are themselves defined in the glossary.

ācārya	A religious teacher, a person of exemplary conduct and authoritative doctrine; a title given by Śri Vaiṣṇavas to a guru who provides initiation into the practices and teachings of the community and authoritative expositions of sacred knowledge. Also an honorific title for the great Advaita philosopher Śaṅkara and several Śri Vaiṣṇava theologians.
Ādiśakti	The Goddess conceived generically; the single, transcendent primeval power or energy extolled in the *Devī Māhātmya.*
Advaita	"Non-dual," a philosophy declaring the complete unity of the godhead and all its creation, associated especially with the philosopher Saṅkara (ca. 800 C.E.) and his school.
ahaṃkāra	"The I-maker," egocentricity, individualized identity, the notions of "I" and "mine."
aiśvarya	"Lordliness, majesty"; the exalted aspects of divinity.
āḻvār	One who is submerged in the qualities of the Lord (*bhagavān*); title given by Śri Vaiṣṇavas to the twelve poet-saints of the seventh to tenth centuries whose four thousand Tamil verses they acknowledge to be the vernacular equivalent of the Sanskrit Vedas.
Amar Chitra Katha	A series of "classic" comic books illustrating stories from the two great epics as well as the Purāṇas and subsequent literature, both Hindu and non-Hindu.

amṛta	"Immortal," the nectar of immortality, for which the gods and the demons contended and the gods won.
ānanda	"Bliss"; along with *sat* (being) and *cit* (consciousness), one of the three predicates of *brahman* considered by Advaita Vedāntins to constitute the essence of ultimate reality; viewed by *bhakta*s both as an essential characteristic of the Lord and as the fruit of spiritual realization.
apsaras	A water nymph, a heavenly courtesan at the court of Indra.
āratī	A graceful form of worship in which an officiant waves a tray of lighted oil lamps or another object in circular patterns before an image of the deity, often to the accompaniment of a song or the ringing of a bell.
Ārya Samāj	A militant nineteenth-century Hindu nationalist organization advocating a return to the Vedas as the true foundation of Hindu teachings and practices.
Aṣṭabhujā	"With eight arms," an epithet of the goddess Vindhyavāsinī in the form in which she is worshiped at the site of that name, which forms one corner of the triangle *yātrā.*
asura	"Lord" among men or gods; a demon, an enemy of the gods. The great feat of Durgā, celebrated on Daśaharā, is her vanquishing of the great water-buffalo demon Mahiṣāsura.
Aśvins	Twin equine gods, sons of Saraṇyū and Vivasvant, the Sun. Half horse and half human in form, they are semidivine. Known for their powers of healing, they serve as physicians to the gods.
avatar (Skt.: *avatāra*)	"Descent," i.e., of a deity, who thus assumes an embodied form. The *avatāra*s of Viṣṇu are his numerous divine "descents" into the phenomenal world. Cf. *avataraṇa.*
avataraṇa	"Descent"; the act of descending, as that of the river Ganges (Gaṅgā) from heaven to earth.
Bhadrakāḷi	A fierce form of Kālī euphemistically called Bhadrā, "gracious" (cf. Śiva). An angry and violent form of Kerala's predominant deity, otherwise known as Bhagavati.
Bhagavati	"The blessed one"; name of the fierce goddess of Kerala, the predominant deity of the region, a form of Kālī. As Bhagavati, she is a benevolent goddess.
Bhairava	A fierce form of Śiva, especially important for Tantric practitioners. The *Vindhya Māhātmya* presents a vision of fifty-two Bhairavas, who protect the sacred region of Vindhyachal.

bhakta — A devotee, one who loves and worships a personal deity, often passionately.

bhakti — Loving devotion; a spiritual path advocated by Krishna in the *Bhagavad Gītā* that flowered into a popular movement throughout India in medieval times. Its main forms are Vaiṣṇava (directed toward Viṣṇu, often in one or the other of his two major avatars, Krishna or Rāma); Śaiva (directed toward Śiva), and Śākta (directed toward the Goddess).

Bhārat Mātā — "Mother India," a goddess promoted by Hindu nationalists.

bhāva — Emotional state; in Sanskrit aesthetic theory, that which, once evoked and refined through an aesthetic medium, serves as the basis for *rasa*, ultimate aesthetic experience; also, one of the devotional modes exemplified by the close associates of Krishna in Vraja. Rūpa Gosvāmī and others enumerated five such *bhāvas*—*śānta, dāsya, sakhya, vātsalya,* and *mādhurya*; these have continued to serve as the basis of much Gauḍīya Vaiṣṇava devotion down to the present day.

bindu — Lit., "drop," "point," the unmanifest central point of the triangle *yātrā* at Vindhyachal in which the Great Goddess dwells, a fact that is reflected in the name Binduvāsinī.

Binduvāsinī — "The dweller in the point," a name of Vindhyavāsinī.

brahman — The absolute; ultimate reality, usually understood as impersonal (the word is neuter) and devoid of attributes (*nirguṇa*), although *brahman* is also described as pure being (*sat*), consciousness (*cit*), and bliss (*ānanda*).

Braj (Skt.: Vraja) — The pastoral country around Mathura, in present-day Uttar Pradesh, in which Braj Bhāṣā is spoken. The entire region is a pilgrimage center for Vaiṣṇavas, for it is identified with the area known as Vraja, the place of Krishna's childhood and youth, which figures prominently in many Purāṇas.

Brindavan/Vrindaban) (Skt.: Vṛndāvana) — A town and pilgrimage center near Mathura in the heart of Braj to which Caitanya is said to have deputed the six *gosvāmīs*. The town is filled with Vaiṣṇava temples and devotees of Krishna.

Caitanya — A passionate devotee of Krishna and Rādhā whose ecstatic devotion inspired a movement that spread throughout eastern India and resulted in the establishment of the Gauḍīya Vaiṣṇava sect. He has been regarded variously as an incarnation of Krishna, of Rādhā, and of the two together in the closest possible embrace.

Caṇḍī	"The fierce one," a name of Durgā, especially in the form in which she destroyed the buffalo-demon Mahiṣāsura, a deed celebrated in the *Devī Māhātmya* or *Caṇḍīpāṭha* and in the festival of Daśaharā.
Caṇḍidās	The name given to three (or more) Bengali poets who wrote on the love of Rādhā and Krishna, especially the earliest of these, Baḍu Caṇḍidās, the author of the *Śrīkṛṣṇakīrtan.*
Dārika/Dāruka	A demon-king slain by the goddess Bhagavati in the ritual possession performance of *mudiyettu* (*muṭiyeṟṟu*) in central Kerala.
dāsya	"Servitude," the devotional attitude in which the Lord is regarded as a beloved master; one of the five primary emotional relations (see *bhāva*) enumerated by Rūpa Gosvāmī; considered by Gauḍīya Vaiṣṇavas and others to be an essential element in all true devotion.
Devī	"Goddess," the most general name for feminine divinity; often used to refer to the wife of Śiva (Pārvatī, Durgā, Kālī, etc.) but applied to other goddesses as well; or specifically, *the* Goddess, ultimate reality conceived as feminine.
Devī Māhātmya	A medieval text, part of the *Mārkaṇḍeya Purāṇa*, narrating the victory of Devī or Durgā over the buffalo-demon Mahiṣāsura; also called the *Caṇḍīpāṭha*, this text is recited during the festival of Navarātrī (Durgā Pūjā).
dhām (Skt.: *dhāma*)	"Abode," one of many places of pilgrimage where the deity is said to have a permanent home.
dharma	Righteousness, virtue, duty, law; the social and spiritual obligations of every Hindu; the order of the cosmos, including norms of social and ritual action.
dhotī	A long, often elaborately pleated loincloth.
Ekātmatā Yajña	The All-India Sacrifice for Unity, which was sponsored by the highly politicized Vishva Hindu Parishad ("World Hindu Council") in 1983.
Gaṇeśa	The elephant-headed son of Śiva and Pārvatī, invoked by Hindus especially at the beginning of all undertakings as the lord who removes obstacles.
Gaurī	"Fair one," a name of the wife of Śiva in her radiant form. It is the goddess Gaurī who presides over the festival of Annakūṭa or Govardhana Pūjā.
ghāṭ	"Step," the steps leading down to a sacred river or temple tank, a place where pilgrims may bathe.

ghī	Clarified butter, poured into the fire as a ritual offering during Vedic ceremonies.
Gītagovinda	The twelfth-century lyric poem of Jayadeva that celebrates the love of Rādhā and Krishna. It inspired a stream of poetic and dramatic compositions in Sanskrit and the north Indian vernacular languages during the medieval period.
gopī	A cowherd woman of Vraja; in the Purāṇas and later poetry and dramas these woman lavish maternal affection upon the baby Krishna and become the amorous companions of his youth. Their intense longing for their beloved in his absence both represents and inspires the yearning of the human soul for the divine. Preeminent among the *gopī*s is Rādhā.
guṇa	"Thread," "quality"; in Sāṃkhya philosophy, one of three constituents or qualities of the phenomenal world (*prakṛti*, "nature"): *sattva* (goodness, purity), *rajas* (passion, energy), and *tamas* (darkness, lethargy). Ultimate reality is often said to be devoid of *guṇa*s (*nirguṇa*).
guruti	"Blood" offering to the evil spirits of the forest in the temple rituals of the fierce goddess Bhagavati in Kerala. Made from turmeric and calcified lime, *guruti* turns bright red when mixed with water.
Harivaṃśa	"The Genealogy of Hari" (i.e., Viṣṇu), a text dating from the early centuries C.E. that recounts the life of Krishna and that was appended to the *Mahābhārata* epic.
hindutva	Lit., "Hindu-ness," a term first given specific ideological content in 1922 by the militant Hindu V. D. Savarkar, who stressed the importance of the struggle against Muslim and British "enemies" for the creation of a Hindu nation.
hlādinī śakti	"Blissful potency," the bliss-filled and joy-giving quality of the Lord; identified with Rādhā in certain Tantric works and by the Brindavan *gosvāmī*s.
īśvara	"Lord," whether earthly or divine; a personal designation of ultimate reality used especially of Śiva; the term emphasizes the Lord's power and supremacy. Cf. *bhagavān*.
Jagannātha	"Lord of the world," an epithet of Viṣṇu especially in the primitive iconic form in which he is worshiped at Puri, together with his brother Baladeva and his sister Ekānaṃśā-Durgā, also called Subhadrā.
jagrātā	In northwest India, an all-night ritual performance of devotional songs and stories about the Goddess's exploits dedicated to her worship.

Jayadeva	Twelfth-century court poet of Lakṣmaṇa Sena of Bengal; author of the Sanskrit *Gītagovinda,* a literary masterpiece that served as the fountainhead of a stream of Sanskrit and vernacular works celebrating the love of Rādhā and Krishna.
kalā	"Art, fabrication," a term used to characterize the creative actions of the goddess Śerāṅvālī of northwest India.
kaḷam	A large multicolored rice-flour picture of Bhadrakāḷi in which the goddess is temporarily installed during a temple ritual.
Kālī	"The black one," the Goddess in a fearsome dark form, usually depicted with lolling tongue, a garland of human heads, and a girdle of human hands.
Kālīkhoh Devī	The Goddess worshiped at Kālīkhoh, "Kālī's cave," a site that forms one corner of the *trikoṇa Yātrā* at Vindhyachal.
kāma	Desire, lust, orgasmic eroticism; personified as Kāmadeva, the god of love whose flower-arrows affected even the great Lord Śiva as he sat in meditation in the Himalayas.
karma	"Action, work," one means or path to salvation (*karmamārga*); according to the law of karma, every action has its inevitable fruit (*phala*) either in this lifetime or in a future one.
Kauśikī	Lit., "[she] of the sheath (*kośa*)"; the dark goddess formed from the sheath of black skin that Umā sloughed off in order to become fair; Kauśikī then slew the demon brothers Śumbha and Niśumbha.
khel	"Play," a term used to describe the exuberantly creative actions of the goddess Śerāṅvālī of northwest India.
laghu	Light, easy, short.
Lakṣmī	"Good fortune," the goddess of wealth and beauty, in later mythology regarded as the wife of Viṣṇu or Nārāyaṇa; worshiped throughout India, especially by the Vaiśyas, during the festival of Divālī.
līlā	"Play"; spontaneous, effortless action, especially that of the Lord in creating and maintaining the universe. The term is used especially by Vaiṣṇavas to designate the graceful actions of Krishna as well as dramatic performances depicting these actions.
liṅga	Lit., "characteristic," a term for the male sexual organ; in particular, the phallic representation of Śiva, understood as symbolizing his transcendent, formless nature.

mādhurya	"Sweetness," the graceful beauty of divinity considered to be most fully manifest in Krishna's form and actions among the cowherds of Braj; also, the amorous emotion represented especially by the *gopīs* in their love for the youthful Krishna.
māna	Rādhā's mixed emotions—including anger, jealousy, hurt, and deep longing—at Krishna's betrayal.
Mahābhārata	The longer of the two great Sanskrit epics, composed ca. 300 B.C.E. to 300 C.E. In some hundred thousand verses, it narrates the story of the great war between the Pāṇḍavas and the Kauravas.
Mahādevī	The Great Goddess, often simply called Devī.
mahāmāyā	"Great illusion"; one possessed of great deluding and creative power (*māyā*); identified with Devī in the *Devī Māhātmya.*
māhātmya	"Greatness," a genre of epic and Purāṇic literature that extols the greatness and power of a deity, a ritual observance, or a place of pilgrimage.
Mahiṣāsura	The buffalo-demon, the great adversary of Durgā, whose death at her hands is celebrated in the *Devī Māhātmya* (or *Caṇḍīpāṭha*) and at the festival of Daśaharā, the culmination of Navarātrī.
mantra	Sacred Vedic formula. These have been employed in a variety of ritual and meditative contexts ever since the time of the *Rig Veda* (ca. 1200 B.C.E.).
Manu	Second son of Saraṇyū and Vivasvant, the Sun; progenitor of the human race.
Mātā	"Mother," a title of the Goddess; applied as well to women in northwest India who are regularly possessed and are therefore worshiped as living goddesses, as manifestations of Śerāṅvālī.
Mātājī	Honorific form of Mātā.
māyā	The mysterious (female) creative power of the Lord, sometimes personified as his consort; in Advaita Vedānta, the illusory superimposition of the phenomenal universe onto the one absolute reality; a force represented as both deluding and redemptive.
mokṣa	"Liberation, release," and, in some Hindu contexts, salvation, freedom from *saṃsāra*, the endless round of birth, death, and rebirth. The last of the four goals of a human being (*puruṣārtha*), the remaining three being righteousness (*dharma*), material well-being (*artha*), and pleasure (*kāma*). Certain theistic groups in India modify or reject the ideal of *mokṣa*, replacing it with *bhakti* or *prema*.

mudi (*muṭi*) — The enormous, heavy, leaf-shaped headdress worn by Bhadrakālī in the ritual possession performance of *mudiyettu* in central Kerala.

mudiyettu (*muṭiyeṟṟu*) — Lit., "the carrying of the headgear" (*mudi*), a ritual possession performance of central Kerala.

Naṭarājā — "King of the dance," an epithet of Śiva as the Lord whose cosmic dance creates, sustains, and then destroys the universe.

nāth (Skt.: *nātha*) — Lit., "master," a name given to one of a group of *yogīs* who wear large, distinctive earrings.

Navarātra/Navarātrī — "Nine nights," the most important festival in honor of the Great Goddess. It culminates in the celebration of Daśaharā, in which Durgā is honored as Mahiṣāsuramardinī, the slayer of the buffalo-demon Mahiṣāsura. In Bengal and elsewhere the festival as a whole is referred to as Durgā Pūjā.

nirguṇa — "Without qualities"; a designation commonly applied to ultimate reality, whether that reality is conceived as transpersonal (i.e., as the neuter *brahman*) or as personal (e.g., as Viṣṇu or Śiva); in a Vaiṣṇava context, *nirguṇa* is usually understood to mean "devoid of limiting attributes" (e.g., by Rāmānuja, 11th–12th c.).

Niśumbha — A demon slain by Kauśikī; twin brother of the demon Śumbha.

nyāsa — Lit., "placing," the embedding of deities within one's own body, a Tantric practice that uses mantras, gestures, and visualization.

pada — One of the numerous lyrical songs, chiefly on the Rādhā-Krishna theme, composed from roughly the fourteenth to seventeenth centuries in eastern India.

padāvalī kīrtan — An elaborate dramatic devotional form of musical performance in which episodes in the love of Rādhā and Krishna are sung and enacted by a male or female lead singer and a troupe of supporting singers and drummers.

paisā — A hundredth of a rupee.

pālā — Lit., "play, turn," a *kīrtan* performance, a three- to four-hour elaboration on a single theme; an episode performed in *kīrtan*, a generally accepted story line that is independent of any given rendering.

paṇḍā — A Brahmin guide at a place of pilgrimage, such as Banaras or Vindhyachal.

paṇḍita (Hindi: *paṇḍit*) — Lit., "learned," a Brahmin trained in one or more branches of traditional Sanskrit learning; in Vindhyachal,

	a religious specialist who recites the *Devī Māhātmya* and other Sanskrit devotional texts for pilgrims.
parakīyā	"Belonging to another," a woman married to someone other than her lover; a type of heroine in Sanskrit poetics. Rādhā is usually depicted in Indian literature as a *parakīyā*, although theologians such as Rūpa Gosvāmī and his nephew Jīva point out that in reality Rādhā belongs to Krishna eternally as his *hlādinī śakti*, his blissful energy. Cf. *svakīyā*.
Pārvatī	Lit., "the one born of the mountain (Himalaya)," the fair, gracious spouse of Śiva.
pavan	"Wind," a subtle form—intermediate between the unmanifest goddess Śerāṅvālī and her full manifestation—that is characterized by motion and breath; the term is used to describe possession by the Goddess.
pavan rūp	"Wind form," i.e., of the goddess Śerāṅvālī. See *pavan*.
prakṛti	"Nature," the phenomenal world; in Sāṃkhya philosophy, insentient yet active matter, as opposed to quiescent spirit (*puruṣa*), but also including much that the West terms psychological (e.g., emotions, dispositions, motives). It has three constituents (*guṇa*s). The term is feminine, in contrast to *puruṣa*, which is masculine, and is often personified.
prasāda (Hindi: *prasād*)	"Purity, grace"; food left over after being offered to a deity or deities, which is then distributed to devotees.
prema	Love, affection; specifically, love devoid of selfish desire.
pravāsa	Lit., "journey," an episode depicting the anguish of Rādhā and indeed all the inhabitants of Vraja at Krishna's departure for Mathurā in order to slay the demon-king Kaṃsa.
premavaicittya	Lit., "the bewilderment of love," Rādhā's temporary delusion, caused by the depth of her love, in which she thinks Krishna has left her when he is right in front of her eyes.
pūjā	A form of worship that is first attested in post-Vedic times: a ritual of hospitality to a deity or deities, in which such elements as water, fruits, a coconut, and cloth are offered.
Purāṇa	Lit., "ancient"; any of numerous medieval Sanskrit compendia of myth and ritual lore. The Purāṇas have been important scriptural sources for *bhakti* communities throughout India.
pūrvarāga	Lit., "first love/redness," Rādhā's or Krishna's yearning love that precedes their first full union.

Rādhā	Consort of Krishna; the most celebrated of the *gopī*s and the one most favored by Krishna; interpreted theologically, especially by Gauḍīya Vaiṣṇavas, as his *hlādinī śakti*, his blissful energy.
Rāmāyaṇa	The shorter of the two great Sanskrit epics, composed ca. 200 B.C.E. to 200 C.E. and attributed to the poet Vālmīki. It narrates the story of Rāma's search for his wife, Sītā, who is abducted by the demon Rāvaṇa and kept captive in Laṅkā.
Rām Līlā	Lit., "the play of Rām(a)," any of a number of dramatic representations of the life of Rāma, usually based on Tulsīdās's medieval Hindi version of the epic, the *Rāmcaritmānas.*
rasa (Hindi: *ras*)	"Flavor, liquid extract"; aesthetic experience. Rūpa Gosvāmī (16th c.) analyzed the highest form of *bhakti* as *rasa,* delineating five primary *bhaktirasa*s that correspond to five emotional relations (*bhāva*s) of the devotee to the divine.
Rig Veda	The most ancient sacred oral text of India (ca. 1200 B.C.E.). It contains more than a thousand hymns to a variety of gods, many of whom are closely connected with natural phenomena. Prominent among these are Indra, god of the thunderstorm, Agni (fire), and Soma, the intoxicating, hallucinogenic drink made from the *soma* plant.
sādhanā	A spiritual discipline, e.g., a form of yoga or of Tantric practice. In northwest India, a spiritual regimen undertaken in order to bring on possession by the Goddess.
Śakta	Pertaining to Śakti, the Goddess; worship of the Goddess; a devotee of the Goddess.
śakti	Energy, power, especially the creative energy that generates and continues to activate the universe. Conceived as female and often personified as the consort of a male deity or as the dynamic, independent Goddess.
sākṣāt darśan	"Direct sight," the unmediated vision of a deity.
*śakti-pīṭha*s	Places infused with the Goddess's special power.
Saṃjñā	Lit., "sign" or "image" or "name"; another name of Saraṇyū.
saṃsāra	The phenomenal universe; the endless round of birth, death, and rebirth from which Hindus seek release, *mokṣa.*
saṃskāra	A mental impression or predisposition from a past life; in northwest India this is given as an explanation for why

	some people get possessed but not others; one of the numerous Hindu life-cycle rituals that stretch from before birth to after death.
sanātana dharma	Lit., "the eternal dharma." The term has come to represent a central core of Hindu belief and practice that is considered to go back to ancient times.
Saraṇyū	Daughter of Tvaṣṭṛ, the artisan of the gods, and wife of Vivasvant, the Sun.
Sanātanī	A Hindu follower of *sanātana* dharma ("eternal dharma"), as contrasted with narrower sectarian forms of worship.
sat	Lit., "being, truth, virtue," in particular, the virtue a *satī* has gained by previous sacrifices of self-will and personal desires.
satī	"Virtuous woman," a wife who is utterly faithful and self-sacrificing, and especially one who joins her dead husband on his pyre; also, the goddess Satī, the wife of Śiva who burned herself to death because her father slighted her husband. Anglicized as "suttee," the term came to signify the practice of self-immolation rather than the woman whose supreme self-sacrifice it honors.
savārī	Lit., "vehicle," a person on whom the goddess Śerāṅvālī "rides" or whom she inhabits and through whom she speaks.
savārī rūp	The goddess Śerāṅvālī as she appears in the form of a possessed person.
Śerāṅvālī	"The one who rides a lion," a name of Durgā especially prevalent in northwest India.
sevā	"Service," especially to a deity or a holy person; the term has acquired a new, political sense with the recent rise of Hindu nationalism.
Shankaracharya (Skt.: Śaṅkarācārya)	Lit., "the learned preceptor Śaṅkara," the great monistic philosopher who lived in South India ca. 800 C.E. The title has been held by each of his successors in four monastic institutions situated roughly at the four compass points around the Indian subcontinent.
siddh (Skt.: *siddha*)	Lit., "perfected," one who is an adept at yoga.
siddhi	A supernatural or supernormal power acquired by a yogi or a Tantric adept.
Śiva	Lit., "auspicious, gracious," a name given to this often-frightening deity in the hope that he will be gracious to his devotees.

Smarta	A follower of Brahmanical tradition, especially that of Śaṅkara; these worship five great deities: Durgā, Śiva, Gaṇeśa, Viṣṇu, and Sūrya.
soma	The elixir of immortality, personified as the moon; in the *Rig Veda*, a liquid pressed from a plant, offered to the gods, and consumed by the priests.
śrāddha	A ceremony performed periodically in honor of a family's male ancestors (*pitṛ*s), in which family members offer them balls of sticky rice.
Śrī	"Radiance, splendor," the deity and consort of Viṣṇu who embodies the qualities of prosperity and beauty; worshiped especially by the Śrī Vaiṣṇavas as inseparable from Viṣṇu.
Śrī Vaiṣṇava	One who seeks access to Viṣṇu by first approaching his divine consort, Śrī/Lakṣmī; an initiate into the Tantric sect of that name, which acknowledges the authority of the *āḻvār*s, their Tamil poems, the *Pāñcarātra* liturgical school, and the unbroken lineage of *ācārya*s, which descends down to the present from the Lord himself.
śṛṅgāra (Hindi: *śṛṅgār*)	Erotic passion; therefore also a woman's adornments and makeup, as might be appropriate for an amorous encounter.
śṛṅgāra rasa	The erotic "mood," the first and, especially for drama, the most important of the eight *rasa*s enumerated by Bharata in the *Nātyaśāstra*. Trasmuted in the theory of Rūpa Gosvāmī into *madhura bhaktirasa*, the "sweet devotional mood" realized in the love of Krishna and the *gopī*s, especially Rādhā.
sthala-māhātmya	A text glorifying a locality deemed sacred, e.g., Vindhyachal.
stotra	Hymn of praise to a deity, written in verse and often sung or recited metrically.
Śumbha	A demon slain by Kauśikī; twin brother of the demon Niśumbha.
Sūrya (Hindi: Sūraj)	The sun, also called Vivasvant, "the Shining One."
svakīyā	"One's own," a woman who is the wife of her lover; a type of heroine in Sanskrit poetics. Cf. *parakīyā*.
svarūpa	"Essential form," the true form of a deity.
tāla/tālam	Cycle of beats, meter.
tāṇḍava	One of the styles of dance performed by Śiva. Unlike its opposite, the slow, graceful *lāsya*, the *tāṇḍava* is an energetic style in which Śiva dances at the destruction of the universe.

Tantra	An initiatory form of religion, often purposely unorthodox, in which the devotee visualizes himself or herself as the deity; Tantric practice has often involved esoteric sexual rituals and the worship of the Goddess. Cf. Śākta.
tapas	"Heat," the fervor of a meditating seer won through intense self-discipline, a source of great spiritual and physical power.
tejas	Splendor, glory, brilliance; semen.
tīrtha	"Ford, crossing," a sacred pilgrimage place where the river of earthly life may be forded to reach the "far shore."
tuḷḷal	In Kerala, any of a variety of possession dances.
Tvaṣṭṛ	Lit., "the Fashioner," also called "the All-Maker" (Viśvakarman), the artisan of the gods. Father of Saraṇyū/Saṃjñā.
Umā	The fair, gracious spouse of Śiva, also known as Pārvatī, the daughter of Himālaya and Menakā.
Vāc	Lit., "speech." Identified with Aṣṭabhujā Devī, the eight-armed goddess, who is married to Mahāviṣṇu.
varṇa	Color; class.
vātsalya	Lit., "calf-love," the love of a cow for her calf; by extension, parental, especially maternal affection.
Vedānta	The "end of the Veda" in two senses: their final portion and their ultimate significance; a name given to the Upaniṣads and philosophies derived from them, usually characterized by a mystic, monistic vision of God and the universe.
Vindhyakṣetra	"Field (i.e., area) of the Vindhya Mountains," the sacred region in which the goddess Vindhyavāsinī dwells and with which Tantrics identify her.
Vindhyavāsinī	"She who dwells in the Vindhya Mountains," a powerful goddess identified with the Great Goddess Devī of the *Devī Māhātmya.*
Vraja	A cowherd settlement; in the Purāṇas, the term designates the cowherd village of Nanda, in which Krishna grows up, as well as the surrounding region. Cf. Braj.
Vṛndāvana	Name of a forest near Gokula in Vraja where, according to tradition, Krishna played his enchanting flute, luring the *gopīs* from their homes to frolic with him in the fields and groves. Cf. Brindavan.
yakṣa	A class of ancient Indian life-energy deities, ordinarily associated with vegetation, particularly trees.

yakṣī	Female tree or water spirit; the term and concept go back to ancient times, and *yakṣī*s are depicted on the railings of early Buddhist *stūpa*s. In Kerala folklore, they are represented as unhappy, seductive, bloodthirsty spirits who seek to entice and destroy virtuous men.
Yama	Lit., "twin"; the first son of Saraṇyū/Saṃjñā and Vivasvant, the Sun, and regarded as the first human being. Inauspicious Lord of death and the underworld, he is worshiped with lighted lamps during the festival of Divālī.
Yamuna (also Jumna)	With the Ganges, one of the two great sacred rivers that flow eastward across the plains of North India; it waters the countryside of Braj and is closely associated with Krishna, whose dark color it shares and many of whose childhood exploits take place near or in its blessed waters. As Yamunādevī she is revered especially by Vaiṣṇavas, and in Vedic, epic, and Purāṇic mythology, she is the daughter of Saraṇyū/Saṃjñā and the Sun, and a twin to Yama.
yantra	A geometric diagram, usually of interlocking triangles and circles, that represents the cosmos in microcosm as well as the human person. Used as a focus for meditation or worship.
yātrā	"Journey," the term used for the temple processions in which images are paraded around on huge carts (*rath*s), as well as for pilgrimages, such as the triangle *yātrā* at Vindhyachal in which one visits the goddess Vindhyavāsinī in each of her principal forms.
yoni	The female sexual organ, a representation of the Goddess; the *yoni* in conjunction with the *liṅga* symbolizes the female aspect of the universe, the *śakti* of the great Lord Śiva.

SELECT BIBLIOGRAPHY OF WORKS IN EUROPEAN LANGUAGES

Agrawala, P. K. *Goddesses in Ancient India.* Atlantic Highlands, N.J.: Humanities Press, 1983.

Agrawala, Vasudeva S., trans. *Devī Māhātmya: The Glorification of the Great Goddess.* Varanasi: All-India Kashiraj Trust, 1963.

Allen, Michael. *The Cult of Kumari: Virgin Worship in Nepal.* Kathmandu: Tribhuvan University, 1975.

Altekar, A. S. *The Position of Women in Hindu Civilisation from Pre-Historic Times to the Present Day.* 1938; repr. Delhi: Motilal Banarsidass, 1956.

Archer, William G. *The Loves of Krishna in Indian Painting and Poetry.* London: George Allen and Unwin, 1957.

Ayyangar, D. Ramaswami, ed. *Stotras of Vedānta Deśika (Stotrāṇi).* Bombay: Sri Vedanta Desika Sampradaya Sabha, 1973.

Babb, Lawrence A. *The Divine Hierarchy: Popular Hinduism in Central India.* New York: Columbia University Press, 1975.

———. "Marriage and Malevolence: The Uses of Sexual Opposition in a Hindu Pantheon." *Ethnology* 9, no. 2 (1970): 137–48.

Bachofen, Johann Jakob. *Das Mutterrecht* (1861). Abridged and translated by Ralph Manheim. In *Myth, Religion, and Mother Right: Selected Writings of J. J. Bachofen.* Princeton: Princeton University Press, 1967.

Bahadur, K. P. *The Rasikapriyā of Keshavadāsa.* Delhi: Motilal Banarsidass, 1972.

Beane, Wendell Charles. *Myth, Cult and Symbols in Śākta Hinduism: A Study of the Indian Mother Goddess.* Leiden: E. J. Brill, 1977.

Bennett, Lynn. *Dangerous Wives and Sacred Sisters: Social and Symbolic Roles of High-Caste Women in Nepal.* New York: Columbia University Press, 1983.

Bhāgavata Purāṇa. See Sanyal, J. M., trans.

Bharati, Agehananda. *The Tantric Tradition.* 1965; repr. New York: Doubleday, 1970.

Bhattacharya, Deben, trans. *Love Songs of Chandidās.* London: George Allen and Unwin, 1967.

———, trans. *Love Songs of Vidyāpati.* With an introduction and notes by William G. Archer. London: George Allen and Unwin, 1963.

Bhattacharyya, Narendra Nath. *History of the Śākta Religion.* New Delhi: Munshiram Manoharlal, 1974.

———. *History of the Tantric Religion.* New Delhi: Manohar, 1987.

———. *The Indian Mother Goddess.* 2d rev. ed. New Delhi: Manohar, 1977. Originally published 1970.

Biardeau, Madeleine. *Autour de la Déesse hindoue: Etudes.* Paris: Editions de l'Ecole des Hautes Etudes en Sciences Sociales, 1981.

———. *Histoires de Poteaux: Variations védiques autour de la Déesse hindoue.* Paris: Ecole Française d'Extrême Orient, 1989.

Blackburn, Stuart H., and A. K. Ramanujan, eds. *Another Harmony: New Essays on the Folklore of India.* Berkeley: University of California Press, 1986.

Bloomfield, Maurice. "Contributions to the Interpretation of the Veda III: The Marriage of Saraṇyū, Tvaṣṭar's Daughter." *Journal of the American Oriental Society* 15 (1893): 172–88.

Briffaut, Robert. *The Mothers: The Matriarchal Theory of Social Origins.* 3 vols. 1927; repr. New York: Macmillan, 1931.

Brooks, Douglas R. *Auspicious Wisdom: The Texts and Traditions of Śrīvidyā Śākta Tantrism in South India.* Albany: State University of New York Press, 1992.

———. *The Secret of the Three Cities: An Introduction to Hindu Śākta Tantrism.* Chicago: University of Chicago Press, 1990.

Brown, C. Mackenzie. *God as Mother: A Feminine Theology in India—An Historical and Theological Study of the Brahmavaivarta Purana.* Hartford, Vt.: Claude Stark and Company, 1974.

———. *The Triumph of the Goddess: The Canonical Models and Theological Visions of the Devī-Bhāgavata Purāṇa.* Albany: State University of New York Press, 1990.

Brown, W. Norman. "Change of Sex as a Hindu Story Motif." *Journal of the American Oriental Society* 47, no. 1 (1927): 3–24.

Brubaker, Richard. "The Ambivalent Mistress: A Study of South Indian Village Goddesses and Their Religious Meaning." Ph.D. diss., University of Chicago, 1978.

Buckley, Thomas, and Alma Gottlieb, eds. *Blood Magic: The Anthropology of Menstruation.* Berkeley: University of California Press, 1988.

Buitenen, J. A. B. van, trans. *The Mahābhārata* [Books 1–5]. 3 vols. Chicago: University of Chicago Press, 1974–78.

Bumiller, Elisabeth. *May You Be the Mother of a Hundred Sons: A Journey among the Women of India.* New York: Random House, 1990.

Caldwell, Sarah Lee. "Oh Terrifying Mother: The *Mudiyettu* Ritual Theater of Kerala, South India." Ph.D. diss., University of California, Berkeley, 1995.

Calman, Leslie J. *Toward Empowerment: Women and Movement Politics in India.* Boulder, Colo.: Westview Press, 1992.

Carmody, Denise Lardner. *Women and World Religions.* 2d ed. Englewood Cliffs, N.J.: Prentice-Hall, 1989. Originally published in 1979.

Carstairs, G. Morris. *The Twice-Born: A Study of a Community of High-Caste Hindus.* London: Hogarth Press, 1957; Bloomington: Indiana University Press, 1958.

Chakravarti, Uma. "Whatever Happened to the Vedic *Dasi*?" In *Recasting Women: Essays in Indian Colonial History,* edited by Kumkum Sangari and Sudesh Vaid, pp. 27–87. New Brunswick, N.J.: Rutgers University Press, 1990.

Chandidās. *See* Bhattacharya, Deben, trans.

Chatterjee, Bankim Chandra. *Ānandamaṭh* (1882). Translated by Basanta Koomar Roy. 1941; repr. New Delhi: Vision Books, 1992.
Chatterjee, Partha. "The Nationalist Resolution of the Women's Question." In *Recasting Women: Essays in Indian Colonial History*, edited by Kumkum Sangari and Sudesh Vaid, pp. 233–53. New Brunswich, N.J.: Rutgers University Press, 1990.
Christ, Carol P. "Symbols of Goddess and God in Feminist Theology." In *The Book of the Goddess Past and Present: An Introduction to Her Religion*, edited by Carl Olson, pp. 231–51. New York: Crossroad, 1983.
Christ, Carol P., and Judith Plaskow, eds. *Womanspirit Rising: A Feminist Reader in Religion.* San Francisco: Harper and Row, 1979.
Claus, Peter J. "Spirit Possession and Spirit Mediumship from the Perspective of Tulu Oral Traditions." *Culture, Medicine, and Psychiatry* 3, no. 1 (1979): 29–52.
Coburn, Thomas C. "The Devī-Māhātmya as a Feminist Document." *Journal of Religious Studies* 8, no. 2 (1980): 1–11.
———. *Devī-Māhātmya: The Crystallization of the Goddess Tradition.* Delhi and Columbia, Mo.: Motilal Banarsidass and South Asia Books, 1985.
———. *Encountering the Goddess: A Translation of the Devī-Māhātmya and a Study of Its Interpretation.* Albany: State University of New York Press, 1991.
———. "Experiencing the Goddess: Notes on a Text, Gender, and Society." *Manushi* no. 80 (January–February 1994): 2–10.
Coomaraswamy, Ananda K. *The Darker Side of Dawn.* Smithsonian Miscellaneous Collections, vol. 94, no. 1. Washington, D.C., 1935.
———. *Yakṣas.* 2 vols. 1928 and 1931; repr. New Delhi: Munshiram Manoharlal, 1971.
Courtright, Paul B. *The Goddess and the Dreadful Practice.* New York: Oxford University Press, forthcoming.
Cutler, Norman, Joanne Waghorne, and Vasudha Narayanan, eds. *Gods of Flesh, Gods of Stone: The Embodiment of Divinity in India.* Chambersburg, Pa.: Anima Books, 1985.
Daniel, E. Valentine. *Fluid Signs: Being a Person the Tamil Way.* Berkeley: University of California Press, 1984.
Das, Veena. "The Goddess and the Demon—An Analysis of the *Devi Mahatmya.*" *Manushi* no. 30 (September–October 1985): 28–32.
Dasgupta, Shashi Bhushan. *Obscure Religious Cults.* 3d ed. Calcutta: K. L. Mukhopadhyay, 1962. Originally published 1946.
De, Sushil Kumar. *Early History of the Vaiṣṇava Faith and Movement in Bengal from Sanskrit and Bengali Sources.* 2d ed. Calcutta: K. L. Mukhopadhyay, 1961. Originally published 1942.
Devī Māhātmya. See Agrawala, Vasudeva S., trans.; Varenne, Jean, trans.
Dimock, Edward C., Jr. *The Place of the Hidden Moon: Erotic Mysticism in the Vaiṣṇava-sahajiyā Cult of Bengal.* Chicago: University of Chicago Press, 1966.
Dimock, Edward C., Jr., and Denise Levertov, trans. *In Praise of Krishna: Songs from the Bengali.* New York: Doubleday, 1967.
Doniger, Wendy. *Asceticism and Eroticism in the Mythology of Śiva.* London: Oxford University Press, 1973.
———. *The Origins of Evil in Hindu Mythology.* Berkeley: University of California Press, 1976.

———. *The Rig Veda: An Anthology*. Harmondsworth: Penguin Books, 1981.

———. *Women, Androgynes, and Other Mythical Beasts*. Chicago: University of Chicago Press, 1980.

———. trans. *Hindu Myths: A Sourcebook*. Harmondsworth: Penguin Books, 1975.

———. trans., with Brian K. Smith. *The Laws of Manu*. London: Penguin Books, 1991.

Downing, Christine. *The Goddess: Mythological Images of the Feminine*. New York: Crossroad, 1981.

Eck, Diana L. *Banaras, City of Light*. New York: Alfred A. Knopf, 1982.

———. *Encountering God: A Spiritual Journey from Bozeman to Banaras*. Boston: Beacon Press, 1993.

Egnor, Margaret Trawick. "The Changed Mother, or What the Smallpox Goddess Did When There Was No More Smallpox." In *Contributions to Asian Studies*, vol. 18, *South Asian Systems of Healing*, edited by E. Valentine Daniel and Judy F. Pugh, pp. 24–45. Leiden: E. J. Brill, 1984.

Erndl, Kathleen M. "The Goddess and Women's Empowerment: A Hindu Case Study." In *Women and Goddess Traditions*, edited by Karen King. Minneapolis: Fortress Press, forthcoming.

———. *Victory to the Mother: The Hindu Goddess of Northwest India in Myth, Ritual, and Symbol*. New York: Oxford University Press, 1993.

Freed, Ruth S., and Stanley A. Freed. "Two Mother-Goddess Ceremonies of Delhi State in the Great and Little Traditions." *Southwestern Journal of Anthropology* 18, no 3. (1962): 246–77.

Freeman, J. Richardson, Jr. "Purity and Violence: Sacred Power in the Teyyam Worship of Malabar." Ph.D. diss., University of Pennsylvania, 1991.

Fuller, C. J. *The Camphor Flame: Popular Hinduism and Society in India*. Princeton: Princeton University Press, 1992.

———. *Servants of the Goddess: The Priests of a South Indian Temple*. Cambridge: Cambridge University Press, 1984.

Gadon, Elinor W. *The Once and Future Goddess: A Symbol for Our Time*. San Francisco: Harper and Row, 1989.

Galland, China. *Longing for Darkness: Tara and the Black Madonna—A Ten-Year Journey*. New York: Viking, 1990.

Gatwood, Lynn E. *Devi and the Spouse Goddess: Women, Sexuality, and Marriage in India*. Riverdale, Md.: Riverdale Company, 1985.

George, Demetra. *Mysteries of the Dark Moon: The Healing Power of the Dark Goddess*. San Francisco: Harper and Row, 1992.

Ghadially, Rehana, ed. *Women in Indian Society: A Reader*. New Delhi: Sage Publications, 1988.

Ghosha, Pratapchandra. *Durga Puja, with Notes and Illustrations*. Calcutta: Hindoo Patriot Press, 1871.

Gimbutas, Marija. *The Civilization of the Goddess*. San Francisco: HarperSanFrancisco, 1991.

———. *The Language of the Goddess: Unearthing the Hidden Symbols of Western Civilization*. San Francisco: HarperSanFrancisco, 1989.

Gold, Ann Grodzins. "Spirit Possession Perceived and Performed in Rural Rajasthan." *Contributions to Indian Sociology* (n.s.) 22, no. 1 (1988): 35–63.

Gold, Ann Grodzins, and Gloria Goodwin Raheja. *Listen to the Heron's Words: Reimagining Gender and Kinship in North India.* Berkeley: University of California Press, 1994.

Goldman, Robert P., et al., trans. *The Rāmāyaṇa of Vālmīki: An Epic of Ancient India.* Princeton: Princeton University Press, 1984–.

Goudriaan, Teun. "On the Goddess' 'Phase of Life' in Some Hinduistic Texts." In *Effigies Dei: Essays on the History of Religions,* edited by Dirk Vander Plas, pp. 69–82. Leiden: E. J. Brill, 1987.

———. "Some Beliefs and Rituals Concerning Time and Death in the Kubjikāmata." In *Selected Studies on Ritual in the Indian Religions,* edited by Ria Kloppenborg, pp. 92–117. Leiden: E. J. Brill, 1983.

Goudriaan, Teun, and Sanjukta Gupta. *Hindu Tantric and Śākta Literature. A History of Indian Literature,* vol. 2, fasc. 2, edited by Jan Gonda. Wiesbaden: Otto Harrassowitz, 1981.

Gough, Kathleen. "Female Initiation Rites on the Malabar Coast." *Journal of the Royal Anthropological Institute* 85, pt. 1 (1955): 45–80.

Gross, Rita M. "Hindu Female Deities as a Resource for the Contemporary Rediscovery of the Goddess." In *The Book of the Goddess Past and Present,* edited by Carl Olson, pp. 217–30. New York: Crossroad, 1983.

———. "I Will Never Forget to Visualize That Vajrayogini Is My Body and Mind." *Journal of Feminist Studies in Religion* 3, no. 1 (1987): 77–89.

Guleri, Vidyadhar Sharma. *Female Deities in Vedic and Epic Literature.* Delhi: Nag Publishers, 1990.

Gupta, Lina. "Kali, the Savior." In *After Patriarchy: Feminist Transformations of the World Religions,* edited by Paula M. Cooey, William R. Eakin, and Jay B. McDaniel, pp. 15–38. Maryknoll, N.Y.: Orbis Books, 1991.

Gupta, Sanjukta. "Women in the Śaiva/Śākta Ethos." In *Roles and Rituals for Hindu Women,* edited by Julia Leslie, pp. 193–209. London: Pinter Publishers, 1991.

———, trans. *Lakṣmī Tantra: A Pāñcarātra Text.* Leiden: E. J. Brill, 1972.

Gupta, Sanjukta, and Richard Gombrich. "Kings, Power and the Goddess." *South Asia Research* 6, no. 2 (1986): 123–38.

Haartman, C. G. *Aspects de la Déesse Kālī dans son culte et dans la littérature Indienne.* Helsinki: Helsingfors, 1969.

Haberman, David. *Acting as a Way of Salvation: A Study of Rāgānugā Bhakti Sādhana.* New York: Oxford University Press, 1988.

Haddad, Yvonne Y., and Ellison B. Findly, eds. *Women, Religion and Social Change.* Albany: State University of New York Press, 1985.

Harding, Elizabeth U. *Kali, the Black Goddess of Dakshineswar.* York Beach, Me.: Nicolas-Hays, 1993.

Harlan, Lindsey. "Abandoning Shame: Mīrā and the Margins of Marriage." In *From the Margins of Hindu Marriage: Essays on Gender, Religion, and Culture,* edited by Lindsey Harlan and Paul B. Courtright, pp. 204–27. New York: Oxford University Press, 1995.

———. *Religion and Rajput Women: The Ethic of Protection in Contemporary Narratives.* Berkeley: University of California Press, 1992.

———. "Women's Songs for Auspicious Occasions." In *Religions of India in Practice,* edited by Donald S. Lopez, pp. 269–80. Princeton: Princeton University Press, 1995.

Harlan, Lindsey, and Paul B. Courtright, eds. *From the Margins of Hindu Marriage: Essays on Gender, Religion, and Culture.* New York: Oxford University Press, 1995.

Harman, William P. *The Sacred Marriage of a Hindu Goddess.* Bloomington: Indiana University Press, 1989.

Hart, George L., III. "Women and the Sacred in Ancient Tamilnad." *Journal of Asian Studies* 32, no. 2 (1973): 233–50.

Hawley, John Stratton, ed. *Sati, the Blessing and the Curse.* New York: Oxford University Press, 1994.

Hawley, John Stratton, and Donna M. Wulff, eds. *The Divine Consort: Rādhā and the Goddesses of India.* Berkeley: Religious Studies Series, and Delhi: Motilal Banarsidass, 1982.

Hazra, R. C. *Studies in the Upapurāṇas.* Vol. 2: *Śākta and Non-sectarian Upapurāṇas.* Calcutta: Sanskrit College, 1963.

Hershman, Paul. "Hair, Sex and Dirt." *Man* (n.s.) 9, no. 2 (1974): 274–98.

Hiltebeitel, Alf, ed. *Criminal Gods and Demon Devotees: Essays on the Guardians of Popular Hinduism.* Albany: State University of New York Press, 1989.

———. *The Cult of Draupadī.* 2 vols. Chicago: University of Chicago Press, 1988, 1991.

Hudson, Dennis. "Bathing in Krishna: A Study in Vaishnava Theology." *Harvard Theological Review* 73, nos. 1 and 2 (1980): 537–64.

Humes, Cynthia Ann. "The Goddess of the Vindhyas in Banaras." In *Living Banaras: Hindu Religion in Cultural Context,* edited by Bradley R. Hertel and Cynthia Ann Humes, pp. 181–204. Albany: State University of New York Press, 1993.

———. "Rājās, Thugs, and Mafiosos: Religion and Politics in the Worship of Vindhyavāsinī." In *Render unto Caesar: Religion and Politics in Cross-cultural Perspective,* edited by Sabrina Petra Ramet and Donald J. Treadgold, pp. 219–47. Washington, D.C.: American University Press, 1995.

———. "The Text and Temple of the Great Goddess: The *Devī-Māhātmya* and the Vindhyācal Temple of Mirzapur." Ph.D. diss., University of Iowa, 1990.

Hurtado, Larry, ed. *Goddesses in Religion and Modern Debate.* University of Manitoba Studies in Religion no. 1. Atlanta: Scholars Press, 1990.

Hymn to Kālī. See Woodroffe, Sir John, trans.

Induchoodan, V. T. *The Secret Chamber: A Historical, Anthropological and Philosophical Study of the Kodungallur Temple.* Trichur, Kerala: Cochin Devaswom Board, 1969.

Ironbiter, Suzanne, *Devi.* Stamford, Conn.: Yuganta Press, 1987.

Jacobson, Doranne, and Susan S. Wadley. *Women in India: Two Perspectives.* 2d ed. New Delhi: Manohar, 1992. Originally published 1970.

Jayadeva. *Gītagovinda. See* Miller, Barbara Stoler, trans.

Kakar, Sudhir. *The Inner World: A Psycho-analytic Study of Childhood and Society in India.* 2d ed. New York: Oxford University Press, 1981. Originally published 1978.

———. *Intimate Relations: Exploring Indian Sexuality.* Chicago: University of Chicago Press, 1989.

———. *Shamans, Mystics, and Doctors: A Psychological Inquiry into India and Its Healing Traditions.* New York: Alfred A. Knopf, 1982.

———. "When Saffron Speaks." *Sunday Times of India.* 19 July 1992.

Kane, P. V. *History of Dharmaśāstra.* 5 vols. Poona: Bhandarkar Oriental Research Institute, 1930–62.

Karlekar, Malavika. *Voices from Within: Early Personal Narratives of Bengali Women.* Delhi: Oxford University Press, 1991.

King, Karen, ed. *Women and Goddess Traditions.* Minneapolis: Fortress Press, forthcoming.

Kinsley, David R. *The Goddesses' Mirror: Visions of the Divine from East and West.* Albany: State University of New York Press, 1989.

———. *Hindu Goddesses: Visions of the Divine Feminine in the Hindu Religious Tradition.* Berkeley: University of California Press, 1986.

———. "The Motherhood of God as Expressed in the Goddess Kālī." *Anima* 8, no. 2 (1982): 131–42.

———. *The Sword and the Flute—Kālī and Kṛṣṇa: Dark Visions of the Terrible and the Sublime in Hindu Mythology.* Berkeley: University of California Press, 1975.

Kondos, Vivienne. "Images of the Fierce Goddess and Portrayals of Hindu Women." *Contributions to Indian Sociology* (n.s.) 20, no. 2 (1986): 173–97.

Kooij, K. R. van. *Worship of the Goddess According to the Kālikāpurāṇa.* Leiden: E. J. Brill, 1972.

Kramrisch, Stella. "The Indian Great Goddess." *History of Religions* 14, no. 4 (1975): 235–65.

Kuhn, Adalbert. "Saraṇyū-'Erinnús." In *Zeitschrift für Vergleichende Sprachforschung,* vol. 1, edited by Theodor Aufrecht and Adalbert Kuhn, pp. 439–70. Berlin: F. Dümmler, 1852.

Kumar, Pushpendra. *Sakti Cult in Ancient India (with Special Reference to the Puranic Literature).* Varanasi: Bharatiya Publishing House, 1974.

Kurtz, Stanley N. *All the Mothers Are One: Hindu India and the Cultural Reshaping of Psychoanalysis.* New York: Columbia University Press, 1992.

Lakṣmī Tantra. See Gupta, Sanjukta, trans.

Lannoy, Richard. *The Speaking Tree: A Study of Indian Culture and Society.* New York: Oxford University Press, 1971.

Leslie, Julia. "Śrī and Jyeṣṭhā: Ambivalent Role Models for Women." In *Roles and Rituals for Hindu Women,* edited by Julia Leslie, pp. 107–27. Rutherford, N. J.: Fairleigh Dickinson University Press, 1991.

Lewis, I. M. *Ecstatic Religion: An Anthropological Study of Spirit Possession and Shamanism.* Harmondsworth: Penguin Books, 1971.

McDaniel, June. *The Madness of the Saints: Ecstatic Religion in Bengal.* Chicago: University of Chicago Press, 1989.

McKean, Lise. *Divine Enterprise: Gurus and the Hindu Nationalist Movement.* Chicago: University of Chicago Press, 1996.

McDermott, Rachel Fell. "Kālī's Tongue: Historical Reinterpretations of the Blood-lusting Goddess." Paper presented at the Mid-Atlantic Conference of the American Academy of Religion, New York, March 1991.

Mahābhārata. See Roy, Protap Chundra, trans.; Buitenen, J. A. B. van, trans.

Mani, Lata. "Contentious Traditions: The Debate on *Sati* in Colonial India." In *Recasting Women: Essays in Indian Colonial History,* edited by Kumkum Sangari and Sudesh Vaid, pp. 88–126. New Brunswick, N.J.: Rutgers University Press, 1990.

———. "Cultural Theory, Colonial Texts: Reading Eyewitness Accounts of Widow Burning." In *Cultural Studies,* edited by Lawrence Grosberg, Cary Nelson, and Paula Freichler, pp. 392–408. New York: Routledge, 1992.

———. "Production of an Official Discourse on Sati in Early Nineteenth-Century Bengal." *Economic and Political Weekly* 21, no. 17 (26 April 1986): WS32–40.

Manuel, Peter. *Cassette Culture: Popular Music and Technology in North India.* Chicago: University of Chicago Press, 1993.

Marglin, Frédérique Appfel. "Female Sexuality in the Hindu World." In *Immaculate and Powerful: The Female in Sacred Image and Social Reality,* edited by Clarissa W. Atkinson, Constance H. Buchanan, and Margaret R. Miles, pp. 39–59. Boston: Beacon Press, 1985.

———. *Wives of the God-King: The Rituals of the Devadasis of Puri.* Oxford: Oxford University Press, 1985.

Mārkaṇḍeya Purāṇa. See Pargiter, F. Eden, trans.

Matsya Purāṇa. See Sastri, S. V., trans.

Meyer, Eveline. *Aṅkāḷaparmēcuvari: A Goddess of Tamilnadu, Her Myths and Cult.* Stuttgart: Steiner Verlag, 1986.

Meyer, Johann Jakob. *Sexual Life in Ancient India.* 1930; repr. Delhi: Motilal Banarsidass, 1971.

Miller, Barbara Stoler. "Rādhā: Consort of Kṛṣṇa's Vernal Passion." *Journal of the American Oriental Society* 95, no. 4 (1975): 655–71.

———, trans. *Love Song of the Dark Lord: Jayadeva's Gītagovinda.* New York: Columbia University Press, 1977.

Mirashi, V. V. "A Lower Limit for the Date of the *Devī Māhātmya.*" *Purāṇa* 6, no. 1 (1964): 181–84.

Mitra, Kana. "Women and the Hindu Tradition." In *Women's and Men's Liberation: Testimonies of Spirit,* edited by Leonard Grob, Riffat Hassan, and Haim Gordon, pp. 83–103. New York: Greenwood Press, 1991.

Mitter, Sara S. *Dharma's Daughters: Contemporary Indian Women and Hindu Culture.* New Brunswick, N.J.: Rugters University Press, 1991.

Monaghan, Patricia. *The Book of Goddesses and Heroines.* New York: E. P. Dutton, 1981.

Mookerjee, Ajit. *Kali, the Feminine Force.* London: Thames and Hudson, 1988.

Mukta, Parita. *Upholding the Common Life: The Community of Mirabai.* Delhi: Oxford University Press, 1994.

Nandy, Ashis. "Sati: A Nineteenth-Century Tale of Women, Violence, and Protest." In his *At the Edge of Psychology: Essays in Politics and Culture,* pp. 1–31. Delhi: Oxford University Press, 1980.

Narayan, Kirin. "Birds on a Branch: Girlfriends and Wedding Songs in Kangra." *Ethos* 14, no. 1 (1986): 47–75.

Narayanan, Vasudha. "Hindu Perceptions of Auspiciousness and Sexuality." In *Women, Religion, and Sexuality: Studies on the Impact of Religious Teaching on Women,* edited by Jeanne Becher, pp. 64–92. Philadelphia: Trinity Press International, 1990.

———. *The Way and the Goal: Expressions of Devotion in the Early Śrī Vaiṣṇava Tradition.* Washington, D.C.: Institute for Vaishnava Studies, and Cambridge, Mass.: Center for the Study of World Religions, Harvard University, 1987.

Neumann, Erich. *The Great Mother: An Analysis of the Archetype.* Translated by Ralph Manheim. 2d ed. New York: Pantheon, 1963. Originally published 1955.

Nicholas, Ralph W., and Aditi Nath Sarkar. "The Fever Demon and the Census Commissioner: Śītalā Mythology in Eighteenth- and Nineteenth-Century

Bengal." In *Bengal: Studies in Literature, Society and History,* edited by Marvin Davis, pp. 3–68. East Lansing: Michigan State University, Asian Studies Center, 1976.

Noble, Vicki. *Shakti Woman: Feeling Our Fire, Healing Our World—The New Female Shamanism.* San Francisco: Harper and Row, 1991.

Obeyesekere, Gananath. *The Cult of the Goddess Pattini.* Chicago: University of Chicago Press, 1984.

———. "Kālī, the Punitive Mother." In *Buddhism Transformed: Religious Change in Sri Lanka,* edited by Richard Gombrich and Gananath Obeyesekere, pp. 133–62. Princeton: Princeton University Press, 1988.

———. *Medusa's Hair: An Essay on Personal Symbols and Religious Experience.* Chicago: University of Chicago Press, 1981.

———. "Psychocultural Exegesis of a Case of Spirit Possession in Sri Lanka." In *Case Studies in Spirit Possession,* edited by Vincent Crapanzano and Vivian Garrison, pp. 235–94. New York: Wiley, 1977.

O'Flaherty, Wendy Doniger. *See* Doniger, Wendy.

Olson, Carl, ed. *The Book of the Goddess Past and Present: An Introduction to Her Religion.* New York: Crossroad, 1987.

———. *The Mysterious Play of Kālī: An Interpretive Study of Rāmakrishna.* Atlanta: Scholars Press, 1990.

Östör, Akos. *The Play of the Gods.* Chicago: University of Chicago Press, 1980.

Pargiter, F. Eden, trans. *The Markandeya Purana.* Calcutta: Baptist Mission Press, 1888–1904.

Payne, Ernest A. *The Śāktas: An Introductory and Comparative Study.* London: Oxford University Press, 1933.

Pintchman, Tracy. *The Rise of the Goddess in the Hindu Tradition.* Albany: State University of New York Press, 1994.

Preston, James J. *Cult of the Goddess: Social and Religious Change in a Hindu Temple.* Prospect Heights, Ill.: Waveland Press, 1980.

———, ed. *Mother Worship: Theme and Variations.* Chapel Hill: University of North Carolina Press, 1982.

Rāmāyaṇa. See Goldman, Robert P., et al., trans.; Shastri, Hari Prasad, trans.

Rao, Velcheru Narayana. "A *Rāmāyaṇa* of Their Own: Women's Oral Tradition in Telugu." In *Many Rāmāyaṇas: The Diversity of a Narrative Tradition,* edited by Paula Richman, pp. 114–36. Berkeley: University of California Press, 1991.

Ratté, Lou. "Goddesses, Mothers, and Heroines: Hindu Women and the Feminine in the Early Nationalist Movement." In *Women, Religion and Social Change,* edited by Yvonne Y. Haddad and Ellison B. Findly, pp. 351–76. Albany: State University of New York Press, 1985.

Renou, Louis. *L'Hindouisme: Les textes, les doctrines, l'histoire.* Paris: Presses Universitaires de France, 1958.

Robinson, Sandra P. "Hindu Paradigms of Women: Images and Values." In *Women, Religion and Social Change,* edited by Yvonne Y. Haddad and Ellison B. Findly, pp. 181–215. Albany: State University of New York Press, 1985.

Roy, Protap Chundra, trans. *The Mahabharata of Krishna-Dwaipayana Vyasa.* 12 vols. 2d ed. Calcutta: Oriental Publishing Company, 1927–32. Originally published 1883–96.

Sahai, Bhagwant. *Iconography of Minor Hindu and Buddhist Deities.* New Delhi: Abhinav Publications, 1975.

Sangari, Kumkum. "Mirabai and the Spiritual Economy of Bhakti." *Economic and Political Weekly* 25 (7 and 14 July 1990), special articles, pp. 1464–75 and 1537–52.

———. "Perpetuating the Myth." *Seminar* no. 342 (February 1988): 24–30.

Sangari, Kumkum, and Sudesh Vaid, eds. *Recasting Women: Essays in Indian Colonial History.* New Brunswick, N.J.: Rutgers University Press, 1990. First published in 1989 under a slightly different title by Kali for Women, New Delhi.

Sanyal, J. M., trans. *The Srimad-bhagavatam of Krishna Dwaipayana Vyasa.* 2d ed. 5 vols. in 2. 1950–54; repr. New Delhi: Munshiram Manoharlal, 1973. Originally published 1970.

Sastri, S. V., trans. *Matsya Puranam.* Delhi: Oriental Publishers, 1972.

Sax, William S. *Mountain Goddess: Gender and Politics in a Himalayan Pilgrimage.* New York: Oxford University Press, 1991.

Scheftelowitz, J. "Śrī Sūkta." *Zeitschrift für die Deutschen Morgenlandischen Gesellschaft* 75 (1921): 37–50.

———, ed. *Die Apokryphen des Ṛgveda.* Breslau: M. and H. Marcus, 1906.

Sen, Sukumar. *The Great Goddesses in Indic Tradition.* Calcutta: Papyrus Press, 1983.

Shastri, Hari Prasad, trans. *The Ramayana of Valmiki.* 3 vols. London: Shantisadan, 1962.

Shastri, J. L., trans. *Śiva Purāṇa.* In *Ancient Indian Tradition and Mythology.* 4 vols. Delhi: Motilal Banarsidass, 1970.

Shinn, Larry D. "The Goddess: Theological Sign or Religious Symbol?" *Numen* 31, no. 2 (1984): 175–98.

Shulman, David Dean. "The Murderous Bride: Tamil Versions of the Myth of Devī and the Buffalo Demon." *History of Religions* 16, no. 2 (1976): 120–47.

———. *Tamil Temple Myths: Sacrifice and Divine Marriage in the South Indian Śaiva Tradition.* Princeton: Princeton University Press, 1980.

Siegel, Lee. *Sacred and Profane Dimensions of Love in Indian Traditions as Exemplified in the Gītagovinda of Jayadeva.* Delhi: Oxford University Press, 1978.

Singaravelu, S. "Sita's Birth and Patronage in the Rama Story." *Asian Folklore Studies* 41 (1982): 235–43.

Singer, Milton, ed. *Krishna: Myths, Rites, and Attitudes.* Honolulu: East-West Center Press, 1966.

Singh, Indu Prakash. *Indian Women: The Captured Beings.* New Delhi: Intellectual Publishing House, 1990.

Sinha, Jadunath. *Rama Prasada's Devotional Songs: The Cult of Shakti.* Calcutta: Sinha Publishing House, 1966.

Sircar, D. C. *The Śākta Pīṭhas.* 1948; repr. Delhi: Motilal Banarsidass, 1973.

———, ed. *The Śakti Cult and Tārā.* Calcutta: University of Calcutta, 1971.

Śiva Purāṇa. See Shastri, J. L., trans.

Spivak, Gayatri C. "Can the Subaltern Speak? Speculations on Widow-Sacrifice." *Wedge* nos. 7/8 (Winter/Spring 1985): 120–30.

Srivastava, M. C. P. *Mother Goddess in Indian Art, Archeology, and Literature.* Delhi: Agam Kala Prakashan, 1979.

Stietencron, Heinrich von. *Gaṅgā und Yamunā.* Wiesbaden: Otto Harrassowitz, 1972.

Sunder Rajan, Rajeswari. "The Subject of Sati: Pain and Death in the Contemporary Discourse on Sati." *Yale Journal of Criticism* 3, no. 2 (1990): 1–23.

"Surya." Retold by Mayah Balse. *Amar Chitra Katha* no. 58, edited by Anant Pai. Bombay: India Book Trust, n.d.

Sutherland, Sally J. "Sītā and Draupadī: Aggressive Behavior and Female Role-Models in the Sanskrit Epics." *Journal of the American Oriental Society* 109, no. 1 (1989): 63–79.

Tagore, Rabindranath. *Collected Poems and Plays.* New York: Macmillan, 1967.

Thampuran, H. H. Kerala Varma. "Kali Cult in Kerala." *Rama Varma Research Bulletin* 4 (1936): 77–97.

Thompson, Edward J., and Arthur Marshman Spender, trans. *Bengal Religious Lyrics, Śākta.* Calcutta: Association Press, 1923.

Tiwari, J. N. *Goddess Cults in Ancient India.* Delhi: Sundeep Prakashan, 1985.

Vaid, Sudesh. "Politics of Widow Immolation." *Seminar* no. 342 (February 1988): 20–23.

Vaidyanathan, K. R. *Temples and Legends of Kerala.* Bombay: Bharatiya Vidya Bhavan, 1988.

van der Veer, Peter. "Hindu 'Nationalism' and the Discourse of 'Modernity': The Vishva Hindu Parishad." In *Accounting for Fundamentalisms,* edited by M. Marty and R. S. Applely, pp. 653–68. Chicago: University of Chicago Press, 1994.

———. *Religious Nationalism: Hindus and Muslims in India.* Berkeley: University of California Press, 1994.

Varenne, Jean, trans. *Célébration de la Grande Déesse [Devī Māhātmya].* Paris: Les Belles Lettres, 1975.

Vaudeville, Charlotte. "Evolution of Love-symbolism in Bhāgavatism." *Journal of the American Oriental Society* 82, no. 1 (1962): 31–40.

Vishva Hindu Parishad. *The Hindu Awakening: Retrospect and Promise.* New Delhi: Vishva Hindu Parishad, n.d.

———. *Vishva Hindu Parishad: Messages and Activities.* New Delhi: Vishva Hindu Parishad, n.d.

Viṣṇu Purāṇa. See Wilson, H. H., trans.

Wadley, Susan S. "The Spirit 'Rides' or the Spirit 'Comes': Possession in a North Indian Village." In *The Realm of the Extra-Human: Agents and Audiences,* edited by Agehananda Bharati, pp. 233–52. The Hague: Mouton, 1976.

———, ed. *The Powers of Tamil Women.* Syracuse: Syracuse University, Maxwell School of Citizenship and Public Affairs, South Asia Series no. 6, 1980.

Walker, Barbara G. *The Woman's Dictionary of Symbols and Sacred Objects.* San Francisco: Harper and Row, 1988.

Wilson, H. H., trans. *The Vishnu Purāṇa.* Edited by Fitzedward Hall. 5 vols. London: Kegan Paul, Trench, Trübner, 1864–77.

Woodroffe, Sir John. [Arthur Avalon.] *The Serpent Power.* 14th ed. Madras: Ganesh and Co., 1989. Originally published 1919.

———. *Shakti and Shakta.* 5th ed. 1959; repr. New York: Dover Publications, 1978. Second edition published 1920.

———, ed. *Principles of Tantra: The Tantratattva of Śrīyukta Śiva Candra Vidyārṇava Bhaṭṭācārya Mahodaya.* 5th ed., pts. 1 and 2. Madras: Ganesh and Co., 1978. Originally published 1914 and 1916.

———, trans. *Hymns to the Goddess.* 1913; repr. Madras: Ganesh and Co., 1964.
———, trans. *Karpūrādi-stotra: Hymn to Kālī.* 3d ed. Madras: Ganesh and Co., 1965. Originally published 1922.
Wulff, Donna M. *Drama as a Mode of Religious Realization: The Vidagdhamādhava of Rūpa Gosvāmī.* Chico, Calif.: Scholars Press, 1984.
———. "Images and Roles of Women in Bengali Vaiṣṇava *Padāvalī Kīrtan.*" In *Women, Religion and Social Change,* edited by Yvonne Y. Haddad and Ellison B. Findly, pp. 217–45. Albany: State University of New York Press, 1985.
———. "Internal Interpretation: The *Ākhar* Lines in Performances of *Padāvalī Kīrtan.*" In *Contacts between Cultures,* vol. 2, *South Asia,* edited by K. I. Koppedrayer, pp. 317–24. Queenston, Ont.: The Edwin Mellen Press, 1992.
———. "The Play of Emotion: *Līlākīrtan* in Bengal." In *The Gods at Play: Līlā in South Asia,* edited by William S. Sax, pp. 99–114. New York: Oxford University Press, 1995.
Yalman, Nur. "On the Purity of Women in the Castes of Ceylon and Malabar." *Journal of the Royal Anthropological Institute* 93, no. 1 (1963): 25–58.
Yocum, Glenn E. "The Goddess in a Tamil Śaiva Devotional Text, Māṇikkavācakar's *Tiruvācakam.*" *Journal of the American Academy of Religion* 45, no. 1, supplement (1977): K369–90.
Young, Katherine K. "Hinduism." In *Women and World Religions,* edited by Arvind Sharma, pp. 59–103. Albany: State University of New York Press, 1987.
Young, Katherine K., and Arvind Sharma. *Images of the Feminine—Mythic, Philosophic, and Human—in the Buddhist, Hindu, and Islamic Traditions: A Bibliography of Women in India.* Chico, Calif.: New Horizons Press, 1974.
Zimmer, Heinrich. *The King and the Corpse.* New York: Pantheon Books, 1948.
———. "The Indian World Mother." In *The Mystic Vision: Papers from the Eranos Yearbooks,* 6 vols., edited by Joseph Campbell, 6:70–102. 1934; repr. Princeton: Princeton University Press, 1968.
———. *Myths and Symbols in Indian Art and Civilization.* Edited by Joseph Campbell. Bollingen Series no. 6. 1946; repr. Princeton: Princeton University Press, 1971.
Zvelebil, Kamil V. "Vaḷḷi and Murugan—A Dravidian Myth." *Indo-Iranian Journal* 19, nos. 3/4 (1977): 227–46.

CONTRIBUTORS

Sarah Caldwell is assistant professor in the Department of Anthropology, Program on Studies in Religion, at the University of Michigan, Ann Arbor, and a postdoctoral scholar in the Michigan Society of Fellows. Her Ph.D. dissertation, "Oh Terrifying Mother: The *Mudiyettu* Ritual Theater of Kerala, South India (University of California, Berkeley, 1995) is currently under revision for publication. She is also the author of several articles exploring feminist, psychoanalytic, and postmodern approaches to the study of ritual.

Thomas B. Coburn is Charles A. Dana Professor and Chair of Religious Studies and Classical Languages at St. Lawrence University. His publications include *Devī-Māhātmya: The Crystallization of the Goddess Tradition* (1985) and *Encountering the Goddess: A Translation of the Devī-Māhātmya and a Study of Its Interpretation* (1991). His current interests include cross-cultural hermeneutics, especially in connection with Goddess traditions.

Wendy Doniger is Mircea Eliade Professor of the History of Religions at the University of Chicago and the author of many articles and books about India, particularly on the subject of mythology. These include three Penguin Classics—*Hindu Myths: A Sourcebook* (1975), *The Rig Veda: An Anthology* (1981), and (with Brian K. Smith) *The Laws of Manu* (1991), all translations from the Sanskrit—as well as several books with the University of Chicago Press: *Women, Androgynes, and Other Mythical Beasts* (1980), *Dreams, Illusion, and Other Realities* (1984), and *Tales of Sex and Violence: Folklore, Sacrifice, and Danger in the Jaiminīya Brāhmaṇa* (1985). In progress are two books, *The Mythology of Horses in India* and *The Bed Trick: Sex, Myth, and Masquerade,* in addition to which she is at work on a novel, *Horses for Lovers, Dogs for Husbands.*

Diana L. Eck is professor of Comparative Religion and Indian Studies at Harvard University. Her work has centered on the comparative study of religion, with particular emphasis on pilgrimage, sacred geography, and religious pluralism in America. Her books include *Darśan: Seeing the Divine in India* (1981), *Banaras, City of Light* (1982), and *Encountering God* (1993). At Harvard, she is also the director of the Pluralism

Project, a mapping of world religions as expressed in communities of worship across the United States.

Kathleen M. Erndl is associate professor of Religion at Florida State University. She is the author of *Victory to the Mother: The Hindu Goddess of Northwest India in Myth, Ritual, and Symbol* (1993), along with a number of articles on Hindu goddesses and the role of women in Hinduism. She is currently engaged in research on women healers in Kangra, North India, and is also working on a book about blood sacrifice and Goddess worship in the Hindu tradition.

Lindsey Harlan, professor of Religious Studies at Connecticut College, is currently at work on a book about hero veneration. Her publications include *Religion and Rajput Women: The Ethic of Protection in Contemporary Narratives* (1992) and (with Paul Courtright) an edited volume, *From the Margins of Hindu Marriage: Essays on Gender, Religion, and Culture* (1995).

John Stratton Hawley is chair of the Department of Religion at Barnard College and was until recently director of the Southern Asian Institute at Columbia University. He is the author of several books on Krishna and the devotional culture of North India: *At Play with Krishna* (1981), *Krishna, the Butter Thief* (1983), *Sūr Dās: Poet, Singer, Saint* (1984), and (with Mark Juergensmeyer) *Songs of the Saints of India* (1988). Volumes he has edited include *Saints and Virtues* (1987), *Fundamentalism and Gender* (1994), *Sati, the Blessing and the Curse* (1994), and (with Gurinder Singh Mann) *Studying the Sikhs* (1993). He was also the coeditor, with Donna M. Wulff, of the forerunner to the present work, *The Divine Consort: Rādhā and the Goddesses of India* (1982).

Cynthia Ann Humes is assistant professor of Religious Studies at Claremont McKenna College. Her publications concern the contemporary use of Sanskrit literature, modern ritual in North Indian goddess worship, political and economic dimensions in Hinduism, and women's roles and experience in world religions. A book entitled *Goddess of Blood, Goddess of Love: Divinity and Power in the Devī Māhātmya and Vindhyachal Temple* is forthcoming from SUNY. She also coedited and contributed to *Living Banaras: Hindu Religion in Cultural Context* (1993).

David R. Kinsley, professor in the Department of Religious Studies at McMaster University, has written several well-known works on the goddesses of India and other religious cultures. These are *The Sword and the Flute—Kālī and Kṛṣṇa: Dark Visions of the Terrible and the Sublime in Hindu Mythology* (1975), *Hindu Goddesses: Visions of the Divine Feminine in the Hindu Religious Tradition* (1986), and *The Goddesses' Mirror: Visions of the Divine from East and West* (1989). He is also the author of *The Divine Player: A Study of Kṛṣṇa Līlā* (1979).

Rachel Fell McDermott is assistant professor of Asian and Middle Eastern Cultures at Barnard College, Columbia University. Her interests include *bhakti* literature, Tantra, the religious traditions of eastern India, the relationship between goddesses and Indian women, and Śākta pilgrimage traditions. She recently completed her Ph.D. dissertation, "Evidence for the Transformation of the Goddess Kālī: Kamalākāṇṭa Bhaṭṭācārya and the Śākta *Padāvalī* Tradition" (Harvard University, 1993).

Lise McKean is the managing editor of *Public Culture* and a research associate in the Department of Anthropology at the University of Chicago. She is the author of *Divine Enterprise: Gurus and the Hindu Nationalist Movement* (1996).

Vasudha Narayanan, professor of Religion at the University of Florida, is the author of a number of works on the textual, ritual, and experiential heritage of Vaiṣṇava religion in South India. These include *The Way and the Goal* (1987), *The Vernacular Veda* (1994), and (with John Carman) *The Tamil Veda* (1989). A coeditor of both *Gods of Flesh, Gods of Stone* (1985) and *Monastic Life in the Christian and Hindu Traditions* (1990), she is also the project director for a complete translation of Nammāḻvār's *Sacred Utterances* (Harvard, forthcoming).

Donna M. Wulff is associate professor of Religious Studies at Brown University. Her publications include *Drama as a Mode of Religious Realization*—a book on the Sanskrit plays of Rūpa Gosvāmī—as well as articles on Sanskrit aesthetic theory, the sacredness of sound and music, and a contemporary Bengali form of religious performance, *padāvalī kīrtan.* With John Stratton Hawley, she was the coeditor of *The Divine Consort: Rādhā and the Goddesses of India* (1982).

INDEX

Page numbers in italics refer to illustrations.

Compositor: BookMasters, Inc.
Text: 10/12 Baskerville
Display: Baskerville
Printer: Haddon Craftsmen
Binder: Haddon Craftsmen